David Farber

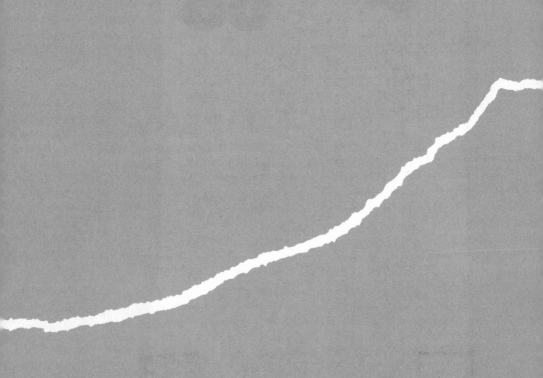

The University of Chicago Press
CHICAGO & LONDON

THE UNIVERSITY OF CHICAGO PRESS, CHICAGO 60637
THE UNIVERSITY OF CHICAGO PRESS, LTD., LONDON
© 1988 by The University of Chicago
All rights reserved. Published 1988
Paperback edition 1994
Printed in the United States of America
97 96 95 94   5 4 3

Library of Congress Cataloging-in-Publication Data

Farber, David R.
  Chicago '68.

  Includes index.
    1. Riots—Illinois—Chicago—History—20th century.
  2. Political conventions—Illinois—Chicago—History—
  20th century.   3. United States—Politics and government—1963–1969.   4. Chicago (Ill.)—History—1875–
  5. Radicalism—Illinois—Chicago—History—20th century.
  I. Title.   II. Title: Chicago sixty-eight.
  F548.52.F37   1987   977.3'11043   87–19071
  ISBN 0–226–23800–8 (cloth)
  ISBN 0–226–23801–6 (paper)

To my mother and father
who taught me to care

Contents

Preface

I grew up in Chicago, not too far from Wrigley Field. The Sunday before the 1968 Democratic Convention began, I walked over to the North Avenue end of Lincoln Park with some friends to see the hippies. I was eleven.

We never got to see them. Between us and them were an endless number of policemen with riot gear and clubs in their hands. Some of us had kind of long hair and the cops started asking us if we were boys or girls which we thought was pretty stupid since we were throwing a football around as we walked. Then a couple of cops who seemed a little younger asked us where we were going and when we said, they told us it could be a real dangerous place to be and that we should get the hell out of there while we could. We were already spooked by all the cops and we left. On Wednesday night, the night when the police and the demonstrators fought it out on Michigan Avenue, I watched the convention on television with my mother and father. When they showed the violence in the streets my mom was furious, my dad wasn't sure what to think except that it was going to make it a lot harder for Humphrey to get elected. I thought it was incredible.

For someone too young to have really lived through the sixties, the whole decade can easily seem incredible; that is to say, unbelievable. I write this book in an attempt to make it credible, to write about the sixties from the vantage point of someone too young to have truly experienced them, to write about it, I think, without any old ax to grind. From me, it's the history I just missed living, much like the New Deal was for some of my teachers. It's the decade that shadowed my coming of intellectual age.

In trying to recover the sixties, I found myself pulled to the 1968 Democratic Convention. I was pulled there, I think, partially for personal reasons; Chicago will always be my city, though I've moved away, and I felt that writing about it gave me an edge. I grew up with Mayor Daley and his people. I knew them and even worked for them. And since I felt the hardest part about writing about the sixties was getting the "silent majority's" perspective straight—in part because there just wouldn't be as much historical material to excavate—writing about the Mayor and his police would be a little easier for me than writing about people I had to feel out from the ground up.

But I was also pulled to Chicago '68 for scholarly reasons. The lines were as clearly drawn at Chicago as they were anywhere in the 1960s. The breakdown in political discourse and practice, that I argue underlay the protests and reactions of the 1960s, were so clearly displayed in the Chicago confrontation, as were the main actors' differing understandings of social order. By writing about the confrontation in Chicago, I feel I can write about the conflict in understandings of both public and private behavior that fueled the 1960s and the decades that have followed. By centering my text so fixedly on the Chicago action, instead of ranging further afield, I feel I can fully give voice to the specific feelings that fired so much rage.

To reveal the conflicting historical voices that gave shape to the 1960s, I have in my narrative sections gone to the unusual length of retaining something of the vernacular and tone of the times. I do this, in part, because the conflicts of the 1960s were not simply about particular political answers to particular questions. Part of the conflict was about representation and form itself. In my narrative section on the Yippies, for example, I show how the Yippies contested authority not simply through alternative policy formations (a very un-Yippie phrase) but through language itself. In order to regain a feeling of genuineness and power in the world, the Yippies and the counterculture in general, like other outsider and dissident groups, felt they had to remake and rediscover their very own way of speaking in the world. To a workable degree, I try to reproduce the ways in which their speech helped focus their world. To a less obvious degree, I do the same in my narrative sections on the National Mobilization to End the War in Vietnam and Mayor Daley and the Chicago police. By hearing how the differing qualities of their voices give shape to their stories, the reader can better feel how different their stories of Chicago '68 are. And by seeing how different their stories are, the reader can better see, I hope, both the ways in which the main actors came into conflict and why they were so unable to settle their conflicts in a more amiable way.

The conflict in Chicago was not at all simply about America's involvement in Vietnam. The conflict was over how the American political system worked and over how Americans found meaning in their lives. In my telling of the stories of Chicago '68, I work to make that conflict clear and immediate.

The researching and writing of this book was made possible by many people. I would like to thank the staffs at the Johnson Library in Austin, Texas, and the Wisconsin Historical Society in Madison for all their help. I specifically would like to thank Russell Maylone, Special Collections,

Northwestern University, for his counsel. The director of the Chicago Police Board, too, was especially helpful in the research stage of this work as were several police officers at the Chicago Police Department. At an early stage of this project, Chuck Olin shared with me the telling films he and his colleagues made about Chicago '68 and I thank him.

My thanks also to the Barnard family who supported this work through the fellowship they established in honor of historian and biographer Harry Barnard.

Over the 1982–1983 academic year, in exchange for the simplest of services, I lived in the beautiful Hyde Park home of Dr. and Mrs. C. Phillip Miller, and by so doing was able to devote more time to the scholarship that laid the groundwork for this book. In part, this book is dedicated to the memory of Dr. Miller and to the engaging spirit of Mrs. Miller.

Without the assistance of Alexandra Speyer, I never would have been able to make such good use of the CBS archives; her special interest in my project meant a lot to me and the book. Bill Katovsky, through complex and clever strategies, helped fund my research trips to Austin and the East Coast; he's a friend for life and I owe him one.

Special thanks also to Sheryl Bailey who came through in the clutch and helped in so many ways.

Barry Karl, over many years, has done his best to teach me how to think hard about difficult intellectual problems. Our many talks on the political problems of mass societies inform much of what I have written about the 1960s in America. While he was not always in agreement with the final results, Barry Karl contributed to every stage of this work.

Special thanks also to Neil Harris, Keith Baker, and Tetseo Najita for the intellectual guidance that made this work possible. Thanks also to David Hollinger, John Shy, Stephen Tonsor, the late Robert Hayden, Stephen Lavine, Sandor Goodhart, Sharon Franco, and Bill Ray, all of whom taught me to love writing and reading and the life of the mind. Harry Harootunian carefully read through the early drafts of this work and made numerous helpful comments, especially on the political meaning of cultural practices.

Mary Sheila McMahon and Edwin Wheeler helped in many ways; Mary Sheila carefully read my final draft and opened my eyes to several historical openings I had failed to follow up—her scholarship served me as a model. Dan Frank read several drafts and his enthusiasm and critical eye kept me going and made this a better work. His friendship helped make the years I spent working on this book golden ones. The years David Cohen and I spent talking about life, literature, and the pursuit of happiness figure on most every page of this manuscript. None of it would have been possible without him.

Beth Bailey read every single word I ever wrote on this subject. At the end of every writing day I read the results to her, she commented and I listened. If this book is any good she deserves much of the credit. If it's bad she can also share in the blame. We had a lot of fun writing this book, so much so that we decided to coauthor a baby, our son Max. Thank you too, Max.

Introduction

The struggle between protesters and protectors of the social order at the 1968 Democratic Convention in Chicago framed the breakdown of both social order and political discourse in the 1960s. At Chicago '68, many of the main performers of the 1960s played out their violently different understandings of political process, daily life, and what it meant to be an American. At Chicago, the rage and the hope, the certainty and the fear, the willfulness and the self-righteousness of both protesters and protectors of the social order were put on display.

In Chicago, late August 1968, approximately ten thousand demonstrating citizens, most of them young, almost all of them white and from the middle classes, confronted almost an equal number of uniformed police and armed defenders of society in public parks and city streets. Other protest events in the 1960s drew more people—by 1968 there had been antiwar protests that had attracted hundreds of thousands of demonstrators. And other protests had resulted in as much or more violence—in California, white demonstrators had been themselves more violent and been just as violently suppressed. Black civil rights demonstrations, in the 1950s and the 1960s, had, of course, included many more people and much more violence. But Chicago '68 was different because it occurred at a time when and a place where the nation watched and knew that what they were watching was themselves. Like President Kennedy's filmed assassination had earlier, it offered Americans an irrefusable opportunity to consider what they thought of themselves and their country.

Chicago '68 was seen by almost all who participated in it and by most of those who watched it on TV as more than just another protest marked by violence, intolerance, and excess. Chicago '68 marked a crisis in the nation's political and cultural order.

For Mayor Daley, aging boss of the City of Chicago, a mass demonstration at the Democratic Convention he'd wooed to his city meant more than a threat to the well-being of the delegates he saw as homage to his power or to the loyal citizens who kept him in power. For Mayor Daley, a mass demonstration at his convention was an insult to what he most believed in. It threatened his politics, a politics in which personal loyalty outweighed loyalty to any policy, and in which power—defined by individual clout and its boons, delivered through jobs, services, and favors—flowed from above to those below who knew the proper ways to ask for them.

Mayor Daley's political machine was self-contained and self-containing. He recognized in the protesters, in all protesters, a threat to the very fabric of his political machine: more than anything else, Mayor Daley feared that these "outside agitators" would ignite and, maybe worse, organize Chicago's powerless blacks who were learning that they lived in the most segregated city in the North. Mayor Daley felt both hate and contempt for the "outsider agitators" whom he knew rejected the form of workable control and the careful balance of power he had constructed. Mayor Daley controlled his city—with the help of the bankers and the bungalow owners—but he could not control the changes that were sweeping the nation. The Mayor knew his political territory was being threatened and challenged by forces that claimed national and symbolic, rather than municipal and civil, jurisdiction.

The Mayor's police, by and large, accepted most of the Mayor's instinct for what was right and wrong. But his problems faded in the face of the police officers' gut concerns. Many of Chicago's police tended to see black and young demonstrators, just as they tended to see members of the press, as a visible sign of what was wrong in their world. More and more, the police saw a world where criminals were coddled by the courts; where hatred, scorn, and even violence against the police were rising uncontrollably; and where hard-working people were ignored and unrespected. At a time when so much—too much—was expected from them, the police felt they were given no support from society. And while they were constantly being admonished by liberal reformers and a short-sighted press to act like professionals—which the police understood to mean: stop beating up Negro criminals and troublemakers—they were becoming increasingly self-conscious that they were paid less than plumbers, glaziers, and any number of other low-status workers.

When the police had to confront ill-mannered, self-righteous college kids, whom they believed came from privileged backgrounds, out protesting in the streets and mixing with and supporting Negroes about whom they knew nothing, the police saw Red. They resented the middle-class demonstrators who talked about equality and freedom but showed no respect for properly designated authority or understanding of those who just wanted to keep the simple things they had worked for so hard. To the police, all the demonstrators, short-haired and long-haired, were dumb, un-American hippies who didn't respect the way real people lived their daily lives. Many police believed that the American political system that maintained stability and order was being destroyed by the enemies of their way of life. At Chicago '68, the police, confronted and provoked by such enemies and unleashed by their superiors, were able to play out their well-developed anger and bitterness.

For the protesters who didn't think or care about the problems of the police or the city administrators, Chicago '68 represented the next obvious step in their attempt to take back Democracy. By 1968, the movement had been marching against the war in Vietnam for over four years and against racism for better than a decade. And as committed activists saw it, they were not being heard by the Establishment. Their efforts to get the United States out of Vietnam *now*, end racism *today*, and to develop a society at peace with itself and the world were not leading to real social change. More and more people were concluding that simple parades and orderly rallies were no longer enough. By 1968, sizable numbers of movement people, especially the young radical leaders who had won their spurs battling for civil rights in the South and beginning the student movement on Northern campuses, believed that more had to be done—and done where it could be seen. They were searching for new means to challenge the Establishment and bring social change. At the Pentagon demonstration at the end of 1967 and at the convention in Chicago they found their new political approach, an almost wholly symbolic one: confront the war makers at their own corrupt institutions. For the antiwar movement, direct confrontation of the war makers presented a clear picture, which they knew the mass media would pass along to the public at large. It presented a simple picture: the war makers versus the people. It was a political statement they believed in and it was a politics they could practice.

This kind of simple picture, and the politics it projected, represented to almost all facets of the fractionated movement a valid expression of their only commonly held ideological position—the government of the United States must be returned to the People. At the core of the New Left, which by and large encompassed all the major factions that organized the Chicago demonstration, was a belief that only through massive participation could democracy be made to work for the People. Participation in a demonstration or an "action" was more important and significant, most argued, than simply casting a ballot every two or four years because it demanded that individual citizens act on their beliefs by expressing their opinions publicly and personally. It demanded that people do something outside of the normal social bounds that they believed constrained people's truer, freer political natures. Participating in demonstrations or political protests was the first step in actively taking back the actual governing process. It was one step—a conscious step—on the long road to a genuine participatory democracy where people really controlled and helped produce their government's public policy.

At Chicago, the many factions of the movement, reduced to those most determined individuals who had not been scared away by Mayor Daley's overt intimidation tactics or been neutralized by the political surprises of 1968, acted out their different understandings of what the new political culture should be.

The Yippies, led by Jerry Rubin and Abbie Hoffman, attempted to use the energy and playfulness of youth culture to wildly redefine radical politics. For Rubin, Hoffman, and their colleagues, who invented Yippie specifically for the 1968 Democratic Convention, the new politics of participatory democracy had to include the new values that rock music, drugs, and the entire nascent hippie culture promised. The new politics had to be more than just a more participatory system of government; it had to include the new freedoms, the new forms of play that American youth were furiously exploring. At Chicago, the Yippies meant to invite the new youth to meet the new politics and by so doing create a "Festival of Life" capable of confronting the dreary, old-fashioned Democratic "Convention of Death."

The Chicago project directors for the National Mobilization to End the War in Vietnam, the multiconstituent coalition that called the Chicago demonstration, had a very different answer to the question of what the new politics should be. They saw the Yippie solution as undisciplined juvenilia that would change nothing. And they dismissed young people who were enthusiastic over the "peace" candidacies of Senators Kennedy and McCarthy as naive or co-opted. As they saw it, the "peace" candidates were unlikely to win and, more important, even if elected would do nothing to change the real faults of the system—the everyday realities of American imperialism and racism. The Mobe's Chicago leaders wanted a revolution—they wanted socialism with a human face, a socialism based on participatory democracy and in league with other non-Soviet socialist and liberationist experiments around the world. Part of their mission, they knew, was to bring those young people, stirred by campus activism but captured by the peace candidates McCarthy and Kennedy, to a new, militant politics that aimed to end all imperialistic wars, not just the one in Vietman. There was much arguing over how this weaning away was to be accomplished, and in the planning for Chicago many tactics were devised, ranging from pamphleteering to creating violent situations that left no middle ground.

In the end, at Chicago, the Mobe celebrated a politics based on a vision of power. The leaders, some more, some less, believed that in this politics of power the catharsis produced by confrontation and polarization could lead more certainly than the practice of compromise or the struggle for reform to real social change and a practical system of self-rule.

The Chicago demonstration turned out as no one who planned for or worked against it would have wished. Yet, despite, or perhaps because, of its unanticipated nature—both possibilities need to be examined—Chicago revealed a great deal about the divided state of American politics in the 1960s.

To give the history of Chicago '68, I tell the story of the convention protest and defense from three major perspectives, one after another. First, I tell the story of the Yippies, who created themselves solely for the purpose of confronting the Democratic Convention. Then I give the story of the Mobilization, the antiwar movement's most important national planning organization, which despite much internal debate about Chicago spent over eight months organizing the convention protest. Finally, I tell the story of Mayor Daley and his police, who did their best to insure that their city was protected from the unwelcome protesters.

I tell each story separately because each set of participants had such very different perspectives on the Chicago protest. At the heart of my history of Chicago '68 is the argument that the conflict at the convention was fueled by the completely different conceptions of political practice and social order the main actors brought to the planning and realization of the convention. I tell each story separately because although all the participants spent many months focused on the same week in August 1968 and reacted to many of the same events prior to the convention week, their stories are fundamentally different and, indeed, separate. Each groups' perceptions, experience, and understanding were so shaped by their very different political visions (and I use political in its widest sense) that an accurate history of the period must radically shift perspective to account for the confrontation that occurred. Though these major protagonists repeatedly and climactically interact, I believe that it is only by presenting each of their stories, in watching how each perceives and reacts to changing circumstances, that one can understand what I have suggested, and intend in what follows to make clear, was a critical juncture in American politics.

To present these three separate stories, all of which climax at the convention, I provide three separate chronological narratives of the staging of the Chicago action and three separate chapters of analysis that assess the motives, the premises, and the beliefs of the main actors in the confrontation.

Let me make this very clear. In the narratives, I essentially give voice—while providing the background material necessary for the reader to follow that voice—*to the actors' own perceptions and plans* as they approach the convention. To put the matter most extravagantly, I aim to present the state of mind the actors brought to their acts. I don't mean to suggest that I'm offering some sort of pyschohistory or, in a formal sense, a phenomenological interpretation. I simply provide a chronology of the actors' most important steps in approaching the protest and give, when I can, a detailed account of how the actors justified those steps to each other, to their followers, and to the public. To make these acts intelligible to the reader, I give, to some degree, the actors' own understandings of the historical circumstances that produced their decisions. To the same end, I sketch the organizational structures and histories that shaped their worlds. Finally, to the degree that my craft permits me, I've also set the tone of the different narratives to reflect the spirit of its protagonists. Very deliberately, however, *I do not attempt to justify or critique the logic or the ideology or the style by which the main actors maintain or develop their roles;* I present that kind of commentary in my analytic chapters.

The tools I used in constructing these worlds are the simple ones of the historian's trade: interview transcripts, private papers, organizational records and files, newspapers, magazines, films and filmed accounts, and books of the times, and a wealth of secondary sources. The historian's problem in writing about the 1960s is not a lack of source material—though there are some very notable exceptions—it is the sifting and sorting through and making sense of the myriad sources available; for example, the National Commission on the Causes and Prevention of Violence, Chicago Study Team, collected well over a thousand accounts of convention week. As I researched, I tried to read the structures and forms as well as the context of these many texts.

In providing narratives so unadorned by the historian's authorial voice I gamble that the reader will address the texts I offer critically. Clearly, the narratives I produce are crafted to produce certain understandings. Like any narrative outside of those composed by Borges's Funes, they mirror only the concerns I wish to raise (or, at times, can't help but raise). But by producing narratives tuned to the historical actors' own voices I do seek to offer texts that are not as predigested as the case study model would insist. The feeling of the past is put ahead of the historian's claim to place such a past in the continuum of history. I attempt to offer the reader the complexity of the past without as firm a guiding hand as historians are now accustomed to giving. I suppress my own voice. My narratives attempt to open up the uncertain worlds the different actors lived in.

In the analytic chapters, I aim to close up, in part, those worlds. Which is to say, I openly interpret what I have chronicled. In my own voice, I place the stories in the larger historical context of American political life. If I have succeeded, my narratives should open up more questions than my analyses can answer, for my analytic chapters are essentially concerned only with answering a few narrowly conceived questions. Above all, I attempt to unpack the problems of political thought and practice I have loaded into my narratives.

In part, the method of presenting the past I have chosen led me to center my texts around an event. To some degree, of course, an event is only another name for periodization or subject. But for historians an event does differ from other objects of organization insomuch as an event seems to be more firmly rooted in the concreteness of fixed action and not in the simulated world of ex post facto categorization or ratiocination. Of course, such differences tend to break down after some consideration and in part, by fixing three very different narratives to what is supposed to be one event, I do attempt to subvert the fixity with which historians tend to use events in their work. Events tend to be more prismatic than we often allow. An event with its seeming fixity provides an ironic opportunity to explore the historian's problem of perspective. I felt this could best be done by offering separate narratives, each attuned to the voice and vision of a different set of historical actors. By mixing event and perspective I hope to reveal the way in which history is contested. My analyses allow me a straightforward entry into the fray.

My analyses center on several interrelated concerns. Fundamentally, I analyze the protesters' decisions to reject electoral politics and to choose street protests and confrontation. In doing this I explore the logic that tied together public protest and self-expression; a logic I see as serving as a nexus between an ideological conception of politics and the praxis of protest in the streets. This concern, in turn, drives me to explore what might be called the politics of style—the demand that one must "live the revolution." Herein, I question the most militant protesters' demands for a politics based on all "Power to the People."

I am also concerned with what might be called the politics of information. I examine the ways the demonstrators tried to portray themselves, both through manipulations of the mass media and through their own media, to what they understood to be their audiences.

Among protesters in the 1960s, the relationship of politics to culture was not clearly drawn. This unclear relationship between "movement culture" and "movement politics" was played out in Chicago and reveals much about the course of protest and resistance in the 1960s. I believe that by analyzing the development of the protesters' logic and the kind of political protest it engendered, I will be able to give a historical understanding to a route radical politics took in the United States during the 1960s and to place that experiment in the larger adventure of American reform and outsider politics.

In contrast to those issues, I will also be examining the claims of those charged with maintaining order when confronted by a citizenry bent on change and upheaval. I will explain and judge the situation of those who saw the protesters as dangerous agents of breakdown and disruption, as a problem in a society where chaos frays at the nerves of a too large, too disjointed corporate body. Here, I will be examining some of the American strategies of reaction that are automatically activated by pressures from outsiders to be let into or to break down the established order.

All of my questions originate in issues that far transcend the crisis of consciousness that exploded in the 1960s. The problem of how to effect and contain political change permeates all of American history, and to understand how it is addressed in the 1960s is to explore the dynamic that underlies much of the American social and political system.

Abbreviations

ACLU	American Civil Liberties Union
COC	Coalition for an Open Convention
CORE	Congress for Racial Equality
CPC	Convention Planning Committee
CPD	Chicago Police Department
DNC	Democratic National Committee
ERAP	Economic and Research Action Project
ESSO	East Side Survival Organization
HUAC	House UnAmerican Activities Committee
JOIN	Jobs Or Income Now
LAPD	Los Angeles Police Department
LNS	Liberation News Service
NAACP	National Association for the Advancement of Colored People
NCC	National Coordinating Committee
NCCPV	National Commission on the Causes and Prevention of Violence
NIC	National Interim Council
NLF	National Liberation Front
SCLC	Southern Christian Leadership Conference
SDS	Students for a Democratic Society
SNCC	Student Non-Violent Coordinating Committee
SWP	Socialist Workers Party
VDC	Vietnam Day Committee
VFW	Veterans of Foreign Wars
YIP	Youth International Party

Narratives

I listen for the sound of cannon, cries
vibrating still upon the air
timeless echoes in echoic time—
imagine how they circle out and out
                    Robert Hayden, "On Lookout Mountain"

1 Making Yippie!

Yippie began as a dope joke, as a half-cocked combination of hippie ethos and New Left activism, only the real joke was that the inventors meant it. They meant to make Yippie! a cry, a myth, a party, a reality that would explode at the 1968 Democratic National Convention in Chicago. Yippie was just make-believe, but Yippie was going to be a joke with which the whole nation would have to play along. Of course, not everybody was going to find the punch line very funny.

Yippie began late in the afternoon, at the very end of 1967, at Abbie and Anita Hoffman's apartment on St. Mark Place. Jerry Rubin, ex-Berkeley activist and most recently project director of the Pentagon demonstration, was there with his woman friend Nancy Kurshan. Paul Krassner, editor and publisher of the *Realist*, was there alone. They were doing a little early New Year's celebrating. Stoned again. Stoned as 1967, the year of the hippie, came to a close. Stoned in the heart of the Lower East Side, in the heart of the home of New York's hippie community.[1]

They were a block away from Gem's Spa, where the hip community met to plot out their collective theater. They were a short walk from the Filmore East, where acid rock was introducing the East Coast to the West Coast. They were right off Thompkin Square, where all summer the long-hair, runaway kids and love-beaded day trippers hung out copping what highs they could between long stares and late-night chills; white kids living on and off the streets. They were voluntarily and quite happily in the middle of one of New York's fiercer collections of low-money people: bitter Puerto Ricans, stolid Ukrainians, and the middle-class dropouts living in a compressed zone of cold-water flats, six-floor walkups, cockroach apiaries, and burnt-out shooting galleries.[2]

Amid this, the Hoffmans had a small but comfortable apartment. No mass media hippie dirt, just clean and uncluttered with put-together pillows for sitting on and leaning against, a handmade loft bed and not much else, just what they'd been able to glean from the streets. Abbie and Anita knew how to live off the streets.[3] As to whether or not many others, less sophisticated or clever, could, that was a complicated question that some of the more thoughtful members of the hip community worried about every so often.

The Hoffmans, Jerry Rubin and Nancy Kurshan, and Paul Krassner were all on the floor, attending to their various highs. They were also planning. For at least a couple of months all of them had known that something had to happen at the Democratic National Convention, that something more than a little surprising had to confront the ugly renomination of the ugly Johnson. The face and structure of what they wanted had to some degree already been decided.

A couple of weeks earlier, Rubin had met up with Ed Sanders and Keith Lampe at a New York movement meeting called to discuss the use of violence at antiwar demonstrations. While hanging around, waiting for things to happen, Sanders, peace activist, second-generation beat poet, and lead singer for the Fugs, started talking about the Monterey Pop Festival. Rubin agreed that it meant a lot that major rock bands would come together and play for free. It was tribal instead of commercial. Sanders suggested they do a free music festival in Chicago, convention time, to defuse all the political tensions. Keith Lampe, older and a little straighter but with the credentials to speak out, agreed completely. They decided to talk with Abbie and a few others and see how it played.[4]

Hoffman liked the idea, but before any real talking and planning could take place Abbie and Anita and Paul Krassner decided to take some time off and go down to the Florida Keys for a month to cool out and work on some obligations. Krassner had to finish up the next issue of the *Realist*, the increasingly political but always satirical magazine he had been publishing and editing for over ten years. Hoffman, who at this point was almost completely unknown outside New York and was, unlike Jerry Rubin, far from being a movement heavy, had just promoted his first book contract on the strength of a few well-publicized cultural/political stunts. He was getting connected into the public system. The modest advance money he'd gotten for the book would pay for the trip and, he hoped, maybe buy him a little time and quiet in which to write part of it.

In the little cottage the Hoffmans and Krassner rented down on Ramrod Key, they all dropped acid, talked revolutionary violence, snorkled the coral reef, and chatted about holding some kind of rock festival in Chicago during the convention that would be political without becoming just another boring demonstration.

The talking didn't get very far and neither did Abbie's writing, and sooner than they expected the charm of Ramrod Key ran thin and the lure of New York came on strong and the Hoffmans and Krassner cut their working vacation short and flew home ready to get going.[5]

So when Rubin and Kurshan and Krassner met at Abbie and Anita's house that afternoon to celebrate the coming of the New

Year, they had all pretty much agreed that having some kind of
youth festival in Chicago during the Democratic Convention was a
good idea. And they knew that they'd have Ed Sanders and Keith
Lampe, and a few other people whom they'd all worked with before, join them in organizing the event. They also knew that in all
likelihood the National Mobilization to End the War in Vietnam would
call for a formal antiwar demonstration in Chicago and that they
would have to make sure that people understood that what they
planned would be an alternative to the straight demonstration the
Mobe would hold. They would not be sleepwalking through marches
or rallies with speechmaking. They were going to have a festival
and it was going to be fun. It was going to be politics of a whole
other kind. Both Rubin and Hoffman saw the Chicago event as the
active culmination of all the changes they had been going through.

Neither Hoffman nor Rubin were kids. As Abbie said, he was fifteen
years older than the runaways he rapped to in Thompkin Square.[6]
Both were men of about thirty who had come of age long before
acid or long hair or even the war in Vietnam. They's grown up
straight, if maybe just a little bit absurd.

Hoffman was born in Worcester, Massachusetts, in 1936. His parents
were middle-class Jews. He was, in the 1950s pool hall and greaser
style, a rebellious teenager, but he did well enough in school and
cared enough to be admitted to Brandeis University. He graduated
in 1959 and then went on to graduate school in psychology at the
University of California, Berkeley.

In 1960, under duress, Hoffman left Berkeley to marry his pregnant
girlfriend, Sheila, in a synagogue in Rhode Island. Abbie wore a
white summer tuxedo and he was not very happy, but he had done
what he felt was right. For the next three years Hoffman worked in
the Massachusetts State Mental Hospital testing patients. There, he
learned that some people really were crazy.

Hoffman had also learned by this time that there were things going
on in the country that he didn't like—and that he cared. In his
autobiography, Hoffman attributes the origins of his political consciousness to the dis-ease of going through childhood a marginal
Jew whose parents never made up their minds about assimilation:

> My parents got sucked into the social melting pot,
> where they were to simmer uncomfortably for the next
> thirty years. Having opted for life in mainstream America
> it became very difficult, even hypocritical for them to try
> to push any strict code of tradition down our throats. . . .
> Deep down I'm sure we felt our parents' generation was
> a bunch of cop outs. Six million dead and except for the

Warsaw ghetto hardly a bullet fired in resistance. . . . I
was shuttled back and forth between Orthodox yeshiva
after school on weekdays and the reform Temple Eman-
uel on weekends. It was getting me pretty mixed up.
Eventually tefillin and torah lessons gave way to dancing classes and discourses (in English) on the nature of
life and how good things were in America.[7]

A whole generation of Jewish political activists (and an overwhelmingly disproportionate number of 1960s, especially early to
mid-1960s, activists were Jewish) tell similar stories.[8]

Hoffman was at two of the first political demonstrations of the sixties.
He held the vigil outside the walls of San Quentin the night rapist
Caryl Chessman was executed and he was at the HUAC demonstrations in San Francisco, the first white middle-class demonstration of
the 1960s that ended with police brutality.

Over the next six years, Hoffman became increasingly involved in
political protests while at the same time trying to hang onto his wife,
two kids, and a straight job. By 1963 Hoffman was putting most of
his energies into the civil rights movement and was one of the
moving forces of the NAACP chapter in Worcester. He spent the
summers of 1964 and 1965 working for SNCC in Mississippi. He got
arrested a few times. In the autumn of 1965 Hoffman helped organize
Worcester's first antiwar march.

Soon after this, Hoffman was turned on to acid and began smoking
marijuana with some regularity. He, slightly ahead of a generation
of relatively free and affluent young people, discovered that he liked
drugs. Things began to speed up.

Spring of 1966, Hoffman was fired from his salesman job at West-
wood Pharmaceuticals for working more hours on political organizing than on selling his products. It was the last straight job Hoffman
would work in the 1960s. He quickly found a paid staff position with
Thomas Adams, who was running for senator in the Massachusetts
Democratic primary on an anti–Vietnam war platform. But Adams
lost and Hoffman was out of work.

He was also out of his marriage. His ex-wife got the house and the
kids. Hoffman left Worcester and moved to New York to be a full-
time organizer.

In New York, Hoffman worked with SNCC in setting up and operating Liberty House, a cooperative store that sold handmade goods
produced by the Poor People's Cooperative in Mississippi. Hoffman
was pretty much in charge and he loved it. He was one of the whites
most hurt and angered by SNCC's winter of 1966 decision to purge
all whites from the organization. Hoffman was so sure that SNCC was

making a big mistake that he wrote a classic leftist attack on black nationalism, insisting that the civil rights movement and poor people's campaign had to be framed in class and not in racial terms. The *Village Voice* printed the piece and a lot of New York liberals praised Hoffman. The praise coming from where it did told Hoffman that something was wrong with his thinking. He talked with Stokely Carmichael, whom he knew fairly well through SNCC, and with Julius Lester. He read Fanon. Spring 1967, Hoffman turned Liberty House over to black management and began again.[9] He realized he needed to find his own community to organize.

He turned to the nascent community growing up around him, the long-hair, dope-smoking, runaway, dropout community that lived uneasily on the Lower East Side. Hoffman was far from the first New York hippie activist. At first, he had fought the new dropout consciousness as a cop–out and believed that its practitioners were easily co-opted by the corporate system. But there was something about the new consciousness with its emphasis on drugs, shifting realities, and absurdity that attracted Hoffman. He tried it on and it worked. It felt a lot better than the nonviolent, almost puritanical, pacificism that governed the New York antiwar movement hierarchy. Hoffman became a hippie activist, borrowing ideas and techniques from the American creators of hippie activism, the San Francisco-based Diggers, when he could and making up a whole lot of others as he went along. He was very very good at it, in part because the changes the new style demanded of him were ones he understood and had already begun to live.

One of those changes was language. Being a hippie activist meant mastering a new approach to speech and communication. It meant, for Hoffman, moving from his well-reasoned, polished graduate school rhetoric to a hip patois—a language redolent with "you knows," all-purpose signifiers like "groovy" and "cool," and swarms of images that aimed to share an experience rather than to state a position. As Hoffman put it later: "See like I learned all that shit and then I had to reprogram myself. It took me about four years to unlearn the English language so that I speak so people can understood it."

More important, Hoffman and his fellow hippie activists began to develop a new kind of public "happening"—a street theater—that aimed to mobilize both the hippie community and develop the consciousness of the general public through focused absurdity, startling put-ons, and straight-ahead community organizing. The inspiration for the street theater came from everywhere—from the live comedies of TV's Golden Age to the New York art scene's return to performance art that aimed to break down the barriers between art and life, performer and audience. In its most distilled and direct form, Hoffman and his friends found what they were looking for in the figures of the Diggers, who had only in the last year begun working their magic in the Haight-Ashbury.

The Diggers had emerged full-blown from the San Francisco Mime Troupe. They saw life and theater as just two words for the same basic thing. Hip to the ways of Brecht and Artaud, and well-schooled by one of the West Coast's most fertile minds, R. G. Davis, founder of the Mime Troupe, the Diggers aimed to be Life Actors who played their parts to the hilt. Costumes, props, improvisations, and skits were moved from the preserve of the theater to where, as they said, life was played for keeps. If much of the world of art and theater was struggling with the distance between culture as elite and mannered contrivance and culture as a collective way of life, the Diggers, grooving to psychedelic visions and the readily available fact that they were living in a community that was fervently trying to create a collective culture, sought to act in, as well as out, the struggle. While straight thinkers like Susan Sontag were talking about similar concerns, it was to the Diggers—artists and political philosophers without portfolio—that Hoffman and other hippie activists around the country would look for inspiration and workable tools.

The Summer of Love, 1967, saw Hoffman and a growing band of like-minded individuals playing out a new style of reality. Equipped with flowers and their very long hair, Hoffman and friends joined the hard-hat, flag-waving Support Our Boys in Vietnam parade. They regularly confronted the local ninth precinct police over harassment of long hairs, Puerto Ricans, and blacks. They sent out hundreds of real joints to people picked out of the phone book as well as a few to local TV newspeople; they wrote and distributed dozens of free leaflets giving the latest on dope, dreams, and street diseases; and they organized sweep-ins, be-ins, and generally good times that brought the community together and on cherished occasions blew the minds of the straight world. Some of this Hoffman did while calling himself a Digger. He pulled off other actions as a part of ESSO, the East Side Survival Organization, and others were pure free lance. That summer, Abbie married Anita in Central Park, the two of them adorned with love beads and flowers, friends and strangers gathered around, and the ceremony performed by their friend Lynn House, a "neo-american boo-hoo" minister. Their photographer was *Time* magazine.[10]

Jerry Rubin's story is not so very different. He was born in Cincinnati, Ohio, in 1938. His parents were Jewish but their class status was less certain than the Hoffmans'. Rubin's mother was well-educated and cultured but his father was a truck driver and later a business agent for the Teamsters. His wife's family looked down on him. Rubin grew up always a little resentful of the more well-to-do Jews who seemed to dominate his small world.

Rubin grew up straight without even the rebelliousness that characterized Hoffman's adolescence. He idolized Adlai Stevenson, was a fanatic supporter of the Cincinnati Reds, participated in extracurricular activities, and dedicated himself to his high school newspaper. He graduated from the University of Cincinnati and by 1960 was a very successful reporter for a Cincinnati newspaper, working as a sports reporter and then as "youth" editor. But Rubin wasn't satisfied. He had a lot of personal anger stored up and he was increasingly but frustratedly aware that the American system was selling too many people a bill of goods. He read a lot and flirted with socialism.

Rubin's mother died in 1960 and his father in 1961. They left Jerry a decent inheritance and the responsibility for his young brother, Gil. Shortly before his father died, Rubin had quit his job and won a scholarship to study in India. The task of taking care of Gil, which Rubin took very seriously, changed his plans. Instead of India, Rubin decided to take Gil to Israel, which seemed a more appropriate move to those family members who were looking over Jerry's shoulder. He went in part to do some graduate work in Jerusalem but mainly to check out Israel and think about the future. Rubin stayed almost a year and a half but he found himself increasingly sympathetic to the Palestinians and repelled by semi-socialist Israel's turn to bourgeois comforts and securities. Rubin mixed with leftists in Israel and became increasingly radicalized, seeing the world more and more from a Marxist perspective. In January 1964, Rubin left Israel in a professional mood and went to Berkeley to begin a Ph.D. program in sociology. He lasted six weeks in the program but he stayed in Berkeley for the next three years.[11]

In the superheated atmosphere of Berkeley, Rubin, now twenty-six years old, became a full-time political activist. Unlike Hoffman, who left Berkeley before the student movement had really begun, Rubin came just as it caught fire. He was a fervent participant in the Free Speech movement and quickly moved into leadership roles in the Berkeley antiwar movement. He also spent two months, that first summer in Berkeley, on a trip to Cuba led by the Progressive Labor party. This, Rubin later said, "was the final step for me. . . . I started to see things the way the Cubans did."[12]

In 1965, Rubin was one of the principal organizers of the first Vietnam teach-in. He then organized, with other hard-core Berkeley militants, the highly successful Vietnam Day Committee. In 1965, the

VDC staged a series of highly charged confrontations with troop trains that were carrying Vietnam-bound soldiers right through the Berkeley area. In one of the very first mass attempts to directly confront the war-making machine, the VDC led a march against the Oakland armed forces induction center. The movement press praised Rubin and his fellow VDC organizers for their imaginative activities and, as Rubin had intended, the VDC also received a good deal of mass media attention. The mass media seemed to take particular delight in the obnoxious behavior, symbolic acts, and wild claims of the movement. Later in the year, Rubin threw a container of blood on the car of General Maxwell Taylor, top military advisor to President Johnson, and earned his first prison sentence—thirty days.[13]

Ideologically, Rubin was in 1966 a member in good standing of the left branch of the movement. He used straight language to make politically correct attacks on America and on capitalism. Like SDS leadership and the older radicals who controlled the antiwar movement, he saw Vietnam as symptomatic of an entire American system that needed revolutionary changes. In the speech he gave at the March 26, 1966, antiwar rally in New York, Rubin said that Vietnam was only a part of "declared world wide American policy, . . . a symptom of our society's sickness." He said, "We are a dangerous country, a neurotic country possessing deadly power."[14]

At the same time, by 1966, Rubin was widely hailed within the movement as one of the most imaginative tacticians of protest. Rubin did things differently. He operated with images and not just with words. For example, to protest the manufacture of napalm just thirty miles outside of Berkeley, the Vietnam Day Committee painted an old truck an ominous gray and then affixed to it a huge bright yellow sign that warned, "Danger, Napalm Bombs Ahead." The truck followed the napalm delivery vehicles all around the Bay area, making sure that people saw concretely and unavoidably what was happening in their own community.[15]

Still in 1966, Rubin, like his fellow radicals, was unsure what to do next. He was comfortable with the basic premises of the movement—participatory democracy, community control, cooperation and not competition, realignment of foreign policy, demilitarization and black power—but like many others he believed that the movement had to communicate these ideas more convincingly. In that March 1966 antiwar speech, Rubin told his fellow marchers that to "talk to people who have never heard our ideas before we are going to have to become specialists in propaganda and communication." He discussed the use of art, music, newspapers, comic books, and movies in this war on consciousness, arguing for the creation of an active counterculture to overcome what he called "the most subtle and far reaching propaganda machine the world has ever seen."[16] The movement, Rubin believed, like other radicals before him, had to enter the twentieth century. Radicals must learn to manipulate the tools of mass communication and the symbols of mass society if they were to bring down the modern warfare State.

Increasingly, Rubin experimented with tactics. In mid-1966, he took the advice of R. G. Davis, leader of the San Francisco Mime Troupe, and answered a House Un-American Activities Committee subpoena wearing the uniform of an American revolutionary soldier. He blew the minds of the committee and grabbed the attention of the mass media.[17]

In early 1967, Rubin took a different tack and ran for mayor of Berkeley. His was a thoughtful, workable, albeit radical platform (it included free heroin for addicts and community control of a dis-armed police force). He wore a suit and a tie and issued a twenty-four-page booklet that used a semi-psychedelic format to present twenty-four carefully worded, well-reasoned one-page stands on lo-cal and national issues. He talked of building "a new political move-ment . . . and a new political party." Though he had started the campaign as a lark, once into it he turned serious, and in a very issue-oriented campaign spoke at shopping centers and shook hands on street corners.[18] Rubin thought he might win and was sorely disappointed when he finished a distant second in a four-man race (he had 22% of the vote, the winner had 69%). He decided that the compromises and the ensuing alienation from his militant comrades that electoral politics demanded were too high a price to pay for the long-shot opportunity to change things from within. Rubin turned his back on electoral politics with a vengeance, and for a long time scorned, as only one who's been there could, the co-optive powers of the American political system.[19]

Indeed, Rubin, who had not started smoking grass until he was twenty-eight and hadn't dropped acid until early in 1967,[20] decided political change was more likely to come from those who completely rejected the system than from those who fought right-wing politics with left-wing politics. Rubin started thinking hard about the political significance of the dropout, hippie community.

In the fall of 1967, David Dellinger, chairman of the Mobilization to End the War in Vietnam, asked Jerry to be project director of the October antiwar march in Washington, D.C. He picked Rubin in order to bring some zip to the unfocused demonstration. Rubin, a little bit at loose ends, agreed and moved to New York in the summer

of 1967. Immediately, he began arguing for a militant, colorful protest. It was his idea to march on the Pentagon and confront the war
makers.[21] In New York, Rubin discovered Abbie Hoffman. Quickly,
the two became partners and close friends.

Thus, by the time Rubin and Hoffman got together late in December
to celebrate the New Year and talk about Chicago, they'd known
each other about four months and had already worked together on
a few different projects. Each knew how the other thought. And that
was important when you're planning a new trip high on grass and
acid.

At the New Year's party, Rubin called on that shared experience,
talking about the last action they'd all pulled off together in late
November—"The War Is Over" demonstration.[22]

The War Is Over had been organized by Hoffman, Krassner, Rubin,
and Phil Ochs, the well-known folksinger and political activist. The
name came from a challenge beat poet Allen Ginsberg threw at the
National Student Association convention in 1966. At the convention
of college student body presidents, Ginsberg ended his poetry reading by screaming at his audience, "I declare the end of the war."
This became a sort of strategy that Ginsberg, who was by then a
prophet figure to both the movement and hippie communities, employed with increasing regularity to challenge the reality and in-
flexibility of power and authority. Ochs saw the poetry of the statement
and wrote a semipopular song that anthematically proclaimed, "I
declare the war is over." The demonstration itself involved about
three thousand young people who massed in Washington Square
and then ran down the streets from Grand Central Station to Times
Square back to Washington Square and over to Thompkin Square,
screaming over and over, "The was is over"—an Armistice Day, only
this victory was completely in the heads of the kids and the people
they got to rethink the war in Vietnam.[23]

This, Rubin said, had been an exemplary action, exciting and
alive and totally participatory; the best kind of guerrilla theater. The
event in Chicago should have the same spirit.

Paul Krassner wondered aloud how they could communicate this
same spirit and protest in the face of what he called the "convention
of death." Rubin, who had the most experience at making sure that
pleasant dope fantasies worked themselves down and into concrete
happenings, jumped on Krassner's wordplay. He wanted to call it
the Festival of Life: it would be open and public, outside in the park,
in the grass, with the trees and flowers, for a whole week a complete
alternative to the convention. Rubin already had the image in his
head: a hundred thousand young people in the park. They'd dance

to rock bands, spill into the streets, terrify the war machine by their very presence, and force Johnson to be nominated by the rubber-stamp convention under armed guard.

Abbie drifted into a long rap on leadership. Young people, he said, didn't want to listen to leaders, so they had to create a situation in which people would participate and so become, in a real sense, their own leaders. Abbie concluded that "this could be done by creating a number of imageries that would conflict,"[24] imageries that when totally added up didn't add up—so that people were on their own to do whatever they felt was necessary to do. In part, Hoffman was airing a central tenet of the hippie credo, the belief that everyone had to do their own thing. But Abbie was also talking out and putting into his own words the newest strategy in movement actions, a strategy that Rubin had helped to develop on the West Coast and Hoffman had helped to deploy only a couple of months earlier at the Pentagon demonstration.

At the Pentagon march, the top organizers of the demonstration had decided that in order to insure the largest possible participation by an antiwar movement increasingly divided as to tactics and even goals they would have to allow for a number of different protest options, ranging from militant confrontation to passive resistence to peaceful, legal assembly. Each demonstrator would decide for him or herself what tactic best suited his or her needs. The more militant and often experienced protestors would carry out their action without formal leadership. Decisions would be made spontaneously by all the participants. At least that was the theory, and in varying degrees it actually worked.

Pushing this multi-option theory of demonstrating, Hoffman, with Rubin's strong backing, had brought an element of guerrilla theater to the Pentagon demonstration by organizing an elaborate exorcise-ment. Hoffman, Ed Sanders and the Fugs, Keith Lampe, Martin Carey (the New York psychedelic poster maker), various members of the Lower East Side hip community, and a whole range of black magic practitioners passed out noisemakers, wild costumes, and witches' hats to intrigued protestors. It was comic theater and a genuine hunger for the liberating force of the irrational lined up against the fierce and deadly reason of the Military Machine. All together they chanted, sang religious songs, and attempted to levitate the Penta-gon three hundred feet in to the air in order to shake out all its evil spirits. The hippie movement was joined to the straight antiwar movement and all understood—do your own thing but make sure you do it where it can be photographed and recorded. It was a mass media hit.[25]

That led the group to one of their favorite conversational topics, the mass media. Hoffman's theory on the subject, which he hadn't had too many chances to act out yet, was that the best way to reach people and spread the new consciousness was by creating a "blank space" in the national media.

Hoffman believed that instead of sending out boring form letters or making tedious telephone calls—or, to take it a step further, instead of marching with picket signs (which made bad TV)—activists should use a kind of street theater that didn't directly come out and say "end the war" or "fight poverty" but instead drew mass media attention through its weirdness, absurdity, and colorfulness. By drawing in the mass media they'd reach an audience that would have never even considered radical politics or a counterculture way of life. They would make the people who saw them on TV or in a scandalized *New York Post* article think again about the way things were through their very absurdity and through the very lack of spelled-out meanings or message in their acts. People would have to figure things out for themselves, which was the start of a whole other way of seeing the world.[26] Hoffman was talking about a public political art form that he and a few other people around the country before him were just starting to pull off. This form and the understanding that educated it were always at the heart of Hoffman's operations. It was, in fact, this tactic that first drew Rubin to Hoffman.

Early in 1967, Hoffman and a few friends had joined a group of tourists for the official tour of the New York Stock Exchange. They remained moderately well-behaved until they were led to the balcony that overlooks the exchange floor. Then they all ran to the railing, took out three hundred—or maybe it was only thirty—one-dollar bills (the number was a part of the theater) and threw them down to the mass of packed stockbrokers. It worked perfectly. The brokers stopped everything and charged after the dollar bills, rooting them off the floor and creating pandemonium for five minutes. The story made the national news even though there were no pictures since Hoffman and friends hadn't tipped their plans to the media.

Later, in one of their first meetings, Hoffman took Rubin to the stock exchange, which in the meantime had built a bulletproof partition along the balcony to prevent any sort of repeat performance, and to the horror of onlookers they burnt some paper money. This time the mass media had been invited along.[27]

All this was part of a hodgepodge theory of mass media and mass society that Hoffman was working out as he went along. The linchpin of the theory was Hoffman's belief that reality, the very perceptibility of reality, was determined by the mass media and one's developmental relationship to it. Information, and much more important, the pattern that made that information make sense, Hoffman believed, came not as much from concrete experiences with everyday life as it did from the world the mass media brought into people's homes in ever heavier and more frequent doses. The changing form of the mass media, Hoffman felt, taking his cues in part from Marshall McLuhan, changed the way people perceived and thus made their way through reality.

Hoffman laid it out to his friends at the party like this: because of radio, people over fifty have to hear it to believe it; because of TV, people thirty to fifty have to see it to believe it; and because of the fact that people under thirty had grown up hip to the ways TV manufactured images, in order to get them to believe in something they needed to do more than just hear it or see it—they have to feel it to believe it and that means that to get the kids right into the new consciousness you can't just give them articles to read or speeches to listen to or even rallies to watch but instead you have to absolutely invent a whole new medium that begins with and depends on involvement and participation, that defines reality through immediacy rather than through passivity, that replaces explanation with actualization. It was the perfect acid epistemology for the TV generation—not quite coherent but piercing beyond the surface facts to an underlying whole.

Krassner had heard almost all of it before but the whole long conversation had him rocking and rolling: hippie as media myth, the "blank space," absurdity, the active spectacle; the irrational, magical possibilities of a youth festival of life confronting, overwhelming, and freaking out the convention of death. From somewhere in primary process land Krassner emerged with the epiphanous sound: "Yippie!"

Yippie! Yippie! He chortled. That's what they would be, the Yippies! The hippies who made yippie. Yip-e-i-o-ky-ya. Yippie is what the festival of life would be all about. All yipped and hooted and knew that it was right. They had found a slogan, childish, irrational, and joyous, the perfect blank space to organize both the mass media and their as yet unformed constituency.

Before the evening was over, Anita played out another idea. She said, our generation will understand Yippie, but for the *New York Times* and the straights, we should have a formal name, like SDS or something that they can relate to and take seriously. And playing around with yippie and words like youth festival and international festival of youth, the words that in part provide Krassner with his inspiration, she came up with the joke formalization, Youth International Party. It had all the right initials and made for a good wordplay

on party: the straights would treat it like the Democratic party and
the kids would know it meant the kind of party where you smoke
dope, get a little crazy, and make some easy trouble.

They spent the rest of the night thinking up ideas and listing people
they could get to help organize the festival. At the top of the list were
their occasional partners Phil Ochs and Ed Sanders, both of whom
had first-rate connections with their fellow rock and folk musicians.
They thought about running a pig as the presidential candidate of
the Youth International Party and putting out a newspaper called
the Chicago Tripune. It all seemed so perfect.[28]

From January through March, Hoffman and Rubin worked full time
organizing Yippie. They held meetings, wrote articles, produced
props, lined up people, thought out the angles.

Right after the new year began, Rubin and Hoffman began a series
of individual meetings and phone calls that produced another,
slightly more formal and larger meeting at the Hoffmans' apartment
on January 11.[29] The main planning group now included Ed Sanders
and Keith Lampe and was assisted by Bob Fass, who ran the most
wide-open, creative, pro–hippie show on New York's burgeoning
FM radio. Collectively, they began working on documents and plans.
Others were contacted.

A large meeting took place in mid-January at the swanky digs of
the very rich Peggy Hitchcock, who among other things was a fervent patron of acid apostle Timothy Leary. Leary, as well as poet/
guru Allen Ginsberg, was there. So was Marshall Bloom, who headed
the highly successful and influential Liberation News Service (a kind
of UPI for underground newspapers), as well as Allen Katzman, editor
of the *East Village Other,* one of the main hippie-oriented underground newspapers. Rubin and Hoffman presented Yippie and described their goal of putting on a joyous festival as an alternative to
the Democratic party convention. Rubin talked of making the Democratic party look like a buffoon circus, which he said would be
easy since "politics was just a circus." The audience of twenty-five
or so was very receptive, and Leary, Bloom, Katzman, and, with
some reservations, Ginsberg, agreed to help promote the Yippie
Festival of Life. The first thing to do, they all agreed, was to get an
office and some money and make Yippie more of a real thing. Very
quickly a three-day benefit dubbed "The Three Ring Yippie" was
arranged at the Electric Circus, one of New York's main dance and
music clubs.[30]

By mid-January, the Yippies had begun their advertising campaign. The first Yippie manifesto, written by Sanders, Krassner, Rubin,
and Hoffman, came out January 16. Distributed by the Liberation

News Service, it got good play in the underground press. Under a LNS headline, "An Announcement: Youth International Party (or Yip!) Is Born," the manifesto read:

> Join us in Chicago in August for an international festival of youth music and theater. Rise up and abandon the creeping meatball! Come all you rebels, youth spirits, rock minstrels, truth seekers, peacock freaks, poets, barricade jumpers, dancers, lovers and artists. It is summer. It is the last week in August and the NATIONAL DEATH PARTY meets to bless Johnson. We are there! There are 500,000 of us dancing in the streets, throbbing with amplifiers and harmony. We are making love in the parks. We are reading, singing, laughing, printing newspapers, groping and making a mock convention and celebrating the birth of FREE AMERICA in our own time.
>
> . . . New tribes will gather in Chicago. We will be completely open, everything will be free. Bring blankets, tents, draft cards, body paint, Mrs. Leary's cow, food to share, music, eager skin and happiness. The threats of LBJ, Mayor Daley and J Edgar Freako will not stop us. We are coming! We are coming from all over the world!
>
> The life of the American spirit is being torn asunder by the forces of violence, decay and the napalm, cancer fiend. We demand the politics of ecstasy. We are the delicate spoors of the new fierceness that will change America. We will create our own reality, we are Free America. And we will not accept the false theatre of the Death Convention. We will be in Chicago. Begin preparations now! Chicago is yours! Do it!

The manifesto closed with Yip's not quite open for business office address at 32 Union Square and a phone number. Twenty-five individuals and groups put their names to the manifesto, including big-time musical performers Phil Ochs, Country Joe McDonald, Arlo Guthrie, and Ed Sander's Fugs. Among others listed were the Bread and Puppet Theatre, the Paegent Players, Allen Ginsberg, Timothy Leary, and writers Marvin and Barbara Garson. Yippie was now a national product.[31]

The manifesto was just one form of Yippie promotion. Throughout January and February the Yippies (and there were just a handful of them) worked on making "Yippie" a household word, at least among the young and the hip. Hoffman took over the ephemera division while Rubin stuck to the articles and debate. These choices of media were revealing. Slowly, the political and tactical differences between Rubin and Hoffman began to emerge.

With the help of Judy Lampe and a few others, Hoffman produced Yippie buttons, flyers, and posters and distributed them around the country. Hoffman also went on a campaign to regularize the spelling of Yippie, which Rubin and the underground press had a way of changing every now and then. As Hoffman later said, "[Yippie] was conceived as an advertisement for a new society," and just "as Coca-Cola is always spelled the same way," so shall it be with Yippie![32] Hoffman put the official Yippie! logo—a psychedelic type climaxed with a roundish, fat exclamation point—on almost fifty thousand buttons. The official colors were pink letters against a purple background. Blank space advertising. According to Hoffman it would work like this: "People would come up and say, 'What does this mean?'" And then the button holder would move from follower to leader as he explained what Yippie was and what it stood for and about going to Chicago in August. Said Hoffman, "It was specifically designed so that everybody would get involved."[33]

Hoffman also produced an $8\frac{1}{2} \times 11$-inch poster that had the officially styled Yippie! with the words August 25th–30th scrawled across a background of almost three hundred typed words that Abbie felt "advertised the kinds of spirits we wanted." In part, it read: "Spree—woweee—Arlo—Guthrie—color—giggle—pleasure—happening—dancing—joy—the politics of ecstasy—Country Joe and the Fish—blankets—poetry—slapstick—venceremos—lights—challenge—yes—Allen Ginsberg—free—tribes—experience—zig-zag."

With Group Image Ltd., a collective of New York artists, Hoffman knocked out a four-color poster that showed a jigsaw puzzle map of the United States—"because it is our feeling that the country is disintegrating and falling apart like a jigsaw puzzle"—with an arrow pointing to Chicago. The only words were: "August 25–30 Chicago   Music Lights   Free Theatre   Magic."[34]

The Yippies also distributed a fairly normal flyer soliciting "conscription into the Yippie army." It asked for name and address and for people to indicate if they'd be interested in helping to do office work, art, organizing, or speaking. But even here the Yippie spirit was in play and the flyer closed by asking, "Who sez these are the only categories? God? Make your own—set up your own thing—fill in the blanks, read the white space. Participate. Initiate."[35] The posters, the flyers, the buttons were the ideogramatic representation of free play. Like the commercials the Yips dreamed of emulating, the Yippie promotions promised only fun, excitement, and fulfillment.

Jerry Rubin, in the articles and speeches he churned out all through the winter months, offered up a different picture of what Yippie and the Festival of Life were all about. His vision was both more explicit and more complex.

Unlike Hoffman, Rubin had been through the entire antiwar scene. And whereas Hoffman used absurdity both to maintain and advocate a freer society in which fun operated as the *lingua franca*, Rubin maintained closer connections to leftist revolutionary goals and was more deliberate in his search for tactics that would bring those goals to realization. At the Pentagon demonstration, Rubin had told a straight press conference, "We're now in the business of wholesale disruption and widespread resistance and dislocation of American society."[36]

Rubin continued to develop this commitment. A few weeks after the Pentagon, December 4–8, Rubin had participated in the unsuccessful attempt to shut down the Whitehall Induction Center in New York. Over five hundred people were arrested at the confrontation and the demonstrators, blocked by hundreds of New York City police, never even got close to the induction center. But at Whitehall Rubin saw much that was good: "The swiftly changing situation frees our thinking. . . . The stated goals of the demonstration are never the real ones." Instead of really shutting down the Whitehall Induction Center, Rubin saw the purpose of the action as being to create "a good fantasy." The action served as more than symbolic protest and more than existential firing for the protestors: "We communicate to the public many emotions . . . . The expressions of those emotions across the nation are the real external goals of the demonstration. We feel deeper than those who support the war. We are shown to be alive."

With these goals in mind, Rubin was very pleased with the general tactic of the Whitehall protest, which West Coast demonstrators had named "mobile tactics." As Rubin said, the demonstrators used their mobility to "spread the cops out, stay ahead of them and stop traffic." In other words, rather than marching in neat columns with picket signs and then perhaps submitting to arrest in the prescribed civil disobedience fashion, those protestors who opted for mobile tactics attempted to storm the induction hall and when rebuffed by strong police opposition ran away, creating havoc as they retreated, regrouped, and then charged again or ran elsewhere, spreading the spirit of resistance and anger. Rubin particularly liked this chaos because it left so much of the decision making up to the individual or small groups of allied protestors. There could be no real central authority or leadership in the streets during a spontaneous set of mobile tactics. It upped the personal ante for all concerned. This, Rubin thought, was the tactic of the future.[37] Many shared his enthusiasm.

At the Labor Forum in New York, in the first week of January, Rubin debated Fred Halstead, a prominent Old Left antiwar figure and the

Socialist Worker party candidate for president, on the direction the
antiwar movement should take. In a rush of words, Rubin left no
doubts about where he stood and what he wanted the antiwar
movement to do: "There's no such thing as an antiwar movement.
This is a concept created by the mass media to fuck up your minds.
What's happening is energy exploding in thousands of directions
and people declaring themselves free. . . . The world laughs at
America's clumsy attempt to defeat peasant warriors called Viet
Cong. . . . In America we are all learning to be Viet Cong." Rubin,
espousing a very rigid anti-intellectualism, then launched into a
direct attack on the sectarianism of the Socialist Workers party and
the old left, in general:

> One lesson learned at the Pentagon and at Whitehall
> is that young people didn't give a hang about the politi-
> cal theories, ideologies, plans, organization, meetings.
> . . . Language does not radicalize people—what
> changes people is the emotional involvement of action.
> What breaks through apathy and complacency are
> confrontation and actions. . . . The Trots are uninspiring,
> they lack music, color, life.

Rubin has a clear alternative in mind: "I support everything which
puts people into motion, which creates disruption and controversy,
which creates chaos and rebirth . . . people who burn draft cards
. . . burn dollar bills . . . say FUCK on television . . . freaky, crazy,
irrational, sexy, angry, irreligious, childish, mad people." These were
the people Rubin believed could reach American youth because
youth knew "instinctively" what the older leaders of the antiwar
movement refused to recognize: that the government was "reacha-
ble only through the language of power and violence. . . . America
understands peace demonstrators fighting in the streets and that's
why we are more dangerous than a hundred Martin Luther Kings."
Rubin ended his talk with a call to Chicago. He presented this
scenario: "Chicago is in panic. The American Youth Festival has
brought 500,000 young people to Chicago to camp out, smoke pot,
dance to wild music, burn draft cards and roar like wild bands
through the streets, forcing the president to bring troops home from
Viet Nam to keep order in the city while he is nominated under the
protection of tear gas and bayonets." When someone asked Rubin
if this sort of action didn't guarantee brutal and heavy-handed
repression, Rubin replied with glee:

> Repression turns demonstration protests into wars. Ac-
> tors into heroes. Masses of individuals into a community.

Repression eliminates the bystander, the neutral observer, the theorist. It forces everyone to pick a side. A
movement cannot grow without repression. The left
needs an attack from the right and the center. Life is
theatre and we as the guerrillas attacking the shrines of
authority, from the priests and the holy dollar to the two
party system. Zapping people's minds and putting them
through changes in actions in which everyone is emotionally involved. The street is the stage. You are the star
of the show. And everything you were once taught is up
for grabs.

In sum, Rubin told his mainly older, working-class audience,
"politics is how you live." Rubin's harangue, as he expected, was
received very, very coolly by the old leftists. Halstead, who was an
old friend of Rubin's and had first suggested him to David Dellinger
for project director of the Pentagon demonstration only a few
months earlier, was angered and disappointed by Rubin's turn
toward anarchy and countercultural extremism. Halsted told
Rubin he'd be lucky to draw a few thousand people to his festival if
he continued to make speeches like that. Still, through the debate,
Rubin accomplished his goal: significant sections of Rubin's
harangue were widely printed in most of the more important
underground newspapers.[38]

Over the next few weeks Rubin fleshed out and continued to promote his politics of action in a series of articles printed by the *Berkeley
Barb* and reprinted in underground newspapers around the country.
Knowing that he was already speaking to the converted, or at least
to those who shared his concerns, Rubin took some pains to explain
his position: "It's getting harder and harder to reach people with
words. Harder and harder to find anything that *is* outrageous. . . .
Logical argument doesn't work. . . . People are emotion freaks.
People are crazy. We've got to involve people emotionally in our
actions."[39] He also wrote that "television has outmoded books." so
those who want a revolution had better learn to communicate ap-
propriately.[40]

Rubin explained why American youth were the natural vanguard
of political change: "Every generation should look to the younger
generation for leadership, because it is the younger generation which
is the most directly and emotionally affected by society's repression.
The younger you are the clearer is your head." Rubin believed that
throughout the West the process of socialization had broken down,
torn apart by a whole set of internal contradictions, and that young
people, increasingly or even already conscious of the contradictions,

could be made a revolutionary force. As the old saying went, all that needed to be done was to heighten the contradictions and then fan the flames.[41] "History has chosen us," Rubin intoned, "born white in middle class America—to reverse centuries of America . . . to vomit up our inheritance. . . . Ours will be a revolution against privilege and a revolution against the boredom of steel–concrete plastic." Chicago would reveal all the contradictions, it would display the revolutionary life force of youth by putting the Convention of Death up against the wall: "Chicago is LBJ's stage and we are going to steal it."[42]

Rubin's first major article on Yippie, published in the *Berkeley Barb* on February 16, gathered together the various threads he had been laying out for the previous six weeks. Rubin attempted to lend Yippie the solid revolutionary credentials he had been known for in Berkeley. He began with the countercultural. The Yippie is, he said, "creating a clean alternative, an underground opposition. He is involved in a cultural revolution. . . . He is seducing the ten year olds with happenings, community, youth power . . . a new style." For his Berkeley readers, members of the most militant community in the country, Rubin spoke directly of political actions the Yippies might pull off in Chicago. Yippies would be "blocking traffic, throwing blood, burning money . . . milling-in, fucking up the draft . . . bottom up revolution . . . [and] you are needed to work on it. . . . A lot of troops will have to watch us . . . and the Yippies being wanderers will be all over the city."

In this article, Rubin fleshed out the festival with absurd possibilities, vague probabilities, and some sincere hopes: the Festival of Life would be a "multi-media experience [with] . . . everything free," performers might include Bob Dylan, the Animals, the Beatles, Janis Ian, the Smothers Brothers, the Who, the Jefferson Airplane, the Monkees; there would be free microphones, mimeos, underground newspapers, teach-ins on film, underground media; living free, guerrilla theater, and the draft. The Yippies would nominate Bancroft P. Hogg for president, Yippie infiltrators would make their way into the convention, Yippie cabs would drive delegates to Wisconsin, and Yippie pep squads would line up and burn their draft cards to spell out "Beat Army." The Yippies, Rubin declared, were moving from the Be-In to the Do-In. In Rubin's scenario rock bands would be sharing the stage with revolutionaries and everybody would be laughing right up to the barricades. Chicago would be the protest event of the year.[43]

There was a good deal more to Yippie than the various promotions of Rubin and Hoffman. And Yippie did exist outside its posters, buttons, manifestos, and articles. The Yippie office at 32 Union Square opened at the beginning of February and served as an "energy center." Hoffman, Rubin, Sanders, Lampe, Fass, Nancy Kurshan, and Jim Fouratt, local hippie activist and sometimes Yippie, were constantly running in and out of the office, talking on the phone, planning meetings, discussing posters, and plotting future Yippie actions. The office staff, which pretty much meant anyone who came in and offered to help, answered the letters that came in from around the country asking about Yip— letters they answered by explaining that a Yippie was anyone who called himself or herself a Yippie and that the writer should just start his or her own Yippie group wherever they were and come to Chicago in August.

Besides Hoffman and Rubin, who were, so to speak, first among equals, Yippie depended on Paul Krassner, Ed Sanders, and Keith Lampe to keep things together. Lampe, from February on, gave almost all his time and energy to Yippie. At thirty-seven, with a wife and daughter, he was the oldest of the full-time Yippies and, though an enjoyer of drugs and occasional costumery, was, relatively speaking, a moderating voice of reason. Lampe had served in Korea but he was a committed pacifist who attempted to cool the talk of violence which Rubin's articles had made a topic of increasing concern among the Yippie organizers.

Like Hoffman, Lampe had worked in the early sixties for SNCC in the South. Later, he'd come to New York and become a dedicated antiwar worker. He had helped with press relations for the Fifth Avenue Peace Parade Committee (the main New York antiwar organization) and had been a part-time staffer for *Liberation*, under the editorship of David Dellinger. Also like Hoffman, Lampe (who had spent the better part of the 1950s traveling around the world, taking in Asian as well as European culture) found much in the new youth culture that was personally liberating.[44] By mid-1967, in movement literature, he called on the antiwar movement to recognize the spirit and energy of the new counterculture. During the planning of the Pentagon demonstration, Lampe was very much aligned with Rubin and Hoffman.

It was Lampe, in *Liberation*, who explained the new sensibilities of the Rubin faction to the straight antiwar movement just before the demonstration:

> The work of the black men of Newark and Detroit has
> freed us honkies (Beep! Beep!) of a few more scholarly
> hang ups and we're getting down into now

> . . . we're getting past the talk and the analysis and the
> petitions and the protests, past the cunning logic of the
> universities and we're heading back down into our-
> selves. The worst trip of all is finally coming to an end.
> . . . We emancipated primitives of the coming culture
> are free to do what we *feel* now because we under-
> stand that logic and proportion and consistency, often
> even perspective are part of the old control system and
> we're done with the old and done with the control sys-
> tems.[45]

Lampe was a valuable Yippie. He wrote well, had a highly developed sense of the absurd, had good connections among the antiwar
movement and the press, and was a hard worker.

Yippie mainstay Ed Sanders was a longtime, hard-core member of
the Lower East Side. Long-haired, a wearer of wild robes, for him
mixing absurdity with political activism was old hat. Through much
of the 1960s, his Peace Eye Bookstore on East Tenth gave home to
some of the most creative energy that flowed through the Lower East
Side.

For several years, Sanders had been editor and publisher of *Fuck
You/A Magazine of the Arts*. At a time when four-letter words and explo-
rations of sex were widely censored in the mass media, Sanders dedicated *Fuck You* to detailed frenzies of poetic exposition on penises,
vaginas, fellatio, and other related subjects. In 1965, Sanders had used
Fuck You to promote a "Fuck-In" for peace at his bookstore. Also in
1965, Sanders founded the Fugs (at the time, the word publishers often
forced authors to substitute for fuck), a rock band devoted to bizarre
mixtures of sex and revolution songs. By 1968 the Fugs had two record
albums and Sanders had three poetry books.

A believer in "non-violent, militant direct action," which was in
essence a form of pacifism, Sanders' antiwar commitment preceded
the Vietnam protests. In 1961, along with David Dellinger, he had
participated in the San Francisco to Moscow Walk for Peace. Later
he spent thirty days in jail for trying to board nuclear submarines in
New London, Connecticut. Sanders had also participated in various
civil rights projects, including the 1962 walk from Nashville to Washington, D.C.[46]

By mid-1967, Sanders's politics were in a total flux and like most
other committed movement people he was on the lookout for tactics
that would be efficacious while at the same time expressive of his
own vision. While in town to play a concert in San Francisco, Sanders
told the *Berkeley Barb*: "My motto is 'Fuck God in the ass.' I don't
have any faith at all in the efficacy of politics. . . . I'm political—I
vote and hustle and hike, fight and scream. Nonviolently. I don't

know what to do. We just try." He added, "I read everything I can read and go to all the demonstrations. . . . I don't know. The way to do it is really be militant, man, and go after them. . . . I don't see how you could disrupt the war machinery with love, because human beings are, like, abstracted from the war machine."[47] The Fugs' big hit song that year was "Kill for Peace." In concert, during the song, Sanders stomped on a large doll.[48]

Sanders had known Rubin since 1965 and had gotten to know Abbie Hoffman early in the summer of 1967 at various Lower East Side community meetings. With the Fugs, Sanders had been an integral part of the exorcisement of the Pentagon, leading much of the chanting and singing.[49]

Sanders had a hand in all facets of Yippie, but his most critical function was lining up the bands that would play at the Festival of Life.

Among the main figures in Yippie, Paul Krassner had the most ambiguous role. Thirty-six years old, moderately long-haired, a hip but not hippie dresser, Krassner was a professional satirist who had turned more and more to politics for his humor. He called himself a participant/observer and regularly wrote for *Playboy*, *Cavalier*, and *Ramparts*. Krassner had begun his career as a hard-edged humorist in the 1950s writing for *Mad* magazine, doing jokes for *Playboy*, and writing material for Steve Allen. In 1958, he started his own magazine of satire, *The Realist*, which became more and more political as the 1960s wore on. Closer in spirit to *Playboy* than Ed Sanders's *Fuck You*, most of all *The Realist* attempted and often succeeded in emulating the absurdist, politically edged humor of Lenny Bruce. One of Krassner's more infamous articles was a parody of William Manchester's book on John Kennedy. Krassner claimed to be printing a censored chapter of Manchester's work: the "censored chapter" had Lyndon Johnson having sex with John Kennedy's corpse while flying from Dallas to Washington, D.C. Krassner was not one for respecting the normal taboos of polite society.

Krassner was an early and enthusiastic explorer of LSD. He was also an early and enthusiastic supporter of the San Francisco Diggers—he arranged with them to publish *The Digger Papers*, which explained how to establish a "free" society.[50]

The essence of Krassner's politics was simple: "My whole style is just laughing at them."[51] He had always preferred absurdity over violence, though by 1968 Krassner was advocating violence in self-defense.

Krassner was a dedicated activist, a longtime speaker at rallies and teach-ins. He had first met Jerry Rubin in 1965 at the Berkeley Teach-In and had met Hoffman in 1966 at Liberty House. Politically aware but indifferent to movement politics or hierarchies, Krassner's long experience with *The Realist* and satirical political writing made him a natural ally to both Rubin and Hoffman.

In on Yippie from the very start, Krassner attended most of the Yippie planning sessions, helped write the manifestos and other advertisements and promoted Yippie at his frequent speaking engagements around the country. Krassner, the only Yippie with a fairly good, steady income, also helped pay printing costs and office rent. *The Realist* and his other professional obligations took up a lot of Krassner's time.[52] Since he wasn't a nuts-and-bolts organizer like Hoffman or an accepted, radical political writer like Rubin, there often wasn't much for Krassner to do.

As winter drew to a close in New York other prominent figures became closely associated with Yippie. In the main, they were less dedicated and less positive of what Yippie hoped to accomplish than Rubin, Hoffman, Lampe, Krassner, and Sanders.

Of these figures, topical folk singer Phil Ochs was the most dependable. As early as January, he had assured Rubin that he'd be in Chicago come what may, a statement no other performer would make. By 1968, Ochs had recorded half a dozen successful, if not Billboard Top Ten, record albums. Ochs was a popular performer at universities and peace and civil rights demonstrations around the country. In style and desire, Ochs was a sometimes uncomfortable mixture of Bob Dylan and Pete Seeger, aiming for the popularity and artistry of the one while trying to maintain the political consciousness and dedication of the other. More often than not Ochs was willing to put his political dedication above his performing career.[53]

Allen Ginsberg also gave his approval and help to the Yippies but far less wholeheartedly. Indeed, much of his participation in Yippie was aimed at neutralizing its violent tendencies and helping to develop its festive, enlightening, and spiritual possibilities. Ginsberg, in the most sophisticated and thoughtful way, represented the hippie pole of Yippie.

Long before Yippie, Ginsberg had been advocating just such a union of political activists and hippies. In early 1967 he stated, "The hippies have deeper insight into consciousness, the radicals more information about the workings and nature of consciousness in the world."[54] He also wrote, "We're back to magic, to psychic life . . . power's a hallucination. The warfare's psychic now. Whoever controls the language, the images, controls the race."[55] Ginsberg understood what Yippie wanted, he had said and lived much of it long before Rubin or Hoffman had dreamed of long hair, marijuana, or festivals of life. And the Yippie style was one he had long been practicing. In April 1967 he declared in *Liberation*, "America's political need is orgies in the park."[56] It was in the getting there that Ginsberg saw the problem.

Ginsberg fervently opposed violence. He did not want to see people manipulated or misled. He did want to see "academies of self awareness," "classes in spirituality," "an official politics of control of anger."[57] But in the speeches and writings of Jerry Rubin and in the shapelessness of Hoffman's scenarios, Allen Ginsberg saw "bloody visions of the apocalypse," and he was wary.[58]

Several other people, most of them either part of the New York hippie or hip community or associates of Jerry Rubin, worked hard to make Yippie happen. Bob Fass, one of the most original and creative radio people in New York, used his alternative, free form radio show on WBAI to promote Yip and he was into the highest levels of planning and participating. Jim Fouratt, a young, gay hippie activist, who long before Hoffman got into the scene was organizing street activities and Be-Ins was part of Yippie. But like Ginsberg he had his doubts about some of the violence talk. He also worried about the national versus local issue and slowly came to believe that Yippie was too interested in the old consciousness of revolutionary politics and not enough into the new head of being free in the here and now. Nancy Kurshan, Rubin's longtime woman friend, took care of a lot of business and made sure that the office wasn't a scene of total chaos. Kate Coleman, a Berkeley vet, who now had a job with *Newsweek*, sided with Rubin and made sure that leftist politics played their part. Stew Albert, another Berkeley vet with a national reputation, did the same. He and Rubin were very tight. Brad Fox was a middleman, a resources person, hustling around, making sure that things happened. There were others like Robin Palmer, Dan Cupid/Peter Rabbit, and David Boyd who worked in the office and on the events.

By the end of winter there were small groups identifying with Yippie in Washington, D.C., Philadelphia, Boston, Berkeley, San Francisco, Los Angeles, and Chicago.[59]

Their numbers were small, but Yippie had captured the imaginations of some of the hippest people on the East and West Coasts. Yippie was happening.

2 The Politics of Laughter

On a day-to-day basis, Yippie tried to do right by the Movement ideas of open planning, community involvement, and participatory democracy. The office on Union Square was open to anybody who came in and wanted to help, and there were regular, free form public planning meetings. The meetings were held every Saturday at 2 P.M. at the Free University at 14th between Fifth Avenue and University Place. As the name implies, the Free University (which added up to two large rooms on the second floor of a loft building) gave away space for a variety of countercultural functions. Later, when the weather warmed up, the meetings were held outside, right in the middle of Union Square. Secrecy was not a Yippie value.[1]

The meetings brought out the people, with anywhere from fifty to several hundred catching at least part of the show. Many knew one another, either from the neighborhood or through politics, and most of the meetings had a festive air with balloons being batted around, smoke in the air, and lots of noise.

Rubin, or one of the other major Yippies, chaired the meetings, but parliamentary proceedings were not observed. There were no motions, no votes, only discussions, arguments, and attempts to produce consensus. More often than not, the meetings served as window dressing for decisions already made by Rubin, Hoffman, Lampe, Sanders, and Krassner, with as always the emphasis on Rubin and Hoffman. The plain people of Yippie were there less to decide policy than to be amused and implicated in the decision-making process. Which is not to say that the meetings went smoothly or were deliberately planned in advance—there was open airing of disagreement and always a high level of chaos.

By the end of the winter, the meetings were revealing some of the tensions that were growing between Yippie's purer hippie wing and its more practical political wing. This tension broke loose in an early March meeting that was supposed to center around the question of where to hold a "straight" press conference.

Rubin chaired the meeting. Kate Coleman and Abbie Hoffman were also up in front of the crowd of over a hundred people.

Rubin began the proceedings, in the midst of the balloon batting and loud talking, by summarizing the press conference situation. The site, he said, was the main problem. The Hotel Roosevelt had turned them down "on the grounds that we're too controversial." The Community Church, a Lower East Side institution, had given them a solid offer at no charge. But Rubin said, "I'm afraid we'd lose forty percent of the press if we used such a down beat location." Kate Coleman, *Newsweek* professional and Yippie stalwart, said she agreed. Tuli Kupferberg, member of the Fugs and a longtime Lower East Side denizen, goofed on the idea of having the press conference at *Time* magazine. But Hoffman deflated the groundswell of support by saying, "But then *Newsweek* wouldn't come."

Keith Lampe argued, "There's nothing wrong with the Community Church. Why give money to the Enemy when we can get a place for free and spend it on the community," to which Rubin angrily replied, "Oh for God's sake, this is our first press conference. It's important we should have it at some formidable place. This isn't just an East Village thing—these writeups will bring all kinds of people into the movement." Hoffman interrupted, "Look, forget about the press conference for a minute." And Rubin did, moving the discussion to a letter he'd gotten from two members of SDS who'd put Yippie down for being too disorganized and unpolitical and who'd said that Chicago was a mistake. Rubin asked the crowd, "Do you want to talk about it?" To which Kate Coleman said, "I thought we'd passed that point." But Jim Fouratt, for one, had not.

Jim Fouratt, longtime New York hippie activist and organizer of the 1967 Be-In, said the SDSers weren't the only ones asking questions: "The Diggers are asking what are we standing for, what are we saying?" The narrow focus on Chicago, Fouratt felt, was warping Yippie and its members, taking too much energy away from the local counterculture. "What are we getting people to Chicago for?" he wanted to know. "Are we going to face them with a lot of cops?"

Ed Sanders couldn't buy that and he shouted back, "Look . . . Chicago is the focus of Yippie and if you don't like it you should get out."

Fouratt retorted, "I see articles about running in the streets and setting things on fire, not talk about a festival. We should project the idea of a festival, not the violence thing." Someone else shouted, that's not Yippie stuff, that's somebody else. Fouratt tried to explain what he meant: "The point is people aren't supposed to stop doing their local thing to work in Chicago. We have to use our ideas here. We have costumes, ok, we should use them now, not save them for

Chicago. . . . Instead of a press conference we should have a community thing at NYU or Stony Brook."

Rubin argued that the press conference was important. Fouratt said, "Why, they'll just lie about us." Kate Coleman hammered the Yippie postcelebrity media message home: "It doesn't matter what the press says about us as long as they say something." Fouratt, holding onto a less cynical attitude toward communication and the formation of consciousness, could only say, "It does matter."

At the end of the meeting, the matter of the press conference seemed to be unresolved. But, of course, it wasn't. The press conference went ahead as scheduled. It was held at the ritzy Hotel Americana on March 17. And it worked. The press gave the Yippies a whole lot of free national advertising.[2]

Fouratt's belief that Yippie should be more than Chicago and the Festival of Life, while not well received at the open meeting, did make sense to Yippie's informal central committee and was in fact a part of the modus operandi. The Yips knew and had always known that Yippie had to be more than a series of advertisements delivered from above. It had to have an ongoing participatory side and that meant doing more than just planning for Chicago. There had to be events and activities which would not only give the plain people a chance to *be* Yippies in the here and now but would also present the mass media and the underground press with something tangible to focus in on and so project the Yippie image around the country.

The first formal Yippie event (there had been an earlier bit of Yippie theater on February 27 at SUNY Stony Brook—about one hundred nascent Yips goofed around the campus, many dressed as Keystone Cops, parodying and protesting a recent campus drug bust) came hard on the heels of the tense early March meeting and the news conference. It was called the Yip-In. It happened March 22 at Grand Central Station.

The Yip-In was loosely based on the Fly-In Bob Fass had promoted the year before at La Guardia Airport. Using his radio show on WBAI, Fass raised the idea of people just showing up late one night at La Guardia for a big party and sort of urbanized be-in. There'd been no organization or real planning or anything but on the night Fass had set for the Fly-In a couple of thousand young people had shown up at the airport, primed for fun. Everything had turned out fine, with the kids goofing with balloons and watching the planes zoom in and out—activities that can be more than entertaining under the right metabolic conditions. There had been no hassles.[3]

The Yips saw no reason why the Yip-In shouldn't work along much the same lines. Hoffman talked to the proper New York City officials so they would know what was going on and Keith Lampe was basically in charge of planning the thing which essentially meant promoting it, getting it into the papers and making leaflets so that people would get the word. Nobody worried about the logistical details as there didn't seem to be any need to. As *Village Voice* reporter Don McNeil put it later, "The promotion was as heavy as the planning was weak."[4]

The Yip-In flyer promised nothing but good times: "Yippie! Yippie! with you performer and audience. . . . Get acquainted with other Yippies now for other Yippie activities and Chicago Y.I.P. Festival . . . bring bells, flowers, beads, music, radios, pillows, eats, love and peace."[5]

As the heralded night took off, it seemed like good times were all the Yippies and quasi-Yippies were going to have. By midnight, over five thousand people had gathered in Grand Central Station for the Yip-In. Neither Lampe nor Hoffman had expected that kind of turnout and the station was packed. Still, everything seemed to be going fine with people singing, dancing, throwing balloons around, sharing food and drink, and just getting high on the crowd and the good spirits. Then too, there were groups of people chanting things like, "Yippie!," "Long Hot Summer," and "Burn Baby Burn." And a member of the Up Against the Wall, Motherfucker had climbed on top of the information booth and with clenched fist in the air unfurled a banner which read vertically, "Up Against the Wall, Motherfucker!" Politics and Fun—Dope and Democracy. The Yippie leadership was congratulating itself. And then things got heavy.

Two people climbed up to the giant clock in the middle of the station and made a poetic statement. They removed the clock hands.

Suddenly, without warning, the fifty or so tactical force police who had been standing around the periphery of the station formed a wedge and charged into the packed crowd with clubs flying. Hoffman ran up to the city officials who were there overseeing things and asked them what in the hell was going on, saying that if they wanted to clear the place out this was an insane way to do it. He asked the officials to get on the public address system and make an announcement or let him make an announcement or anything to calm things down and stop the police. The official said he had no control over the police and would not let Hoffman get on the p.a. system. Abbie tried the same thing with the police officer who seemed to be in charge and was told, "It's too late now. You had your chance. Now we have ours."

The police went through the crowd arbitrarily clubbing people and almost chanting the refrain, "Get the fuck out of here, get out." A few people responded to the police rampage by throwing bottles and garbage at the police. Most people were simply terrified, trapped by the crushing crowd and the police, who offered no exit. Several of the cops went through the crowd screaming, Where's Hoffman? Where's Rubin? Soon enough, they found Hoffman and clubbed him to the ground. Ron Shea, a Baltimore Yippie, tried to protect the prostrate Hoffman with his body. The cops picked Shea up and very deliberately threw him through a plate glass door; the shattering glass severed the tendons in Shea's left hand.

The violence went on and on for more than an hour and a half with the police retreating every now and then for no apparent reason. The police seemed to take particular pleasure in clubbing credential-displaying members of the underground press. They arrested fifty-seven people, mainly for disorderly conduct and resisting arrest, and sent over twenty, including Hoffman, to the hospital. Yippie, having expected neither violence nor arrests, had set up neither legal nor medical aid.

The police never succeeded in completely clearing the station, although it's not clear that that was their purpose since they never tried systematically to do so. At 3:30 A.M., there were still a thousand or so celebrants in the station. Together, as was originally planned, they made their way over to Sheep Meadow in Central Park and watched the sunrise.[6]

The Yip-In put the Yippies on the national map for good. They made the TV news and, if not the headlines, at least the front section of most major newspapers in the country. Yippie, "the blank space," was entering into the national consciousness, and although this was not the incident by which the Yips would have made themselves known, it would have to do.

Among movement people and fellow travelers, the reaction to the Yip-In was mixed. Although no one blamed Yippie for provoking the police into their attack—indeed, the New York Civil Liberties Union issued a report unequivocally castigating the New York police for "systematic and indiscriminate assault upon both demonstrators and innocent bystanders"[7]—people did blame Yippie for setting up a situation in which unprepared people could be stomped so easily. Don McNeil, who at twenty-three was probably the most influential writer on the counterculture and the youth movement in New York, wrote in the March 22 *Village Voice* that the Yip-In amounted to "a pointless confrontation in a box canyon and somehow it seemed to be a prophecy of Chicago."[8]

By 1968, anybody who'd been to a serious demonstration or wore their hair over their ears, whether in New York, Los Angeles, Oakland, or Detroit, knew that the police were always looking for any kind of an excuse to beat up some "hippies." The Yippies, people were saying, should have known better. They should have been better prepared and they should have thought the whole thing out a lot more carefully. The days of the bucolic be-ins were over.

But of course Jerry Rubin knew that the peace and love days were over, days, of course, in which he had never participated. In the *Voice* he responded subtly and ambiguously to the anti-Yuppie remarks that had followed the Yip-In. First, he castigated McNeil by name, accusing him of being far too negative and possibly frightening people away from Chicago. If the Yip-In "seemed to be a prophecy of Chicago," Rubin wrote, "can't an argument also be made that a police riot against the youth festival during the time of the Death Convention would be the worst thing that could possibly happen to the Democratic Party in 1968?"[9] Just as Rubin had reasoned during his debate with Fred Halstead, so Rubin reiterated three months later: violence and repression are part of the revolutionary process; they help get done what's necessary.

This was exactly the kind of talk that so infuriated some members of the movement, and not just older and more careful folks like the prominent chairman of the Socialist Worker Party, Fred Halstead. SDS, even before the Yip-In, had blasted the Yippies for being irresponsible and dangerously misleading. In the March 4 *New Left Notes*, an editorial stated that Yippie's "intention to bring thousands of young people to Chicago during the DNC to groove on rock bands and smoke grass and then put them up against bayonets—viewing that as a radicalizing experience—seems manipulative at best. The idea would not be so bad were it not for the National Guard and the Chicago Police."[10] Yippie worried a lot of people.

Then too, Yippie had its champions. Julius Lester, columnist for the independent socialist newspaper the *Guardian*, and one of the clearest, least dogmatic radical commentators writing in the 1960s, understood what the Yippies were trying to do. He countered the uproar that followed the Yip-In by giving them a big vote of confidence. He ignored the specific problems of the Yip-In and gave a pithy description of all that was right about Yippie:

> In a country where the picket sign march and demonstration have become respectable, other means of communicating a political point of view must be found. Regis Debray talks of armed propaganda. . . .

The Yippies have begun to explore the techniques of
disarming propaganda. They have their roots not in
Mao or Che but in the Provos, rock and Lenny Bruce.
They ignore what a man thinks and grab him by the
balls to communicate their message.

They seek to involve people in an experience, not
argue with them. They are like Zen monks who never
answered a question directly, never set forth a list of Dos
and Don'ts, Rights and Wrongs but answered students
with a hard slap. The Yippies are a hard slap, a kick in
the crotch, a bunch of snipers pinning the enemy down
and making him afraid to move."[11]

There were people around and good people who exactly understood and appreciated what the Yippies were trying to do.

Jon Moore, in the influential underground paper *Rat*, also countered some of the bad press the Yip-In had produced. He wrote
that Yippie could very well "project the convergence of 'cultural'
and 'political' consciousness as clear as hippies-flower-love-Haight
has last year." But on Chicago, he warned, "if you go, go with
your eyes open."[12] The Yip-In had not harmed the Yippies so
much as it opened people's eyes as to what they were up to.
And at the time that seemed like a good thing to the main Yippies,
a good counter to the overly romantic, overly dropout oriented
kind of rhetoric writers like Lawrence Lipton in the *LA Free Press*
had draped around the Yippie altar.[13] It all just deepened the
myth, put more into the blank space.

The day after the Yip-In, Hoffman, Rubin, Fouratt, Krassner, Fass,
and Marshall Bloom, head of the Liberation News Service and Yip
supporter, all flew to Chicago to attend the National Mobilization
meeting at nearby Lake Villa; a meeting called to decide whether
or not the Mobe, the umbrella organization for almost every
American antiwar group, should sponsor a call to demonstrate in
Chicago during the Democratic National Convention.

Up to that point, Yippie had had very little to do with the Mobe
or Mobe plans. Tom Hayden, Mobe coproject director for Chicago,
had stopped in on a couple of the early, public Yippie meetings
but he had had no substantive discussions with the Yippies. In the
other direction, Keith Lampe had continued to attend New York
movement meetings and on at least one occasion, a March 14
Greenwich Village meeting sponsored by the Resistance (a militant
group of draft resisters), spoke to the crowd about Yippie plans for
Chicago, stressing that their purpose was nondisruptive.[14] In addition, the "Convention Notes" mailer the Mobe's Convention

Committee put out February 27 included a two-page piece by Hoffman, Rubin, Sanders, and Krassner that outlined the Festival of Life and emphasized that Yippie sought not to disrupt but to present an alternative to the Democratic Convention of Death.[15] But that was about it in the way of direct communication between the two groups. They were on somewhat uneasy terms with one another.

The Yippies came to Lake Villa almost directly from the Yip-In. Abbie Hoffman still had on the Indian costume he'd concocted, and none of them had had much sleep, which was not unusual. Though they had been formally invited, Hoffman was later to say, "We were treated like niggers, you know, like we were irrelevant."[16]

The Yippies, for their part, practiced what they preached, goofing on the meeting and mixing a few moderately straight moments with plenty of more flipped out ones. On the straight side, they met with Davis, Hayden, and Dellinger, the main moving forces behind the Mobe Chicago plans, and with them the Yippies got along moderately well. Rubin gave a moderately serious speech to the assembly of two hundred or so people on youth solidarity, telling the crowd of old and new leftists that they should support Polish students in their protests against Russian imperialism. Hoffman in his speech said that politics was "the way you lead your life, not who you supported," and that Yippie didn't have any particular kind of program for Chicago but that they intended to present a new kind of life-style.

More characteristically, the Yippies went around the meeting passing out Yippie buttons and posters. Jim Fouratt freaked out some of the delegates by frequently breaking into song, giving out such lyrics as, "Bullshit, this is all bullshit. You are doing a dance with a dead lady, the Democratic Party." Hoffman attended a sober workshop on capitalism and gave a long rap about the crime of pay toilets and how something had to be done about them.

Most of the Yippies stayed throughout the entire conference, demonstrating their particular brand of politics and becoming increasingly disgusted and bored with the Mobe's long debates and cautious maneuverings. By the end of the meeting the Yippies told the Mobe that they were not interested in this "particular format," that they'd be in Chicago and if the Mobe was there, "good, it would be a good time."[17]

From Lake Villa, the Yippies went to Chicago to coordinate things with a local group of "hippie leaders" and to try to get all the permits or whatever they needed from the city to make everything legal and hassle free. Jerry Rubin had gotten this particular ball rolling several weeks earlier when he'd flown into Chicago and met with several of the locals, talking up Yippie and laying the groundwork for a working relationship. The night of March 25 marked the first time the local hippies, who were supposed to be in the process of becoming the local Yippies, and the New York Yippies met as a group.

They met backstage at the Cheetah Club, in Uptown, where a benefit was going on for the nascent Yips and the *Seed,* Chicago's relatively new underground newspaper and headquarters for many of the local Yippies. The Chicago Yips were nowhere as politically oriented or as experienced in the ways of organizing or promoting as the New York Yips. There was a little bit of tension in the air between the two groups as they established their respective identities. It quickly became apparent that the New Yorkers expected to control all the action while they were in Chicago. They succeeded, and maybe not on purpose, in intimidating at least a few of the local Yippies.

During and after the benefit, the New York Yippies discussed sites for the Festival of Life with locals, including Valerie Walker, Al Rosenfield, and John Tuttle, and then drafted the permit application. Both the locals and the New Yorkers signed the application. The joint signatures were a strategic move aimed at offsetting cries of "outside agitators." The permit requested the use of Grant Park, Chicago's main lakefront park, located just east of the Loop and, at the time, the hotels in which the delegates would be staying. The permit went on to explain that the festival would be the "nation's biggest music festival" and that the Yippies wanted to sleep in the park and have the city provide sanitation facilities and health department aid in setting up kitchens in the park.

The next morning the fun began in earnest. At 9 A.M. the Yippies held a press conference at the *Seed* office. They told the assembled reporters, including Chicago notables Mike Royko of the *Daily News* and Jack Mabley of the *American,* that they had completed an application for the use of Grant Park during the convention and that they would now present said application to the Park District and to Mayor Daley. Over twenty Yippies then proceeded to Soldier Field, where the Park District offices were located, and without much fanfare presented the application. They held another press conference, taped by local TV, and then made their way to City Hall to confront Mayor Daley.

Daley, of course, was "out." But the Yips were able to meet with Deputy Mayor David Stahl and they graced him with the full treatment they'd hoped to spring on Daley.

In full view of the local press and Nicholas Von Hoffman of the *Washington Post,* who was doing a big story on the Yippies, the

Yippies' well-orchestrated performance unfolded. Helen Running Water, who was a white girl from New York dressed up in hippie-Indian, presented the application to Stahl rolled up in a Playmate of the Month gatefold upon which was scrawled, "To Dick with love, the Yippies." After presenting it to him, Helen kissed Stahl and pinned a Yippie button to his suit. Stahl quickly retreated into his office and the Yippies left City Hall in high spirits, reassembled in front of the Civic Center next to the new Picasso statue, and talked to reporters while passing out leaflets to startled passersby.

The New York Yippies flew home that night, satisfied with the proceedings. The Chicago Yippies had enjoyed the action too, and that week's issue of the *Seed* included a major feature on the Yippies, written by Abe Peck, which gleefully promoted Yippie's "politics of ecstasy" and broadcast Yippie's message that the festival was a Do-In and not a Be-In. Peck explained that though there would be entertainers like Country Joe, Phil Ochs, Steve Miller, Judy Collins, and others, people must do their own thing; the Festival was to be an "occasion for personal creativity," for "leaders are frauds," he went on to say, and it was time for everybody to do it on their own. In spite of some tensions, the locals and the New Yorkers seemed to be in good communication.[18]

Back in New York, winter turning into spring, the Yippies got down to business. Rubin and Sanders sent out a letter to as many people as they could think of explaining the Festival of Life—"a statement that goes beyond protest, a statement that reaffirms our commitment to life"—and asked for money, saying that they needed one hundred thousand dollars to make the whole thing happen.[19]

At the very end of March, a select group of Yips met to discuss what went wrong with the Yip-In and figure out what to do next. The problem, everyone agreed, was that they just hadn't expected so many people to show up and that the space was all wrong. Rubin counseled that they should try again but this time have something more like Chicago, kind of a trial run with bands, good equipment, a park setting, and city cooperation. The key, all agreed, was getting the city to cooperate and arrange to have the cops stay away. They decided to call it the Yip-Out and to hold it on Easter Sunday, which was only a couple of weeks away.[20]

Out of necessity, the Yippies worked fast. They held a press conference and announced that in cooperation with the city they'd be holding a free music festival and gathering. The underground press practiced a quick forgive and forget and the *Voice*, in Howard Smith's "Scenes" column, promoted the Yip-Out as a "joyous reunion of the tribes" and the "resurrection of free."[21] The city, meanwhile, gave no indication that it was interested in cooperating. As Easter drew closer the Yippies were getting more and more worried about the city's refusal to allow critical equipment into the park or to guarantee police cooperation.

On April 10, thirty Yippies went to Mayor Lindsay's office and held a kind of sit-in, refusing to leave until terms were reached. The Yippies negotiated with Sid Davidoff, the Mayor's aid, and after a while he agreed to what the Yippies wanted: the Yippies could bring trucks into the park and they would be allowed to use amplified sound. The Yip-Out was on.[22]

And it went like a charm. Over ten thousand people showed up, the vast majority of them under twenty-one. They heard some local bands play, shared food and drugs, and got free Yippie posters. Some, as per Yippie requests, even brought canned goods which were being collected for the Poor People's Campaign. The weather was good and the police stayed well in the distance, ignoring the drugs that were being used openly.

The Yippie fix on the event was strong. All day, Yippies in quasi-official purple satin t-shirts with Yippie! scrawled across the front in luminescent pink moved through the crowds carrying Day-Glo painted buckets, soliciting money. Between musical sets, Yippies gave regular pitches for money and for the Festival of Life in Chicago. The crowd was complacent and mainly sat in the grass, listened to the music, and watched each other.

On the one hand, the Yip-Out went without a hitch and proved that the Yippies could organize a peaceful, stoned-out day in the park. The Liberation News Service disseminated the good vibrations to all of its subscribers.[23] On the other hand, the Yip-Out opened the door to some unpleasant speculations.

Sally Kempton, in the *Village Voice*, which was printing more and more nasty things about Yippie, gave vent to some of those unpleasantries. Her featured piece on the Yip-Out was almost entirely negative. It asserted that the Yip-Out produced nothing so much as "a sense of malaise." She peopled the Yip-Out with "fat teenyboppers," "boys with acne scars," girls who looked "tired and strained . . . flaccid." And she concluded that this cast of uglies and burnouts wasn't even "having a very good time." Yippie, she said over and over, wasn't very hip, wasn't very cool and, most of all, wasn't accomplishing much of anything.[24] Equally unpleasant from the Yippie perspective was the fact that the Yip-Out—peaceful, calm, and without controversy—had captured almost no mass media attention.

The mixed reception of the Yip-Out didn't help to quell the crisis that was fast moving through Yippie's leadership ranks. The withdrawal of Johnson, the success of Eugene McCarthy in the primaries, and the entry of Bobby Kennedy into the presidential race all had damaged a number of Yippie hopes and understandings. Johnson's March 31, prime time announcement that he would not seek reelection totally baffled the Yippies. As Abbie Hoffman wrote a couple of months after the fact, "Remember a guy named Lyndon Johnson? He was so predictable when Yippie! began. And then pow! he really fucked us. He did the one thing no one had counted on. He dropped out. 'My God,' we exclaimed, 'Lyndon is out flanking us on our hippie side.' "[25] Yippie, after all, counted on the power of myth. A workable myth, they all knew, demanded a mythically evil bad guy. LBJ had been playing that part to perfection. Without him the whole scenario, the whole game plan of the Festival of Life confronting the Convention of Death could dissolve.

Even before LBJ's surprise move, Yippie had been reeling under the double whammy of McCarthy and Kennedy who seemed to be offering the middle ground that Yippie knew made myths seem only like fantasies. McCarthy, while problematic, seemed from a mythical point of view controllable. From the very beginning to the very end, the Yippies knew he never stood a chance. Hoffman said rooting for McCarthy was like rooting for the Mets: "One can secretly cheer for him . . . knowing he can never win." McCarthy might turn a few potential Yips "clean for Gene" but come the convention, the Yippies figured, the disappointed McCarthyites would just swell their ranks. But Bobby Kennedy was another story. He hit Yippie where they lived.[26]

In a piece that got a lot of play in the underground press, Jerry Rubin wrote, "We expected concentration camps and we got Bobby Kennedy. I am more confident of our ability to survive concentration camps than I am of our ability to survive Bobby."[27] Kennedy, as Hoffman wrote just after the fact, was a "challenge to the charisma of Yippie!"

> Remember Bobby's Christmas card: psychedelic blank space with a big question mark—"Santa in '68?" Remember Bobby on television stuttering at certain questions, leaving room for the audience to jump in and help him agonize, to battle the cold interviewer who knew all the answers and never made a mistake. Come on, Bobby said, join the mystery battle against the television machine. Participation mystique. Theater-in-the-streets. He played it to the hilt. And what was worse, Bobby had the money and the power to build the stage. We had to steal ours. It was no contest. . . .

When young longhairs told you how they'd heard
that Bobby turned on, you knew Yippie was really in
trouble.[28]

Insult seemed to be added to injury when Hubert Humphrey entered the race exalting a new "politics of joy." Yippies Rubin and
Hoffman suddenly wondered if the whole plan of attack hadn't
suddenly grown irrelevant.

At first, Rubin took the high road and aimed a barrage of political
rhetoric at the new order of things. "Elections," he wrote, "are authoritarian, the subjects elect their King. . . . Elections in America are
a mind poison." America, Rubin insisted, needed a massive populist
revolution, not just a changing of the guard in which the people are
really "little more than bystanders." What had to be changed was
not "celebrity" leadership but "the quality of American life, the
distribution of power, the content of culture, the forms of decision
making, the top heavy organization of institutions and the tiny influ-
ences individuals have over their own lives."[29] But this was not
Yippie talk. It was running scared. The Yippies were filling in their
own blanks, de-mythifying as they discovered that President Johnson
could be more outrageous than they, that Kennedy could outcharm
them, and that McCarthy could outrighteous them. After a while,
Rubin, especially began to wonder what purpose Yippie served if
there wasn't going to be a Lyndon Johnson–Devil to confront in
Chicago.

Self-doubt began to permeate Yippie's top figures. By the end of
May both Rubin and Hoffman had begun to wonder if Yippie wasn't
"too funny, too cute."[30] Throughout April and May Yippie slowed
down to a crawl as Rubin and Hoffman thought about just calling
the whole thing off.

This lassitude and doubt was not publicly admitted. Indeed, for
many of the Yippies, who saw the Festival of Life as essentially a
celebration of an alternative style of life, the political vicissitudes
seemed more or less irrelevant. What they worried about was the
lack of cooperation and wholesale hostility that was emanating out
of Chicago.

Everything seemed to be going wrong in Chicago. In particular,
the newly formed Chicago Yippies, who were supposed to be working out the local angles, found themselves the focus of some very
heavy police harassment. The harassment began at the very first
open Yippie meeting in Chicago.

The night of April 25, seventy people met on the near north side
of Chicago to discuss local implementation of Yippie. Before the
meeting even began, police burst in, lined everybody up, and in a
decidedly unfriendly way searched and questioned every single

person in the room. Eighteen people were arrested for "disorderly conduct," which amounted to anything from not following orders fast enough to talking back. They also got one person for "resisting arrest" and another (brother of John Mrvos, one of the main locals) for possession, a charge he denied. Needless to say, the meeting that followed all this was not the one that had been planned.[31]

Abe Peck, who was a moving force behind Chicago Yippie, tried to go on a gentle counteroffensive. A few days after the big bust, he wrote an "Open Letter to Mayor Daley," which he sent Daley and also had distributed around the country by the Liberation News Service: "You must realize that it is too late to stop thousands of young people from coming to Chicago. . . . [We] share a common desire to avoid bloodshed and needless hardship." He added that he personally, or the *Seed* in general, very much wanted to discuss any problems and quickly work out all permit requirements.[32]

But things only got worse. Starting in May, the police regularly arrested *Seed* vendors, booked them at the station, and then later, after bond had been arranged, quietly dropped the trumped-up charges. Police also began regular weekend roundups of long-haired young people all along Wells Street, the main drag of Chicago's underdeveloped hippie quarter. One late May weekend, the police hauled in seventy-four people, almost all of them for disorderly conduct. Again, when the cases were called, all charges were dropped.

The harassment reached tragicomic proportions on May 20. In order to pay the lawyer's fees accrued from the April 25 bust, the local Yippies had formed a nonprofit corporation, the Free City Survival Committee, and scheduled a benefit at the Electric Theatre. Shades of the Yip-In, everything started off great, with over 1750 people paying three dollars a head to listen to music, dance, and help out the cause. But while everybody inside grooved to the music, outside the police massed. The minute curfew struck, the police raided the theater and arrested scores of underage kids, booked them at the Twentieth District Station even though Chicago's curfew statute stipulates that first-time offenders are only to be sent home to their parents with a note. Of course, all charges were later dropped. The police also smashed several cameras and announced that under fire department orders they were closing down the theater and everybody had to leave. The fire department later denied that they had ever issued such an order.[33]

Jerry Rubin wouldn't have been surprised but the local Yippies were. This wasn't the game they'd bargained for. Still, they learned fast and fought back, mobilizing the American Civil Liberties Union, friendly lawyers, and neighborhood people to protest the harassment. But Chicago was not New York, and the reality of Chicago life came out in the classic words of one young lawyer who said he'd be glad to offer discreet counsel but that he couldn't help Free City in direct negotiations with the police department or with city officials. "I have to practice law in this town," he said, and the Mayor's political cronies on the bench remember everything.[34]

Meanwhile, the negotiations seemed to be going nowhere fast. As of June 1, more than two months after the permit request had been submitted, neither the Park District nor the Mayor's office had given any sort of reply. When Abbie Hoffman had flown into Chicago in late April to do a local radio show (more free advertising) he had tried to get some answers from the city but had only gotten the runaround. The locals had done no better. Finally, in early June, Abe Peck and a few others were able to schedule a meeting with Deputy Mayor Stahl. The gist of the meeting, according to Peck, was Stahl's declaration, "Gee guys, you can't expect the Mayor to allow dope and fornication in his front yard." The meaning was clear; Grant Park was not going to happen. Over the next month a little progress was made but most of the news was bad. The good news was that maybe the Yippies could use Lincoln Park for something as yet undefined. Lincoln Park was well north of the Loop and all the main downtown hotels where the delegates and party nominees would be staying, but it was roomy, near Lake Michigan, and right by Old Town, the center of Chicago's hip and hippie scene. The bad news was that nothing had been guaranteed and that all negotiations were now officially in the hands of Al Baugher, a low-level city employee who worked with the Chicago Youth Commission. The Yippies were sure that Baugher had no real power to negotiate anything. They were right—in the almost three months that followed no higher city official ever asked Baugher his opinion on the permit situation or anything else.[35]

Other news from Chicago was, if anything, worse. Movement people all around the country were freaking out over the "shoot to kill" order Mayor Daley had issued at the height of the West Side rioting that followed Martin Luther King's assassination April 4. If he's willing to say that publicly, plenty of people wondered, what does he have in mind for us privately. Moreover, newspapers around the country carried statements by Cook County Sheriff Joseph Woods in which he explained his plans for handling demonstrators during the convention, plans which included deputizing civilian vigilantes and using the sewers as temporary holding tanks to handle mass arrests. The same newspapers carried smaller stories on the fierce, even brutal police action that had crushed a small antiwar demonstration in Chicago's Loop. As Country Joe McDonald told Abbie Hoffman in late April, the vibrations coming out of Chicago were getting uglier and uglier and the musicians were getting scared.[36]

The lack of permits, in particular, was scaring away the musicians. Even a Yippie stalwart like Judy Collins explained that she couldn't perform if there were no permits. She had to have proper lights and equipment, she said, or she just wouldn't go on. Most other bands and theater groups were just plain-out scared of all the hassles and potential violence and as June rolled around and the permit situation remained unresolved many of them started copping out. A few of the big rock 'n roll bands had been willing to play at a free festival but almost no one wanted any part of political hassles or mixing it up with police and arrest situations.[37]

Hoffman, after some futile telephone calling, had flown back to Chicago in mid-May to try to straighten things out. Mothers' Day, May 13, Hoffman and the local Yippies met and discussed the stalemate. Steve Mrvos told Abbie that from what he could tell the city officials were much more open to negotiating with the local Yippies than they were with the New York people, feeling that if anything went wrong they at least could have somebody to take the fall. Hoffman had respected the advice and had flown out without trying to see any city officials.[38]

In the first week of June, Abe Peck and a few others flew to New York and at a Yippie meeting in Union Square explained the new situation. Peck said that the new site was Lincoln Park and that things looked pretty good for it. He'd been meeting with the police, trying to cool things out with them, and though things were still extremely tense—the police had said that they would close the whole park down if they caught even one person smoking dope—at least communication seemed to be opening up and everybody, the police and the city, were talking about Lincoln Park as if the festival was really going to happen there. The consensus was that the city would really put on the stall but in the end the permits would be granted.[39]

Back in Chicago, Peck and company were a little less optimistic. By June, Peck was very aware that Yippie was not always what it seemed. Jerry Rubin, he realized, was a lot less interested in a joyous festival of life than he was in creating a solid, forceful protest against the war in Vietnam and the system that engendered it. Hoffman, he believed, could go either way, straddling the fence, so to speak, between a Festival of Life and a confrontation. Peck also knew that there was a lack of unity among Yippies leadership—a split between what he thought of as the "cultural people" like Ed Sanders and Bob Fass and the "political people" like Rubin. In general, through May and June, the communication between the New York people and the Chicago people was terrible. By late June, Peck believed that the whole thing should be canceled, but the other locals disagreed and they all kept plugging away.[40]

Part of the reason communication was so bad during this critical period was, of course, due to the fact that Rubin and Hoffman were also thinking of canceling the festival. So that while they somewhat desultorily scheduled a few meetings, in general they spent most of the spring playing around with other things, dealing with their own problems and trying to figure out where their own politics, and not their sense of the absurd, should lead them.

One place their politics led them was to the Columbia University takeover in late April. Both Rubin and Hoffman were enthusiastic supporters and both were arrested there. Columbia, they realized, was the kind of theater they really liked; the leaders of tomorrow acting like the radicals of today and getting stomped on by the police like the niggers of yesterday. And all of it appearing nightly on everybody's color TV as the Communards of Columbia versus the Molochs of Death City: serious but not boring business. It definitely put Yippie out of the news.[41]

Jerry Rubin also started getting interested in the doings of the Peace and Freedom Party, a radical group that started in the Berkeley area and was attempting to go national. The party intended to nominate state and national candidates and get on the November ballot. By mid-summer it looked like the party intended to nominate Eldridge Cleaver, the Black Panther party minister of information, for president. Cleaver, in turn, had told Rubin that he wanted him to run for vice-president. Rubin told the New York chapter of Peace and Freedom that he wanted the spot and that he'd bring the Yippies into Peace and Freedom and help the party capture people's imaginations. It was a long way from some other people's imagined vision of the Festival of Life.[42]

Rubin also received the attention of another interested party, the New York City Police. On June 10, warrant in hand, they busted into Rubin's apartment and caught him with three ounces of marijuana, enough so that they could charge him with ''felonious possession with intent to sell.'' While ''searching'' for the dope, they also went through Rubin's files and ransacked his apartment. Later, in jail, he was kicked in the lower back hard enough to fracture his coccyx. A new auxiliary was added to Yippie, the Rubin Defense Fund. Rubin made bail. The bust probably had little or nothing to do with Yippie in particular. It seemed instead to be a part of a general crackdown on ESSO, the East Side Survival Organization, which did most of the local hippie and hard core political organizing on the Lower East

Side. Both Rubin and Hoffman were prominent members of ESSO. Fifteen members of ESSO were arrested at around the same time. Repression was intensifying and everybody knew it.[43]

Early June decidedly marked the low point of Yippie. As Abbie said, "We didn't know what the fuck to do. We were saying we're not even going."[44] And then with the murder of Bobby Kennedy early in the morning June 5, things changed. It wasn't just that a powerful rival had been removed, though that was certainly critical (Jerry Rubin, with an ironic smile declaimed, "Sirhan Sirhan is a Yippie").[45] It was more that everyhing Yippie depended on had been proved right again; the world was out of control, the system, one way or another, was going to perpetuate itself and the only way out was through absurdity and recognition, exploration, even celebration of alienation and anomie. The mood was Yippie! again. Or at least more so. A couple of weeks after the assassination Hoffman was back into full-time Yippie organizing. According to Hoffman, it took Rubin, whose dope case took up a lot of his energy, a few more weeks to decide that Yippie really could be made relevant.

In early July, Hoffman wrote his first piece on Yippie! Published in Krassner's *Realist,* it reaffirmed Yippie's call to Chicago and attempted to explain both what Yippie had gone through in the last few months and what it was up to now. It was, for Hoffman, a kind of throwback. It was serious and it was carefully reasoned.

Hoffman began by explaining Yippie's relationship to myth. He wrote that Yippie had four main objectives: "the blending of pot and politics," the creation of a "gigantic national get together," and "the development of a model for an alternative society," "the need to make some statement, especially in revolutionary action-theater terms, about LBJ, the Democratic Party, electoral politics and the state of the nation." The points were numbered. "To accomplish these tasks," Hoffman explained further, had "required the construction of a vast myth, for through the notion of myth large numbers of people could get turned on and in the process of getting turned on, begin to participate in Yippie! and start to focus on Chicago. *Precision was sacrificed for a greater degree of suggestion* . . . and distortion became the life blood of the Yippies. . . ." Hoffman then went on, in an almost academic call on higher authority, to quote Marshall McLuhan at some length on the TV generation's dependence on myth for creating a "participation mystique," a feeling of belonging in the world. "Myth," Abbie asserted, "can never have the precision of a well oiled machine . . . it must have the action of participation and the magic of mystique. It must have a high element of risk, drama, excitement and bullshit."

The problem, Abbie wrote, was that things had changed since Yippie began. He wrote of the near demise of Yippie in the face of LBJ's pullout and the rise of Kennedy and McCarthy and then of the recent reversals—Kennedy's assassination and Hubert Humphrey's lock on the nomination. Yippie was once again relevant, he stated, but it must approach the convention differently. Explaining that since "the United States political system was proving more insane than Yippie," and that "reality and unreality had in six months switched sides," Yippie must now use "the direct opposite approach from the one we begin with. We must sacrifice suggestion for a greater degree of precision. We need a reality in the face of the American political myth. We have to kill Yippie! and still bring huge numbers to Chicago."

Then Hoffman, in moderately straight language, laid out the plans for Chicago. He saw a "Constitutional Convention" where both poets and "technologists," artists and community organizers, indeed "anyone who had a vision," would attempt to formulate "the goals and means" of the new society; a free rock and theater festival, that "contrary to rumor" was going to happen; workshops on draft resistance, drugs, commune development, guerrilla theater, and underground media, all of which would be "oriented around problem solving while the Constitutional Convention works to develop the overall philosophical framework." Then, too, Hoffman said, "There will probably be a huge march across town to haunt the Democrats."

Hoffman was backing off the Yippies' original "blank space" organizing principle but not haphazardly. He knew that the time had come to give Yippie a structure that could stand up to the hostility and potential violence that he knew awaited it in Chicago. He had to offer some vision of order and preparation, even if it was really no more than another myth. However, Hoffman held on to the crux of the Yippie! vision: "People coming to Chicago should begin preparations for five days of energy exchange. Do not come prepared to sit and watch and be fed and cared for. It just won't happen that way. It's time to become a life actor. The days of the audience dies with the old America. If you don't have a thing to do, stay home, you'll only get in the way."

According to Hoffman, the Yippies wanted to avoid a confrontation, they didn't want to disrupt anything ("What could we disrupt? America was falling apart at the seams"), and very much the Yippies wanted a legal permit. Hoffman stressed, "All of these plans are contingent on our getting a permit and it is toward that goal we have been working." But he warned his readers that the city, ''knowing this would decrease the number of people that descend on the city,'' would probably not grant the permits until the very last minute. In the end though, Hoffman assured, the permits would come through because it really was in the city's own self-interest: ''They can ill afford to wait too late, for that will inhibit planning on our part and that will create more chaos. It is not our wish to take on superior armed troops who outnumber us on unfamiliar enemy territory. It is not their wish to have a Democrat nominated amidst a bloodbath. The treaty will work for both sides.''[46]

Abbie got down to work trying to keep the bands from dropping out and began to line up figures like Buckminster Fuller and Allen Ginsberg for the Constitutional Convention. At the same time, he knew that because of the city's hostility, Yippie's own unfocused program, and all the other protest activities scheduled for convention week, the probability of some kind of violence was fast increasing. He knew that Yippie somehow would have to prepare its people for more than a few carefree days in the park.

Meanwhile, back in Chicago, the local Yippies had heeded Deputy Mayor Stahl's suggestion that they apply for permission to use the southern tip of Lincoln Park for the Festival of Life. Lincoln Park was over ten miles from the International Amphitheater, where the convention was going on, and more than two miles from the nearest delegates' hotel. So on July 15 they resubmitted their permit request, using the same careful, accommodating language they had employed in all their requests and negotiations. They asked this time for twenty-five or so acres of Lincoln Park from 11:59 P.M. August 24 to 11:59 P.M. August 29, ''for a youth convocation to be known as the Festival of Life . . . dedicated to the sharing of life experiences.'' The permits reiterated the requests for sleeping in the park, sanitation facilities, and Health Department aid. They also asked for the use of Soldier Field all day August 30 for a concluding rally. The rally would be, they pointed out, a practical way to get everybody out of Lincoln Park once the permit expired. In this request, the local Yips estimated that 25,000 people would attend the festival.[47] By August 1, the city had made absolutely no comment on the status of the permit request.

Jerry Rubin, who had given up on Yippie in June, was back in the fold in July. But if Hoffman came back attempting to modify or at least explain more carefully what he believed Yippie was all about, Jerry Rubin continued to make the kind of wild remarks that had typified his end of Yippie from the beginning.

At a July 23 demonstration outside the Waldorf Astoria, where Hubert Humphrey was appearing at a five hundred dollar a plate fund-raiser, Rubin loosed a monumentally vituperative harangue.

Hubert Humphrey was an "asshole," Rubin exclaimed, and had sold his soul to the "corporation" which is America. Rubin said that political power in America is just "kissing ass" because America is run from the top down, that the elections in November are meaningless with pigs nominating other pigs and that people must show their contempt for the whole thing by demonstrating every time the candidates appear, especially at the Chicago convention. People must disrupt the pig election system, make it so that the candidates cannot even go out on the streets anymore. Rubin also noted that there was more freedom for a Cuban in one day than for an American in a lifetime because the Cuban worked for a collective enterprise whereas the American worked for the ruling elite and was alienated from himself. He ended by turning to the Waldorf and screaming, "Open up the jails. Let everybody out and then put the pigs in. America the great power, is over. Come out with your hands up, motherfuckers." And then he gave the hotel the finger. A variety of national and local security agencies took down every word.[48]

In Chicago, August 5, after meeting with other members of Free City, Abe Peck said, Enough. Rubin, Hoffman, Krassner, Sanders, and the Fugs had breezed into town August 3 and 4 for a Fugs concert at the Electric Theatre. They'd met with the *Seed* people and rapped about the need to keep things flexible, saying that they couldn't really lay down a schedule yet but that it didn't really matter because "the structure is more important than the content." But Hoffman warned the locals that they might better prepare for a bloody scene: if the permits didn't come down—and they just might not—Yippie was still going on and the city wasn't going to make that easy. He then, very loosely, sketched out a scenario that concluded with Thursday as caring-for-the-wounded day. Peck had been appalled: "Abbie's schedule freaked out Free City. Suddenly self defense classes were a major activity."[49]

Through the Liberation News Service, Peck distributed "A Letter from Chicago," that got wide play throughout the underground press. It hit like a bomb. He began: "The entire Yippie thing has become a Zen experience with no leaders, a no-structure, and a no-philosophy [and] . . . no real sign that the thing can come off as originally planned—IT CAN'T HAPPEN HERE." He publicized his feelings that the New York Yippies had something in mind that he, at least, couldn't go along with: "The New York feeling is that Yippie is a golden opportunity to shit all over the Old Men, while the Chicago ethos, specifically that of the Free City Survival Committee is that a festival . . . can be carried off despite the choice of convention week, as the time for fun and frolic." There was nothing wrong with a political protest, he wrote, but "it is a black piece of action if it involves masquerading as the Pied Piper of Peace." The city, he wrote, was freaked out by Jerry Rubin, the talk of dope and public fornication, and fear over what the city's blacks were going to do. The atmosphere in Chicago was anything but festive. Peck concluded, "This is my rap and my rap only . . . there's a chance that this letter could become a classic piece of underground paranoia. I hope so, but don't bet on it. . . . If you're coming to Chicago, be sure to wear some armor in your hair."[50]

Peck had warned Abbie Hoffman, back in New York, about his feelings the night before he sent the letter. He had also reported, in shock, that the city had just told him that they had not realized that the Yippies wanted to sleep in the park and that that was obviously impossible since it was illegal to sleep in the park. Peck had been flabbergasted because the city had allowed other groups like the Boy Scouts and the National Guard to sleep in the parks and had for years looked the other way when city residents sought relief from summer heat waves by bivouacing along the lakefront. Peck was also overwhelmed that it had taken the city over two months even to realize that the Yippie permit had requested the right to sleep in the park. He told Hoffman the *Seed's* windows were being broken regularly by rock-throwing policemen. In sum, the local Yippies were probably going to withdraw their permit application and call it quits.[51]

Hoffman quickly gathered together Rubin, Sanders, Krassner, and Richard Goldstein, a *New York Times* music critic and part-time Yip. Together they flew to Chicago. Before leaving, Rubin called up Deputy Mayor Stahl and set up a meeting for the following afternoon.

The meeting with Stahl was a disaster. It began badly enough when Stahl demanded that the *Look* photographer who was following the Yippies everywhere (paying the Yippies for the privilege) be excluded from the meeting. The Yips felt obligated by their agreement to have the photographer with them. Finally Hoffman asked the photographer to leave, and with bad vibrations already in the air they got down to business.

Rubin and Hoffman did most of the talking, insisting that the Mayor was crazy if he didn't give the Yippies the permits they wanted, that they were going to have their festival whether they got the permits or not, with Abbie adding in anger that he was willing to die for his right to assemble in Lincoln Park. Stahl responded that the permit decision wasn't up to the Mayor, and the Yippies laughed. Stahl said that if they wanted the permits they could help their case by submitting a schedule of their plans for the week. Hoffman retorted that Yippies don't have schedules, that people do what they want but that Yippies didn't believe in marches and rallies, that they just wanted to do their thing in Lincoln Park, just present their own politics of being without leaders. Somewhere in this exchange Hoffman added that the city should help pay for the festival, give Yippie a hundred thousand dollars to make sure that it had enough money to be well-organized and run. Then, as was his way, Abbie added that if the city was really smart they'd pay him a hundred thousand dollars to get out of town, a comment Stahl took dead seriously. Hereabouts, Al Baugher, the low-level city employee who had been entrusted with day-to-day communications with the local Yippies, broke in to say that the local Yippies were withdrawing their permit request because the city had been so uncooperative and because they knew that the New Yorkers were set on political confrontation.

Hoffman said no, no we just want to swim naked in the lake and make love, Krassner quickly adding, and listen to poetry and music. Jerry Rubin, seeing the writing on the wall, called out angrily, we're not getting anywhere, let's get out of here. Before they left Stahl agreed to set up another meeting for the Yippies the next day with the heads of the city departments that Stahl insisted had jurisdiction over the permit request.[52]

In a foul mood the New York contingent made their way over to the *Seed* office to have it out with the local Yippies, who were fast on their way to being the local ex-Yippies. They met for seven angry hours.

After exchanging insults and angry rhetoric for several hours, Jerry Rubin suggested that they call up Tom Hayden, the Mobe's coproject director and a man all regarded with great respect, and ask him to come over and act as an arbiter. Hayden came in his slippers and, after listening to both sides, cuttingly remarked to Peck, "This sounds like a case of drug paranoia." He then announced that he had little regard for the whole Yippie thing and that they should just serve as a sideshow at the convention, as entertainment for the real protest events being carried on by the Mobe. He also declared that there would, in fact, be little real violence, although there well might be mass arrests. "The city can't afford a massacre," not in the presence of the TV cameras and so many reporters. Hayden then left.

Somewhat taken aback by Hayden's cool condescension, the Yippies came to an agreement: the locals would withdraw their permit application but at the same time the New York and Chicago Yippies together would submit a new proposal. The locals got the New

Yorkers to be more up front publicly about the probability of violence and, in general, to be more straight and serious. All agreed the *Seed* office would continue to be used as the Chicago Yippie headquarters. Although everyone knew that no real rapprochment had been made, at least it looked like Yippie could count on a modest appearance of local support.[53]

While the Yippies worked out their problems, down in Miami Richard Nixon accepted the Republican nomination for president of the United States, saying among other things: ''It's time for a new leadership to restore respect for the United States of America.''[54] The Yippies didn't listen to the acceptance speech.

Instead, operating on little or no sleep, they drafted a new permit application, signed by the New Yorkers and the locals (Peck not included), and very formally presented it to the Park Department. They then went back to the *Seed* office and had a well-attended press conference. At the press conference they aired their gripes with the city, saying it was acting like an ostrich, sticking its head in the sand and hoping all the trouble would just disappear. The trouble wouldn't go away, they said, the Yippies were coming no matter what. The group then went over to City Hall to meet with the heads of the various departments the deputy mayor had agreed to round up.

But of course, there were no department heads, only Stahl and a team of city lawyers who wanted to know what the Yippies intended to do. The discussion got nowhere.

The Yippies, angry, frustrated, and worried, walked out of the conference room into a crowd of waiting reporters. The Yippies told them the city was refusing to cooperate.[55] The next day's *Sun-Times* reported that the city had so far not ruled on the Yippie permit request and then quoted at some length Abe Peck's warning that ''the chance for confrontation with repressive agencies had increased'' and that those people who are looking for ''music and love'' should not come to Chicago.[56]

The Yippies were about at the end of their rope. They talked and it was decided that Hoffman would stay in Chicago, continue to negotiate with the city, and also begin preparing for whatever came down. The rest would fly back to New York and take care of business at that end.[57]

Over the next two weeks Hoffman ran around and around and around, plotting, planning, speculating, grandstanding, sleeping three hours a night—doing what he liked best. Later he said, ''I was very stoned on it all and I really dug it . . . it was a big challenge.'' He spent some of the time trying to make some connection with the black community, most specifically with the Blackstone Rangers, the largest street gang in Chicago. Like many large street gangs in the 1960s, the Rangers had learned how to play the political game and periodically had made small attempts to organize activities for the community. And like many others they had capitalized on their extremely modest forays into respectability by receiving a host of War on Poverty jobs. Already warned by the police to have nothing to do with the protesters, the Stones, who were anything but cultural revolutionaries, were not interested in joining up with the Yippies in the alien northside territory of Lincoln Park. Nor were any other black groups, which didn't make Abbie too happy but, as he reported later, "this was a honky revolution."[58]

Abbie also spent a fair amount of time catching up with the Mobe activities, to which he and most of the Yippies had been paying very little attention since the Lake Villa conference in March. It wasn't as if Abbie exactly wanted to go into partnership with them, but he was fast becoming aware of the order of things and it looked like some sort of common cause needed to be mounted. He promoted a deal in which the Mobe agreed to have their corps of marshals help the Yippies protect Lincoln Park from potential violent scenes, like white street-gang harassment and maybe police vamping. He also worked out an arrangement with Mobe coproject director Rennie Davis to share the Coliseum, a beat-up, old indoor stadium just south of the Loop, on August 27 for a mutual Yippie-Mobe rally entertainment hoopla. The Mobe was still keeping their distance from the Yippies, but as Abbie put it later, everybody wanted to "keep from stepping on each other's toes."[59] Things looked bad enough without any more internecine quarrels.

There was more than enough of that coming from the local Yippies, who put out another public don't-come-to-Chicago letter only a few days after the big New York–Chicago Yippie showdown. This one was signed by practically all the main figures of Free City. Among other nasty and frightening and absolutely prescient things, it said, "The word is out. Many people are into confrontation. The Man is into confrontation. Nobody takes the Amphitheater. Cars and buildings will burn. Chicago may host a Festival of Blood. . . . Many people will play in the streets. The cops will riot. The word has gone down. 'Brutality be damned.' "[60] Abe Peck wrote an article answering some of Hoffman's published criticisms of him. It ended with a word from William Blake: "The hand of vengeance found the bed to which the purple tyrant fled / The iron hand crushed the tyrant's head and became a tyrant in his stead."[61]

Despite the intensely hostile vibrations, Hoffman kept at it. He looked for housing, free food, and a parkside headquarters. He wrote and distributed to the press the final draft of Yippie's convention plans. Across the top of the mimeographed statement Abbie wrote, "Daring expose. Top secret Yippie plans for Lincoln Park." The "top secret" plan looked like this: August 20–24, snake dance, karate, self defense training; August 24, "Yippie Mayor Richard J. Daley presents fireworks"; August 25, welcoming of the delegates at the hotels; August 25 P.M., music festival in Lincoln Park; August 26 A.M., workshops on drug problems, underground communication, live free guerrilla theater, self-defense and draft resistance, communes; August 26 P.M., beach party at the lake—singing, BBQ, swimming, love-making; August 27 dawn, poetry mantras, religious ceremonies; August 27 A.M., workshops and scenario sessions, film showing and mixed media; August 27 P.M., benefit concert at the Coliseum, rally, nomination of Pigasus and LBJ unbirthday party at Lincoln Park; August 28 dawn, poetry and folk singing; August 28 A.M., Yip Olympics, Miss Yippie contest, Catch the Candidate, Pin the Tail on the Donkey, Pin the Rubber on the Pope, and "other normal and healthy games"; August 28 to be announced, 4 P.M., Mobe rally at Grant Park and march to convention; August 29, depends on Wednesday night—to park for sleeping. The plan then gave directions for getting to Chicago by car, subway, raft, and waterways. On the back of the mimeo was a map of Yippie's area of Lincoln Park, now retitled "Dream City." Following the natural geography of the park, Dream City was divided into three main sections: Free City, which was to include the Hog Farm headquarters (Hog Farm being the name of the group of the well-known California hippie-theater commune that was supposed to be bringing Pigasus, the Yippie pig presidential hopeful); Future City, the site of the music and theater activities; and Drop City, which included a special park for "Bikers."[62] The plan and map were heavily publicized by both the straight and the underground press.

The underground press also issued warnings. The *Berkeley Barb*, for example, noted that "Yippies will need to be a tough breed. . . . Flower children may be quickly 'radicalized' by having their heads busted by a cop's billy club." The schedule, with its emphasis on self-defense, marches and rallies, and its lack of celebrity entertainment made clear what most people already knew. As a sign on Berkeley Yippie's open-air headquarters proclaimed, Go to Chicago only "if you are committed enough to suffer for it."[63]

In Chicago, Abbie was still trying to reverse what was looking like the inevitable. Tenaciously, he made the round of friendly, movement-type lawyers until he found one willing to take on the city in court, challenging the city's right to deny the Festival of Light the permits they needed to bring the musicians to Chicago and to keep the cops at a distance.[64]

Back in New York, Ed Sanders attempted to combat all the heavy
political trips and violence talk that was fast accumulating around
Yippie, the Festival, and Chicago by distributing a crazy quilt schedule of Yippie events to the underground press. It was pure Sanders:

> Poetry readings, mass meditation, fly casting exhibi-
> tions, demagogic Yippie political arousal speeches, rock
> music and song concerts will be held on a precise time
> table . . . a dawn ass washing ceremony with tens of
> thousands participating will occur each morning at 5
> a.m. as Yippie revelers and protesters prepare for the 7
> a.m. volley ball tournaments . . . the Chicago offices of
> the National Biscuit Company will be hi-jacked on prin-
> ciple to provide bread and cookies . . . the Yippie ecol-
> ogy conference will spew out an angry report
> denouncing Chicago's poison in the lakes and streams
> . . . and exhaust murder from a sick hamburger society
> of automobile freaks. . . . Poets will rewrite the Bill of
> Rights in precise language detailing 10,000 areas of free-
> dom . . . to replace the confusing and vague rhetoric of
> 200 years ago . . . universal syrup day will be held on
> Wednesday when a movie will be shown at Soldier's
> [sic] Field in which Hubert Humphrey confesses to Allen
> Ginsberg his secret approval of anal intercourse . . . filth
> will be worshipped . . . there will be public fornication
> whenever and where ever there is an aroused appen-
> dage and a willing aperture . . . 230 rebel cocksmen
> under secret vow are on 24 hour alert to get into the
> pants of the daughters and wives and kept women of
> the convention delegates. . . . Demand respect from the
> stodgy porcupines that control the blob culture.[65]

Key passages of this attempt to give the ailing Yippie Festival "myth-
opoetic meaning"[66] found their way to angry and appalled eyes.

By August 20, the main core of the New York Yippies had made
their way to Chicago. Almost all of the music and theater groups
had, due to lack of permits and the hate waves they felt emanating
so steadily from Chicago, copped out.[67] The Yips still hoped a court-
ordered permit might lure some of them back.

August 22, the Yippies had their day in court. Presiding over their
suit against the city was Judge Lynch. The first thing the Judge said
was that the Yippies' dress was an affront to the court. He then
pushed the trial off for a couple of hours to give the Yippies and the
city officials one more chance to talk things over. But rather than
talk things over the Yippies met with their attorneys, were informed
that Judge Lynch was Mayor Daley's ex-law partner, and unanimously decided to withdraw their suit.

The Yippies held another press conference. By this time, with the convention news front-page material, the huge press corps was treating the Yips like full-out celebrities. The Yippies responded to the limelight by acting like even bigger braggarts and showmen than usual. Hoffman stated that the Yippies had no faith in the fairness of the judicial system and since they were sure that Lynch would only have issued a court order forbidding any of them to enter Lincoln Park they were withdrawing their suit. He added, we saw Lynch and we got lynched, we met Stahl and we got stalled, like in a comic book. Hoffman, who had figured that nothing was really going to come out of the lawsuit, had already prepared a long statement that he distributed and then read to the press.[68]

It was the final preconvention Yippie manifesto. It read:

> This is my personal statement. There are no spokes-
> men for the Yippies. We suggest to all reporters that they
> ask each and every Yippie in Lincoln Park why they
> have come to Chicago. We are all our own leaders. We
> realize this list of demands is inconsistent. They are not
> really demands. For people to make demands of the
> Democratic Party is an exercise in wasted wish fulfill-
> ment. If we have a demand it is simply and emphati-
> cally that they along with their fellow inmates in the
> Republican Party cease to exist. We demand a society
> based on humanitarian cooperation and equality, a so-
> ciety which allows and promotes the creativity of all
> people, especially youth.

A list of eighteen demands followed, including legalized marijuana, an end of all forms of domestic and foreign imperialism, abolishment of money, ecological development that would foster decentralization and encourage rural living, full unemployment, open and free use of the mass media, national referendums broadcast on television and conducted by a phone vote. The eighteenth demand was blank, so "you can fill in what you want." The document ended: "We recognize that we are America; we recognize that we are free men. The present day politicians have robbed us of our birthright. The evilness they stand for will go unchallenged no longer. Political pigs, your days are numbered. We are the second American Revolution. We shall win. Yippie." The document was signed, A. Hippie. At the top of the pamphlet was the Paris, May '68 slogan, "Be realistic—demand the impossible."[69]

There was nothing left but to do it.

Courtesy of the Kaye Miller Collection,
1968 Democratic Convention,
Northwestern University Library.

Jerry Rubin
(Chicago Sun-Times, Inc. 1987)

Bobby Seale
(Ted Lacey photograph)

Rennie Davis
(Ted Lacey photograph)

David Dellinger
(Chicago Sun-Times, Inc. 1987)

Abbie Hoffman
(Chicago Sun-Times, Inc. 1987)

Courtesy of the Kaye Miller Collection, 1968 Democratic Convention, Northwestern University Library.

ON THE WALL

DON'T GET BUSTED TWICE

Two people were arrested on Wells Street Sunday for putting up "Handwriting." They pasted the paper without taking any special precautions. Changes were dramatically costlier—released on bond.

When you go out to post the paper, don't go at night. If you know the city, or under less-militarized conditions, it might be easier, or safer to hang paper there; here, given the instructions under which cops are operating, it should be suicidal. You could be "mistaken for a looter" and shot. And it could go harder on you without bystanders around if you're caught.

During the day, though, keep off main streets—Wells, Clark, North, et cetera are all heavily patrolled, and the traffic on those streets is so thick that you often can't spot approaching squads.

Side streets, with much less traffic, give you a lot more time.

The faster the method you use for sticking them up, the safer you'll be.

Both thumbtacks and paste seem to take a long time. (Wide) packing tape is quicker. Staple-guns are ideal if you can get them (!).

The people on the streets of the community took a great interest in the paper. As soon as it was posted, groups gathered around to read it. This kind of medium is really good for getting real news around the city in the most immediate way, and making it clear what's going down.

Be careful, though, when you're posting "Handwriting".

The Red Squads in all major cities have located the cops here on activists from their areas.

DON'T GET BUSTED TWICE. NO MATTER WHAT FOR!

Be cautious, but remember that the point of caution is not to stay innocent, but to stay active. Good guys don't get caught.

NEWS MEDIA

These newspapers, TV/radio talk about news blackout in Chicago right now. Media blackout: no live TV outside the Convention, camera blitz no mobile trucks or cameras allowed in the streets and all the other choking "restrictions" that go with "security." Cronkite and Severeid complain Chicago with Prague. Cool. See something about not having covered real USA before, naked power. Liberals outraged—talk of defying restrictions and all that jive, see the power we're faced with all along being used against them for the first time maybe. Truth is in the air. They may, finally, have petty reasons—these professional men with their professional working arrangements and relations and deals getting fucked over—but still, the truth we have all along is in the air.

What do we think? Many things.
(1) That the news blackout in Chicago isn't surprising. It is only a logical extension of the concentration camp that Chicago has become. More than that, Chicago and USA have always been concentration camp/armed garrison.

only revealing themselves concretely to many people in certain situations. So there's nothing surprising in all this, only readjustment.

(2) That this situation is dangerous for us. Direct TV eliminated, less liberal outrage against the necessary violence of the pigs, or the nonepidated fear of National Guard/Regular Army faced with their own people. No record, no cameras—we're in the street and the pigs are all around us. Got to watch your ass and be good place. Black is up against it all the time. Got to begin to practice for the time when we don't have much liberal space to move in.

"Liberal outrage" wasn't ever much to count on; was unhealthy to protect ourselves with. We're learning not to beg, so we act accordingly.

(3) That we ought to think about possible relations with the established media during this Chicago time.

There is no "free access to information" in USA and there never has been. There is "free access" for those who pay; who agree, who are "objective", who play the right games. But now, Chicago Daley and

ruling structures local and national have hampered "free access" even to those paying members of the club who have always played the game acceptably. The stakes were high enough this time. (Why?)

OK. So repression has been unleashed—probably just for this week—by another group in the society. As they feel that weight we got something to talk to them about. When people feel the heat we know about—the truth about USA—then you can start to talk.

Could talk about media organization alot. How it's broken up into packs: lawyers and presidents, liberal program directors and front men, union crews. Each one another problem, each one situated differently in the society. But there isn't time to talk about that now. We got things to do.

The main thing. You're going to see TV and reporters on the streets, in Movement centers, wherever there's any action. They're going to come to you. And we can move on them, we can push because right now the truth about USA is all coiled up through the asphalt. Not soft subtle sly obsequious talking, but it's hard line. How are they going to put up now?

BLACKOUT

SATURDAY NIGHT FIGHTS

The cops and the Yippies held field maneuvers Saturday night in Old Town in preparation for the big confrontation Sunday. The cops, and the moderates on North Wells, lost.

The confrontation started about 10:30 p.m. when pigs began massing in the east side of Lincoln Park, apparently ready to charge at the singing, chanting crowd didn't split by the 11 p.m. curfew. Teams of plainclothes cops in nervous approval groups of six to eight circulated on the fringe of the crowd, while 20s and Yippie people tried to figure out what to do.

Suddenly a police van moved into the crowd, and the pigs boiled out. Yippie! The crowd fled divided for a minute, fight began to run, but soon settled down to moving slowly out in the pack to the west.

But the pigs weren't prepared for what happened next. The crowd split, only to re-form a few minutes later on North Clark, and began streaming straight toward North Wells, the main drag of Old Town, Chicago's attempt at a West Village. One smaller group lined up on the sidewalk, facing a line of advancing cops, shouting "Red Rover, Red Rover, send Daley right over!"

Traffic was heavy on North Wells, and in five minutes the crowd, joyfully circulating through and down the middle of the lines of stalled cars, had everything at a total standstill. Yippies and SDSers quickly passed out all their SLN and began shouting "Stop the Democratic Convention." The moderates seemed puzzled, amused, only a few bodied. Crowds soon massed on the sidewalks from the rinks, and many young kids with McCarthy stickers joined

the street melli-in. No cops at all showed up for half an hour.

The only cops to arrive hit the main intersection and split up the crowd, a few of whom quickly shot down side streets to re-form on North Wells several blocks up. The cops busted one or two Yippies at the intersection, but were unable to deal with the main Yippie crowd, which would melt onto the sidewalk crowd as cops appeared near them.

The Yippies suffered from their disorganization, and only a few were together enough to systematically outflank a few of the pigs of the main intersection. But the possibility of successful traffic tie-ups in an area where other crowds made heavy boats impossible was proven. The streets of Old Town belonged to us Saturday night, and it wasn't just rhetoric.

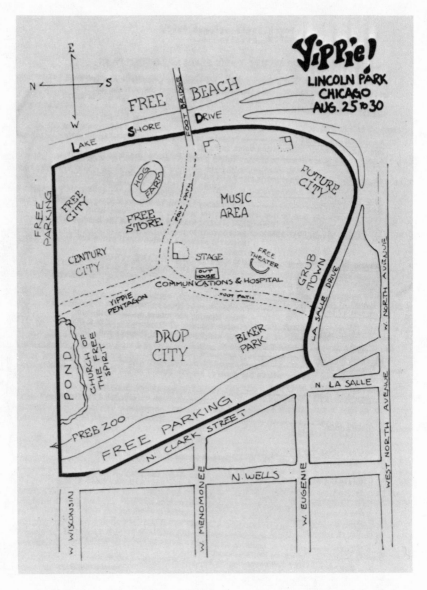

Courtesy of the Kaye Miller Collection, 1968 Democratic Convention, Northwestern University Library.

Contact sheet (Chicago Historical Society. Photographer unknown. ICHi-18362)

3 Gandhi and Guerrilla

On October 21 and 22, 1967, antiwar protesters, armed with the certainty that they were right, assembled at the Lincoln Memorial and then laid siege to the Pentagon. Both the demonstrators and the government knew what the Pentagon protest meant: the stakes were being raised. Many in the antiwar leadership, frustrated and angry, saw no other choice.

The pentagon action was the National Mobilization to End the War in Vietnam's first mass implementation of a new confrontational, multitactical strategy. "From Dissent to Resistance" was the slogan.[1] A few, but an important few, really meant it. No more would the antiwar movement resort simply to orderly civil disobedience or tentative street marches. The tactics were, as several writers put it, "Gandhi and Guerrilla":[2] half joke, half truth—people were challenging the government of the United States. Americans were burning their draft cards, disrupting public places, and shouting down government speakers. The antiwar movement was beginning to force the issue. Suddenly, people had to decide, and publicly, what they were going to do about the war their government was waging.

Politics was no longer simply the private business of casting a vote once every other year. Politics was a public affair, revealed by the buttons you wore everyday, the length of your hair, the signs you carried down the middle of city streets.

The purpose of the National Mobe was to offer support to all protest, to any sign of disgust or rejection of the State or, at least, the President. At the Pentagon the Mobe approved of it all. The skittish housewives and businessmen could listen to the speeches and be counted, the veteran pacifists could sit-in and be arrested, the student radicals and committed revolutionaries (a very few) could confront and even disrupt.[3] Maris Cakars, who'd been protesting for so long, wrote, "It is time to take the Movement we have built and direct it so that it actually disrupts the war machine. It is time to use direct action."[4]

Direct action. What did that really mean? Twenty-two years earlier, Mobe chair Dave Dellinger had put out a pacifist-anarchist sheet called *Direct Action* that called for "strikes, sabotage and seizure of public property" as well as "civil disobedience of laws which are contrary to human welfare."[5] Was that what it would take? Cakars didn't know, not really. It was all tentative because no one really had any idea where to go.

They saw themselves as the creators of a new American politics—a democracy of direct participation, based in part on the already legendary heart of the Civil Rights movement and in part on the vision of a generation born to unprecedented individual opportunity. They saw themselves as the vanguard of a New America, unfettered by the old fears—scarcity, racism, anti-Communism. They were free to create a global consciousness based on internationalism and brotherhood. But to get there, they knew, would be to overturn the Old Order and the ugly world it perpetuated.

It had been over two and a half years since the first national antiwar in Vietnam march had been called. Yet, there were almost half a million American soldiers in Vietnam and no sign of de-escalation or peace. The bombs and napalm fell like rain on the Vietnamese. The means to stop what was so vividly wrong remained painfully unclear. All that the Mobe leadership knew at the end of 1967 was that it was time to raise the ante. That was all anyone really knew.

A key section of the antiwar movement—its younger leaders, in particular—was leaving behind careful, law-abiding respectability. These were people who could not accept what they saw as the venality and stupidity of the system that perpetuated the war they watched on television. These people—who watched on TV and in a very few cases saw the results of the saturation bombing, the napalming, the slaughter of Vietnam—had built up a wellspring of anger and outrage that, they felt, had to be loosed publicly, where the State—a distant, bureaucratic State they were learning to loathe—could somehow be made to listen. By the end of 1967 there were white radicals in the leadership of the movement who felt at least a part of the anger that tore at the small group of black activists who had categorically said: Enough. (And a few even saw hope in the ghetto riots that were inflaming Watts, Detroit, Harlem, and Newark.)[6] On at least one front of the movement the need for action, hard action, was welling up and spilling over. And some of these people were making their presence felt.

A few weeks before the Pentagon demonstration, the National Mobe released a press statement that said in part:

> We live in a society which trains its sons to be killers
> and which channels its immense wealth into the busi-
> ness of suppressing courageous men from Vietnam to
> Detroit who struggle for the simple human right to control

their own lives and destinies. We Americans have no
right to call ourselves human beings unless personally
and collectively we stand up and say no to the death
and destruction perpetuated in our name.[7]

There were plenty of people in the leadership of the movement who
thought of the American government as a "bully and an outlaw,"
and who were resolved not to be "good Germans."[8]

Many disagreed with this spirit of militancy, a militancy they
thought preposterous and counterproductive. Many feared it would
tear apart the movement's fragile solidarity. Members of the Old
Left—of the Communist party and the Socialist Workers party—some
of whom worked long and hard in organizing various antiwar actions, actively opposed the new militancy, sure that it would drive
away any working-class support the movement might gain. Members of old line antiwar and antinuclear groups like SANE (the Committee for a Sane Nuclear Policy) and Women Strike for Peace, some
of whom had worked through the 1950s and had lucid memories of
Joe McCarthy and quiet college campuses, were afraid of the confrontational language and worried about all its ramifications.

Others too, who personally could understand the desire for militancy, worried that the new militancy was premature and that a
hollow rhetoric and a few ineffective acts would drive a wedge
between a tiny activist vanguard of the movement and the mass of
rank and file who were not revolutionaries or militants but at this
point only wanted to voice their outrage over what they saw as an
illegal and stupid war. The new spirit that had taken over the hearts
and minds of some young militants and a few older men, the spirit
summed up in the slogan, "From Dissent to Resistance," was not for
everybody.[9]

Chairman Dave Dellinger didn't think the new militancy had to
endanger the antiwar movement's mass following. In planning for
the Pentagon demonstration he stated over and over, in a leaderly
fashion: "We must maintain the fraternal ties of solidarity."[10] At the
Pentagon demonstration, as Dellinger saw it, solidarity had been
maintained because all styles of protest had been welcomed and
supported. "The Mobilization had a maximum impact because it
combined massive action with the cutting edge of resistance,"[11] said
Dellinger. He wanted to up the stakes without driving anyone out of
the game. It was a tricky and not totally consistent position to hold
but it was Dellinger's and he wasn't alone.

The Pentagon demonstration was a great success. After receiving
permits at the very last moment, a hundred thousand protestors
massed at the Lincoln Memorial. They heard speeches by Dr. Ben-

jamin Spock, the world-famous baby doctor, and other mainly older, moderate antiwar figures. There was also a moment of silence for Cuban guerrilla fighter Che Guevera, who had recently been killed in the mountains of Bolivia. The rally ended and some of the moderates dropped out. But a much larger group lined up and marched on the Pentagon. As the huge crowd reached the building (actually a Pentagon parking lot), another less moderate rally was set up.

Some were ready for more. Militant protestors, a group that included Students for a Democratic Society (SDS) and the Revolutionary Contingent (a couple of tiny militant organizations),[12] spontaneously jogged up the Pentagon mall. They faced themselves off against a line of bayonet-wielding troops. Soon others left the rally and joined the first wave of militants. A few people walked along the line of soldiers and put flowers in gun barrels. Some people, a few over the loudspeaker system, talked to the troops and explained that the protests weren't aimed at them or their fellow soldiers in Vietnam but rather were aimed at the war-making machine, at the system that was their enemy, too. Some people pushed at and sometimes through the troop lines in an existential attempt to reach the dull gray walls of the Pentagon itself. These people federal marshals arrested, sometimes with much clubbing and kicking. A group of several hundred split the confrontation line and stormed a barricade which enabled them to mass illegally in a parking area close to the Pentagon.

There was even a hippie contingent that, with the mixed blessing of the Mobe leadership, attempted to levitate the Pentagon and so exorcise it of evil spirits.

As night fell many left the Pentagon grounds but thousands stayed and maintained the siege. At night they spray painted slogans, pissed on the Pentagon grass, and maintained their symbolic stand. Late at night, the federal marshals used clubs and tear gas to regain "illegally" occupied territory. The next day, thousands of people returned to continue the siege until the demonstration permits expired that night. Over eight hundred demonstrators were arrested, mainly for trespassing on the Pentagon grounds.[13]

The Pentagon marked the first time that the antiwar movement under the national sponsorship of the Mobilization to End the War had symbolically and, no matter in how nonthreatening a fashion, literally confronted the war machine. Symbolic, confrontational action had been occurring on the West Coast for well over a year with induction centers as targets, and several years earlier pacifists had targeted military installations for nonviolent acts of civil disobedience, but those were, relatively speaking, vanguard actions.[14] The Pentagon action, above all, was a multifactional protest.

A Mobilization action was, by its very nature, supposed to be acceptable to all Mobe members, from militant groups like SDS to more moderate, multiconstituent organizations like the Fifth Avenue Parade Committee, New York's largest antiwar group. The Mobe was the only national force dedicated to consensus in the antiwar movement—a movement fractionated by ideological, tactical, and generational differences. And as such, the Mobe's move away from rallies in public spaces and marches down well-policed downtown streets and toward a more confrontational style that advocated resistance, a term always vaguely defined and even more vaguely applied, represented a major step for the entire movement toward increased militancy—at least in theory, since in practice the vote was really not yet in.

After the Pentagon, Sid Lens, a middle-aged, longtime Chicago union leader and prominent antiwar organizer, applauded the increased militancy. He said, "We implanted the notion . . . that this government is not only immoral but illegal," and this, he continued, must be the real goal of the antiwar movement: "Our task . . . is to create a mass disidentification with a counter-revolutionary, racist and unrepresentative society."[15] David Dellinger, the Mobe chairman, while warning against the extremes of what he called a crude "Gandhianism" or a crude "Guerrillaism," had praise for all the participants, even the SDS who had led the most militant action at the Pentagon and about whom the more traditional and careful Mobe had long worried. Dellinger, who, while a careless writer, often showed deep insight in the many articles he wrote for *Liberation,* the movement magazine he edited, described the protest as an "existential unity between words and deeds."[16] Confrontation had triumphed at the Pentagon, at least in the minds of many of the antiwar movement's most committed and well-spoken leaders.

The immediate question was, What next? Eric Weinberger, the young treasurer of the National Mobilization and administrator of the Fifth Avenue Parade Committee, said later that the answer "occurred to millions of people simultaneously." They would confront the head war maker himself, LBJ, at his renomination party in Chicago.[17] In the *Mobilization Report* published by the Mobe shortly after the Pentagon event, David Dellinger wrote:

> One of our continuing aims must be to disrupt and
> block the war machine. There may be a need for other
> well conceived "disruptions," as well, which will make
> it increasingly difficult for our society to conduct "busi-
> ness as usual" while the war continues (We might dis-
> cuss the implications of trying to disrupt the nominating

conventions of the Republican and Democratic parties in order to expose their hypocritical and undemocratic nature).[18]

David Dellinger's suggestion that the movement escalate to large-scale societal disruption did not come from a natural impetuousness. David Dellinger was fifty-two years old when he orchestrated the siege on the Pentagon. He had been an activist all his adult life, consistently practicing forms of radical pacificism and communism.

During World War II, though a seminarian and an assistant minister and thus entitled to a deferment, Dellinger had refused to register for the draft. He spent three years in jail. Just before entering Lewisberg Penitentiary, Dellinger tried to explain the beliefs that had caused the American government to sentence him to three years in prison—beliefs that were not to change in any fundamental way over the years:

> I believe all war is evil and useless. Even a so called war of defense is evil in that it consists of lies, hatred, self-righteousness, and the most destructive methods of violence that man can invent. . . . The rest of the world has been driven to desperation by the economic cruelty of the United States with its Big Business Empire, and of England with her colonial Empire. We produced the economic, social, and psychological conditions that made war inevitable.[19]

Dellinger's critique did not stop with the West.

He had contempt, too, for the Soviet Union: "Russia, for all her social reforms, is a bloody dictatorship . . . she has subsidized political parties all over the world that have poisoned the left wing movement with dishonesty, opportunism, and violence."[20]

Dellinger was never for a moment to waver, at least publicly, from these understandings of world economics and politics. His opposition to the "bad" war in Vietnam, he later wrote, always and totally stemmed from the same reasons that led him to oppose one of America's "good" wars—World War II.

Dellinger began his activism within the radical pacifistic Protestant tradition that had inspired an older generation that included Norman Thomas and A. J. Muste to oppose the brutalities and inequities of industrial capitalism and to seek a cooperative community of love. In tune with this tradition, Dellinger was a communist "with a little c," an unequivocal, unbending opponent of capitalism and a firm, principled opponent of Soviet totalitarianism. The beliefs that put Dellinger behind bars in the 1940s would lead him to oppose all

American wars, declared and undeclared, covert and overt, as well as all acts of direct Soviet expansionism. In his opposition Dellinger was uncompromising and unrelenting.

During the early 1950s, along with many other adherents of the now small but stalwart group of radical white Protestant and Catholic activists, Dellinger became an active participant in the civil rights movement. Throughout the unceasing, violent attacks by organized gangs of racists, Dellinger, like almost all of the civil rights leaders, stuck to the principles and practices of nonviolence.

While Dellinger was uncompromising in his own practices and principles, he did recognize the importance of using tactics that met the current situation and the needs of his allies, potential allies, and, critically, his opponents. An extreme idealist, Dellinger was also a hard-nosed pragmatist when it came to working out the strategies and tactics he and his fellow organizers might employ. In late 1963, while participating in the Quebec-Washington-Guantanamo Walk, just after Georgia police officials had brutally assaulted or callously allowed others to assault the walkers, Dellinger wrote:

> . . . nonviolence has the power to win tangible victories
> against seemingly overwhelming odds, if its practitioners
> are prepared to make almost limitless sacrifices [but] . . .
> I came away from Albany [Georgia] newly aware of the
> fact that it would be possible to carry on such a struggle
> . . . and yet leave the situation worse than at the begin-
> ning. For despite the importance of making the first hole
> in the dike . . . the key questions for the future are the
> readiness of others to pour through that hole and the
> willingness of the more enlightened members of the
> white community to prevent its being forcibly closed
> again.[21]

The danger, Dellinger believed, was in demonstrators holding too rigid, too uncompromising a position. Self-righteousness, ab-solutism, and demands for total conversion of the enemy, Dellinger stated, produce only ill feelings, misunderstandings, and even disasters. They only ''lead one to become insensitive to the com-plexity of the situation in which one's allies find themselves [and] . . . turn one's opponents into cardboard representations of evil . . . that merely stiffens their resistance and blocks their openness to new understandings.''[22]

Dellinger, even through the thin years of the 1950s, was not inter-ested in mere moral witnessing. He wanted to change the way things were. He was willing to work on an issue-by-issue basis with almost anyone who was interested in world peace, justice, and equality.[23]

One place those beliefs took Dellinger was to the "Assembly of Unrepresented People" in Washington, D.C., in August of 1965. Out of this assembly, to put it somewhat simplistically, grew what would eventually be called the National Mobilization to End the War in Vietnam, the umbrella organization Dellinger would lead in 1967 and 1968.

The evolution of the Mobe from its inchoate beginnings in the summer of 1965 to its triumph at the Pentagon is a convoluted story told effectively and carefully in Fred Halstead's *Out Now*.[24] But a brief outline here, based essentially on Halstead's account, will provide a context for some of the more critical actions and actors that I will be discussing later.

The Assembly of Unrepresented People arose out of a complex set of needs. The most important of these was the feeling among many key activists, who represented a variety of small pacifist and antiwar groups, that antiwar protesters needed a national umbrella organization that would give the antiwar movement a national framework and focus. At the same time, the activists wanted to maintain a local focus in keeping with their belief in local autonomy. Thus, the umbrella organization would not accept individual memberships but instead would consist of representatives from its many and different constituent groups who would collectively and consensually work out any national policy decisions. In essence, the activists decided to create an organization not unlike the National Council for the Prevention of War and the American League against War and Fascism which had led the peace movement in the 1920s and 30s. Until the creation of the assembly in 1965, anti-Vietnam protests were, on the left, a kind of political hot potato.

The leadership of SANE—the Committee for a SANE Nuclear Policy, founded in 1957, and the most influential antiwar group in the United States in the early 1960s—vehemently opposed and largely succeeded in suppressing the introduction of Vietnam into their large antiwar, antinuclear proliferation marches and rallies. The moderates who controlled SANE believed in moral suasion and were extremely wary of leftist politics. They felt that the Vietnam issue would taint their "more important" message with the dangerous stain of anti-Americanism and, even worse, communism. At this time, President Johnson had already sent over twenty thousand American troops to Vietnam.[25]

At the end of 1964, the national office of the Students for a Democratic Society, in accordance with the organization's anti-imperialism stance, decided to grab the hot potato. SDS was at this time a campus-based organization with only 2500 members in forty-one chapters but with a fast-growing reputation. They decided to sponsor a national march in Washington, D.C., on April 17, 1965, against the burgeoning war in Vietnam. SDS also decided to kick over the anti-Communist policy that had been governing the antiwar movement up until then. They declared that this march would be organized on a basis of nonexclusion, which meant that the communists, who SANE and other moderates had absolutely refused to work with, would be welcomed as organizers and participants in the march.

For the older antiwar workers, who had long been organizing antinuclear and antiwar marches, this was a serious move. They not only remembered the McCarthyite red-baiting that had destroyed so many lives and weakened so many liberal organizations in the 1950s, they also remembered the Communist party tactics of the 1930s and 1940s; tactics like block voting, the establishment of phony front groups to manipulate coalition and umbrella organizations, and uncompromising, unwavering tactical and debating positions, sometimes dictated by the Soviet Union, that eventually weakened the resolve and the morale of less dogmatic reformers. Many anti-Communist moderates were appalled by SDS's nonexclusion policy. But as the SDS and many others saw it, both the sectarian squabbling of the last few decades and the Red Scare tactics of the more recent past had to be forgotten. There was much work to be done.

At any rate, the SDS-sponsored march went very well, no doubt helped by President Johnson's February 7, 1965, decision to begin sustained bombing of North Vietnam and to dramatically increase United States troop strength through large-scale draft call-ups. About twenty thousand demonstrators marched from the White House to the Washington monument. The historian and pacifist activist Staughton Lynd, the independent journalist I. F. Stone, SNCC leader Robert Parris (formerly Bob Moses), SDS president Paul Potter, and Senator Gruening were among those who spoke. Phil Ochs, Judy Collins, Joan Baez, and others sang for the crowd.[26] As Fred Halstead reports in his account of the SDS-sponsored event, on the day of the march the *New York Post*, the largest daily circulation newspaper in the United States, printed an editorial stating that if the reports were true that the Vietnamese have installed antiaircraft missles around Hanoi to protect it from U.S. air attacks then the "sensible thing for our side to do is . . . give two hours warning to everybody in the area to get out of the way, then blow the whole layout to Kingdom Come with hydrogen or conventional bombs."[27] That an editorial of such extreme proportions could be printed, even in the easily exercised *Post*, demonstrated just how far the antiwar movement had to go.

After the march, SDS leadership, though pleased by their success, decided not to continue their preeminent role in the antiwar movement. The leaders were afraid that SDS would become a single issue operation just at the time they were most interested in expanding SDS from a small, campus organization to a large grass-roots movement dedicated to fundamental social and political change. SDS wanted to stop the system that produced the war, not just the war itself.

Other radical leaders, however, were heartened by the large turnout and saw the need for establishing some sort of ongoing organization that could effectively carry on the antiwar struggle on a national scale and a nonexclusionary basis. Out of this concern, in part, came the Assembly of Unrepresented People which met August 6-9, 1965—a date chosen to commemorate the twentieth anniversary of the atomic bomb explosions in Hiroshima and Nagasaki. At a workshop arranged by Jerry Rubin of Berkeley's Vietnam Day Committee (VDC)—at the time the most successful and active local antiwar group in the country—the National Coordinating Committee to End the War (NCC) was established.

Most concretely, the NCC was set up to provide a structure for the International Days of Protest, a demonstration the VDC had scheduled for October 15 and 16. The NCC steering committee included a few prominent antiwar figures, David Dellinger for one. But in the main, the NCC deliberately avoided creating a powerful central committee or staff since its purpose was only to help coordinate and issue the call for the October 15 and 16 protest and not to set policy or determine strategy. The emphasis was on local organizing and local decision making.[28]

The International Days of Protest produced demonstrations in over sixty cities, all of them moderate and all of them nonviolent. The largest demonstration was in New York City where over one hundred thousand people participated. There were also protests in Europe, South America, Canada, Mexico, and elsewhere.

In making their protest, the demonstrators knew they were picking a real fight. McCarthyism still simmered. A few days after the marches, Senator Thomas J. Dodd declared, "We have to draw a line and draw it soon and draw it hard, between the right of free speech and assembly and the right to perpetuate treason." J. Edgar Hoover, director of the Federal Bureau of Investigation, called the demonstrators "halfway citizens who are neither morally, mentally nor emotionally mature." *Time* magazine ran an editorial entitled, "Vietniks—Self Defeating Dissent." In their informal, seemingly impartial, seemingly reasonable tone, the *Time* editorialists revealed just what the movement was up against and how far from the so-called middle they stood: "The fact is the Vietniks, by encouraging the Communists' hope and expectation that the United States does not have the stomach to fight it out in Viet Nam are probably achieving what they would least like: prolonging the war and adding to the casualty lists on both sides."[29]

The fact that the Vietnamese had been fighting for decades, the fact that many Americans indeed did not have the stomach to fight it out, the fact that the editorial never discussed the morality or reason of the war—none of that seemed to bother the *Time*-niks. But it did bother many of the protesters. In some ways, the superficial "reasonableness" of the *Time* editorialists was more infuriating than the clearly drawn line of the radical right. Antiwar activists could neither understand nor accept the simpering tone or the callous ethnocentrism of the editorial—just as they couldn't fathom the benign faith so many seemed to have in the American state. Many in the movement had left the basic attitudes and premises of the American establishment behind them. There were now almost two hundred thousand American troops in Vietnam.

Over the next year the antiwar movement struggled with internecine quarreling and sectarian disputes, some of them promoted by the FBI's Cointelpro campaign.[30] Despite these sometimes bitter fights, the National Coordinating Committee began to function as an umbrella organization to a large spectrum of antiwar groups. However, due to personnel problems and to the extreme difficulty of working with such widely divergent groups as the Communist party and SANE, the NCC was not very successful in creating a workable coalition of antiwar groups.

As the NCC became increasingly nonfunctional, a second International Days of Protest took place around March 26, 1966. Almost all the activities were organized locally. The more conservative organizations like SANE and Women Strike for Peace began to fade in importance as the movement pushed toward more outright opposition to the war. Fifteen thousand marched in New York, five thousand in Chicago, and over one hundred cities had significant demonstrations. There were demonstrations against U.S. involvement in Vietnam in dozens of countries around the world.

Despite the success of these locally organized marches many felt the need of an effective, multifactional national mobilizing force with a stronger leadership role. Among those who felt this way were a group of moderate professors affiliated with the Inter-University Committee for Debate on Foreign Policy. Sidney Peck, a sociology professor at Western Reserve University in Cleveland, led the way in organizing two major meetings of antiwar activists in Cleveland on July 22 and September 10–11.

The second of these meetings was heralded as a National Leadership Conference (as compared to the original Assembly of Unrepresented People) and drew representatives from most major antiwar groups, including the American Friends Service Committee, CORE, New York's Fifth Avenue Committee, Women Strike for Peace, Committee of Clergy Concerned about Vietnam, Committee for Nonviolent Action, SNCC, Socialist Workers party, and many other smaller groups. Approximately 140 people attended: some, dedicated pacifists who had been active for decades; others, younger people brought to the movement by recent events. No one representing national SDS or national SANE registered for the meeting.

The Cleveland meetings, after much give-and-take, resulted in the formation of the November 5–8 Mobilization Committee. This committee, in turn, issued a call for four days of protests featuring marches and rallies in New York and San Francisco. In tone and temper the Mobilization was still essentially moderate, seeking a consensus position. The Mobilization's call for the demonstrations did not come out and advocate immediate troop withdrawal but instead listed a hodgepodge of assorted reasons to be against the war; all were listed under the less than poetic title, "Sick of the War in Vietnam?"

The chairman of the November 5–8 Mobilization was A. J. Muste, a kind of living saint to the antiwar movement. Muste had been the leading pacifist in the United States for almost half a century—he was a direct link to the religiously oriented and widely popular peace movement of the post–World War I years—and almost all of the older movement people gave him their love as well as their respect. As Fred Halstead wrote, "In effect, the implementation rested on Muste, on his great personal authority, and on the confidence that most of the people present had in him as a fair arbiter. No one else could have carried it off."[31]

The November 5–8 actions, due in part to the lack of enough time for proper organization, were not a great success. But all of the participating antiwar factions were pleased with the new organizational format and were prepared to continue it. There were now, toward the end of 1966, 340,000 U.S. troops in Vietnam, and President Johnson had learned to expect antiwar demonstrators at all his public appearances in the United States and abroad.

Once again in Cleveland, the leaders of the antiwar movement met. They decided to continue the Mobilization and use it, retitled the Spring Mobilization Committee to End the War in Vietnam, to organize major demonstrations in New York and San Francisco on April 15, 1967. Muste was renamed chairman and David Dellinger, Sidney Peck, and two others were named as vice-chairmen. Besides calling for the two major demonstrations, the founding document of the new Mobe stated that the organization "shall be charged with suggesting, stimulating and/or organizing actions of a more limited and more localized nature . . . as long as these actions clearly fall within the consensus reached by the diverse viewpoints of the conference."[32] The Mobe was maintaining its consenual base while trying to reach out toward a more permanent and influential position in the antiwar struggle. But staying within the "consensus reached by the diverse viewpoints" of the Mobe's many members was getting harder and harder to do for some of the antiwar leaders.

Certainly David Dellinger, at this point, held a much more radical view on Vietnam than the publicized positions of the Mobe, as did many of the other prominent activists. Dellinger had missed the November 5-8 Mobilization activities because he was at that very time in North Vietnam, a visit that led many establishment figures to label him a traitor.[33] By 1965, Dellinger had already called for "immediate unconditional withdrawal" of all American troops and stated that the United States should offer economic aid to a united Vietnam as an "indemnity." America, he said in the same article, must stop running counter "to the mainstream of world politics." The civil war in Vietnam, he said, was just another part of an "Asian self-liberation" movement.[34]

With each visit Dellinger made to the ravaged cities and countryside of Vietnam—and he made several—the more adamant, the more passionate he became in demanding an end to what he saw as the American perpetuated decimation of a land and a people.[35] But for many other antiwar supporters Vietnam remained a complex abstraction, a tragic reification of the interstices of spreading third world communism, dying imperialism, and a voracious American capitalism. For them the problem remained vague and the answers unclear.

The Johnson administration, however, did its part to try to clarify the issues. In mid-December 1966, the world press reported that Hanoi was being bombed by American planes. The administration said it was a lie. A couple of weeks later, Harrison Salisbury, a *New York Times* editor on special assignment, reported from Hanoi that it was the American government that was lying.[36] He had seen the damage caused by the bombing attacks and had surveyed the carnage. For the antiwar movement, the Salisbury reports were a breakthrough. They demonstrated that it was the more militant and radical factions of the movement that had been telling the truth and they made the more moderate factions who had trusted in the good intentions of the Johnson administration look like dupes.

The Spring Mobilization's official call for the April 15, 1967, demonstrations left little doubt about the direction in which the antiwar movement was heading. No longer did the Mobe equivocate about negotiations and timetables. The Mobe stated: "We march to dramatize the world wide hope that the United States remove its troops from Vietnam so that the Vietnamese can determine their own future in their own way." The call went on to tie Vietnam to American domestic policy: "We call for the enlistment of the men, money and resources now being used to maintain the military machine in a fight against the real enemies of man—hunger, hopelessness, ignorance, hate, discrimination and inequality. As the war cruelly destroys in Vietnam so it denies hope to millions in the United States." The call ended by declaring that the April 15 actions would be "not merely a protest but a new beginning."[37] And though SANE refused to sign this more radical call, more and more moderates were making common cause with the Mobe's more radical adherents. The moderates, too, were seeing in Vietnam more than just a mistaken policy.

A. J. Muste died February 11, 1967, at the age of eighty-two and David Dellinger took over as chairman of the Mobe. The ascension of Dellinger, who believed in a "creative tension" between a militant vanguard and a more moderate rank and file, moved the Mobe even further toward militancy. And it is important to understand that militancy is not synonymous with "left wing" in the 1960s; it is very difficult to define 1960s groups using the old labels of left and right. The Communist party, for example, was one of the more moderate groups in the Mobe coalition.

The Spring Mobilization reached the American people. Four hundred thousand people marched against the war in New York City. Seventy-five thousand marched in San Francisco. But the bombing of Vietnam escalated and, in 1967, 9419 Americans were to die in military action. Establishment voices labeled the protestors as traitors and Communists.

The antiwar movement escalated the struggle too. As noted at the beginning of this chapter, in October 1967 the protesters marched on the Pentagon and accepted the necessity of direct confrontation and more and more forceful civil disobedience. Moderation no longer seemed possible. As the war escalated in the face of the rapidly expanding antiwar movement, more and still more, the protest leaders saw, needed to be done and, critically, seemed possible to do. The protesters had the numbers, the will, and, they totally believed, the right and truth on their side and their side only.

It was with this history and this scenario in mind that David Dellinger, in a private communication, stated that "one of our continuing aims must be to disrupt and block the war machine. . . . We might

discuss the implications of trying to disrupt the nominating conventions of the Republican and Democratic Parties."[38] The war makers
had to be made to listen. They had to be made to see, Dellinger
and his compatriots believed, that the American business of business
would not be allowed to carry on blithely while the barbaric crime
of American destruction of Vietnam went stupidly onward, leading
nowhere.

After the Pentagon, the Mobilization was still an organization without a clear structure or established policy-making procedure. And
though the Mobe had come a long way in just over a year, its
position in the antiwar movement was still unstable and its leadership
not at all sure what it should do.

Chairman David Dellinger insisted, "Mobilization generally does
not think of continuous national action because the national actions
really come after actions and focusing on local institutions and teach-
ins."[39] In fact, both the Spring Mobilization and the Pentagon demonstration had been instigated without much local groundwork or
local predecessors. But Dellinger still talked about such a practice—
which was the means by which the Mobe's first actions had been
initiated—because National Mobe did not want to be seen, or see
itself, as some sort of authoritarian national policy making body for
the whole movement.

Dellinger wanted both the movement and the general public to
understand that the Mobe was still essentially a consensual, administrative body and that the real antiwar organizing effort had to and
did in fact occur on the local level. The Mobe was not a membership
organization per se but was only a coalition of over a hundred small
and large antiwar groups. And it was those groups, Dellinger was
saying, which had to establish policy and decide if, when, and
where a national action would be called. This was the Mobe's policy
and had, at least until the Pentagon, been very much in effect.

But after the Pentagon, Dellinger later explained, there had been
a change, an excited urgency that precipitated Mobe action:
". . . after the October event there were a lot of people who kept
saying, 'Well, where do we go next?' You know, and so at that
point we talked about the convention."[40] Some talked about
demonstrating at both national party conventions. But logistically
it would have been impossible to launch major demonstrations in
both Chicago and Miami, site of the Republican Convention, in
the same month. Besides which, everyone was sure Johnson would
be renominated; in early November it seemed extremely unlikely
that he would even be opposed. And it was Johnson above all
others whom the antiwar movement saw as the symbol and the
reality of the hypocritical, barbaric war-making machine.

In the eyes of the men and women who made up the broad base of the antiwar movement, he was the great betrayer—the liberal liar who ran in 1964 promising to end the war in Vietnam. He was the one who had appeared as a genuine alternative to the "Bomb Hanoi" right-wing fanaticism of Barry Goldwater. It was he who had run with the support of every liberal university group on his side—it was he who had bombed Hanoi. It was Johnson, the antiwar activists said, who let the napalm rain down on women and children, burning their flesh down to the bone. It was Johnson, they believed, who permitted the saturation bombing that destroyed a whole way of life in the mocking name of free choice, and it was Johnson who gave free reign to the Pentagon generals and let them drop antipersonnel bombs on civilian areas, bombs that shredded human flesh while they left structures intact. And then lied about the fact. It was Johnson. And the antiwar movement would hound him at every public appearance he dared to make and would turn his renomination "celebration" into something very, very different. At least, that is what Dellinger and more than a few others hoped.

Rennie Davis was certainly one of those who so hoped. Davis was one of a growing number of young, left activists who had gone to North Vietnam, talked with the people there, witnessed the atrocities, and at home hammered away at the lies perpetrated by the United States government. Like many other young new leftists who had met with members of the National Liberation Front, either in Vietnam or in meetings set up in Europe, Davis had come to identify more with the revolutionary forces in Vietnam than what he had come to see as the imperialistic forces of the United States. Davis, who had worked on the Pentagon demonstration, was from the beginning one of those who wanted to see the antiwar movement confront Johnson and the war party in Chicago.

At a meeting of the Resistance on November 20, 1967, at the University of Chicago, Davis and David Harris, the founder of that militant group of draft resisters, and two others spoke about the war. Davis told the small group of what he had seen of the bombing of North Vietnam, of the fragments of antipersonnel bombs he had been presented, and of the giant craters that stood witness to the American government policy of lying to its own people. Davis, in his careful, undramatic fashion, closed his prepared comments by saying that the movement should confront Johnson at the Democratic Convention and protest the lying and the rigged electoral system.

When asked about the shape of that protest, Davis advocated forceful civil disobedience combined with large-scale demonstrations that could include people who had never before publicly protested the war. Davis left the scope and style of the civil disobedience ambiguous. It is likely that he himself was not sure exactly how far the protest could, would, or even should go.[41] But like a growing number of people, he knew that there had to be a protest at the convention and that it had to demonstrate the increasing militancy of the movement. He also knew, by late November, that he would be one of the principal organizers of the Chicago protest if it came off.

Davis, at the end of 1967, was only twenty-seven. But he had come a long way fast. He was born in Lansing, Michigan, in 1940. His father was an economics professor at Michigan State. During the war, his family moved to Washington, D.C., and for the next several years his father was a major economic advisor—from 1947 to 1953, a member of the Council of Economic Advisors. Davis grew up knowing how the system worked, or at least how it was supposed to work.

A brilliant high school student, Davis went on to Oberlin College. At Oberlin, he helped to found a radical, campus political party, one of several such parties that were popping up at many of the country's best colleges and universities.

Davis was not a charismatic leader. But from his early college or-ganizing days he showed himself to be a hard-working, dedicated, intelligent, and extremely serious organizer. By 1962, Davis was a leading member of the newly emerged SDS. Over the next few years, he half-heartedly pursued graduate degrees in political science at the Universities of Illinois, Michigan, and Chicago. Most of Davis's energy and enthusiasm went into student organizing.[42]

At the beginning of 1964, Davis took over SDS's main program, ERAP (Economic Research and Action Project). SDS leader Tom Hayden had pushed this program to the front of the SDS agenda. In theory, ERAP (Ee-rap) was to take SDS from the campuses to the cities, from organiz-ing students to organizing the poor. The idea was that small groups of SDSers would set up informal centers in poor areas and use local issues like housing problems and employment practices to organize the poor and slowly move them into increasingly complex, political issues. The United Auto Workers and the Packinghouse Workers Union both liked the idea and provided modest funds to get the project going.[43]

Davis proved to be a superb organizer and against the odds turned the plan into a real functioning operation. ERAP began with centers in Chicago, Newark, Cleveland, and Hazard, Kentucky, and soon expanded. Davis, only half-jokingly, called his work "organizing with mirrors." By this, he meant that he often had to make—for the sake of both those involved and those who were being served—what was in reality only a small group of uncertain, young people seem like a large, professional organization. It was a technique that would serve Davis well for years to come.[44]

By late 1967, Davis was living in Chicago and working with the successful, local branch of ERAP, JOIN (Jobs or Income Now). Davis was widely recognized in the movement as a top administrator who knew how to work with people and get things done. By the end of November 1967, he was a key member of the Mobe staff. As a long-time Chicago resident and organizer, familiar with the city's political machine, he was a natural for project director of a major Chicago demonstration.

During November no concrete planning or formal meetings on Chicago occurred. David Dellinger was in Denmark during the later part of the month participating in the second session of the War Crimes Tribunal. The tribunal had been established by Bertrand Russell to investigate American atrocities in Vietnam and as such had stirred up some debate in the American left. Pacifist Staughton Lynd had refused to attend the Tribunal because it would be investigating solely American atrocities while ignoring National Liberation Front and North Vietnamese activities. But Dellinger was there, as was ex-SDS president Carl Oglesby and Black Power advocate Stokely Carmichael. Dellinger came back to the United States in early December and in a *Liberation* article stated: "I doubt if Americans will ever be able to comprehend the depravity represented by U.S. actions in Vietnam."[45] The American mass media totally ignored the reams of evidence the Tribunal turned up disclosing American atrocities.

On December 27, in New York, more than two months after the Pentagon protest, the Administrative Committee of the Mobe met to discuss the future. Over fifty people attended the meeting. Most every person represented a different group of antiwar protesters. Chicago was the main topic of conversation and people came at it from every possible direction.[46]

Rennie Davis began by giving the perspective on Chicago from Chicago. He was 100% in favor of a Chicago action. According to the minutes of the meeting, he declared that protesters should "not try to prevent the convention from taking place but should show people an 'escalation in militancy' by the peace movement." He also warned that Chicago activists believed that the city would get a "blanket injunction" preventing any and all demonstrations. Linda Morse, a young pacifist who had been a leading activist for a few years and was most recently a moving force in the newly created Student Mobilization Committee, agreed with Davis on the necessity of a Chicago action. She added that the demonstrations should "disrupt and demand" and that they should concentrate on racism as well as the war.

Fred Halstead, leader of the Socialist Workers party and a key figure in the Mobe, felt that things were moving too fast and that it would be better to hold off on Chicago for a while and to plan instead for spring demonstrations in a number of cities. Somebody else wanted to demonstrate in Chicago and Miami. Lew Jones of the Young Socialist Alliance, an affiliate of the SWP, not surprisingly agreed with Halstead. He, too, wanted to decentralize the protests. Bob Greenblatt, a Cornell math professor and Mobe co-chair, spoke against the decentralization move. He said *national* mobilization is the whole point of the Mobe. Halstead pushed for a large-scale conference to discuss spring actions. Others said, let SDS—who at their recently held national convention had decided to protest the war with "Ten Days to Shake the Empire" in April—figure out the spring actions.

David Dellinger also spoke out against Halstead's call for a mass conference to discuss spring protests. Dellinger said, "Everytime there's a conference there's also a power scramble which with time could cause a fiasco." Dellinger meant that whenever there's a mass conference Old Left groups try to pack the meetings and use block-voting techniques to try to get their way. Dellinger much preferred smaller meetings in which a consensus position could be worked out slowly. Old Left organizers like Halstead knew that that is what Dellinger meant and they didn't like it.

Somewhere in all this arguing, Tom Hayden, a newcomer to Mobe meetings, spoke up. He urged that a planning group be set up for Chicago that could outline a more specific agenda that could be discussed at a later date. Dellinger, who had long known and trusted Hayden, put his weight behind the suggestion. and without any sort of vote or outright approval certain vague plans were worked out.

The Mobe would work toward spring demonstrations but it would also begin working out plans for a Chicago convention demonstration. The Chicago demonstration would protest the state of electoral politics, racism, and the war in Vietnam. All of this would help to promote local organizing efforts which in turn would help establish a mass coalition dedicated to radical social change. Not everyone approved of these plans and not everyone accepted the fact that these plans were indeed to be implemented. It was generally understood that all of these plans would be discussed again before anything happened. Nothing was very clear when the meeting broke up. Davis and Hayden, however, left the meeting knowing that they would be the ones working out the plans for the Chicago demonstration and they knew what they wanted.[47]

Tom Hayden, while a newcomer to the Mobilization staff, was anything but a new arrival to the movement. More than anyone else, Tom Hayden could take credit for founding and directing the development of the American New Left. Not that he would lay such a claim—that was not Hayden's style.

Hayden's friend, the prominent liberal journalist Jack Newfield, described Hayden as "the New Left's protean equivalent of Andre Malraux . . . a radical activist, writer, international adventurer, politician and myth."[48] While that description is a bit overstated, Tom Hayden was the New Left's busiest worker, most forceful thinker, and best-traveled man behind Communist lines.

Hayden was born in 1939 and grew up in Royal Oak, Michigan, a Detroit suburb. His parents were middle-class Catholics who divorced while Hayden was still young. He went to a Catholic grammar school and public high school.

In high school, he was editor of the school paper. The last editorial Hayden wrote before graduating seemed like just another high-minded, banal exhortation. In fact, it spelled out all the anger and frustration Tom Hayden had been fast accumulating. The first letter of each paragraph announced Hayden's real message—"Go to hell," the letters spelled.

In 1957, Hayden went to the University of Michigan, one of the largest universities in the country. In Ann Arbor, he later said, "I had to live in a dorm with thirteen hundred guys that was worse than a public housing project. There were no written rules . . . [only] absolute, arbitrary authority." Hayden organized protests.

He also drove a motorcycle and hitchhiked around the country. After his junior year, he drifted cross-country to check out the HUAC demonstrations in Berkeley. He also visited the National Student Association headquarters and met up with a bunch of students, black and white, who meant to do something about what they saw going on around them. Hayden explained it this way, "I didn't get political. Things got political."

In his senior year, Hayden was editor of the university newspaper, the *Michigan Daily*. He had also become involved with the Students for a Democratic Society, which at that time was a tiny, liberal, campus group with no clear agenda or political orientation.

Primarily in his role as journalist, Hayden went down to Atlanta in October, 1960, to check out the Student Non-Violent Coordinating

Committee. He went with them to Fayette County, Tennessee, where he saw sharecroppers demonstrating for their right to be free men.

Right after graduation, Hayden went back down south as SDS field secretary. He was beaten in Mississippi, jailed in Georgia, but kept at it. He wrote reports about the voter registration campaign, reports that the tiny SDS national office reprinted and distributed to university campuses around the country. Students read the reports and some of them joined SDS and some even traveled to the Deep South to help. Hayden later described the period as "a creative, revolutionary period . . . tremendous energy . . . great optimism . . . a state of religious fervor. I began to unlearn everything I had been taught at college. Mechanics, maids, unemployed people taking things into their own hands." The slogan of the time was, "Let the People decide."[49]

In December of 1961, Hayden wrote most of the "Port Huron Statement," the SDS manifesto that served as the American New Left's first, clear credo. The manifesto began with a full-out critique of American society. Redolent with the thinking of C. Wright Mills, it spoke not to the working class or the poor but to white, middle-class college students. Its critique centered not so much on poverty itself as on a poverty of vision, and it was not so much about oppression as about apathy: "America rests in national stalemate, its goals ambiguous and tradition-bound instead of informed and clear, its democratic system apathetic and manipulated rather than 'of, by and for the people.' . . . America is without community."

The manifesto did more than just outline the problem. It presented a detailed examination of the arms race, the Cold War, racism, big business, unions, and much more. It also suggested answers. Some of these answers were simple kinds of reformism, in essence, expansions of the emerging welfare state. But there was more to the message than simple reformism. The statement linked all of America's problems together and stated that more than just reforms would be necessary to correct the underlying problems. The "Port Huron Statement" declared that the practice of democracy itself had to be changed:

> We seek the establishment of a democracy of individual participation, governed by two central aims: that the individual share in those social decisions determining the quality and direction of his life; that society be organized to encourage independence in men and provide the media for their common participation. In a participatory democracy, the political life would be based in several root principles: that decision making of basic social con-

sequences be carried on by public groups; that politics
be seen positively, as the art of collectively creating an
acceptable pattern of social relations; that politics has
the function of bringing people out of isolation and into
community.[50]

This vision of participatory democracy would rule the New Left
throughout the 1960s.

Over the next few years, Hayden continued to guide SDS, which
was growing rapidly. He was president from 1962 to 1963. In 1964
he helped to develop and implement the aforementioned ERAP.
And soon after its inception, he and a handful of others moved into
the heart of black Newark.

In 1965, historian and Communist activist Herbert Aptheker was
asked by the North Vietnamese government to come to Hanoi during
Christmas with two non-Communists. Aptheker picked pacifist
Staughton Lynd and he, in turn, selected Tom Hayden. Ignoring a
State Department travel ban, and amid much publicity, they be-
came the first Americans to go to Hanoi since the war began. With
Staughton Lynd, Hayden wrote a book about his visit to Vietnam
called *The Other Side*. Their book presented the NLF and North
Vietnamese side of the war.[51]

In part as a result of this visit, but also out of the frustrations endemic
to local organizing, Hayden expanded his efforts to a full-out attack
"against capitalism and bureaucracy."[52] Hayden was beginning to
target his enemies more clearly. By 1967, he was prepared to leave
the Newark project he had headed for over two years. He wanted
to work full time on national and international issues.

But on July 12, the Newark ghetto exploded for six days and Hayden
stayed to try to make sense of all the anger and deaths. He wrote a
book about the riot called *Rebellion in Newark*. "A riot," he argued,
"represents people making history."[53] Violence, Hayden stated, was a
necessary ingredient of any revolution.

Hayden continued to travel around the world, meeting with leftists
in Cuba, Europe, and elsewhere. At the North Vietnamese's request,
he helped organize a conference in Bratislava, Czechoslovakia. At
the conference, young Americans could meet with their Vietnamese
counterparts. At the end of 1967, Hayden, again at the North Vietnamese's request, flew to Hanoi and Cambodia to work out the
"goodwill" release of three American prisoners of war. Worldwide,
Hayden was the best-known young American radical. He was de-
spised by much of the American government and establishment
press and honored, respected, and listened to by substantial portions
of the movement.[54]

By late 1967, the Mobilization, indeed the national antiwar movement, finally seemed to Hayden to be a viable form of antiwar
protest. It was finally firm enough in its commitments to make a
strong, uncompromising protest be heard. And so, Tom Hayden was
ready to join forces with it.

After the December 27 meeting, Hayden and Davis, old-time SDS
partners, began working out what shape the Chicago action could
take. Over the next couple of weeks, they wrote a five-page, single-
spaced paper titled, "Discussion on the Democratic Convention
Challenge." Labeled "not for circulation or publication," the document was distributed to the Mobe staff and a few other people Davis
and Hayden wanted to get involved in the protest.[55]

The first two pages of the "Discussion" outlined a basic critique of
American society beginning with what they saw as its stupefied
reliance on electoral politics: "American society is being destroyed
by its unrepresentative government. . . . Democracy is reduced to
the sorry event of people trooping to polls every four years to vote
for candidates who offer no serious choices."[56] They went on to
attack racism, urban blight, the media, health care, party politics,
and bureaucracy. Almost any movement document longer than a
few pages began with this sort of attack. Here, the attack also served
as a means for justifying the Chicago protest.

After three pages of attack, Davis and Hayden stated that Chicago, the site of LBJ's renomination, was the natural site for
protesting the failures of the American system. A protest at the
Democratic Convention, they wrote, would "dramatize to the
world"[57] that the government doesn't represent the American people and that electoral politics were nothing but a mockery of real
democratic practice.

Davis and Hayden went on to describe the protest possibilities.
First, they went along with the idea of a Spring Action, April 21–
30. But, they said, the Mobe organizing effort should be oriented
strictly toward creating mass demonstrations in Chicago during the
Democratic Convention. Davis and Hayden wanted "a week of
demonstrations, disruptions and marches . . . clogging the streets
of Chicago demanding peace, justice and participation in government." Each day, they said, the protests should escalate and
on August 28, the day Johnson was to be renominated, a "half
million" people should march on the convention hall, "pinning
the delegates in the International Amphitheater until a choice is
presented to the American people." Then, too, somewhat incon-
sistently, Hayden and Davis warned, "The movement must not
play into Johnson's hands by attempting to prevent the convention

from assembling, a position few Americans would accept or understand."[58] In sum, Hayden and Davis declared that the Chicago protest should be a militant, mass demonstration that attacked not just Johnson's war policies but the entire panopoly of policies and practices that made the war possible and even predictable. Racism, they said, should be as much the target of the demonstrations as the war itself.

David Dellinger was one of the first to read the Hayden-Davis plan. While he very much approved of the general scenario, he did not like some of the language or some of the implications. The phrase "pinning the delegates in the International Amphitheater" particularly aggravated him. It was just the kind of needless hyperbole that alienated moderate followers and lit up the eyes of law-and-order types. Dellinger wanted a nonviolent demonstration and he made that very clear to Hayden and Davis.[59]

In essence, Hayden and Davis agreed with Dellinger's belief that Chicago had to be a nonviolent demonstration. But they had their own reasons. As they saw it, violent confrontation would be counterproductive and in all likelihood would produce nothing more than some pointless martyrs. Davis and Hayden believed that the vast majority of the demonstrators, as well as society at large, would be repulsed, and not turned on, by violent tactics. Then, too, they firmly believed that any violence stirred up by militant demonstrators in Chicago would be crushed and brutally crushed by the armed might of the well-organized and prepared State. So although Davis and Hayden would remain ambivalent about the use of violent tactics in Chicago, in part due to their own understandings and in part due to pressures exerted by Dellinger, they did stop using language, at least in public, that suggested its implementation.

The subject of violence would, however, remain a particularly touchy one for the Chicago planners from the beginning to the end. And many movement people around the country knew it and they knew that Davis and Hayden, unlike Dellinger, accepted the eventual necessity of violence. And movement people worried about what that would mean for Chicago.[60]

4 Mobilizing in Molasses

In late January, Davis, Hayden and Dellinger all gathered in New York for a couple of small meetings to discuss Chicago. The first meeting, on Janaury 26, brought the Chicago organizers and a few of their friends together with a dozen or so members of the National Lawyer's Guild—a leftist–liberal group established in the postwar era to provide legal aid to demonstrators. Bernardine Dohrn, a young lawyer fast moving from liberal to revolutionary, helped to organize the meeting.[1]

According to the minutes of the meeting, Hayden said that tactics for the protest were not yet clear but he thought that they "should have people organized who can fight the police, people who are willing to get arrested. No question that there will be a lot of arrests. My thinking is not to leave the initiative to the police. Have to have isolated yet coordinated communication. Don't want to get into the trap of violence versus passive action."[2] Hayden anticipated police violence. And he did not want to see such violence go uncontested.

By that, he did not mean that he wanted demonstrators to make unprovoked attacks on policemen. Rather, he meant that if, or more accurately when, police attacked demonstrators there should be trained people prepared to stop the police. This was not a new idea. West Coast demonstrations usually had such people. They were volunteers who underwent an informal, usually only half-serious bit of training that taught them how to move crowds and protect demonstrators from hecklers and police. Generally, they interposed their bodies between attackers and the demonstrators.

Bernardine Dohrn ended the meeting by suggesting that, though it would take a little money, they should establish an ongoing legal committee for Chicago. Davis, always the nuts-and-bolts man, agreed and said he would work on it.

The next day, Davis, Hayden, and Dellinger met with about twenty-five other major movement people, including Sid Peck, Sid Lens, and ex-SDS president Carl Oglesby, who Hayden had specifically invited. They met to lay out the purpose and strategy of the Chicago protest, a protest about which many still remained unsure. Some people were wondering how appropriate a demonstration at the convention would be now that a major peace candidate—Senator

Eugene McCarthy of Minnesota had announced his candidacy November 30—was running for the nomination.

Davis did most of the talking at this meeting and he met the McCarthy thing head-on. Presidential politics, he says, distracts people from the real issues. The campaigners might talk about peace and civil rights but after the election the talk just fades away. Dellinger added that while a McCarthy might mean well when he said that he wants to end the war, in fact, he wouldn't do it because he couldn't; he's too dependent on the party machinery which is run by special interests who don't want the war stopped. The job of the antiwar movement is to educate people about the real practices of politics so that they will understand that the mere casting of a vote for a peace candidate is not enough—after all, Johnson was the peace candidate in 1964. Davis, Hayden, and Dellinger all agreed that no matter who was running for the nomination the "People" had to be in Chicago during convention week to tell the Democratic party and the rest of the country that vague rhetoric about peace would not be enough. They wanted action; they wanted the war stopped. And more important, they wanted the whole system that perpetuated such a war to be changed and changed now.

On the whole, most of the twenty-five or so activists in the room listened sympathetically. But many remained unsure that an action at the convention would best serve the needs of the movement. Already some opposed it outright.[3]

SDS's national leadership was from the beginning ambivalent about Chicago; such ambivalence surprised no one, not even Hayden or Davis who had at one time been a part of that national leadership. Starting with the 1965 decision not to continue SDS's antiwar leadership role but to concentrate instead on keeping SDS a multi-issue grassroots organization, SDS leadership had grown even more opposed to nationally organized marches and rallies. In 1966, Jeff Shero, at that time SDS vice-president, wrote, "We must develop political programs that go beyond marches, fasts, personal witnesses, and other symbolic forms of protest. We must deal with questions of power rather than act out our generational alienation."[4] Based on the same assumptions, SDS had more or less opposed the Pentagon protest, saying, "We feel that these large demonstrations—which are just public expressions of belief—can have no significant effect on American policy in Vietnam. Further they delude many participants into thinking that the 'democratic' process in America functions in a meaningful way."[5]

SDS's first public statement on the Chicago action appeared in the January 8, 1968, *New Left Notes*, the official SDS newspaper. In part, the brief editorial stated:

> SDS recognizes the importance of entering coalitions.
> . . . However, in the context of a national electoral
> campaign, it is also aware of the danger of cooption by
> liberal elements within the anti-war movement . . . the
> same role that McCarthy had admitted is his own—to
> channel dissent that is potentially radical into Demo-
> cratic Party confines.[6]

The editorial concluded that national leadership (the National
Interim Council) had resolved to send NIC members to all Mobe
meetings and then decide at the spring and summer national SDS
conventions what SDS should do in Chicago.

The NIC was treading carefully. They had essentially not participated in organizing the Pentagon action—even though SDS members
had participated in the most militant actions—and some in the NIC
had later regretted that decision. However, almost everything SDS
had been doing and saying for the last few years indicated that
they would not endorse the Chicago protest. And would not, even
though ex-SDSers Davis and Hayden were directing the action and
bringing a sizable number of "graduate" SDSers into the organizing
effort.

Back in Chicago, Rennie Davis asked one of those "graduate"
SDSers, Clark Kissinger, the 1963–1966 national secretary, to help
organize what would be, in part, a trial run for the convention
protest. Davis wanted Kissinger, who had been a community organizer in Chicago for the last few years, to plan the spring antiwar
march and rally in Chicago. The protest would be one of many
antiwar protests held around the country on or around April 27. These
spring protests were now almost a tradition and were the protests
Halstead and others had in mind when they pushed through the
vague Mobe decision of December 27 to support spring actions.

Kissinger, who like Davis was a first-rate administrator and organizer, agreed to plan the march and rally. With the support and
leadership of the Chicago Peace Council, the local multiconstituent,
consenual organization that traditionally planned Chicago antiwar
protests, Kissinger got to work on the demonstration, working out of
the Mobe's new Chicago office.[7]

Davis had opened the office February 1, on the third floor of the
Old Colony office building in the heart of the Loop, at 407 South
Dearborn. The rent money—Davis paid one thousand dollars up
front—came in part from one of the Mobe's more generous supporters, Dan Kalish, a UCLA philosophy professor, who was also one of
the Mobe's several cochairs.[8] The 407 South Dearborn office quickly
became the center of operations for the Chicago action and as such

attracted a number of volunteers, some of whom worked for various government security agencies.

The office provided a quick and dirty introduction to movement style and practices for those who were new to the movement. The Old Colony Building had only two to four offices a floor and, like many other movement organizations, the Mobe shared their floor with fellow activists. The American Friends Service Committee, a Quaker antiwar group with years of experience, was just down the hall. The Mobe's space consisted of three rooms, one a tiny cubicle and two others filled with used desks and filing cabinets which had been donated by a sympathetic businessman. Scattered around the rooms were typewriters in various states of disrepair, a few telephones, a beat-up mimeograph machine, a small refrigerator, a coffee maker, and a broken radio. Davis, Donna Grippe—who among other things managed the office—and a very few others worked for subsistence wages. When they could, Davis or Grippe or anybody else in the office would hit up snooping newspapermen for a little money to buy baloney or peanut butter and jelly for office meals. Proper appearances were not thought worth maintaining. Nobody kept regular hours and people came in and out all the time, with more people arriving as the day progressed. There was no effort made or interest expressed in excluding intelligence agents or eavesdropping reporters. The door was open to newcomers, albeit they were not greeted with any particular enthusiasm.[9]

One volunteer, who was in fact a somewhat sympathetic spy for *Chicago American* star columnist Jack Mabley, later recounted that when he first walked in his only welcome was a laconic announcement, "We have a volunteer."[10] And that after filling out a card giving his name, address, and telephone number he was immediately put to work calling up people for a fund-raiser. He also reported that the workers were friendly and laughed a lot. He noted that Davis, who smoked a lot of Pall Mall menthols, was very much in charge and, in general, used his low-key, unflappable manner to help keep everyone else in the office calm; Davis kept things together.[11]

On February 11, 1968, an ad hoc Mobilization Committee of thirty-four met in Chicago, at the somewhat larger offices of the American Friends Service Committee, to discuss the convention demonstrations. Davis and Carlos Russell of the Congress on Racial Equality cochaired the meeting. The committee addressed two central problems: the need to prepare an agenda for a large movement conference to discuss Chicago and the need to figure out the role of black people in the protest.

Dellinger began by reporting that there had been no blacks present at the January 27 meeting on Chicago and that he was pleased
that this problem had now been rectified. He and several others
present wanted Russell and the other blacks in attendance to explain
to them what role they saw blacks playing in the Chicago protest.

After conferring with his fellow activists, Russell told the whites much
of what they already knew. He said, "We are working from separate
concerns." For blacks the war was not the central issue, survival
was. Russell added, "Blacks are focusing on Black Liberation . . .
any preparation for the Convention would see blacks organizing
around Black Liberation locally and whites reaching out to their own
communities around the issues of war and imperialism." Chicago, if
it came off, would be, like almost every other antiwar protest, a
white affair.

It was not that black leadership was indifferent to the war. Everyone from Martin Luther King, Jr., to Black Panther Chairman Huey
Newton had spoken out against it again and again. It was just that
they believed that they had more important issues to organize
around. Moreover, as Russell stated, at this point in the struggle dual
organization best suited the needs of the black people; by which he
meant that blacks would work together on their thing and whites
could work together on their thing—which meant that whites could
work on the war but they had better work on racism, discrimination,
and inequality, too. This separatist and somewhat hostile attitude
was very much the sentiment of an increasing number of black
activists and no one at the meeting was surprised. And although
Rennie Davis emphasized that he thought it essential to have a
sizable black presence at the Chicago action, it seemed from what
Russell was saying that this would not happen.

The meeting continued with Davis laying out four paths the Chicago protesters might follow: they could disrupt the convention, they
could use the convention to demonstrate for a peace candidate,
they could stay home and protest locally, or they could demonstrate
against the war and the system that created it. They could have a
mass march on the convention hall as well as a week of smaller
protests organized by the Mobe's diverse membership. Sid Lens, with
no protest from the others, quickly dismissed option number one:
disruption. He said, the Mobe must draw people into the movement
and not scare them away: "Americans must learn that the chairman
of the Democratic Party is also the president of Commonwealth Edi-
son." Hayden elaborated, saying that they "must project a nonviolent legal face . . . . Although violence is a major method of
change in this society . . . a national mobilization must be legal and

have a particular kind of political meaning. It must be designed to reach out to new people.'' Even Fred Halstead of the Socialist Worker party, who had been very hesitant about a Chicago action, now approved of it and added that, even if the demonstration was not legal, that is, was somehow repressed by the government, "we should definitely go ahead with an action.'' Publicly, at least, all the delegates seemed to be in favor of planning for a convention protest as outlined in option number four. Hayden concluded by suggesting that the Mobe host a major conference in late March to further plan and promote the demonstration. All agreed.[12]

Over the next few days, Hayden, Davis, and a few others, under the newly devised name, the March 23rd Convention Committee (the date they had chosen for the big Mobe conference), published and distributed a brief newsletter, "Convention Notes.'' The newsletter printed the minutes from the February 11 meeting and announced the March 22–23 conference, which was to be held in Lake Villa, a small campground outside Chicago.[13]

At approximately the same time, the National Mobilization staff, which David Dellinger headed, sent out a new issue of the *Mobilizer*, the Mobe's official, irregularly published newsletter. The *Mobilizer* covered several topics. As usual, it described American atrocities committed by American forces in Vietnam, including the napalm devastation of parts of Cholon, which was compared to tactics used by the Nazis. Another article discussed the somewhat unfocused spring antiwar activities. In general, the Mobe was calling for local, multitactical protests: "The major objectives of these days of protests are to accelerate the growth of the opposition and to keep it viable *in all its depth and diversity.*'' There would be no nationally coordinated marches or rallies. Local groups were to organize on university campuses and cities around the country.

Finally, the *Mobilizer* formally announced plans for the March 22–23 conference at Lake Villa. The notice directed all interested parties to direct papers and proposals to Davis in Chicago. It also said that the Mobe needed to assess the relationship between the antiwar movement and black liberation. Blacks, in particular, were invited to the conference.[14]

Over the next month, Hayden and Dellinger promoted the convention demonstration in New York. Davis worked in Chicago, and movement groups around the country began mobilizing either for the March 22–23 conference or for the Chicago action itself. In Boston and the Bay area, special committees of area antiwar activists and community organizers were set up to discuss Chicago and to send representatives to Lake Villa.[15]

The Resistance, a national organization of highly committed draft resisters, well-respected by most factions of the antiwar movement, issued a position paper on Chicago titled, "The Long March." In the paper, the Resistance leadership declared that though "many agreed that the Resistance would become lost and sacrifice the independence of its position" in Chicago, they had decided to participate in the demonstration. They stated that it was important for the resisters to break out of the isolation the act of draft refusal created and to participate in the larger antiwar community. Moreover, they would participate in their own special way; starting in San Francisco, well before the convention, fifty to seventy-five members would form a "traveling medicine band" and walk and caravan all the way to Chicago, explaining draft resistance and their politics as they went.[16]

The February 27 "Convention Notes" enthusiastically passed along these and other descriptions of organizing efforts aimed at Chicago. Without comment, it also printed a short piece by Jerry Rubin and his new associates describing Yippie's plans for the convention.[17]

The two weeks before the March 22–23 Lake Villa Conference exploded with unforeseen news. On March 12, the voters of New Hampshire, in the nation's first presidential primaries, shocked the political pundits, President Johnson, and the antiwar movement when 28,791 New Hampshire voters rejected Johnson and his war. The people of New Hampshire, one of the most conservative states in the country, split their votes almost evenly (though Johnson did have a slight plurality) between Johnson and antiwar candidate Eugene McCarthy—a liberal senator from Minnesota, short on charisma and political savvy but long on integrity and courage. Four days after McCarthy's dark horse "victory," Senator Robert Kennedy—who was strong in just those areas where McCarthy was weakest—changed the tune he had been playing for the last half year and announced that he, too, would seek the Democratic presidential nomination in Chicago. Suddenly, Lyndon Johnson, who had hoped that he would run virtually unopposed, and thus would not have to face a campaign trail crowded with protesters and hecklers, was in the middle of a serious political contest.

The sudden viability of not one but two antiwar candidates in the Democratic party created problems for the antiwar movement in general, and for the Chicago protest planners in particular. Thousands of young people were flocking to the McCarthy and Kennedy campaigns. Many were cutting their hair and dressing up in their straight Sunday best—known as going "Clean for Gene"—in an attempt to make the system work for them while they worked for it.

Suddenly, some antiwar people were joining the campaigns and worrying about alienating the electorate.[18] Others, more radical, worried that McCarthy and Kennedy would co-opt the movement for half-way reformist ends. The movement, by and large, was perplexed by the changing political situation.

Divided to begin with, the two hundred invited delegates came to Lake Villa on March 22 knowing that the chances of reaching a consensus were now worse than ever. The twenty-five or so blacks who came to the conference caucused separately. And that presented only the most obvious division—a division, however, the blacks seemed to enjoy demonstrating and even exacerbating. There were also clear differences of opinion between the Mobe's moderate forces and its smaller, radical wing—the wing that very much controlled the conference.

The small black caucus quickly made it apparent that they were not very much interested in demonstrating in Chicago. They did state that they did not *oppose* such a demonstration. In their own position paper they announced their agenda of black liberation. They declared that their liberation movement was an ''integral part of liberation struggles throughout the third world . . . . We also see that those white people who have verbalized an affinity with the Black and Brown Liberation Struggle have failed because of an internalized racism, to understand this crucial relationship.''[19] Black militants had reached the last stop on the radical vanguard express. More specifically, their position paper declared that their first goal was total control of their own community. A list of thirteen recommendations followed, including the freeing of all political prisoners (which sometimes meant all incarcerated blacks), the repeal of all gun laws (so that blacks could defend themselves against the police, a la the Black Panthers), the creation of community review boards, jobs and income for all oppressed minorities, the return of all Indian lands, the rejection of all War On Poverty programs (because they were paternalistic reformism), and the rejection of all presidential candidates. As was evermore typically the case, most of the whites at the conference supported the black caucus's demands. Some supported the demands because they had worked in the South or in the ghettoes and knew that the blacks were playing this game for keeps; others supported the demands because the blacks intimidated them or made them felt guilty.

While the small group of blacks went about their separate business, the one hundred and seventy-five or so whites heard papers, broke into smaller discussion groups and debated resolutions and future plans. The makeup of the white delegates was decidedly unusual for a major Mobe conference. Many of the delegates were under thirty.

Lew Jones, a young delegate himself, representing the Young Socialist Alliance—the youth branch of the Socialist Workers party—declared that the meeting was overwhelmingly packed by SDS types.[20] Actually, there were very few current SDSers at the conference. On March 9 and 10 at the National Interim Committee meeting, SDS leadership decided to send only six people to the Mobe conference. And they were sent with strict instructions: "Under no circumstance were they to vote on the final endorsement of the call—The NIC also requested that one of the six make explicit to the people printing up the call that SDS's name should not appear on it anywhere."[21] Real SDSers were at the conference but only a few, and for all the reasons already discussed they were holding off on any kind of endorsement of Chicago. But as for SDS "types," they were indeed at the conference in significant numbers—and in leadership positions.

Eric Weinberger, the Mobe functionary and a non-SDS "type," agreed with Jones that the Lake Villa Conference delegates were not the usual Mobe people. He described it, however, as:

> an attempt to bring youth spokesmen into the Mobilization. . . . Lots of people, the not very militant people, you know, the old line peace groups, the labor unions, the religious groupings, etc., played a decision making role that ignored the feeling from the young people, that there had to be more representation of the young people. . . . There was a feeling that too many of these offices had become bureaucrat ridden.

Lake Villa, he concluded, was an attempt at a deliberate "regrouping of forces within the coalition."[22]

As has been stated, Hayden and Davis, with the full support of David Dellinger, were behind this shift. They were the SDS "types" who had brought so many of their one-time colleagues into the conference and into positions of power. The list of SDS vets included Kathy Boudin, Constance Brown, Clark Kissinger; Corina Fales, John Froines, Carol Glassman, Vernon Grizzard, Mike Locker, Paul Potter, Jeff Shero, and Lee Webb—not everyone of whom was at the conference but who were all decidedly participating in and organizing for the Chicago action. And almost without exception, all of them wanted to see the Mobe move in the direction of militant confrontation.

There was another group of young people (young at heart, at any rate) at the conference who Hayden and Davis did not particularly care to see. The Yippies, led by Rubin and Hoffman, had come to show the Mobe that they were for real and to check out what the "serious" protesters meant to do in Chicago. With very few exceptions, no one was pleased with the appearance of the Yips.

Eric Weinberger, in retrospect, put it diplomatically when he said he mistrusted the Yippies because he worried that they were apolitical and would only water down the antiwar actions.[23] Lew Jones of YSA, younger than many of the Yippies, put it less diplomatically in a report he drew up a couple of days after the conference. The Yippies, he said, are "a totally regressive development . . . [part of a] sick escapist milieu. This new organization can only be viewed as an opponent and its 'festival' as degenerate" (of course, it must be remembered that Jones didn't think much of SDS, Davis, Hayden, or anyone else who fell outside of "correct" Marxist-Trotskyist views).[24]

Long after the conference, David Dellinger would say of the Yippies: "Like the society they criticize they are too often victims of their own rhetoric and their own failure to think through the consequences to other people of the things they say or do." Dellinger was repulsed by the Yippies' irresponsibility and hedonism. He saw in all the Yippie rhetoric way too much "ego-tripping . . . fantasies and . . . bullshit. . . . Their revolution is largely rhetorical. . . . [Their] culture turns out to be distressingly like the mirror image of the culture [they] . . . thought [they were] . . . rejecting."[25]

Generally, at the conference, movement people just tried to steer clear of the Yippies. As a *Chicago Tribune* reporter later wrote—his disappointment evident—"The meetings were all business and most of those attending wore conventional clothing. . . . The only one seen wearing beads was a Negro."[26] Many of the Mobe delegates were young but they were hardly hippie types interested in the sex, drugs, and rock 'n roll revolution Yippie was promoting. They were interested in a path to power.

Davis and Hayden tried to give the conference just that kind of answer. In their twenty-one-page report, "Movement Campaign 1968: An Election Year Offensive,"[27] they told the delegates what kind of actions they thought should happen preparatory to and in Chicago. Not everyone liked what they were promoting either.

The program they called for was, to say the least, ambitious. Hayden and Davis wanted to launch a locally organized nationally administered movement dedicated to challenging the Democratic party. Each branch of this grass roots movement would challenge the local Democratic party. A variety of strategies were to be used: protesting the convention delegate selection procedures, setting up teach-ins on the party during the spring antiwar protests, organizing people for the convention week protests, establishing training schools for "street leadership during the Chicago action," holding "People's Platform hearings," and, finally, preparing their own protest agenda for Chicago. The structure of this grass roots movement was extremely hazy, a fact recognized by Davis and Hayden: "Discussions and program development should be decentralized as much as possible."[28]

On the Chicago protest itself, Davis and Hayden, as compared to their first planning report, had adopted a much more cautious rhetoric. The Chicago protest, they wrote, "should be non-violent and legal . . . we must make an absolutely clear commitment to non-violent tactics, develop a simple and clear political message that large numbers of Americans can understand."[29] Hayden and Davis were not, however, merely looking for some sort of lowest-common-denominator demonstration. Like Dellinger on the Pentagon protest, they thought they could have it both ways: "The tendency to intensify militancy without organizing wide political support is self defeating. But so is the tendency to draw away from militancy into milder and more conventional forms of protest."[30] They wanted a broad coalition that could include the most moderate member of Business Executives against the War and the most radical member of SDS.

One thing Davis and Hayden decided they didn't want was disruption. And not so much because they opposed the idea of disruption per se—they didn't—as because they knew it wouldn't work in Chicago. They admitted it straightforwardly enough: "The campaign should not plan violence and disruption against the Democratic National Convention. . . . The right to rebellion is hardly exercised by assembling 300,000 people to charge into 30,000 paratroopers. . . . Any plan of deliberate disruption will drive people away . . . little would be served except perhaps the political hopes of Johnson, Nixon, and Wallace."[31] Rather than disruption, the goals of the protest, they stated, should be fourfold. First, the protest would put pressure on the Democrats to revise their war policies. Second, the protest would demonstrate both to the rest of America and to the rest of the world that the resolve of the peace movement was firm. Third, organizing and participating in the Chicago action would help "unite and radicalize" the deeply divided peace movement. And fourth, the grass roots organizing before the convention could strengthen local movement activities all around the country. All of these things were more important than a possibly suicidal disruption of the Democratic Party Convention—even if it was a very tempting objective.

As for the Chicago protest itself, Davis and Hayden were vague. Possibly, they suggested, there could be a mass "People's Platform Hearings," protests against poverty and racism, a national day of resistance and a big march to the convention hall. Maybe each day of the convention the protests could revolve around a specific subject like racism one day and the war next. Specific ideas, they said, should come from as many parts of the movement as possible.[32]

The conference ran all day and night Saturday and half the day Sunday. In small groups and all together, the delegates talked and talked about the possibilities. Though this conference was somewhat different from the usual large-scale Mobe conference in that it was a by-invitation-only affair and because some effort had been made to exclude the straight press, procedurally it was a typical Mobe production. As David Dellinger said, "We don't offer a parlimentary procedure in votes. If a thing isn't overwhelming, why we then talk about it some more . . . people drop in and out."[33] The Chicago "thing" was not "overwhelming." And the discussions went on and on.

On Sunday morning, with the assembly down to about one hundred and fifty participants, David Dellinger spoke at length, trying to convince what was clearly an ambivalent crowd to support the Chicago action and to create a broad, activist coalition. A demonstration in Chicago, he said, would not be so much a negative, oppositional act—just another protest—as it would be a representation and expression of the American people's desire for a new direction. The demonstrators would pose the desire for a positive, humanitarian, and peaceful society against the shoddy choices of the Democrats and the Republicans.

Hayden spoke, too. He said that he had been traveling around the country and he knew that the American people wanted to end the war and stop repression at home. What was needed, Hayden said, was large-scale, grass roots organizing. He supported the Resistance's plan to send a caravan of folks around the country acting out anti-war skits. People needed to hear about the real issues of war and imperialism, hunger and racism. Hayden pushed once again for the creation of local assemblies to discuss the issues and free political discourse from the boss-controlled parties. All these grass roots efforts, he concluded, could then be brought together at a massive demonstration in Chicago.[34]

After long discussion and debate, the conference was able to pass a few resolutions. The most important stated, "We call for an election year organizing campaign to be carried into cities and towns and counties across America. . . . We need to develop independent electoral alternatives based on radical programs centered on local organizing." It was also resolved not to support McCarthy or Robert Kennedy but instead to have a "stance . . . that makes us relevant to the political energy they have released." Finally, following up on a suggestion by Rennie Davis, the conference resolved to have another conference in June to discuss the Chicago action in more detail.[35]

The conference ended with nothing clearly decided and with nothing clearly planned. There were no plans for implementing "an election year organizing campaign." No one defined what was meant by a "stance . . . that makes us relevant" to the enthusiasm created among young people for RFK or McCarthy. Even the Chicago action remained formally unsupported. What was clear was that the antiwar movement was very much afraid of being co-opted by the Kennedy and McCarthy forces and that they were badly divided over the question of what was to be done next. All this was made much worse by what happened exactly one week after the conference ended.

"I have concluded that I should not permit the Presidency to become involved in the partisan decisions that are developing in this political year. Accordingly, I shall not seek, and I will not accept, the nomination of my party for another term as your President."[36] At 9:35 P.M., in Washington, D.C., on March 31, Lyndon Johnson withdrew from the 1968 Democratic presidential nominating process. Outside of a small circle of friends, almost no one had known or even suspected that Johnson would not seek renomination.

There were many reasons behind Johnson's decision. A fundamental reason was simply that the president suffered from ill health and was exhausted. As presidential aide and confidante Bill Moyers said, "The Presidency is a long distance race and Lyndon Johnson had been running it like a hundred yard sprint."[37] Worried about a number of life-threatening ailments, for several months the president had been talking to friends and family about not seeking reelection. He had considered making a withdrawal statement during his State of the Union address in January. But he had not. And though he says differently in his memoirs,[38] it seems likely that he would not have renounced renomination on March 31 either were it not for something more problematic than mental and physical exhaustion. And that was the fact that the president of the United States had lost control of the political process and he knew it.

He had already "lost" the New Hampshire primary and his most trusted aides were telling him that he was going to lose again, in the April 2 primary in Wisconsin. The rest of the primaries didn't look any better. Moreover, the president knew that the Gallup Poll that was to be released March 31 showed that only 35% of the American voters approved of his actions. Johnson probably could have still won the Democratic nomination using party rules and backroom deals to thwart the outcomes of the state primaries. But he knew that by following that uncertain course he would have split the party and raised the ire of the electorate.[39] President Johnson, who really did want to end the war in Vietnam honorably, chose to play the role of statesman. He would put politics aside and concentrate on winning a "just peace" in Vietnam.

Seemingly, Johnson's withdrawal left the race to Kennedy and McCarthy. But seasoned political observers knew better. Richard Nixon, perhaps the nation's most savvy political observer and by March the almost certain 1968 Republican nominee, told reporters, "We must assume that someone within the Democratic Party who represents the Johnson viewpoint will be the candidate."[40] Everyone knew he meant Vice-President Hubert Humphrey.

The peace movement greeted Johnson's withdrawal with euphoric feelings of victory. David Dellinger wrote that Johnson's decision was "added proof that his policies and those of his military and industrial advisors had collapsed in Vietnam and have been repudiated by the American people." But Dellinger, too, knew that Johnson's withdrawal was far from a decisive victory. Dellinger, and most every other militant antiwar activist, feared Johnson's withdrawal almost as much as they celebrated it. Without the sure renomination of Johnson as a target, the liberal reformism of Kennedy and McCarthy would, the militants knew, seem to many less committed members of the movement to be an attractive alternative. And so Dellinger stated the day of LBJ's withdrawal:

> The powerful forces that got us involved in Vietnam are still in basic control of our country. They have suffered a setback but until they are repudiated there is danger of further military adventures at home and abroad. . . . In view of the weakness of the potential candidates and the danger that the American people will relax their vigil, it may be all the more important that there be demonstrations across the nation on April 27th and at the Democratic Convention in August. We must continue to insist not just on an end to the war in Vietnam, but on a reversal of the American domestic and foreign policies of arrogance and paternalistic interference in the economic and political affairs of foreign countries and of blacks and poor people in the United States.[41]

Delilinger knew that Johnson's surprise withdrawal had put the 1968 antiwar offensive in serious jeopardy and he was worried.

He was right to be. Immediately after the withdrawal, enthusiasm for the Chicago action waned among both the leadership and the rank and file of the antiwar movement. Sid Lens, a Mobe leader, major Chicago activist, and longtime labor leader, said that after the withdrawal "I concluded . . . and so did others, that any demonstration in Chicago would be small and probably uneventful."[42] Lens planned a trip to North Africa and Eastern Europe. The peace candidates' sudden viability, Johnson's simultaneous withdrawal and declaration that peace talks would be initiated in Paris, all these events, as the ex-SDS vice-president Paul Booth said, "depoliticized the whole situation . . . for the mass."[43]

Less than a week after Johnson's withdrawal, on April 4, in Memphis, Tennessee, Martin Luther King, Jr., was assassinated. Urban blacks, in anger and in frustration, rioted in over one hundred American cities.

Chicago was one of the hardest hit cities. Over twenty blocks of the West Side ghetto burned down. Mayor Richard Daley, angered by his police commissioner's cautious response to the arson and looting, demanded that the police "shoot to kill any arsonist . . . and shoot to maim or cripple anyone looting."[44] In Chicago, nine blacks died in the rioting.[45]

While some Mobe supporters reacted to the death of King and the withdrawal of Johnson with lethargy and shock, Dellinger, Davis, and Hayden continued to promote the Chicago protest. Throughout April, Dellinger continued to make the same kind of statements: "It would be a mistake to think that the fight against the war can be won in the ballot box. It still has to be won on the streets."[46]

At the end of April, antiwar protests blanketed the country. Dozens of cities had marches and rallies on April 27. And while most were fairly small affairs, in New York well over one hundred thousand marched, and in San Francisco better than twenty thousand assembled. Over a thousand universities and high schools participated in a national student strike on April 26, with an estimated one million students staying out of school.[47] Both SDS and the National Mobilization steered clear of any national coordination or support of the protest activities. Both organizations, however, watched the Chicago spring peace march very carefully.

Organized by Clark Kissinger and the Chicago Peace Council, the Chicago march ran into some portentous trouble which began with the parade permits. Though Kissinger had applied for the permits weeks before the parade date, the city, week after week, refused to

rule one way or the other on the permit request. Otto Liljenstople of
the Chicago Peace Council was familiar with this routine. Since 1966,
the city had been going through the same stall tactic every time the
antiwar movement wanted to hold a march or a rally. The Parade
Board, made up of various city department superintendents, always
waited until the last possible moment before granting demonstration
permits, thereby assuring that more moderate and cautious marchers
would be scared off.[48] Kissinger, after being stonewalled by the city,
turned to the judiciary. And on April 26 he got a court order allowing
the march.[49]

Once the parade got going, the police—there were about five
hundred assigned to the demonstration, which was incomprehensi-
ble to the protesters—indicated their contempt by forcing the marchers to use the sidewalk instead of the street. They also kept the six
thousand to eight thousand marchers stopped at street corners for
two or three series of stoplights. But it was only when the marchers
reached the Civic Center and the rally began that the real trouble
erupted. The police attacked the demonstrators.

The formal reasons for the police attack are hazy. They seem to
revolve around the fact that a handful of demonstrators broke a
string surrounding a small section of the Civic Center plaza that was
under repair. But the police did not just attack the small group who
had broken the string. They attacked the entire, absolutely peaceful,
absolutely nonprovoking, non-stone-throwing, nontaunting crowd.
Dozens and dozens of people were clubbed, slugged, kicked, and
Maced by the Chicago police. After the string incident and after the
police had already moved in, the crowd was ordered to disperse.
But the police who surrounded the demonstrators allowed no exit
and attacked any demonstrators who broke into the streets in an
attempt to escape the melee. A few police took special pleasure in
throwing people, on this cool spring day, into the reflecting pool that
stood in the middle of the plaza. A few police chased long-haired
demonstrators several blocks in order to club them.

Despite all the clubbing and beating, the police arrested only
approximately fifty people. Those arrested faced a gauntlet of FBI
agents, army intelligence officers, and police subversive unit men,
all of whom were looking for "soldiers absent without leave, known
communists and communist sympathizers."[50]

Because the local newspapers and TV stations had expected a
peaceful march, almost none had sent any reporters. Only the Tribune, the city's most conservative news source, had sent a major
reporter. And while his story described the marchers as "noisy but
peaceful," the small front-page headline read, "Anti-war Protesters
Battle the Police: 15 Hurt 50 Arrests."[51]

Later, a blue-ribbon panel reported that

> the police badly handled their task, brutalizing demon-
> strators without provocation. . . . Yet to place primary
> blame on the police would, in our view, be inappro-
> priate. The April 27th stage had been prepared by the
> Mayor's designated officials . . . to communicate that
> "these people have no right to demonstrate or express
> their views."[52]

This view was exactly in accord with that of the organizers of the
demonstration. And while Clark Kissinger had insisted that the April
27 march was not a "trial horse" for the convention protests,[53] movement people around the country took the city's actions as a threat.
The Mobe organizers knew that this show of force, combined with
Daley's nationally broadcast "shoot to kill" order and his announce-
ments that the convention would be protected by tens of thousands
of police and soldiers, had scared off a great many of the Mobe's
moderate adherents, who would not participate in a demonstration
in which they might be hurt or even killed. On the other hand, there
were protesters who welcomed Daley's approach.

These more militant, more radical protesters welcomed the clarity
Daley's position seemed to offer. Otto Liljenstolpe later commented,
"My position was that I realized there was a risk of violence but I
wanted exposure to occur. I wanted a confrontation . . . so it would
be broadcast internationally . . . a visible exposure of what to me is
a developing police or militaristic state in this country."[54]

Chicago SDS, who had been completely indifferent to the April 27
march, also welcomed the police brutality that it had produced. On
May 4, a small group of SDSers protested the brutality by marching
around the Civic Center. A few of them carried water pistols filled
with ammonia for self-defense. But the police in attendance did
nothing and the march broke up without incident.[55]

Hayden and Davis knew that these militant responses to the police
brutality were a minority view and one that they did not want to
publicly foster. But as May came, they were not sure what they did
want the Chicago protest to be. And though they did keep working
on the demonstration, it was work without clear purpose.

Hayden, as was his way, had spent the first few months of the year
traveling around the country. While Davis worked out of Chicago
setting up and organizing the Mobe operation, Hayden had been
making speeches, doing some writing, and being where things were
happening. He had planned to come to Chicago in late April and
work with Davis. But just as he set out, the Columbia University

takeover began. And in a rare bit of humor, Hayden later said, "It would be terrible if the revolution actually started out and I was driving across the country."[56] Hayden hung around Columbia for the next few days, coming and going, moving from occupied building to occupied building. To some degree, he led the takeover and organization of the mathematics building.

Hayden, like almost all movement militants, was extremely pleased with the Columbia takeover and months-long student strike. He used a version of Che Guevera's line about two, three, many Vietnams to title a *Ramparts* article, "Two, Three, Many Columbias." In the piece, Hayden jubilantly declared:

> Columbia opened a new tactical stage in the resis-
> tance movement which began last fall, from the
> overnight occupation of buildings to permanent occupa-
> tion, from mill-ins to the creation of revolutionary com-
> mittees, symbolic civil disobedience to barricaded
> resistance. Not only are these tactics already being du-
> plicated on other campuses, but they are sure to be sur-
> passed by even more militant tactics. In the future, it is
> conceivable that students will threaten the destruction of
> buildings as a last deterrent to police attacks.[57]

Hayden was joking when he talked about being on the road and missing the revolution, but he and a number of others believed that the well-supported student takeover and strike at Columbia University signaled a major escalation in the struggle. And while Hayden very much understood that a student action at Columbia and a mass demonstration in Chicago were two very different kinds of protests, the spirit of militance, confrontation, and even violence that permeated the Columbia action became a part of the attitudes and expectations that Hayden and other militants brought to both the formal planning and informal discussions of Chicago '68.

Throughout most of May and early June, among important and substantial elements of the Mobe, interest in the Chicago protest waned. Mobe stalwarts like Donald Kalish and Sid Peck, both Mobe cochairs, were hopeful that an antiwar candidate would take the Democratic nomination. This hope caused them to fear the negative impact a militant antiwar demonstration might have on the chances of the peace candidates at the nominating convention.[58] Similarly, substantial numbers of the young people who helped to make up any successful national demonstration had turned their energies to the candidacies of McCarthy and Kennedy. They were convinced that the system itself, rather than street actions, could be used to

create an alternative to the war policies of Johnson and his min-
ions.[59]

In reaction to this peace candidate enthusiasm, substantial numbers of Old Left adherents rejected the Chicago protest. The Socialist
Workers party and its youth affiliate, Young Socialist Alliance, concluded that without Johnson as a target a demonstration in Chicago
could too easily "be seen as support to the doves within the Democratic Party, in particular as pro-McCarthy demonstrations." Fred
Halstead, the SWP presidential candidate, decided to tour South Vietnam during the planned protest. He and his party wanted no part in
a demonstration that did not absolutely and in the clearest terms
repudiate liberal, mainstream politics.[60] And while these Trotskyites
were small in number, they were extremely committed organizers
and their working abilities would be missed.

The SDS national office, while opposed to the ideology and practices of the Trotskyites, essentially agreed with their position on Chicago. They, too, saw the convention protest as being too close to
the McCarthyites, too open to the possibility of liberal co-option. At
the beginning of the year, the National Interim Committee had said
that final decisions on the Chicago action would be reached during
the spring and summer national SDS conventions. But at the spring
convention, June 10–14, in East Lansing, Michigan, the Chicago
protest was ignored. SDS was much more concerned with establishing their own program for the future. One of the more popular
proposals to come out of the convention was written by Tom Bell,
Bernardine Dohrn, and Steve Halliwell. In part, it stated: "[SDS must]
change the emphasis from building a radical movement to using
the radical movement in the work of making revolution." Dohrn,
who declared at the convention, "I declare myself a revolutionary
communist," was elected inter-organizational secretary. National SDS
was losing interest in coalitions. More and more influential members
were pressing for SDS to fully accept the status and responsibilities of
being at the vanguard of the forthcoming revolution.[61]

During this period of uncertainty, Davis and the small Mobe staff
kept busy. Part of their energies were diverted to organizing the
"Summer of Support," a program aimed at fostering antiwar senti-
ments among soldiers by establishing "coffee houses" around military bases. But Davis and his coworkers also kept at the Chicago
protest. Davis went around speaking to local antiwar groups, describing the protest as a nondistruptive mass protest, and asking the local
people to help in the planning and organizing. Specifically, the staff
started rounding up housing for the fifty to one hundred thousand
demonstrators they expected to arrive around August 26.[62]

Davis also made contact with the Medical Committee for Human Rights—a progressive organization of doctors, nurses, and other health professionals active in civil rights and antiwar work—and asked if they would provide medical aid during the Chicago protest. After the April 27 police attack and the mounting evidence of Daley's absolute intransigence about any sort of convention week protest, Davis wanted to make sure that the demonstrators could be guaranteed prompt medical attention. Davis also maintained contact with the National Lawyers' Guild and began setting up legal aid for the demonstrators.[63]

By late May, Hayden was also working out of the Chicago office. He, too, spoke to local groups and phoned around the country, trying to, and often succeeding in, getting people involved in the protest.

Shortly after midnight, June 5, in celebration of his narrow California primary victory, Robert Kennedy—"at once broker of power, magic leader, desired sexual object, protagonist of aspirations, liberator and hero"[64]—gave a short and magnanimous victory speech. A few minutes later he was shot twice, once glancingly in the shoulder and once mortally in the head. He died the next day.

For the next few days all the nation mourned. Even though Kennedy had been shot by a Palestinian-American angered by the senator's Middle East policies, conservatives and radicals vied with one another in suggesting how the Kennedy assassination demonstrated what was wrong with America. For the conservatives, Kennedy's assassination seemed perfect proof of the breakdown in law and order—a phrase they used as shorthand for demanding that blacks and other undesirable elements be more vigorously and harshly treated by the police and the court system. A few days after RFK's burial, California Governor Ronald Reagan, who was running for the Republican presidential nomination, used Kennedy's death to push the law-and-order issue harder than all the others. At an Indiana campaign stop, he sadly but angrily told his supporters that "in this week of tragedy, six policemen in Chicago had been killed in the line of duty." Something, he said, had to be done to stop the lawless in their murderous disregard for authority. Reagan's fact was a complete fabrication. In all of 1968 up till then only two Chicago policemen had been killed. But few seemed to care about the truth.[65] Powerful fears and angers simulated facts that made sense.

Tom Hayden, too, was affected by Kennedy's death. He went to the funeral at St. Patrick's Cathedral in New York and was for a brief moment part of the honor guard at the coffin. Hayden knew Kennedy and some of his aides. He felt the loss, the stupidity, and like most of his generation, the tragedy, even if he did not at all agree with the dead man's politics. Hayden, a man who usually worked coolly and, seemingly, dispassionately, wept—a fact well reported and manipulated in the mass media.[66] For most radicals, Kennedy's assassination was another clear sign that the American system was drowning in shapeless violence, alienation, and anomie.

Kennedy's assassination stirred up some parts of the antiwar movement. Many, like Donald Kalish and Sid Peck, who had believed that Kennedy or McCarthy could win the nomination, saw that it was not to be. And they decided that the Chicago demonstration was good and was necessary.[67]

But others, including a number of relatively moderate activists, believed more than ever that, "objectively," a Chicago action would be a demonstration for the remaining peace candidate, Eugene McCarthy.[68] And for these people McCarthy was just another phony liberal, too scared to do what was really necessary to end U.S. imperialism or to create justice and equality.

With less than two months to go before the August 26 convention, the Mobe had issued no official "call" for Chicago. The protest advocates could not get the divided, weary, and battered antiwar movement to focus its attention on Chicago. As Tom Hayden said, the "crazy series of developments that begin with Johnson's announcement" had acted as a "sedative" on the peace movement.[69] Some people were now waking up, others clearly were not.

On June 29, the self-proclaimed Chicago steering committee acted. Without meeting with the rest of the Mobe leadership or consulting with the representatives of the many organizations that made up the Mobe coalition, Dellinger, Hayden, and Greenblatt in New York and Rennie Davis in Chicago held press conferences and announced that the Chicago protest was on and that the full Mobe Administrative Committee would meet July 20 to set and define the demonstration.[70]

By July 1, most people realized that Hubert Humphrey was going to win the nomination. Despite the fact that he had not entered a single primary, he was sewing up almost all the delegates selected through caucuses or committed to party bosses and favorite-son candidates. He was also picking up many delegates who had been committed to Kennedy but were now free to support the regular party's candidate.

Al Lowenstein, the liberal Democrat and onetime president of the National Student Association who had almost singlehandedly begun the antiwar challenge within the Democratic party that had produced McCarthy's candidacy, decided not to go down peacefully. With other young, committed McCarthyites, Lowenstein founded the

Coalition for an Open Convention, dedicated to contesting the nomination in Chicago. They operated, however, without the support of McCarthy or his national campaign staff, who were "leery of the plan," worried that it would result in violence. The COC meant to bring one hundred thousand young McCarthy supporters to the convention to put pressure on the delegates and also, less optimistically, to provide the so-called McCarthy kids with some well-structured focus for their more than likely bitter disappointment.

COC officials met with Rennie Davis but only to avoid overlaps and to discuss the possibilities of sharing medical and legal services.[71]

In late June, Rennie Davis began attempting to reach Mayor Daley or his representatives in order to negotiate permits and other arrangements for the convention week protests. Davis called the Mayor's office day after day and left more and more urgent messages. He got no response. July 2, he assigned one of his assistants, a young law student, to keep calling until he got through. Davis told his assistant to concentrate on contacting Deputy Mayor David Stahl, whom previous antiwar organizers had found a reasonable, open, and understanding man. The assistant, Mark Simon, called everyday for the next two weeks. He, too, got no response.[72]

Davis tried an end-around play. He talked with an old friend in the Justice Department and asked him if there was any way the department (which Davis knew had a special unit for dealing with recalcitrant local officials—usually white ones causing problems for local blacks) could help him set up a meeting with city officials. His friend said he would give it a try.[73]

During some of this time, Tom Hayden was in Paris. He had been invited by the North Vietnamese to assist in the release of three American prisoners of war. After successfully carrying out his part in the release, he returned to the United States and gave an interview in which he blasted the Paris Peace Talks as nothing but a blatant attempt to "neutralize and defuse" the antiwar movement. Hayden declared that the National Liberation Front and the North Vietnamese would win the war by December 1968. He ended the interview with the customary, "See you in Chicago."[74]

In Chicago, Davis and the Mobe staff were moving ahead on several fronts. Using area colleges as a base, they had begun to organize a corps of marshals who would be assigned to the various protests as peacekeepers and march coordinators. Davis also spoke to local antiwar groups like the Chicago Peace Council, keeping them abreast of developments and maintaining their commitment to the August demonstrations. Davis had also organized a couple of local fundraisers for the Mobe. These events were hosted by a local rich person—self-described "parlor liberals"—who would gather together a few other well-to-do liberals, and then Davis or another name activist would give a talk and collect checks. These events didn't produce much money, but then the Mobe didn't need much either.[75]

July 17, Davis met with Roger Wilkins, director of the Justice Department Community Relation Service—which had been set up by Title 10 of the Civil Rights Act of 1964 to help local communities settle racial disputes. Wilkins made it very clear to Davis that he worked well inside the law and would have nothing to do with violent or disruptive activities. Davis made it equally clear to Wilkins that he was in full agreement with such a stance. He outlined for Wilkins the Mobe's plan: a peaceful march to the Amphitheater, a rally at Soldier Field, a series of workshops held by all the different groups that would be participating in the protest, and a number of smaller actions spread out over the convention week. Davis added that he expected very little black participation but that the Mobe was counting on "tens of thousands" of demonstrators. He ended by stating that the Mobe would have a single, unified command and that he hoped the city would too. Could Wilkins help the Mobe in their attempts to negotiate with the city?

Wilkins said he would have to see. He went back to Washington to confer with his superiors.[76]

A couple of days later, Davis took off too. He, Hayden, Dellinger, Bob Greenblatt, the rest of the Mobe Steering Committee, and a variety of other Mobe delegates—about seventy-five in all—met in Cleveland to discuss the Chicago protest.

Many at the meeting still fought against the Chicago demonstration. Lew Jones, of YSA, said Chicago would be co-opted by the McCarthy Kids. More moderate members worried that the demonstrations would harm McCarthy's chance for the nomination. David Dellinger, as always, argued for the demonstration, telling the delegates not to be afraid of their diversity but to embrace it.

Dellinger, Hayden, and Davis then got into some more of the details of the protest. They talked about setting up working spaces—movement centers—for a range of affinity groups—like-minded individuals bonded by organizational affiliation or personal belief. At these centers, the different groups would plan their own convention week activities. They also told the delegates that they had paid three thousand dollars for a special convention newspaper to be put out by *Rat* and edited by ex-SDSer Jeff Shero. Davis and Hayden then discussed the August 28 march on the Amphitheater which everyone agreed would be the focal point of the Chicago demonstration. Davis said it would be no problem and that they'd easily be able to surround and block all the entrances to the convention hall. Hayden emphasized that the blockage didn't have to be deliberate—the sheer number of protesters would ensure it. Some found this strategy abhorrent and said so. The issue was left unresolved. In general, however, it seemed that most of the delegates approved of the actions outlined by the Chicago project directors.[77]

Not far away, in Chesterton, Indiana, the National Interim Council of SDS also met and talked about Chicago. By the summer of 1968, SDS was easily the largest membership organization in the movement with upward of fifty thousand active members in approximately three hundred and fifty chapters. SDS was on every major campus in the country.[78] By this time, Mike Klonsky, Fred Gordon, and Bernardine Dohrn held the national offices of SDS. All of them considered themselves revolutionaries, dedicated to overthrowing the American system.

Klonsky started the discussion by stating that as many as half a million people might show up in Chicago and that that was too many people to ignore. So Klonsky proposed, "We should have a program of political education and influencing decisions that are made. We should try to organize and recruit people." Gordon and Dohrn jumped in with some specific ideas. Wayne Heimbach of Chicago SDS, who unlike almost all the others knew what was going on in Chicago, interjected the fact that McCarthy headquarters seemed to be telling the McCarthy volunteers not to come to Chicago—indicating that the crowd would probably not be anywhere near half a million. But the others who had been denigrating the Chicago protest for better than a half year were no longer interested in negatives. They wanted a piece of the action. As Eric Mann stated: "If we go into this, we should run it."

Still, the SDSers were being cautious. They were still worried about being co-opted by the McCarthy forces, either literally or "objectively"—which meant that a large convention demonstration, regardless of its intended purpose, might be seen by the delegates, the mass media, and the public as pro-McCarthy. Most people argued that they should only bring a few hundred of their best organizers to "educate the kids," to talk to them in the park and explain things to them so that they wouldn't ever "be fooled again" by liberal reformers.

Several others believed that since "Hayden and Davis are pushing for us to push people into confrontation . . . we must be prepared to handle a street situation. We must be responsible for the streets

because no one else will do it." For some of the SDSers, this meant
helping the kids escape from the cops—"tactics to break through
police lines." For others, it meant organizing the disruption of traffic,
instigating the infiltration of the hotels where the delegates were
staying, and planning citywide protest actions.

Several of the SDSers, including Jeff Jones, one of SDS's most militant
strategists, believed that the action in the streets would be rough,
much rougher than Hayden was predicting—which was not at all a
bad thing. Indeed, it would give SDS a chance to show the McCarthy
kids in Chicago who was and was not able to exercise leadership
in tough situations. The SDS, and not Hayden or the cops or anyone
else, could determine when and where confrontation took place.
Others doubted that SDS could so control the street action and argued
for a less "formal" role.

After hours of discussion, the National Interim Committee decided
not to issue a general call to Chicago. They would bring in several
hundred organizers who would basically work on "kids" who'd been
co-opted by McCarthy. Carl Oglesby, ex-SDS president, would write
an open letter to McCarthy supporters that would explain to them the
error of their ways. There would be no formal SDS guidelines or orders—
SDS just didn't work that way—but it was assumed that the corps of
organizers would hold a leadership role in any street actions.[79]

A few days later, in the SDS organ, *New Left Notes*, Klonsky broadcast the message. He blasted the Mobe, calling it the "We Are Right
Politics," and said that its followers were just a bunch of cop-out
liberals who think "that the society we live in is basically just." SDS,
he said, would not endorse the Chicago action because "any radical message which SDS would want to put forth concerning the War
and imperialism would merely be blurred by the massive confusion
surrounding the McCarthy campaign." He added, however, that
SDS would use the protest as an educational opportunity.[80]

This message was followed up August 11 with a letter sent to the
membership. In part, it read, " . . . we have to concentrate on
getting our best organizers from around the country to come here
and do what they can to get the McCarthy kids out of their bag and
into SDS chapters in the fall. . . . This will be an organizing job and
not a picnic—Chicago is pig city and they are uptight."[81] SDS was
sticking to its chosen path. They would not support protests that
merely mobilized the masses; they were interested in organizing. But
they would be in Chicago and with many of their most experienced
and dedicated people.

The Mobe's people most dedicated to the Chicago protest, after
the Cleveland meeting, intensified their organizing efforts. Hayden

went to New York and talked to the Fifth Avenue Vietnam Peace Parade Committee. He blasted Johnson's "peace" initiatives as trickery, an ugly attempt to "end the anti-war movement rather than ending the war itself." He warned that the United States was seriously considering the use of nuclear weapons and other genocidal tactics. The antiwar movement must stop the genocide, he said, and in Chicago, in order to make their voices heard, they must be ready to face police violence and mass arrests.[82]

In San Diego, David Dellinger gave much the same speech, telling a crowd of students to burn their draft cards, resist the draft, and do everything they could to stop the insane war. He ended, "I'll see you in Chicago."[83]

In New York, Eric Weinberger, the mild-mannered Mobe administrator, tried to light a fire under the divided national Mobe staff. He wanted them to print up and distribute the formal call to Chicago that had been approved at the July 20 meeting. But the Mobe staff, many of whom were uncertain about the demonstration and some of whom felt handcuffed by the declared policy that organization would be done locally, did nothing. Finally, in exasperation, Weinberger produced the flyers himself, but he succeeded in getting out only fifty thousand—for the April 27 March in New York, five hundred thousand flyers had been issued.[84]

Back in Chicago, Davis led the efforts to convince the city to give the Mobe permits and cooperation. By August 1, he still had not been able to meet with any important city officials. A few days earlier, though, he had talked with Roger Wilkins, Wesley Pomeroy, Clark Roberts, and Tom Foran of the Justice Department. They told Davis that they had met with Daley and discussed the permit situation. Unfortunately, they said, it seemed the Mayor was not interested in the subject. Davis entreated the Justice Department officials to tell Daley that the Mobe's plans were peaceful and nondisruptive. Foran, the local U.S. district attorney, said he'd pass the information along to Daley and see if he couldn't get him to enter into some kind of negotiations.[85]

The day after the meeting, Davis's assistant, Mark Simon, was finally allowed to speak on the telephone to Deputy Mayor Dave Stahl. Stahl told Simon that he was not pleased with Davis's remarks to the Justice Department and CBS that he wanted the Chicago police investigated before the convention. Stahl, Simon later reported, added something to the effect of, "one doesn't invite another over to dinner and then publicly criticize him." Simon responded by asking for a meeting to discuss matters. Stahl said to call back in a few days.[86]

Davis and his staff filed permit applications at City Hall the day before the legally prescribed thirty–day limit. They had wanted to discuss the applications with the city before filing them but they'd run out of time. They requested permits for two marches and rallies on August 28. They wanted a midday march from the Loop to the bandshell in nearby Grant Park and then permission to march to the Amphitheater, where they would hold a massive rally.

The Mobe also contacted the Park District and told them they would need parks for sleeping and assembling. They designated eleven parks, including the south end of Lincoln Park, Grant Park, and several smaller parks, most of which were just north and south of the Loop. The Park District said to submit a memo and they'd discuss it at their August 13th meeting. The Mobe submitted the memo but the Park District never even brought the matter up at their meeting.[87]

Mobe staffers Vernon Grizzard, Paul Potter, and other committee heads kept working. Potter contacted friendly churches and unions and began setting up spaces for movement centers. He also sent out a letter describing the centers as "a way of responding flexibly to events during the Convention," and as places for "long range political and programmatic discussions [which] may not draw the most people but [which] . . . may have the most telling effect."[88] Grizzard began devising schedules for marshals' meetings and training sessions—the first to begin August 9. The legal and medical committees met and prepared for trouble—figuring out procedures for mass arrest situations and traveling emergency medical crews. The Chicago Peace Council was setting up a bail fund. After the April 27 march, the post-King assassination shoot-to-kill order, Mayor Daley's huge military build-up, and the permit snafu, the Mobe knew they had to be prepared for harsh treatment. Some even wanted to warn prospective protesters that they should bring protective clothing like helmets, bulky sweaters, and bandanas for the tear gas, but it was decided that this might overly alarm would-be protesters.[89]

Over the next three weeks, Mobe officers held a series of increasingly frustrating meetings with city officials and with each other.[90] Stahl had finally agreed to an informal meeting with Davis on August 2. They met for breakfast at a Loop coffee shop. Stahl listened politely as Davis outlined the Mobe plans. He told Davis that he doubted the parks could be used as a campground. He also said that for security reasons a march on the Amphitheater was not a good idea; maybe the Mobe could march somewhere else. Davis said that the protesters had to be at the convention, that that was the whole idea of the demonstration and that if the city didn't grant the permit and even if the Mobe didn't lead the march, people would still try to get to the convention to make their protests heard. Better, he said, to have an organized march than to have two or three hundred thousand white demonstrators chaotically making their way through the Negro section of Chicago in order to converge on the Amphitheater. Stahl listened politely and said he would report back to Davis but that he should know that all decisions on the permits were up to the Park District, the Police Department, and the Department of Streets and Sanitation. Davis pointed out that he was a longtime resident of Chicago—maybe he and the Mobe administration committee could meet with Mayor Daley? Stahl said he would get back to Davis.[91]

Two days later, the Mobe Administrative Committee came in from around the country and met in a hotel in Highland Park, an upper-class suburb north of Chicago. Approximately fifty people came, including Sid Peck, Don Kalish, Bob Greenblatt, Mike Klonsky, and, of course, Davis, Hayden, Dellinger, and the rest of the Chicago staff. Davis presented the final Chicago plan: August 24, people's assembly at forty movement centers; August 25, workshops and picketing at the delegates' hotels—this action would indicate what the police and National Guard were up to; August 26, meetings in Lincoln Park, Grant Park, and Hyde Park; August 27, Yippie Festival, decentralized actions, rally at the Coliseum; August 28, marches and rallies in Grant Park and at the Amphitheater; August 29, decentralized actions "aimed at institutions representing militarism, exploitation, racism."

The committee then discussed the McCarthyite Coalition for an Open Convention rally scheduled for August 26 and decided not to formally endorse or participate in it. Dellinger warned that the antiwar movement must not compromise itself. Dellinger went on to say that they must go to the Amphitheater because that was where the mass media would be and that the "necessity of having the military surround masses of people at a Democratic Convention would lend political context to the action." They must march with or without a permit.

The various committees reported and Don Duncan, an ex-Green Beret who'd been with Army Intelligence, warned that the security forces might use CS gas—a new, more powerful tear gas—on the demonstrators. He suggested that the medical teams carry large quantities of water with a 5% solution of sodium bisulfate to alleviate the painful effects of the gas. Tom Hayden laughed as Duncan finished and told Davis he didn't think the medical people were ready to hear that kind of talk.[92]

The next day, the Administrative Committee held a well-attended press conference. After outlining the Mobe protest, Dellinger reiterated the Mobe desire for a nondisruptive demonstration. He predicted that

a hundred thousand Americans would march on the Amphitheater:
"The anti-war movement is going back in the streets and will stay
there no matter who the candidate is until the U.S. troops are withdrawn from Vietnam." Sid Peck also asked that the police withdraw
from the march route and the rally in order to avoid the kind of police
violence that erupted at the April 27 protest. The Chicago papers
buried the story.[93]

That same day, Davis again met with the Justice Department officials and asked them to set up an August 12 meeting between the
city and the Mobe leaders. Richard Salem, of the Community Relations Unit, told Davis that they had just talked to the Mayor who had
said that communication between the groups was just fine as it was.
The Mayor had also said that there would be no permits for sleeping
in the parks. Davis replied that that was the first straight, negative
reply they'd gotten. The Justice Department officials said that they
would try to set up a meeting.[94]

Also that day, Davis's assistant, Mark Simon, sent a letter to Superintendent of Police Conlisk asking him to let the Mobe's own marshals
"act as the only peace keeping group at the park and beach sites"
as well as during the August 28 march. He also requested that Conlisk
"disarm the peace officers who will be encircling the International
Amphitheater. . . . The well trained marshals will work with the
disarmed officers to prevent . . . assaults."[95] Davis and Simon figured
it didn't hurt to ask.

That night, privately, several of the Mobe leaders met in Hyde
Park. Hayden told them that he didn't think they'd get a single
permit. The others disagreed, citing the Pentagon and other protests,
saying that the permits always came through at the last minute.
Hayden said, not this time. He was called cynical by the others and
they all talked about parade routes and general strategy. As a
compromise gesture, they decided to simplify their permit application; they'd only make one march on the twenty-eighth, from Grant
Park, near the Loop, to the Amphitheater.[96]

Over the next few days, the Chicago staff sent out letters and made
phone calls trying to set up the major August 12 meeting. They also
met with various members of the Police Department and tried to
explain their situation and to seek cooperation. The police officials
they met with were noncommittal but didn't seem hostile.[97]

Marshal training began in earnest August 13 and continued right
up to the convention. Vernon Grizzard was officially in charge, but
the actual training sessions were run by a variety of veteran marshals, including Ben Radford of the American Friends Service Committee, Dave Baker, a Detroit activist, Pat Toddy and Craig

Shimbakuro of Los Angeles, and, to a lesser degree, John Froines, a young Oregon University professor. Lee Weiner, a graduate student at Northwestern University, who knew his way around Chicago, also helped to keep things organized. The Mobe wanted to train two hundred marshals before the convention. They were getting about thirty to sixty people at most of the training sessions.[98]

Each marshal was given a five-page set of instructions outlining procedures. They were told that their central purpose was to help organize the marches by providing directions and overseeing spacing and rhythm. They were also to guide demonstrators to safety in confrontations and help to stop panic from spreading. Through the use of skirmish lines and other defensive formations they'd also protect demonstrators from hecklers and other violent situations. But they were instructed, "We are not police. It is not our duty to prevent a brother from exercising his free will (as in the case of civil disobedience). Nor are we a para-military group designed to engage in physical combat with law enforcement personnel."

The marshals were told in their instruction booklet that the "Chicago Police will probably operate from a strategy of containment and mass arrest rather than indiscriminate brutality." As a result, the marshals should use their self-defense training against the police-skirmish lines and the snake dance formation only as a last resort. But the marshals were also taught how to minimize the damage of a club-swinging cop—the best defense was to fall down and cover up. The marshals would be given walkie-talkies and should wear work shirts, Levi's, and work boots—cups, helmets, goggles, and Ace bandages were listed as optional equipment.

The actual training sessions were informal, humorous, friendly get-togethers. Snake dance training—a kind of marching accompanied by rhythmic chanting used most effectively by students in Japan to break through police lines—was a comical routine accompanied by much tripping over one anothers' feet; it looked so bad that Davis talked a CBS camera crew out of filming it. The marshals were, however, given fairly serious instructions on how to treat bleeding, leg injuries, and gas victims. The marshals were also told, usually by Davis, to scout out parade routes to the Amphitheater and make maps of Loop locations where demonstrations and picketing might be held.[99]

Everybody was worried about the parade route to the Amphitheater. Davis and Hayden feared that black people might get angry at a large crowd of white people, accompanied by a sizable force of hostile police, marching through their neighborhood. They equally feared the reactions of the working-class white people who lived in the neighborhoods immediately surrounding the Amphitheater. Much time and effort went into finding the safest possible parade route and to figuring out how to best deploy marshals along that route to keep hostile forces away from the white, middle-class marchers.

Hayden also made an effort to let the marshals know that there might well be no parade permits, which could result in a very heavy mass arrest situation. It would be the marshals' responsibility to keep people out of that situation. If the police started a confrontation, the marshals should use mobile tactics to disperse the march and organize multiple, moving protests.[100]

On August 12, in Los Angeles, Senator McCarthy formally announced what his staff people had been saying for weeks. Don't come to Chicago, he said. "The pressure of large numbers of visitors amidst the summer tensions of Chicago may well add to the possibility of unintended violence or disorder. This would be a tragedy, a personal tragedy for anyone hurt or arrested and a tragedy for those of us who wish to give the political process a fair and peaceful test."[101]

The McCarthyite Coalition for an Open Convention was shaken by McCarthy's statement but decided to continue their efforts to get a permit for a large rally in Soldier Field on August 25. On August 14, the ACLU filed a suit for the COC in U.S. District Court. The suit stated that the Park District, owners of Soldier Field, by refusing to rule favorably (in fact, to rule at all) on the COC permit request were denying the group their constitutional right of free speech. Judge Lynch, Mayor Daley's ex-law partner, was the presiding judge. The COC lost their suit and Al Lowenstein, chairman of the COC, called off all planned COC activities in Chicago. He said he viewed the convention with a sense of dread. Mayor Daley, he concluded, was inviting violence.[102]

After the McCarthy statement and the COC decisions, the Mobe knew that their chances for drawing upward of one hundred thousand people were extremely slim. Even a few days before McCarthy's announcement, at a Mobe sign-up table at the Hiroshima Memorial March in New York, it had become plain that Daley had scared away a number of moderate protesters; of the hundreds of charter bus tickets available for Chicago, only a few were sold.[103]

To lure moderates to Chicago, the Mobe leaders knew they had to have the permits which would give the protest at least the possibility of being peaceful. They kept after whatever city officials they could find. Davis kept talking to Deputy Mayor Stahl who kept saying he'd do what he could.

On August 12, the Mobe Administrative Committee made their way to Chicago for what they thought was a scheduled meeting with top city officials. At City Hall they were shocked to find only Stahl, the corporation counsel David Elrod, and flack catcher Al Baugher. Davis, angry and embarrassed, asked where everybody was. Stahl mumbled something about everyone being busy and that maybe they could meet tomorrow. Elrod, a second-generation City Hall insider working with the Police Department on convention security, started asking over and over, What was the Mobe going to do if they didn't get any permits? Elrod was also willing to discuss alternatives to a march on the Amphitheater. But the Mobe was not interested in marching anywhere but to the Amphitheater; that was, after all, the central idea of the protest. Elrod also stated that he didn't like the Mobe's planned usage of marshals. Why were they needed? he wanted to know. Would the Mobe advocate breaking the law? David Dellinger, fed up, said that they would not obey any law that violated their civil rights. Davis tried to give the Mobe schedule. The meeting broke up after a few minutes—a total failure.[104]

By this time, everyone directly involved in organizing the protest knew what was happening. August 10, Hayden and Davis sent a fund-raising letter out stating, "Chicago will be difficult—strategically, logistically, and politically." And instead of talking about hundreds of thousands of demonstrators, they now hoped for "thousands."[105] Hayden and Davis had opened up communications with McCarthy youth leaders and Abbie Hoffman of the Yippies in order to coordinate and maybe make more effective those demonstrations that could still be organized.[106] The American Friends Service Committee, which was strictly pacifistic, distributed a memo to members decrying "strategies of disruption and provocation which have . . . become dominant," they said, in the rhetoric and actions of both the Chicago police and certain activist groups.[107] Conflict, confrontation, and violence were in the air.

At mid-August marshals' meetings, Davis and Hayden talked about defensive tactics and how to respond to the city's provocative stance of total noncooperation. They said that if, or more likely when, the police start to arrest campers in Lincoln Park, the marshals should take charge. They should help the protesters avoid arrest by forming small groups, breaking out of the park, and then moving into the Loop. There the protesters could fight back against the city by tying up traffic, running through the streets and stores, and generally wreaking havoc. Davis also declared at one meeting, according to one marshal, that if the city refused to grant any permits it was as good as "a declaration of war." Davis warned that no matter what the legal situation a confrontation with the police seemed almost certain. The marshals were going to be faced with a heavy set of tasks; they were going to have to take charge of whatever situations came down. There weren't going to be any orders from above; it was going to have to be up to everybody to make the demonstrations work.[108]

As a last-ditch effort, the Mobe, like everyone else, brought suit against the city. Everybody else—the Justice Department, the Democratic National Committee, as many branches of the city government as could be reached—had failed to come through. It was the courts or nothing. Judge Lynch presided. Raymond Simons, the city corporation counsel, said the Mobe was "unreasonable" and that the city would be glad to discuss a variety of protest alternatives. In the judge's chambers, the city said it would allow the Mobe to rally in Grant Park on August 28 and then repeated its old offer of an alternative march in and around the Loop. The Mobe accepted the Grant Park offer but insisted on a march at least within eyesight of the Amphitheater. August 23, Lynch denied the Mobe request for an injunction allowing them to march to the Amphitheater.[109]

Jay Miller, executive director of Illinois ACLU, had already told reporters that by denying all permits Chicago had insured that "the most radical elements among the dissenters will gain ascendancy."[110]

Around the country, moderate and radical organizations tried to mobilize their people for Chicago. After all the confusion and the rush of events, antiwar organizers tried to remind their people of what was at stake. Activists reminded the less committed that despite Johnson's bombing halt the brutal war lurched on; the War Party more than ever needed to hear the voice of the People. The New York Fifth Avenue Parade Committee printed thousands of last-minute leaflets calling Chicago "a vital place for the anti-war movement to be—Join Us!" They sold round-trip bus tickets for thirty-four dollars. The Committee of Returned Volunteers (ex-Peace Corp volunteers) promoted Chicago in their August 15 mailer and stated that three hundred and thirty members were going or considering going to Chicago. The moderate Women for Peace had chartered several buses leaving from around the country. Coalitions in Boston, Detroit, and Ann Arbor prepared for the protest, as did Vets for Peace, Clergy and Laymen Concerned about Vietnam, People against Racism, Women Strike for Peace, Resistance, the Radical Organizing Committee, and many others. The Mobe organizers were still hoping for at least twenty thousand people.[111]

The Mobe organizers were also very much aware of the possibilities of violence. In Lincoln Park, the marshals practiced forming skirmish lines that could be used to keep police away from demonstrators. Lee Weiner, one of the head marshals, told J. Anthony Lukas of the *New York Times:*

> Obviously things are going to be getting rough here. We've got to be prepared. . . . We're still dedicated to peaceful methods but I can tell you there are some doubts in the movement these days about the old-time nonviolent stance—you know, rolling yourself up in a little ball . . . and getting clubbed. Some of the guys who've done that had been very badly hurt. . . . We're planning some more active and mobile forms of self-defense.[112]

· Stuart Glass, however, another Mobe trainer, told the marshals, "We're not teaching you how to fight. . . . We're not prepared to fight Daley's cops, the National Guard and the Army. . . . What we can teach you is how to protect yourself and other demonstrators in the case of attack by the cops or by a hostile neighborhood group."[113] The main method taught was how to look imposing by linking arms, clenching fists, and standing with legs shoulder width apart. Marshals also practiced throwing their bodies across the arms of "policemen" dragging off "arrested demonstrators" and thus freeing the "arrestees." But like the snake dance, this tactic was practiced more for fun and morale than for actual use.[114]

The Mobe slogan was, "Confront the Warmakers."[115] The final pre-Chicago issue of the *Mobilizer* showed a pig wearing a police helmet, waving a club, and dancing on a map of Chicago. The image was clear; Chicago was to be the pigs against the people—the barbaric war machine against the unarmed forces of peace. Still, a last-minute Mobe editorial was mailed out stating: "Mobilization in Chicago seeks not to disrupt . . . but to demonstrate and use direct action on behalf of the issues."[116] David Dellinger and other Mobe leaders spent much of the last few days running around City Hall and on the phone trying to get city officials to change their minds and issue permits.

Dellinger still hoped that the demonstrators could march on the convention without creating a violent confrontation. At a press conference August 22, he stated, "When those thousand persons come here, they will constitute a permit."[117] Most of the older leaders still hoped that a massive assemblage of demonstrators in front of so many representatives of the mass media would force the city into allowing the demonstrators to sleep in the parks and make their peaceful march.

Just before the convention and the protests were to begin, in the special convention issue of *Rat*, paid for by the Mobe, Tom Hayden, the coproject director, set the scene: "We are coming to Chicago to vomit on the 'politics of joy' [espoused by Hubert Humphrey], to expose the secret decisions, upset the night club orgies, and face the Democratic Party with its illegitimacy and criminality." The protests, he said, were not aimed at reforming or changing the Democratic party—the party of genocide and racism—they were aimed at destroying it: "The government of the United States is an outlaw institution under the control of war criminals."

To those who feared liberal co-option, Hayden said, yes, McCarthy is just another trick and a dangerous one. But he warned militants not to scorn the protest out of a simple fear of co-option: "Too great a fear of co-option can lead radicals to a shrill purism or to a fear of any mass action." Militants should come as a vanguard and carry red or black or NLF flags and interject their "radical presence into a complex political drama." This demonstration, Hayden argued, could include all factions and incorporate all tactics. In the multiple protests and actions leadership could be, indeed had to be, carried out by the range of represented organizations and positions—things would be moving too fast and too wildly for orders from above to be useful or appropriate. Actions must be formed from below to meet the changing nature of the week's protest.

Daley and the security forces were trying to scare the demonstrators away. Their schemes, Hayden said, "reveal the mentality of the bully." And he warned that there was a "sadistic and provocative element" within the police force. Demonstrators, he made clear, must indeed by ready to face jail and "suffering." Chicago would be difficult, Hayden warned, but "frequently we need a dramatic national experience as a common point of reference, as a way to make a leap of consciousness."[118] Caught between Daley and McCarthy, the Mobe was ready to make their stand.

5 The Mayor and the Meaning of Clout

The Democratic Presidential Nominating Convention hadn't been held in Chicago since 1956. Mayor Richard J. Daley had only been in office for one year. Then, he was just another local pol to be placated, even if his fellow Illinoisian and one-time boss Adlai Stevenson was the nominee. Eleven years later, among Democratic power brokers, Daley was thought by most in the know to be without peer.

In national terms, the Kennedy election of 1960 had done that for him. He'd been the man who'd turned out just enough Chicago voters to give Illinois to Kennedy—and Illinois had been the difference between victory and defeat. With a mixture of pride and love in his heart, Daley had put the first Catholic into the White House. Some said he'd stolen the election. Be that as it may, he'd turned out the votes. He had made the difference. That was his national clout—as Mayor and as head of the Cook County Democratic party, a party more tightly controlled by its leader and better organized, from the ward level down to the city's more than three thousand precincts, than any other local party in the country. It seemed to be a fact that he could or would not turn out the vote in Chicago, producing either victory or defeat in Illinois for the Democratic presidential nominee. And Illinois, with its twenty-seven electoral votes and its long history of being a swing state, was a critical commodity in any tight presidential race. Everybody knew that 1968 was going to be close.

So Richard J. Daley knew he had considerable clout going into the October 8, 1967, meeting in Washington, D.C., to decide who got the convention. Daley wanted that convention. He wanted it for the status, as his rightful due for the party organization he'd controlled for more than a decade. And of course, he wanted it for the city—for the money, thirty to fifty million dollars, and the jobs it would bring. It would show the world, as the Mayor liked to say, "that Chicago is the number one convention city." Keeping it that way was part of the Mayor's job, a part that the State Street and La Salle Street interests couldn't get enough of.

Since the middle of 1966, the Chicago Citizens' Committee—composed of various politicos and big money men—had been flying in and out of Washington, D.C., lobbying the National Democratic Site Selection Committee and bringing its members to Chicago for tours of the city. The red carpet had been rolled out and committee members got a taste of the best Chicago had to give. To sweeten their offer, the committee had also raised $650,000 in cash from hotel keepers and other interested parties to use for bidding purposes. The Mayor had also authorized a special 2½% convention hotel tax which would contribute another quarter of a million dollars to the total bid package.

The Citizens' Committee had also worked on the Republicans—back in 1952 Chicago had hosted both party conventions. By the fall of 1967 they'd already lost that one to the sun and surf of Miami. But it was the Democratic Convention that Daley really wanted.

The trouble was that proud Texan Lyndon Baines Johnson seemed to be favoring Houston. And since it was his party, in the end it was pretty much up to the president to decide where the convention would be held. Of course, the president was willing to listen to other reasonable suggestions. One of those was coming from the television networks.

The networks wanted the Democrats in Miami, same as the Republicans. By leaving their set-ups and equipment in Miami, the networks would save over a million dollars. And while placating the networks did not translate directly into votes, other things being about even, it was a serious factor to consider. Also, the Miami committee was claiming that they had the safest possible site—by which they meant that their Negroes were less trouble than Chicago's. That was another factor to consider but not critical either since both Houston and Chicago had come out of the seething 1967 summer of black ghetto riots without major incident. Still, the week before the host city was to be chosen, rumor had it that Miami, in deference to the networks, was favored by the Site Committee.

October 7, the night before the Site Committee was to award the convention, President Johnson held a thousand-dollar-a-plate fundraiser in Washington, D.C., for his reelection campaign. Over twenty-five hundred guests attended the affair, including Mayor Daley. Sometime that night, Daley, exercising some of his clout, had a private meeting with Johnson and Daley gave a hard pitch for Chicago. Alluding to the Democrats' disappointing showing in the Midwest in the 1966 congressional races, he told the president that without the convention in Chicago the president might lose Illinois. But if the convention were in the city, Daley said, the president could get enough good press to turn things around. Daley also argued that it'd be a waste to hold the convention in Houston because the president already had Texas in the win column.

By this time, Johnson had pretty much turned away from Houston, perhaps in part because he had already accepted Daley's position on Texas but more certainly because the Texas Democratic party was feuding. And that feud seemed almost to promise trouble that the president wanted no part of. The president's war policies had already produced more than enough party division in the country. He didn't need to confront any more in his own backyard—and have the mass media broadcast that confrontation—during his renomination celebration.

The next day, Mayor Daley already back home, the Site Committee announced that they had unanimously selected Chicago for the 1968 Democratic Presidential Nominating Convention. Committee head David Wilentz, the New Jersey Democratic national committeeman, gave the official reason for selecting Chicago: ". . . because it is centrally located geographically which will reduce transportation costs and because it has been the site of national conventions of both Parties in the past and is therefore attuned to holding them." Chicago did indeed know how to host political conventions; twenty-three out of the last fifty-six had been held there. But the *Chicago Tribune* and other newspapers told the rest of the story, too. Somebody had leaked the conversation between Daley and Johnson the previous night.

At City Hall, Mayor Daley held a press conference. Graciously, he stated in his low, clipped tones, "It is a great honor for our city and gives the people of Chicago another opportunity to show why it is the finest and friendliest convention city in the nation." Daley also declared his total commitment to the president, stating, "He's been a great President. All you have to do is look at the record." And the Mayor recounted Johnson's great domestic successes. The Mayor supported Johnson up and down. He was a Democratic president and that was all there was to it and if there was anything you didn't like about the president, the Mayor didn't want to hear about it.

At the press conference, with the Mayor in a very good mood, some reporter asked about potential demonstrations at the convention. Patiently, Daley tried to explain how things were in Chicago: "We have a great city. All our people are playing a positive part. In 1967, we had a positive program, we'll have one in 1968. We had more people working with us on our programs than any other city in the country." The blacks, Daley was saying, were happy in Chicago, they were taken care of, there weren't going to be any demonstrations to worry about. There'd been no riots in 1967, the Mayor was saying. Not like Detroit or Newark or any of those other cities. Chicago had a program. In 1967, when things looked bad and the blacks on the south side and on the west side were so angry, the Mayor's program—putting dozens of swimming pools and sprinklers in the ghettoes—had worked. In Chicago the people were "positive." Nobody was left out in Chicago.

One man, however, who was, politically speaking, a Chicago outsider, put another twist on the selection of Chicago for the convention. Timothy Sheehan, the savvy but almost powerless Cook County Republican chairman, saw the selection as an anti–Robert Kennedy pro-Johnson move—not that Kennedy had at that time given any indication that he would challenge Johnson, but it didn't take a genius to predict that he just might. He believed that Johnson picked Chicago because the Mayor, better than anybody else, could control the convention setting. Daley and his people, Sheehan said, "[will] make sure that no strange outsiders, including Kennedy forces, pack the gallery. They'll pack them themselves."[1] Sheehan knew what he was talking about. He'd been watching the Mayor for a long time.

Richard J. Daley controlled Chicago as no other city in the 1960s was controlled. The critics, and in Chicago there weren't many, called it machine politics. The Mayor insisted that he simply had a well-run organization.

Daley had been chairman of the Cook County Democratic party since 1953. He'd been Mayor since 1955. Through local control of the nominating process and through the old-time electoral efficiency of the precinct-by-precinct political organization, which in turn was perpetuated by an extensive patronage system, Daley and his coterie controlled all but a handful of the city's aldermen, judges, state representatives, and other elected officials. Since he had no real opposition in the city council, his control over appointed officials was absolute. And all of them, elected and appointed, payed off regularly. In Chicago, Mayor Daley was the Democratic party, and in Chicago almost nobody got anywhere in public life—and in Chicago public life had a very long reach—without the Democratic party.

Nationally, Chicago was known as "the city that works." The national print media and a host of writers and intellectuals acclaimed Daley party kingmaker and the beneficent boss of an efficient political machine. Under Daley, Chicago had avoided the municipal employee and trade union strikes that had paralyzed so many other cities, especially New York. Under Daley, the city had an excellent financial record, again, so unlike New York. And as of October 1967, it was true that in Chicago the blacks had not rioted (at least, not seriously), unlike New York, Los Angeles, Detroit, Newark, and so many other cities. David Kennedy, Chicago bank chairman and later secretary of treasury under Nixon, spoke for many when he said in 1968, "I don't think there is a mayor anywhere who is doing more for his city in an intelligent, forthright, objective way than Mayor Daley."[2] State Street businessmen, La Salle Street financiers, a coterie of University of Chicago professors, and most every Bridgeport bungalow owner believed that the city worked because of Mayor Daley's efficient Democratic organization. Nationally, as well as locally, Mayor Daley was giving machine politics a good name.[3]

As most Chicagoans knew, the organization predated the Mayor. In fact, Richard Daley had been a part of the Democratic organization since before he was old enough to vote. He'd started as a precinct captain, got a city job, and slowly ascended the party hierarchy. The only worlds Mayor Daley knew firsthand were the Irish Catholic working-class neighborhood life he never really left—born at 3602 South Lowe, fifty-six years later the Mayor lived at 3536 South Lowe—and the grand bazaar of Chicago city politics—a clearinghouse for every kind of corruption, deal making, power brokering, clout accumulating, hard-nosed fragile governance—which was supposed to keep a line on the city's three and a half million people, seven hundred thousand of whom were poor.[4]

Mike Royko in *Boss Richard J. Daley of Chicago*, Bill Gleason in *Daley of Chicago*, Len O'Conner in *Clout*, and Milton Rakove in his books on Chicago politics go a long way toward evoking both of those worlds and the vision of politics they offered, and I'm not about to try here to present either in all its complexity. But a few words, in the main borrowed from these works, will help to explain much of what went on in Chicago in 1968.[5]

Richard Daley, like the two mayors that preceded him, was born in Bridgeport, a working-class, south side Irish neighborhood of bungalows and small apartment buildings. Most of the people of Bridgeport worked in the nearby stockyards (the effluvium of which scented the air), neighborhood factories or industries, the trades, or for the city. These were people strong for the unions and strong for the Church. And like the Irish in all of America's big cities, they were from the start a powerful force in city government.[6]

But Richard Daley's family was not a political one. Second generation Americans, his father was a hardworking sheet metal worker, and his mother, thirty years old when Daley was born, did volunteer work in the parish church and took care of her family. Daley was a rarity in Irish Catholic Bridgeport; he was an only child.

He went to a Catholic grammar school and then to the De LaSalle Institute, a three-year commercial school run by the Christian Brothers. He learned office skills like bookkeeping. It was a ticket out of the working class.

After graduating, Daley took a job at the stockyards—mainly desk work—and immediately began to save his money. At twenty, he had enough to enroll at De Paul University night school. It took him eleven years of going to work all day and studying at night to get his law degree. But the Mayor did it; he pulled himself up by his own bootstraps.

By the time the law degree came through, Daley was long gone from the stockyards. Like a lot of other young men in Bridgeport, he tied his fortune to the Democratic party, starting as a precinct captain in the local ward organization. Daley made it pay off because he had what it took. He was smart, he worked hard, he was ambitious, and he knew how to look the other way. For several years young Daley had been personal secretary to Joe McDonough, the charismatic alderman of the Eleventh Ward. Then he'd been appointed City Council clerk, a patronage job supplied by McDonough.

Through a good part of the 1920s and 1930s, Daley was also president of Bridgeport's most important social and athletic club, the Hamburg. The club members were equal part young men on the make and rowdies looking for a good time—with the two parts often found in the same young Irishman. The Hamburgs were intensely loyal to one another and, working together, were a potent political force in the neighborhood, helping to elect aldermen, state representatives, and other local officials. They'd help to elect their president, Richard J. Daley, too. In all the years that followed, Daley never forgot his Hamburg friends.

In 1931, McDonough was elected county treasurer. Daley followed his boss and became his administrative assistant. Since Big Joe was not keen on monkeying with numbers all day, Richard Daley ran the business side of the county treasury. And he ran it well. While he waited to move up the party ladder, Dick Daley studied municipal finances day in and day out.

Besides being a harder worker and smarter than most of his fellow party members, Daley was also more honest than most of them. During most of the twenties and thirties, Chicago was a wide-open town. Kickbacks, payoffs, "honest" graft, and straight graft were the name of the game in every branch of city government. Gangsters and their front men helped run the city while they lined politicians' pockets. Through it all, Daley stayed clean. Of course, he also obeyed the unwritten rule—he stayed quiet, too.

In 1936, Daley won his first election—as a Republican write-in candidate. He'd been a last minute stand-in for a candidate for the state legislature who'd died days before the election. Through a political deal, the candidate had been running unopposed. With his death, all deals were off. But since the ballots had already been printed up showing no Democratic candidate Daley had to run on the Republican side as a write-in candidate. With the organization behind him he won easily. Once in Springfield, Daley was allowed to cross the aisle and join the Democrats. Soon, he moved up to the state senate. He was quiet and uncontroversial in his years downstate, following the party line. Inasmuch as he presented a political perspective, he was a solid New Dealer who supported legislation favorable to the workingman. He kept working hard, specializing in revenue matters.

Back home, while a state legislator, Daley was appointed Cook County comptroller, a job usually treated as a sinecure by its holder. But Daley took it seriously and learned how every cent of the county's budget was spent. By studying the numbers and seeing who got what contracts and who had whom on the payroll, Daley furthered his education in municipal realities. He learned, as he liked to say, that "good government is good politics."

By this time, Daley was a married man. He had waited until he was almost thirty-five to get married but not out of any kind of "sow your wild oats" attitude. The Mayor was a good Catholic who went to Mass almost everyday of his life. He and Eleanor (known to everyone as Sis) waited until he felt himself financially and politically secure enough for the responsibilities of raising a family. From the beginning to the end, Daley was a loyal husband and dedicated family man and he never could really put up with anybody who wasn't the same way.

For the Mayor, the years in Springfield were just stepping stones to higher political office back in Chicago. So in 1946, when he'd gotten enough clout with the party leaders, he got himself slated for Cook County sheriff, a plum job with lots of patronage. But Daley lost the election, victim to a post–World War II anti–Democratic party surge that was heightened in Chicago by a series of local scandals. It was a bitter setback to be sure—it would be the only election he ever lost—but Daley kept at it. He managed to maneuver himself into the Eleventh Ward committeemanship and so became a key member of the Cook County Democratic Central Committee. It was a good time to be entering the committee because after the postwar electoral defeats it was reforming its ranks. Daley managed to keep on the good side of most of the old-timers—he had after all come up through the ranks as a protégé of Big Joe McDonough—while at the same time he built a reputation among the party reformers and press as a fellow progressive—after all he appeared to be uncorruptible and he knew municipal revenue issues as well, if not better, than anyone around.

In 1948, Daley continued his climb by combining his strong ties to the party organization and his legislative experience with his proven ability to untangle complex revenue issues. He became state director of revenue under the reform administration of Governor Adlai Stevenson. For the first time, Daley became a well-known public figure. Scandal-free and with a first-rate record as revenue director, over the next few years Daley picked his way through the dirt and power scrambles of city politics. He kept coming on stronger and stronger. In July 1953, now county clerk and ward committeeman, Daley got himself elected chairman of the Cook County Democratic Central Committee. Two years later, he was the Mayor.[7]

He was the Mayor of the most ethnic city in the country and of the country's most racially segregated city. But through a political organization that was based on local loyalties built by precinct captains who held patronage jobs and through small favors efficiently carried out (and there was vote stealing and other political chicanery but it really only played a minor part), Daley kept the city united behind the Democrats. Year after year, the poor black communities gave Daley and his ticket the biggest votes. Little favors and promises of a few jobs mean the most to those who have the least.[8]

By 1968, thirteen years after taking office, the Mayor's hold on Chicago was rock solid. True, in the mid-sixties, with the civil rights movement, a few blacks had challenged Daley's people. And in the 1967 aldermanic races, two black independents had eked out victories over the organization. Still, that same year, in the mayoral, some black precincts had given Daley over 95% of their votes. So while it was obvious to everybody that the city's blacks had their complaints and had started to do more than grumble about them, they seemed to be under control. They would bear watching and for the Mayor they were his number one political problem, but still, they were under control.[9]

And since there was nobody else in the city who seemed likely to raise a stink, the Mayor and his people expected no problems at the convention.

Of course, in a city as large as Chicago, there were bound to be some troublemakers. And on December 26, in some sort of tie-in to the day of goodwill toward all men, one of them started threatening to create trouble during the convention. Dick Gregory, a black comedian with a national reputation, and a longtime civil rights activist, told a group of newsmen that unless the city of Chicago passed an open housing bill and got itself some top black police officers, he was going to lead a massive, nonviolent protest during the convention.[10]

The Mayor responded characteristically to the threat to Chicago. He was livid. His Chicago accent asserting itself, he told reporters, "No one is going to take over the city—now or in July or at any other time. They won't take over the Convention or any street. . . . We'll permit them to act as American citizens and in no other way." Cooling down, the Mayor tried to explain: "We live in an age of spreading hatred and violence. We are forgetting the spirit of friendship and love. . . . We need respect for law and order, we need a unification of our citizens." Tom Keane, the city's most powerful alderman, added that talk of nonviolence was nothing but a front for violence and that Martin Luther King—who had had a series of run-ins with the Mayor in 1966 and with whom Gregory had worked—and his ilk, with all their talk about freedom, never paid any attention to anybody else's right to be free of him and his people.

"I think the great mass of the American people has had enough," he said, ". . . and are getting fed up with the cry of police brutality."[11]

Adding a coda on police brutality to a discussion of civil rights marchers' lack of respect for other people's rights might sound like a non sequitor, but it wasn't. For Tom Keane and a lot of other white people, any discussion of civil rights automatically brought to mind what they saw as civil rights activists' incessant claims that the police, as a matter of course, brutalized black people. For Keane and others, the police brutality charges showed just how wrong the whole civil rights agitation was. Keane and a good many other Americans were sick and tired of hearing that blacks were repressed and that everything was the fault of the police. What the police needed, presidential aspirants Governor George Wallace of Alabama and Governor Ronald Reagan of California and, later, Republican nominees Richard Nixon and Spiro Agnew said at one campaign stop after another was not more restrictions and interference but more support and more freedom to do their thankless job. Already by January 1968, after too many riots, too many violent protests, and too many disruptions, the cry for law and order was ringing from coast to coast.[12]

Between the two coasts, Mayor Daley was getting the word from his intelligence people that Dick Gregory wasn't the only one who was talking about making trouble in Chicago during the convention. Police informant reports and other intelligence reports received by the Mayor's people indicated that the antiwar movement was planning to march on the convention. The possibility of Gregory leading tens of thousands of poor blacks through the streets while "subversive and militant" antiwar protesters tried to disrupt convention activities was an ugly picture.[13] It meant that the city was going to have to plan extraordinary security precautions. After the riots and the campus upheavals anything could happen, even in Chicago. But in early January, the Mayor still hoped it wasn't going to happen. Publicly, the Mayor kept repeating the same message when reporters asked him about the likelihood of demonstrations in his city: "No thousands will come to our city and take over our streets, our city and our Convention."[14]

Privately, the city began to mobilize. Richard Elrod was one of the city officials upon whom the responsibility for convention security fell most heavily. Elrod was the head of the Ordinance Enforcement Division of the city's corporation counsel's office, which meant, among other things, that it was his job to assess and prepare legal procedures for civil disorders and mass arrest situations. Elrod was also the son of Arthur Elrod, who was the last of the tough-guy Jewish committeemen in what had become the all black Twenty-fourth Ward. Elrod, Senior, had also been an important member of the Cook County Board of Commissioners.

The younger Elrod had graduated from Northwestern Law School and then gone to work for the city. Daley trusted him and he moved up fast. He was looking, in January 1968, to move up a good deal further.[15]

Soon after the New Year, Elrod was spending a good part of his time preparing for the convention. One of the first things he did was to tell his people that there'd be no August vacations. He also started meeting with his opposite numbers in the Police Department in order to coordinate efforts and plan strategy.[16] The February issue of the *Chicago Police Star* featured an interview with Elrod in which he explained his job and then told the police, "Our division is willing to do everything possible to make sure that the city is peaceful this summer, that the city is open to all. I do think there will be stepped up attempts in civil rights demonstrations because of the focus of the nation on Chicago this summer." Elrod made his position on such demonstrations clear when he concluded, "There is something wrong when people interfere with other people's rights."[17] The police, Elrod was saying, were likely to be facing a long, hot summer, but at least the city was going to be on their side all the way.

By early January 1968, the Chicago Police Department had also begun to plan for the convention. Superintendent James Conlisk, in his January 12 yearlong forecast report to the Police Board, outlined a number of steps aimed at preventing riots during the summer and especially during convention week. He planned to increase ten-man tactical teams—made up of policemen whose everyday experience of handling violent situations seemed to make them the best officers for controlling civil disorders—from thirty-two to sixty-seven. He reported that he would set up a civil disturbances critique and planning seminar to acquaint all department units on civil disturbance procedures and to "increase command level competence in tactics." The report also specified that by early spring all tear gas weapons would be reevaluated and updated, that before the summer began all Task Force and District Tactical Unit personnel would undergo crowd control training, and that a new set of General Orders on crowd control would be issued. Further, he hoped to buy new equipment to analyze LSD specimens and to purchase helicopters. July 1, he stated hopefully, the police operating procedure for the convention would be completed and plans implemented "to assure protection, convenience and safety to all Convention participants."[18] Conlisk and his commanders went into 1968 confident that the force could handle their assignment. They had good reason for this optimism.

Over the last eight years, the Chicago Police Department had undergone a set of far-reaching reforms administered by the best police mind in the country—O. W. Wilson.[19] And while Wilson had retired from the superintendency in August 1967, Conlisk was his protégé and knew the system. Many, both in and out of the department, believed that the Wilson reforms had made the Chicago Police Department one of the nation's best. The director of Professional Standards for the International Association of Chiefs of Police rated Chicago as "the best equipped, best administered police force in the United States."[20]

A number of facts seemed to indicate that the CPD was not only in better shape than police departments in other urban areas but was also in far better shape internally than it had been only a few years earlier. Morale had certainly improved; in 1960, 40.8% of Chicago policemen said the department was well run; in 1965, 77% thought so.[21] Along the same lines, whereas better than one-half of the Chicago police surveyed believed that the public rated them higher than they did twenty years earlier, in Boston and Washington, D.C., only one-fifth of the police believed that their ratings had improved. Surveys also showed that 64% of Chicago's blacks believed that the police did at least "fairly well" in treating Negroes, which was a higher percentage than that earned by New York or Atlanta police. In part, this relative good will might be explained by the fact that O. W. Wilson had very actively recruited and promoted black police officers. In his first year, Wilson appointed one hundred and twenty-five sergeants and fifty of them were black. By 1968, the police force was one-quarter black, which was a higher percentage than New York or Los Angeles.[22]

In his better than seven years as superintendent, Wilson had restructured and rebuilt the police force. Immediately after taking over, Wilson successfully "encouraged" many incompetent and sometimes corrupt senior officers to retire. At the same time, Wilson and his non-Chicagoan aides created new police districts to break down political interference and promote greater efficiency. Wilson also used the redistricting to create the Task Force, a special group of officers who moved from high crime area to high crime area. All police were put through regular in-service training (something never done before), in which they were instructed in new police techniques and tactics. Wilson also purchased new equipment and built new facilities. Then, too, Wilson completely reorganized the department's administration, in the main to cut down on corruption, to remove politically appointed officers, and to make the department operate more efficiently. As part of this structural reform, Wilson created the Internal Investigations Department, whose sole purpose was to stamp out police corruption.

Police corruption was what had brought Orlando Wilson, the uncorruptible California police chief–scholar to Chicago. And it was the scandal of police corruption that had forced Mayor Daley to give Wilson an open hand in dealing with the department. If by July 1968 the Chicago Police Department was one of the best in the country, there is no doubt that in 1960, when Wilson took over, it was one of the most corrupt, politically influenced police departments in the country.

The scandal that precipitated Wilson's hiring was a particularly embarrassing one. In a plea bargaining move, a small-time thief implicated eight policemen in a number of burglaries. It seemed likely that other policemen had, at the very least, known about the burglary ring and done nothing about it. The Mayor was vacationing in Florida when the scandal broke and the newspapers—it was an election year—played it up big. There was a public outcry.

Of course, there had been public outcries before and reforms, too. In the 1920s it was hard to tell who was paying the police more, the city or the mobsters. And when that situation had gotten just a little too brazen there had been a big reform. It had even been relatively effective, clearing out a lot of the shady characters whose first allegiance was to the mobsters. But the Police Department, like the Park District or the Fire Department, was still, in 1960, far from an independent force for professional public service. It was, by and large, just another branch of the patronage system, which meant that the department was larded with political influence. That wasn't exactly a secret.

In 1960, 53.7% of the force admitted that politicians had "a lot" to do with who got promoted and 32.9% said that the politicians had "some" influence. The police knew that a little corruption and a little inefficiency were not going to bother anybody's "Chinaman" (their political sponsor in or out of the department) who all were, after all, playing the same game. Moreover, the police were just playing along with everybody else. Not to be corrupt might put you in wrong with the system, which ran on petty corruption and payoffs. There were no incentives in the department to be honest or efficient.

Of course, there were other reasons for the corruption. Police professionals, including Wilson, while arguing that political interference underlay a good deal of police corruption and mismanagement, also pointed to the lack of modern bureaucratic oversight, inferior applicants and training methods (the former due to poor salaries and benefits and the latter to low budgets and mismanagement), and the use of too many police for nonpolice functions (like chauffeuring politicians or being lent to prominent and sometimes disreputable businessmen), which normalized corruption and goldbricking. The rank and file blamed another problem: there were too many laws that prosecuted people for doing things that were "natural," like drinking, gambling, and whoring. Such unenforceable laws only created confusion and cynicism among both the police and the public. In the main, these morally ambiguous activities were what police took payoffs to protect.

Of course, there were many police who, while maybe looking the other way at brother officers' misdeeds, did solid, honest police work. But in 1960, when O. W. Wilson took over the superintendency, the CPD was in sorry shape.[23]

Many policemen, especially the younger ones, as the aforementioned statistics indicated, were pleased with the revamping of the police force. But while they enjoyed the general improvements, which included salary raises, better equipment, and nicer facilities, there were some things few policemen liked. Many of the police resented the rigid, hierarchical controls over everyday police actions that Wilson tried to implement. But even more, the rank and file hated Wilson's Internal Investigation Department, especially its use of entrapment to bag officers on the take. Frank Carey, president of the Patrolmen's Association, loudly rejected Wilson's zealous attempts to stamp out corruption. To him, Wilson was nothing but an ivory tower puritan.[24] Many of the police also disliked Wilson's Negro policy, quite simply because they didn't like working with Negroes.[25]

It is hard to measure the total effect of Wilson on the CPD. Writing at the end of Wilson's administration, William Turner, ex-FBI agent turned law enforcement critic, stated that Wilson's good efforts were "more of a face lifting than a fundamental reform."[26] Another sympathetic observer wrote:

> Wilson held that policemen, if not closely controlled, would avoid work, engage in extralegal behavior and would subvert the administrative goals. It is an idea which has been disputed by a great mass of social science research data which indicates that men want to work and derive great satisfaction from it. . . . Wilson's theory failed to allow for the complexities of the human condition. . . . Wilson contributed to rank and file alienation by applying ruthless disciplinary action. . . . The result was a continuing program of selling an image of reform without engaging in the indepth reform needed to cure the malaise. . . .
> More change in form than in substance.[27]

Certain pieces of evidence indicate that there was something to these charges.

Despite Wilson's efforts to improve applicants, when he left only 2% of the police were college graduates.[28] And despite Wilson's Negro policy (or perhaps because of it), a large majority of the white policemen—a 1967 study said three-quarters of them—were racists.[29] Several years into O. W. Wilson's administration, 86% of the police still believed, albeit not so strongly as in 1960, that politicians influenced who did and did not get promotions. And whereas in 1960, 66.5% of the force believed that being a policeman made you cynical, near the end of Wilson's administration 69.5% thought so. In the same years the percentage of policemen who believed that a policeman should be liked by the citizens with whom he came in contact fell from 79% to 59%.[30] The Police Department was, in August 1967 when James Conlisk, Jr., took it over, more efficiently administered and better equipped than it had been in 1960. But the attitudes of many of the police officers were being shaped by forces a lot stronger than fancy reforms that to them often meant little more than extra paperwork, less freedom and autonomy on the job, and the fear that a snitch would turn you in for taking five dollars to help out a friendly merchant. By 1968, the rank and file believed, more than ever, that they were between a rock and a hard place and that the only person you could really trust was another cop.

The police were not just imagining things. All through the 1960s, from every angle, the police were catching flack. As New York Police Commissioner Howard Leary said, after battling student protesters, "Too often [the police are] caught in the middle, criticized for being too aggressive and not aggressive enough."[31] L.A. Police Chief Parker, after the Watts riots of 1965, put it another way when he said police were "the most downtrodden, oppressed, dislocated minority in America."[32] In every major city, the police saw themselves as being made to play the scapegoats for social problems they had nothing to do with causing, and they bitterly resented it.

Their list of enemies was long. Somewhere near the top was the Supreme Court, which in a series of decisions that included *Miranda v. Arizona* (1966—the right to remain silent and have counsel) and *Escabeda v. Illinois* (1964—the right to a lawyer once the accusatory stage of the process begins) seemed to give every break and every benefit of the doubt to the criminal. As O. W. Wilson said, in an address titled "Police Authority in a Free Society," "The scales of justice are getting out of balance. . . . I plead only for the rule of reason. Let the police have the authority to do what the public expects them to do in suppressing crime."[33] Almost 90% of all policemen believed that the Supreme Court had gone too far in protecting criminals.[34] To the police it just didn't make any sense; crime was growing five times faster than the increase in population and yet the police were being given less and less authority to do anything about it.[35] And what was worse was that whenever the police did try to do anything, do-gooder liberals, politicians, and the press raised a stink, broadcast cries of police brutality in every direction, and further tied the policeman's hands.

To the police, by the mid-sixties, the situation in the ghettos had gotten completely out of hand. So-called civil rights leaders, many policemen

believed, with the help of liberals and the press, had made it impossible
to follow normal police procedure without producing outraged cries of
police brutality. Of course the police used physical force in handling
suspects and troublemakers in the ghettos. As they saw it—and they,
not the do-gooders, were there everyday seeing the rape victims, the
gangbangers, the junkies, and the thieves—without force, without the
no-nonsense approach that produced fear and respect, there could be
no law and order in the ghetto crime jungle. The longer policemen served
in the ghettos the more they felt this way. They were the ones putting
their lives on the line—in 1967 one of eight policemen nationally was
assaulted—and all they got from the press for their trouble was scan-
dalmongering and the headlining of every claim of police brutality.[36]

Quentin Tamm, executive director of the International Association of
Chiefs of Police, put the matter simply: "The better we do our job of
enforcing the law the more we are attacked. . . . The state of our so
called objective press is sad to behold. . . . Subtly, too many so called
objective news writers attempt to excuse the actions of minorities." The
mass media, he went on to say, cause "the police to be singled out by
virtually all factions as the symbol of all society's failures."[37] O. W. Wilson concurred: "The press [is] primarily directed at incidents that tend
to discredit the police. Small wonder that those who read the papers . . .
conclude that the police are evil."[38]

What was worse, in the eyes of many police, was that it seemed almost
like there was a conspiracy between the mass media and the rioters,
protesters, and other agitators. After a series of civil rights protests, the
New York police commissioner, practically a liberal in police circles,
told reporters that police were "puzzled, bitter, and deeply resentful . . .
that the public image of law enforcement . . . was unfairly distorted and
smeared today as never before in our history . . . [by] certain groups
determined to weaken the democratic process."[39] In 1965, two-thirds of
all Chicago police sergeants surveyed agreed that the city's newspapers
were too critical of the force.[40] By 1968, that figure almost certainly would
have been a good deal higher.

Worst of all, of course, were the liberals and "communists" who seemed
dead set on keeping the police from preserving law and order. An overwhelming number of policemen identified themselves as conservatives
and forthrightly admitted to being against the radicals and liberals who
wanted to change the way things were. Experts said police were prone
to conservative and bigoted beliefs because they were uneducated working-
class people. They were people who, the experts said, out of status insecurity and other developmental problems were intolerant of change and
of people different from themselves. The same experts also claimed that
the particular sort of lower-class, uneducated people drawn to the police

force often suffered from what they called "authoritarian personalities." For psychological reasons, police highly valued order, predictability, stability, and safety; and they believed that when it was necessary, using violence to maintain these conditions was justifiable. The experts further stated that the police force, like the army and other male subcultures, produced a highly valued sense of internal loyalty and an "us versus them" mentality that created paranoidal tendencies. Most police didn't think much of these experts.[41]

Most did respect J. Edgar Hoover, LAPD Chief Parker, and Berkeley Chief of Police Fording, all of whom believed that the ACLU type attacks on police procedure, the civil rights agitators' claims of police brutality, and the students' attacks on police and all proper authority were quite simply part of a comprehensive Communist conspiracy to destroy legally designated authority in the United States. Many police around the country agreed.[42] Policemen made up approximately 3% of the John Birch Society's membership. In 1964, the Oakland police, from the chief down, actively campaigned for Barry Goldwater. In early 1968, John Harrington, national president of the Fraternal Order of Police, endorsed George Wallace, who had stamped Support Your Local Police on Alabama license plates.[43] In December 1967, the Chicago Police Departments' Internal Investigation Department found a Ku Klux Klan cell equipped with guns, ammunition, and hand grenades in the force.[44] Gerald S. Arenberg, founder of the American Federation of Police, in referring to the civil rights protesters, the civil liberties advocates, and the student protesters, warned, "We are at war with an enemy just as dangerous as the Viet Cong in southeast Asia."[45]

A few police, like O. W. Wilson, took a more moderate view and believed that the antipathy to police was caused by a pervasive breakdown of civic consciousness and a general fear of encroaching social problems.[46] Attorney General Ramsay Clark called 1968 "The Year of the Policeman" and said, "We are living in a time of change the likes of which history has never before seen." The police, he went on to say, were unfairly forced to act as peacekeepers between the conflicting forces of those changes.[47] "Damned if you do, damned if you don't," was how one veteran cop put it.[48]

Certainly by January 1968, that damned if you do, damned if you don't feeling was shared by a good many Chicago policemen. They had learned that lesson well during the 1965 and 1966 civil rights marches and during the small ghetto riot that had erupted in the summer of 1966.

Mayor Daley had been outraged by the marchers who were parading through white neighborhoods in support of an open housing bill, and he demanded that O. W. Wilson arrest the participants. But Wilson, who had been promised when he took over the scandal-ridden Department that he would have a free hand, told police to overlook minor violations of the law and instead to control the angry white crowds. "Chicago," Wilson said, "would not be another Selma or Watts." Wilson did the same thing when a group of nuns, in favor of civil rights, sat down in the street at State and Madison; Wilson simply ordered the police to reroute traffic.

Wilson and his police were praised by civil rights leaders but were angrily condemned by the Mayor, his people, the *Chicago Tribune*, and— this is conjecture—a good portion of Chicago's whites. According to one Daley intimate, the Mayor's response to Wilson's tactics was to "sit there blowing his stack and shouting that Wilson was a dumb sonofabitch." Indeed, after Wilson's handling of the 1966 west side flare-up, numerous city officials and anti-Wilson police officers made an extensive investigation into the causes of the riot, trying to dig up proof that the whole thing was a part of a Communist conspiracy or was directly produced by outside agitators. Such proof, they felt, could be used to press for much harsher treatment the next time the Negroes rioted.[49]

During most of this trouble the police caught it from all sides. The liberals and civil rights activists blamed the police for starting the 1966 riot and used it as a springboard for more demands that police brutality and harassment of blacks be stopped. They demanded investigations and called for more civilian control of the police, including a civilian police review board. The Mayor and his aldermen, on the other hand, wanted the police to be more aggressive in their treatment of miscreants. One alderman lectured Superintendent Wilson on New York City police tactics in the 1950s; there the police handled troublemakers by "breaking their heads both figuratively and literally." Wilson asked the alderman, "Are you suggesting that Chicago policemen go out and break the heads of people?" The alderman said that the People of Chicago would support any policeman who broke the head of a lawbreaker. Later, the independent alderman Leon Despres stood up and condemned police brutality. Another alderman interrupted Despres by shouting that the "police brutality lobby" should shut up and let the police do their job.[50]

In Chicago and throughout the country, as ghetto violence and student protest increased throughout 1967, more and more people, especially policemen, were repeating the alderman's demand that the "police brutality lobby" shut up and let the police stop the breakdown in law and order. In January 1968, after the Miami police chief announced a crackdown on ghetto criminals, he was asked by reporters if he didn't fear massive complaints about police brutality. He replied, for publication, "We don't mind being accused of police brutality."[51] In Chicago, an unofficial police spokesman appeared on a local TV talk show and complained that due to court decisions the policeman's job had become almost impossible. But the public, he said, instead of blaming the courts, blames the cops, saying that they're too soft. It isn't right, he said, to blame the cops for what isn't their fault.[52]

More and more police were coming out against the "kid gloves" treatment being given to rioting blacks and students. The law, they said, must apply to everyone. A New York policeman, angered by his liberal mayor's policy of having the police overlook minor violations of the law during riots or tense situations, spoke for the vast majority of policemen when he wrote: "It was never intended that a responsible police administration would be directly or indirectly required to operate under a policy or philosophy that encourages, permits or condones serious violations of the law."[53] Seeing that the American people were getting fed up with the agitators, rioters, and other criminal elements, prominent public officials, including presidential aspirants Ronald Reagan, Richard Nixon, and George Wallace, spoke in favor of unleashing the police from what they saw as the dubious restraints imposed upon them by the Supreme Court, the liberal press, and the gaggle of bleeding hearts, most of whom, they liked to say, lived in the suburbs and didn't have any idea of what urban violence was really like.

In the midst of this national debate, sixty-seven-year-old O. W. Wilson decided to retire, citing health reasons for his decision.[54] He recommended that his protégé, head of the Bureau of Field Services, James B. Conlisk, Jr., be named in his place. Conlisk took over the department the summer of 1967—the summer of the nation's worst ghetto rioting.

Superintendent Conlisk was a different sort of man from Wilson and he took over the department without the guarantee Wilson had that he would be free to run it without political interference. Conlisk was no "California knight in shining armor" come to save the Chicago Police Department from disgrace. He was a career officer whose father before him had been a politically well-connected assistant superintendent of the force.[55] James Conlisk, Jr.—an excellent police officer—like the superintendent of the parks, the fire commissioner, and every other municipal department head, owed his job to the Mayor. One observer of the department wrote that Conlisk was "a capable commander who functioned well under supervision but who lacked initiative and technical expertise [and the ability] . . . to exercise independent judgment and firm leadership."[56]

That's what the critic said, but Conlisk got the department and the city through the red hot summer of 1967 without incident.

Courtesy of the Kaye Miller Collection, 1968 Democratic Convention, Northwestern University Library.

Mayor Richard J. Daley

Deputy Mayor David E. Stahl *(Chicago Sun-Times, Inc. 1987)*

Police Superintendent James B. Conlisk

Police Superintendent Orlando W. Wilson

Sheriff Richard Elrod *(Ted Lacey photograph)*

6 The City of Broad Shoulders

January 1968, Conlisk exercised the kind of administrative planning he learned from O. W. Wilson and set up a Convention Planning Committee. This committee included high-ranking officers from the patrol, community relations, traffic, youth, communications, and planning divisions. Eight months before the convention was to begin, the group began working on such logistical problems as traffic flow, parking, communication between various security forces, Amphitheater security, perimeter security, and manpower requirements. They also began to consider how to handle any protests at the Amphitheater.

At one of the first meetings, Sgt. Thomas of the Youth Division, who'd worried about arresting youths at civil rights demonstrations before, suggested that no arrested juveniles be housed openly in the Amphitheater area. He'd learned from experience that "older people tend to become hysterical when they see youngsters become involved with the police."[1]

By early February, the Convention Planning Committee began scheduling regular meetings approximately every other week. By late February, the CPC had set up working relations with the Secret Service, Military Intelligence, the Illinois National Guard, the Democratic National Committee, the Chicago Convention Bureau, and other private and public agencies. Intelligence reports began to come in from the department's own intelligence unit, as well as from federal sources, warning of massive antiwar demonstrations. Assistant Corporation Counsel Richard Elrod began meeting with Deputy Superintendent James Rochford, who was in charge of the police convention security, and Chief John Kelly, who was in charge of the CPC. They talked about mass arrest situations and worried about housing thousands of prisoners.

The CPC considered using railroad cars and mobile schoolroom trailers (called, by some, "Willis wagons" after the Chicago school superintendent who'd introduced them to overcrowded black schools in order to keep blacks out of underused white schools) as temporary holding cells. They also tried to figure out a means of inconspicuously transporting all the arrestees from the Amphitheater holding facilities to the city's jails.[2]

While the police went very quietly about their business, Republican Cook County Sheriff Joseph Woods decided to go very public with his convention plans. In early February, he held a press conference and announced that he was forming a one-thousand-man volunteer posse to help keep order during the convention. He also announced that his office was considering the use of Chicago's underground steam tunnel system for holding troublemakers. Woods's plans made the headlines in Chicago and were carried in newspapers across the country. (In New York the depressing news of another strike by garbagemen dominated the head-lines.) Almost immediately, Woods's office was swamped with volun-teers, all of whom were willing to furnish their own guns, helmets, and uniforms and were willing to work without pay.[3]

The Mayor was not pleased by Woods's political showboating. He and Conlisk held their own press conference. The Mayor told off Republican Sheriff Woods: "We don't need the Sheriff's group in Chicago. We do need positive programs and the cooperation of people." The Mayor re-peated that he expected no disorder during the convention. Conlisk con-curred and told the press and the public to ignore "the apostles of doom and gloom."[4] A few days later, the ACLU used a lawsuit to stop Woods's formation of a posse comitatus; Circuit Court Judge O'Brien said such a posse could only be formed in an emergency.[5]

Through February and March, the police kept to their quiet prepara-tions, ironing out logistical problems, and planning convention week assignments. February 29, the Convention Planning Committee flew Professor Miesner, an expert on police activities at the 1964 Republican Convention in San Francisco, in from California to talk to all area deputy chiefs. The police listened quietly to Miesner's description of police procedure at the 1964 convention and to his recommendation that only police officers of proven emotional stability be used for convention duty. When he finished, the area deputy chiefs plied him with questions about San Francisco hippies: Where do they get their money? Are they all students? Are most students hippies? Will the hippies come to Chicago? Miesner, though a Californian, was only a police expert and he couldn't tell the officers much about hippies.[6]

As Conlisk had planned at the beginning of the year, police also began taking refresher courses in crowd handling and crowd psychology. By the end of March, 705 members of the Task Force and of the expanding district tactical units had gone through a one-day in-service training course which began with a lecture by the city commissioner of human relations who outlined the city's racial problems. Robert McCann, the director of police training, then spoke to the men, stressing that they must not respond to verbal insults. As he told a reporter later:

> We explain to the officers that the agitated person who is
> facing them sees them not as they see themselves but
> merely as agents of the government, examples of unreason-

able restraint. . . . It is up to the officer, unless he is being
physically assaulted, to avoid making a personal issue out
of the insult, to be firm but yet use some degree of
persuasion.

The police were also shown how to perform proper "come-alongs":
from arm grips to arm locks. Some time was also spent on demonstrating
proper club techniques. Clubs, the officers were told, should be used to
jab protesters below the shoulders in order to move them and also to
defensively ward off blows. The police practiced all of these maneuvers
on each other. They also practiced minimum-force techniques useful in
disarming and taking a prisoner. Finally, they enjoyed a session on removing limp picketers.

Director McCann said that "police have learned from the errors of
Los Angeles, Detroit, and other cities and are developing new tactics."
The new emphasis, he said, was on learning how to be strong-minded
and not strong-armed. One veteran of the Task Force, however, told a
watching reporter, "If the fight starts, don't expect it to last long. We'll
win in the first round and there won't be a rematch."[7]

Also in March, Superintendent Conlisk appointed Frank Sullivan director of the Public Information Division. Sullivan had been a veteran
Chicago Sun-Times reporter and was a savvy Chicago insider. By ap-
pointing Sullivan, Conlisk gave the department a top man for what he
knew was going to be an important position. No matter how smoothly
the summer went, the police were going to need a man who could convincingly present the police side of any story to the press and, thus, to
the public. Conlisk knew that the convention would mean intense press
scrutiny of the department all summer long. The same month, Conlisk
issued General Order 67-18c which authorized the wearing of chemical
Mace as a part of the official police uniform.[8]

Everything the department did through the winter months to prepare
for troubles before and during the convention was perfectly consistent
with the recommendations made in early March by President Johnson's
National Advisory Commission on Civil Disorders. In their report, commonly known as the Kerner Report after the commission's chairman,
Illinois Governor Otto Kerner, the commissioners recommended that
during "incidents which could lead to disorders," police should use
"maximum police manpower" and not "lethal weapons" to maintain
order. The report also stressed police training "in the prevention of
disorders" and police use of "alternative . . . control equipment" in the
case of a riot; the police should use tear gas–type weapons and not guns
on rioters.[9] While the Police Department brass took the Kerner Report
recommendations in stride, other members of the Chicago law-and-order
community were appalled by its findings.

The Kerner Report, prepared under the direction of presidentially appointed Republican and Democratic officeholders, representatives of labor, business, and the Negro community, flew in the face of conservative common sense. "White racism," the report concluded, "is essentially responsible for the explosive mixture which has been accumulated in our cities." Further, the report declared that not a single ghetto riot was caused by any sort of Negro or Communist conspiracy. The report added that *the police are not merely a 'spark' factor.* To some Negroes police have come to symbolize white power, white racism and white repression. And the fact is that many police do reflect and express these white attitudes . . . in a 'double standard' of justice and protection—one for Negroes and one for whites."[10]

Mayor Daley treated the president's commission with mild condescension. And while he suggested that it went a little too far in blaming the police and elected officials for the Negroes' problems, all in all, he told reporters, it was "a good report." They should "put that at the top" of their stories, he said.

The Mayor, as one Chicago reporter later phrased it, "understood the fact that really mattered. The report was not about Chicago."[11] The report was about the riots of 1967. Chicago had no riots in 1967. As the Mayor saw it, he had nothing to learn from a bunch of so-called experts talking about how to stop urban riots when he'd already done it.

The *Chicago Tribune*, however, did not treat the matter so cavalierly. Speaking for most of Chicago's disgruntled whites—especially the rank-and-file police officers, who once again were being made to shoulder a lot of the blame—the *Tribune* blasted the report:

> [It] is awash with tears for the poor oppressed rioters.
> . . . The blame must be placed on those who have been
> preaching anarchy, letting people think they can violate
> laws which they think are wrong and encouraging Negroes
> to believe that all their troubles are the fault of somebody
> else. If this activity has not been an organized plot to pro-
> mote violence, what was it? Furthermore, it is impossible to
> believe that wholesale arson, gunfire, and looting are spon-
> taneous, unorganized, undirected or unprepared.

Police investigation, the *Tribune* concluded, proved that the riots in Newark and Plainfield, New Jersey, and Detroit were all planned and directed by the same "agitators." "The police on the scene of riots are as well qualified to discuss them as the Kerner Commission's psychologists and sociologists."[12] Nobody in Chicago wanted any advice from national commissions or liberal university professors.

Throughout the winter months, Mayor Daley had stood squarely be-
hind President Johnson. In early January, when the Democratic National
Committee met in Chicago, he had helped the party chairman William
Bailey stop Senator Eugene McCarthy from speaking to the committee.[13]
The Mayor wanted the party to stay united. During the Illinois Demo-
cratic party slatemaking sessions he made that clear.

Adlai Stevenson III, the very popular state treasurer and son of 1952
and 1956 Democratic party presidential candidate Adlai Stevenson II,
wanted to be slated for governor but was willing to take a shot at the
very conservative and very popular Republican Senator Everett Dirkson.
During the slatemaking process, Stevenson told the assembled party
chieftans that if he was elected to either office he would oppose Johnson's war policies. Later, the Mayor pulled him aside and asked him to
explain what he meant. Stevenson reiterated and explained his opposition to the war. The Mayor listened and then, as Stevenson remembers
it, asked "Does this mean that you will support the President on Vietnam?" Taken aback, Stevenson refused to recant and Daley refused to
support him. Stevenson was not slated.[14]

Throughout the winter months, Daley and Johnson stayed in close
touch, talking or seeing one another at least fifteen times. In mid-
January, Daley invited the president to be the guest of honor at his big
April 24 fundraising dinner.[15] When the president decided on March 31
not to run again, nobody was more surprised than Mayor Daley.

The Mayor's first reaction to the turn of events was to say that he still
stood by the president and hoped he would reconsider his decision. So,
too, did two of the Mayor's congressmen, adding that LBJ would be
drafted by the Chicago convention.[16] The Mayor did not just make his
comments for public consumption. Behind the scenes, he and Mayor
Alioto of San Francisco got busy trying to convince other party leaders
to stand behind the president.[17]

President Johnson and the War on Poverty had been good for the
Mayor's city. The Johnson domestic programs had pumped tens of millions of dollars into the city's ghettos. And except for one small grant
(which was quickly cut off) to the Woodlawn Organization, a local black-
controlled group, and a very few other programs tightly overseen by
federal authorities, the Mayor had virtually total control of all the federal
money coming into the city.[18] The War on Poverty money helped the
Mayor keep Chicago's blacks thinking "positively" about the Democratic party.

The day after his withdrawal speech, President Johnson sent a telegram to the Mayor's alma mater, now called the De LaSalle High School,
where the Mayor was being honored. It read: "My own admiration for

Dick is second to none. Throughout the long friendship we have shared, he has more than proved his unquestioned devotion to America and his dedication to the highest national ideals."[19] Later in the day, the president quietly flew into Chicago, where he was greeted by two hundred Chicago policemen as well as an enlarged force of secret service and FBI agents—by now a typical security precaution. After giving Daley a very public bear hug, the president conferred privately with the Mayor for over an hour. Afterward, neither man would comment on the substance of the meeting but the Mayor did suggest that it was likely that he would wait until August 26—the day of the convention roll call vote—to announce his candidate for the presidency. Political insiders speculated that Johnson had come to Daley in order to convince him not to support Robert Kennedy. On that Daley would not comment.[20] However, the next day, one of the Mayor's congressmen called for the nomination of Hubert Humphrey.[21]

While all this political maneuvering was going on, pushed off the front pages by the press of dreary news from Vietnam, Martin Luther King, Jr., publicly stated that he was going back to Memphis to give his support to striking black garbagemen. He'd left the city only a few days earlier after suffering a strategic defeat.

Though the story was given only a few lines, deep in the newspaper, the *Chicago Tribune* featured King's decision on its editorial page. Quoting J. Edgar Hoover, the paper called King "the most notorious liar in the country." "Sanctimoniously," the editorial went on, King claims to believe in nonviolence, "while clandestinely conspiring with the most violent revolutionaries in the country." Using the FBI as its source, the *Tribune* stated that King was involved in the 1967 black riots which were part of a Communist conspiracy. The *Tribune* went on to condemn the Kerner commissioners as "blind demagogs" for ignoring this Communist conspiracy and for idiotically asserting that ghetto riots were caused by white racism. In concluding their remarks about Dr. King the *Tribune* stated, "The communists have sowed the seeds of discord and hope to reap in 1968 a year filled with explosive racial unrest."[22] Though few, if any, well-informed people would have agreed that the "communists" could take credit for the "explosive racial unrest," the *Tribune* was dead right that "the seeds of discord" were about to explode.

Three days later, they did—and you could say, if you followed the logic of the *Tribune*, that it was King's fault. April 4, seconds after 6:00 P.M., King was assassinated. Within hours, across the country, ghetto blacks began to riot.

In Chicago, at first, nothing happened. On the south side, in the older, better-organized black belt communities, black leaders moved through the ghetto preaching peace and urging the people to respect Dr. King's memory. On the west side, in the more desolate, anomic black ghetto, where the political leadership was almost all white, there were that first night no public signs of trouble.

The Mayor's immediate reaction to the assassination was to order all flags at municipal buildings flown at half-mast. He also called for a memorial service to be held the next morning in the City Council chambers. Deputy Superintendent Rochford, in charge of police field operations, reacted by cutting all police days off, effective immediately, and by assigning three to four officers to ride in all police cars.[23]

The next morning, Chicago's ghettos—unlike those in Baltimore, Washington, D.C., New York and an increasing number of other cities—still quiet, the Mayor presided over the City Council memorial service for King. In life, the Mayor had not liked King, who had come to Chicago in 1965 and 1966 to protest the city's school and housing segregation. In private, according to one insider, the Mayor called King "a rabble rouser, a troublemaker," and, more from the gut, "a dirty sonofabitch, a bastard, a prick."[24] The Mayor blamed King and his staff for the small, West Side ghetto riot that had flared up during King's attempt to change the city's public housing policies in the summer of 1966. To Daley, King was in life not much more than a well-spoken outside agitator who offered Chicago nothing but trouble. One time, he said so for the record, "He comes up here for one purpose—to create trouble here and in every city he has visited."[25] But usually, when the Mayor spoke publicly about or to King it was all politeness and respect. Still, politeness aside, when it came down to brass tacks, the Mayor had never given in to a single one of King's demands for major reform.

In death, the Mayor accorded King—publicly—even more respect. At the City Council memorial service, Daley called on the city's Negroes to honor their dead leader: "All of us must help soften the grief of Dr. King's family and associates by demonstrating that his life was not sacrificed in vain. We must advance those programs which he so courageously stood for and accept his doctrine of nonviolence." But another speaker at the service, who was in fact one of Dr. King's most trusted associates, saw it all very differently. Jesse Jackson, only twenty-six years old but already head of the Southern Christian Leadership Operation Breadbasket in Chicago, and who was at Martin Luther King's side when he was assassinated, looked out at the crowd of aldermen and cried out, "The blood is on the chest and hands of those that would not have welcomed him here yesterday."[26]

Approximately five miles due west of City Hall, in the middle of Chicago's most desperate pit of slums and poverty, a crowd of high school students, grade school students, and a few older people gathered in Garfield Park to hear speakers mourn King and voice their anger. Quickly, the mourning and the anger mixed into hate and the young people moved into the streets and began to destroy Madison Street, the commercial heart of their own neighborhood. Hundreds and thousands of people joined them. They smashed windows. They looted the stores—almost every one was white owned—that lined the street. At 3:49 P.M., a rioter started a fire at a furniture store at 2235 West Madison. A minute later, a rioter put the torch to a building a block away. In twenty minutes, firemen were battling fires in an area a mile-and-a-half square. In the next twenty-four hours they logged 599 fires.

Even before the fires began, Superintendent Conlisk had asked the Mayor to get the governor to call out the National Guard and by 2:45 the Mayor had done so. But it would take time for the guard to mobilize. For the first few hours there were only the police.

They confronted a blazing world gone mad. Rioters filled the streets of Lawndale, thousands of them. Yelling, screaming, laughing, they smashed cars, stores, stoplights, anything that would break. They torched buildings. Ladies pushed shopping carts down the street filled with shoes, sports coats. People ran by carrying cases of beer; a few lugged sofas, chairs, whole bedroom sets down the middle of the street. Children threw bricks and ran in and out of shattered store windows, looting. The entire block of 2300 West Madison was on fire.

White people in the Loop, less than three miles away, could see the smoke. Rumors of black snipers and of mass destruction filtered through the city. Whites fled the Loop, avoiding the expressways that ran through the black ghettos, and clogged the Outer Drive that runs along the city's lakefront. Some white people, twenty miles away from Lawndale, barricaded their suburban homes and waited. The TV showed footage of the city burning.

At 4:20 P.M., the Mayor spoke on radio and television:

> Stand up tonight and protect the city. . . . I ask this very
> sincerely, very personally. Let's show to the United States
> and the world what the citizenry of Chicago is made of. . . .
> Violence in a free society leads to anarchy. Anarchy accom-
> plishes nothing. We must have respect for the rights of all
> people. . . . Be proud of the grateful city . . . which has
> given opportunities to all.

The Mayor then did his best to stop all the rumors by outlining the situation—he was precise and accurate, stating that the riot was re-stricted to the Lawndale area and that the rest of the city was under control—and he reported that the National Guard was on its way to the riot area to restore order. When he finished speaking the pack of re-porters wanted the Mayor to explain why the blacks were rioting. The Mayor could only say, "I don't know what it is. But I hope to God it subsides." Mayor Daley had been elected to his first term of office exactly thirteen years earlier.

Until 11 P.M. of the first night of the riot, for better than seven hours, the police alone stood off the mob. Approximately five thousand police were on the streets, but most of them were protecting the Loop and white neighborhoods adjoining the riot area, or patrolling the still peaceful south side black ghettos. Those in the riot zone, under Superintendent Conlisk's orders, followed the procedure set by O. W. Wilson. They tried to contain the riot and to stop only the most flagrant law breakers. Guns were to be fired only as a last possible resort and, overwhelmingly, the police obeyed that order.

At first, the police tried to use riot control formations—the wedge, diagonal, and skirmish lines—to clear the streets. But none of them worked because the crowd was not trying to go anywhere in particular; the mob would just break into another set of stores or run through the alleys. The police also found that they couldn't make "symbolic arrests" to cool out the crowd because there were just too many "troublemakers." The mob was virulently antipolice and the command personnel on the streets were worried any aggressive acts might just increase the level of violence; they knew about the "blind pig" raid in Detroit, the "traffic arrest" in Newark, and the "pregnant woman" arrest in Watts. Arresting looters was also complicated by a few other factors. First, in all the chaos, the police could not discriminate between looters and people fleeing burning buildings with their possessions. Second, arrests took time and many police officers felt that they were more useful in the streets than they would be detaining and processing suspected looters.

Even more important, many of the officers in the riot zone were needed to protect the better than two thousand firemen and one thousand sanitation workers who were being stoned and jeered while they tried to put out the fires and clear the debris. Soon after the riot broke out, somebody shot a fireman in the leg and both police and firefighters were anxiously waiting for more shots and more casualties. The mainly white police, firemen, and city workers were surrounded by tens of thousands of hostile, drunken, hysterical rioters. Despite the riot helmets and their handguns, the police knew that they were sitting ducks and that there wasn't much of anything they could do if a sniper wanted to knock off a few firemen. But the police held on, courageously wading through the rioters and doing their best to clear the streets so that the fire engines and ambulances could get through. By nightfall, the police had succeeded in turning the arsonists and looters away from the Loop, which some police and city officials wrongly assumed was the rioters' goal.

During all of this, the police arrested only a few hundred rioters. One policeman, shortly after the riot, explained, "Arresting them doesn't

seem to help because they don't care. . . . It's been my experience that
they beat me out of the court back onto the street. I believe one good
crack on the head does more good. If you give them a headache they go
home and usually stay there."

The police did shoot and kill four rioters and others were wounded by
police gunfire. But compared to Detroit in 1967, when forty-three blacks
were killed, the Chicago police—all of whom were on twelve-hour shifts—
were a model of coolness and compassion.

Downtown, the police had heavy guards around the department stores
and the financial district. In the late afternoon, a gang of black boys,
the *Tribune* said four hundred, ran through the Loop and broke several
windows. But other than that, the Loop was quiet and secure. Four
hundred police surrounded City Hall and the entire fifth floor, the May-
or's office, was lined with police officers. More stood in reserve in the
City Hall basement. There were more policemen in the Loop than there
were in the riot zone.

By midnight, sixteen hundred National Guardsmen were in the streets.
Soon after, the city was fairly quiet. But the Mayor continued his vigil
in City Hall. He had the television on and the radio tuned to police calls.
City officials continued to stream in and out of his office. At 2:30 A.M.,
the Mayor, with a heavy police guard, drove through the riot area. He
spoke to the police and other city workers who were still fighting the
fires and trying to clean up the rubbled streets. It seemed like the worst
of the rioting was over.

The next day, however, looting and rioting broke out on the south side,
just south and southwest of the University of Chicago. And again, the
streets of the west side filled with people and more fires were set and
more stores were smashed into. Police and twenty-four hundred more
National Guardsmen were deployed, and although arrests did go up
dramatically they could not stop the rioting. The Mayor called President
Johnson and asked for army troops. Several thousand were rushed to
Chicago. The Mayor also imposed a 7 P.M. curfew for all people under
twenty-one. He also ordered a ban on all liquor in the riot area as well
as a citywide ban on the purchase of guns, ammunition, and gasoline in
portable containers.

By the end of the day, nine people were dead in riot-related incidents—
but still only four due to police gunshots. Three hundred people were
injured. Twelve hundred and fifty people had been arrested. Twenty
thousand people were without electricity. Two miles of West Madison
were burned out and firemen were still battling blazes on the west side.
Some west side streets were still mobbed. Many of the people were just
fleeing the fires, but as the second day of the rioting came to a close
there were some people still looting and smashing.[27]

April 7, the *Chicago Tribune*, the city's most powerful newspaper, damned the rioters and the city's response. The *Tribune* editorialists had ignored King's death but they were not about to ignore the riots. In an editorial titled, "Law and Order First," the *Trib* declared:

> . . . the rioters here have taken advantage of the wave of sentimentality and assumed guilt that has swept the country. . . . The Mayor conceded yesterday that the city not only underreacted at the outset of the crisis but that it did not move with sufficient speed. . . . The lesson of all recent riots has been that when public officials and the public at large lean over backwards in an attempt to appease the lawbreakers cities are in deep trouble. . . . Permissive attitudes in Chicago and elsewhere can only lead to more and worse rioting. . . . Here in Chicago we are not dealing with the colored population but with a minority of criminal scum. . . . We hope Mayor Daley will not fall into the same category as spineless and indecisive mayors who muffed early riot control in . . . Los Angeles and Newark.[28]

The *Tribune* spoke for many; to call the city's blacks the "colored population" was not just a slip back to an older terminology. It was a deliberate attack on everything blacks and pro–civil rights whites had been fighting for over the last fifteen years.

Sunday morning, after Mass, the Mayor and Fire Commissioner Robert Quinn flew over the riot areas. The Mayor saw the devastation. He saw the firemen still putting out fires on the west side. He also saw that the streets, lined with armed security forces, were finally calm.

There were sixteen thousand police, National Guard, and army troops on duty in and around Chicago. Twelve hundred soldiers, many of them Vietnam vets, were camped out in Jackson Park, just southeast of the University of Chicago. After forty-eight hours of rioting, eleven blacks— but still only four at police hands—were dead. The police had shot forty-eight people. Ninety policemen had been injured, none seriously. Approximately 2150 people had been arrested—thirteen hundred for riot-associated misdemeanors, and eight hundred and fifty for felonies. Three hundred and sixty-eight juveniles were in custody. Richard Elrod, with remarkable efficiency, had run the mass arrest operation.

When the Mayor got out of the helicopter, looking noticeably shaken, he told the people of Chicago, "It was a shocking and tragic picture of the city. I never believed this could happen here. I hope it will never happen again."[29] The Mayor, along with Commissioner Quinn and Superintendent Conlisk, then went on to praise the police and firemen who had acted so courageously in containing and eventually stopping the arson and rioting.

April 8, the streets quiet, the police arrested five Black Power leaders and charged them with arson. Undercover agents of the Police Intelligence Unit had fingered them.

The Mayor responded to the arrests by claiming what many other big city mayors had said after rioting broke out in their cities: much, though not all, of the rioting was caused by a conspiracy. The Mayor said, "Certainly, the arsonists were organized."[30]

The *Tribune* also reported that FBI agents had uncovered a plot to turn a King memorial rite in Grant Park, planned for April 9, into another riot. The leader of the plot was Rennie Davis, "a black power advocate [who] . . . participated in secret black power meetings in Lake Villa."[31] The next day, the rally—six hundred people, most of them white members of SDS or the Mobe staff—was allowed to go on surrounded by several hundred heavily armed troops. A *Tribune* editorial stated that "the demonstrators must be working for communist North Vietnam. It is an outrage that this country has to deal with a second front at home against rioters and beatniks when the fighting men are risking death overseas." Another editorial declared that the Republican party "should campaign for the return of moral values and common sense" and concluded by quoting Richard Nixon, "Until we have order, we can have no progress."[32]

Over the new few days, the Mayor tried to restore normalcy. He lifted the curfew and had hundreds of city workers clear the riot areas of rubble and bulldoze the dozens of burnt-out buildings. In only a few days, the most obvious signs of the riots were turned into smooth vacant lots.

The Mayor, those first few days after the riots, let his sadness and uncertainty show. Despite his best efforts, his city had burned. He showed how much the riots had affected him when he was asked by reporters if he felt the Democratic Convention could go on without more disorders. The Mayor, who had been replying to that question before the riots by stating over and over, there will be no disorder in Chicago, could now only say that, "we hope there will be no further disturbances and we feel that this has been one no one could anticipate. We hope the Convention will be conducted in an orderly manner."[33]

Alongside his sadness, the Mayor also began to let some of his anger show. He told reporters that Superintendent Conlisk had better be able to explain why he couldn't stop the looters. Rumors began to circulate that the Mayor was furious with the Police Department's handling of the riots and that the Mayor had blasted Conlisk at a cabinet meeting. There were rumors that when Daley and Quinn had helicoptered over the city Quinn had told Daley that the police hadn't adequately protected his firemen.[34]

One week after the riots had been quelled, the Mayor put all the rumors to rest by, in essence, verifying them. The Mayor, who had hated O. W. Wilson's kid gloves handling of civil rights marchers and picketers, was disgusted by Superintendent Conlisk's "minimum force" approach to the riots. In a rush of words, with his syntax careening around heartfelt beliefs, the Mayor told the people what he felt. He condemned Conlisk and the rank-and-file police for being too soft on the rioters. He stated that he personally had issued orders to the Police Department outlining new tough measures for riot control.

> I have conferred with the superintendent of police this
> morning and I gave him the following instructions which I
> thought were instructions on the night of the Fifth that
> were not carried out:
> I said to him very emphatically and very definitely that
> an order be issued by him immediately and under his signa-
> ture to shoot to kill any arsonist or anyone with a Molotov
> cocktail in his hand in Chicago because they're potential
> murderers, and to issue a police order to shoot to maim or
> cripple anyone looting any stores in our city. Above all, the
> crime of arson is to me the most hideous and worst crime of
> any and should be dealt with in this fashion.
> I was disappointed to know that every policeman out
> on the beat was supposed to use his own decision and
> this decision was his [Conlisk's]. In my opinion, police-
> men should have had instructions to shoot arsonists and
> looters—arsonists to kill and looters to maim and
> detain. . . .
> I assumed any superintendent would issue instructions
> to shoot arsonists on sight and to maim the looters, but I
> found out this morning this wasn't so and therefore gave
> him [Conlisk] specific instructions.[35]

The Mayor didn't stop there. In his own, indirect way, he attacked the black schoolchildren who'd set off the west side rioting: "The conditions of April 5th in the schools were indescribable. The beating of girls, the slashing of teachers and the general turmoil and the payoffs and the extortions. We have to face up to this situation with discipline."[36] If the black people could not discipline themselves then the Mayor would do what was necessary with the full weight of the forces of law and order.

The next day, the *Tribune* praised the Mayor's resolve. The president of the Fraternal Order of Police sent a telegram expressing "our deepest respect and admiration." The Mayor's office reported that they had received ten thousand letters and one thousand telegrams and that by a fifteen to one ratio the people approved of the Mayor's speech.[37]

There were, of course, some who protested against the "shoot to kill" order. U.S. Attorney General Ramsey Clark, the ACLU, the conservative City Club of Chicago, a host of church leaders, and even some of the city's traditional black leaders attacked the Mayor's order as barbaric, illegal, and racist.[38]

By the next day, his political acumen overcoming his anger, the Mayor began to back away from his statement. The first thing he did was to complain to reporters that he had been misquoted: "There wasn't any shoot to kill order. That was a fabrication."[39] But the Mayor had spoken in front of the cameras and the "shoot to kill . . . shoot to maim or cripple" order was there for all to see.

So the next day, in the City Council, the Mayor gave a speech announcing the city's observance of Law Day on May 1. He used the speech to reformulate his remarks. First, he softened his attack on the Police Department policy of "minimum force" and then he reworded his "shoot to kill" order:

> Certainly an officer should do everything in his power to make an arrest to prevent a crime by utilizing minimum force necessary. But I cannot believe that any citizen would hold that policemen should permit an arsonist to carry out his dangerous, murderous mission when minimum force necessary cannot prevent or deter him. Nor do I believe that any citizen supports the theory that in times of riot and chaos any person has the right to willfully and maliciously throw a brick through a store window . . . encourage mob behavior and urge persons to become burglars and thieves. . . . Again, that such a person should be restrained if possible by minimum force necessary—but he cannot be given permissive rights for his criminal action.[40]

No longer was the Mayor demanding that police shoot to maim a fifteen-year-old boy running down the street with a radio in his hands. Few policemen, familiar as they were with violent crime, could live with such a policy. But they very much could learn to live with the Mayor's suggestion that the O. W. Wilson policy of minimum force—never very well observed on a day-to-day basis anyway—need no longer be strictly observed in tense or riotious conditions. That was a welcome message.

The City Council did their part in strengthening the police officers' ability to stop riots before they got out of control. April 11, they passed new disorderly conduct, trespass and resisting arrest ordinances, all of which gave the police far more leeway in making arrests. Among other things, the new ordinances made it illegal to "make any unreasonable or offensive act, utterance, gesture or display which . . . creates a clear and present danger of a breach of peace." Superintendent Conlisk made sure that the rank and file got the message—the new ordinances were read at roll call four days in a row.[41]

The same day the city passed its new ordinances, President Johnson signed a bill that gave the forces of law and order a major new weapon for their war on the riot agitators. The new antiriot law brought almost all civil disturbances under federal law. Most important, the new laws created a new federal crime, conspiracy to cause a riot. Though somewhat vague, the new law did make it clear that anyone stating that people had a right to riot, or who taught people how to make molotov cocktails or techniques capable of causing injury as well as more direct planning of a riot could be charged under this law. Senator Strom Thurmond of South Carolina, one of a group of southern senators who sponsored the riot provisions, stated in the Senate: "The government must be empowered to deal firmly and actively with those harbingers of anarchy." Congressman O. C. Fisher of Texas made it clear whom the bill was aimed at stopping: "The enactment of this bill would cramp the style and make subject to criminal prosecution the Stokely Carmichaels, the Martin Luther Kings, the Floyd McKissicks and others of their kind who preach anarchy or disobedience to the law."

The nation's top law enforcement officer, Attorney General Ramsey Clark, a most reluctant warrior in the "law and order" battles, opposed the bill. He asserted that riots were local, not federal concerns, and that "government has an absolute duty to do what it can to enlarge the opportunities of its people to speak, and a bill like this does just the opposite. . . . It makes it exceedingly dangerous." But Clark's boss, fellow Texan Lyndon Johnson, closer to the pulse of the people, disagreed. He signed the bill, which provided penalties of up to five years in jail and a fine of up to ten thousand dollars—the same penalties provided in the anti–draft card burning bill LBJ had signed into law less than three years earlier—for conspiring to cause a riot.[42]

Back in Chicago, Superintendent Conlisk, in direct reaction to the riots, quickly made and implemented policy to equip every police officer with a riot helmet and a personal aerosol tear-gas dispenser. He also put a shotgun in every police car. He also ordered the immediate purchase of more tear gas and gas masks. The intelligence unit was rewarded for their fingering of the Black Power arsonists by being given more money to buy more photo supplies. Conlisk's purchases put the department two hundred thousand dollars over their equipment and supplies budget. But no one protested.[43]

If Conlisk and the police rank and file came out of the riots without the Mayor's full approval, the police intelligence unit emerged very well indeed. The *Tribune* did a special feature on the unit's undercover operatives who infiltrated subversive organizations in the city. The *Trib* called the men "unsung heroes."[44] And it's very likely that the Mayor, too, was extremely pleased by the work they did in implicating the five Black Power advocates in the west side fire bombings.

The intelligence unit had a long history of keeping an eye on the city's dissidents. Known to everybody as the "Red Squad," it was started in the 1920s to spy on union organizers. After World War II, its purview was enlarged, allowing it to hunt down Communists wherever they could be found. By the 1960s, the unit divided its attention between black organizations like the Woodlawn Organization and the Black Panthers and the expanding forces of the "communist" left, which included groups like the American Civil Liberties Union and the Communist party. A good deal of the Red Squad's energies was spent on taking pictures of individuals going in and out of a great variety of meetings and of infiltrating black and "communist" or "communist front" groups; all this "in search of conspiracies to disrupt the city."

Since the mid-sixties the Red Squad had been increasingly concerned with the antiwar activists and New Left organizers operating in the city. They began to carefully monitor their activities and to do what they could to minimize their impact on the citizens of Chicago.[45]

Starting in the spring of 1965, they began to harass SDS's Chicago community organizing project, the so-called Jobs or Income Now (JOIN), that was creating trouble by organizing tenants and complaining about police brutality in Uptown, a poor white neighborhood. None of the JOIN agitators were indigenous to the neighborhood. To make life difficult for the outside agitators, the Red Squad set up a police raid on the JOIN office and the apartment where many of the agitators lived. The police ripped through the office and apartment, destroying office machinery and furniture. During the raid they planted narcotics and hypodermic needles and then hauled the agitators in. No drug convictions were gained in these operations—the cases were thrown out of court—but they let the neighborhood knew how much trouble you could find yourself in if you belonged to a "subversive" organization.

The Red Squad also kept a close eye on antiwar activists. And by carefully monitoring their activities, Red Squad officers were able, at various times, to arrest several activists for disturbing the peace, criminal trespass, littering, and disorderly conduct. One night, in September 1967, in order to increase their understanding of antiwar activities in the city, the Red Squad burglarized the offices of the Chicago Peace Council, Women for Peace, and the Fellowship for Reconciliation. They took mailing lists, files, typewriters, mimeo machines, and money. To throw the dissidents off their scent and in order to spread racial discord, the operatives wrote "Black Power" and "You're next Rosen" (John Rosen, an ex-Communist, owned the building at 1608 West Madison that housed the activists) on the walls. The mailing lists and files kept the unit abreast of the antiwar activists' plans and strength.[46]

By late fall of 1967, the intelligence unit knew that with the convention in Chicago they had to increase their monitoring of the antiwar activists. They got lucky. They found a perfect undercover agent in Irving Bock, a resourceful police recruit fresh from nine years in the navy. At police request, he joined Veterans for Peace and became a full time antiwar activist. Bock was good, and in a few weeks he became the Vets for Peace representative on the Executive Board of the Chicago Peace Council. He was privy to much of the leading antiwar activists' convention plans.[47]

By the middle of the winter, the unit was also able to get good information from a young police officer who masqueraded as a college student. The young officer became a member of the Northeastern Illinois State College Peace Council, the Student Mobilization Committee, SDS, and a Mobe volunteer. Though not high up in any of these organizations, he was, due to the New Left's open meeting practices, able to give the unit good reports.[48]

The Red Squad also served as the city's main conduit for FBI and other security agency reports on subversives' plans to disrupt the convention. Across the country, the FBI had informants attending most every antiwar and Chicago planning meeting.[49] By March 21, the FBI agent in charge of assessing the Chicago situation was able to report to J. Edgar Hoover that the SDS, Communist party, and Mobilization to End the War planned a "massive demonstration . . . [which] will represent a substantial threat to the national security." Hoover, in a March 22 memo to Attorney General Ramsey Clark, requested, for the second time, wiretaps on the Mobilization offices in Chicago—the FBI was already wiretapping Hayden, Rubin, Dellinger, and several other Chicago planners. Hoover informed Clark that two to five hundred thousand demonstrators would be in Chicago "with the objective of disrupting the Convention and forcing the government to utilize Federal troops to contain the demonstrators."[50]

Attorney General Clark, however, continued to maintain an unprecedented narrow interpretation of wiretapping laws, and the FBI was not able to do the kind of surveillance of the Mobe J. Edgar Hoover believed he needed to insure American security. Nonetheless, the FBI passed on what information it had to Chicago's intelligence unit. In April, an FBI agent was able to inform the unit that Communist party members and supporters were planning massive protests to disrupt the Democratic convention. He warned, "The New Left wants publicity and will go to any length to get it. They want to discredit law enforcement and have demonstrated ability."[51] The Red Squad passed the information along to the Convention Planning Committee and to the Mayor's office.

Besides the information garnered from the FBI and their own intelligence unit, the city saw other sinister signs of Mobe activity in Chicago. Bail money for Fats Crawford and the other Black Power advocates, who had been arrested for their part in organizing the arson during the King riots, was provided by Lucy Montgomery, a well-to-do Lake Shore Drive liberal. Montgomery, under the guidance of Rennie Davis, was helping to finance Mobe activities in Chicago. Richard Elrod, who'd been overseeing arrest procedures during the riot, added one and one together and came up with the obvious: the Mobe and the Black Power advocates had, as he put it later, "gotten together." He and other city officials feared that the April riots were only a prelude to the convention disruption.[52] This was the Mayor's darkest nightmare.

If that wasn't bad enough, by this time the city also had to contend with the Yippies, a group of New York and local hippies led by a known Communist, Jerry Rubin. Intelligence reports indicated that the Yippies were far less worrisome than the antiwar activists and the Black Power advocates but they did represent a problem.

Deputy Mayor David Stahl had met a delegation of the Yippies on March 26 and had requested the Chicago Youth Commission to find somebody who knew something about hippies to keep an eye on the Yippies.[53] The commission came up with Al Baugher, who worked with black youths under the auspices of the Community Organizing Division of the Chicago Youth Commission. Baugher was serious about his work. To understand the hippies, he wrangled a trip to San Francisco where he learned about the hippies' venereal disease problem, drug usage, and high crime rate. For Baugher, the hippies were "interesting, foolish, lovable and disgusting." Of course, in terms of the city, it didn't matter what Baugher—a total outsider—thought of the hippies because nobody higher up asked him his opinion about anything to do with the Yippies. Still, Baugher was useful.

Over the next few months, he spoke with the members of Free City, the local Yippie group, on a regular basis. He did his best to convince them of what they really knew, that they had very little in common with the violent, revolutionary politics of Jerry Rubin and Abbie Hoffman. It is probable that he let the locals know what the city had already decided, that there would be no deals with Jerry Rubin, whom intelligence reports revealed as a dangerous revolutionary dedicated to disrupting the convention.[54]

By late April, the Mayor had pretty much worked out his response to all the protesters. The city would not cooperate. Earl Bush, who had been the Mayor's press secretary for as long as the Mayor had been the Mayor, said the plan was simple: "Our idea was to discourage the hippies from coming."[55] More specifically, the Mayor's strategy, according to Earl Bush, "was not to give a staging ground" to the protesters. There would be no park permits. As Bush said, why should the city tell "people from outside of Chicago . . . [that] you can come to Chicago, plop on the ground, and you'll be taken care of?"[56] As the Mayor saw it, there was no reason in the world for the city to be accommodating to outside agitators whose sole purpose in coming to Chicago was to disrupt the city and its convention.

The city demonstrated its resolve when a group of local peace protesters demanded that the city give them permits to hold an antiwar march and rally in the Loop on April 27. The city refused to cooperate. William McFetridge, president of the Park District and a longtime intimate of the Mayor, announced that it was Park District policy to "keep unpatriotic groups and race agitators from using the parks."[57] The Department of Streets and Sanitation, which controlled parade permits, stated that because there already was another parade—a loyalty march—scheduled for the same day the protesters could not march. Finally, the Public Building Commission, which was in charge of the Civic Center plaza, the marchers' end point, stated that construction made it impossible for the marchers to use the plaza for their activities. But the marchers brought a lawsuit and forced the city to make a compromise: the protesters could have a rally in Grant Park, march on the sidewalks, walk around the Civic Center, but then must disperse.

But, of course, the demonstrators refused to play by the carefully spelled-out rules. The march went fine but when the protesters reached the Civic Center plaza they began to congregate. Some of them broke through a restraining rope onto the part of the plaza that was under repair.

The police officers on the scene then made it clear that they had heard the message the Mayor had given them after the King riots. Rather than wait for agitators to make real trouble, the police, under the command of Deputy Superintendent James Rochford, ordered the marchers to disperse immediately.

Rochford, who was to command field operations during the convention, was a total police professional. He was in his twenty-third year on the force and had done well under the reform administration of O. W. Wilson. But like many of the police, Rochford was an army veteran and had little stomach for the antiwar protesters. As he said later in the year, "American boys are dying over there every day," and he just could not agree that the demonstrators were right in their actions.[58] His superior, Superintendent Conlisk, felt the same way. Indeed, earlier in the day, the superintendent was on the reviewing stand for the city's loyalty march. And when a VFW banner went by reading, "We will pay for a one way ticket to Red China or Russia for any draft card burner or draft dodger," Conlisk had applauded vigorously.[59]

Immediately after several police ordered the crowd to disperse, most of the five hundred or so riot-helmeted officers began to move the crowd, many using their clubs. However, because the police were not trained like soldiers to operate as a unit, but were instead used to operating on their own initiative, their efforts to move the crowd were not very well organized. Indeed, the police came at the packed crowd of marchers from every direction and provided no clear means of egress. The police did, however, back up their hard-to-follow order to disperse with some old-fashioned firmness. By using their newly acquired Mace and their clubs, in a matter of minutes the police had most of the large crowd running in every direction. During the confrontation, several of the demonstrators tried to spit on the police and one female demonstrator succeeded in hitting Police Captain Michael Riordan with a picket sign. Several police responded to the provocations and to the general provocation the antiwar protesters represented by their very presence by using their Mace, clubs, and street-fighting tactics in a retaliatory manner. In order to forestall the protesters' usual claims of police brutality, some policemen removed their badges and nameplates during the fracas. Other police confiscated film from protesters' cameras.[60]

Only three days before the Police Department display of firmness and resolve, Mayor Daley had been doing his own bit of postriot recovering. As had been scheduled in January, President Johnson flew into Chicago as the Mayor's "surprise guest" for the Cook County Democratic party fundraising dinner held at the Conrad Hilton. Before four thousand party members and supporters, all of whom had paid one hundred dollars to be there, the president praised the Mayor and the Democratic party. Though there were seven or eight hundred protesters outside the hotel— the president rarely had less—as Mayor Daley had promised, security was so tight and effective the hecklers never even glimpsed the president as he was whisked in and out of the Hilton.[61]

Over the next month, the police continued their preparations. The intelligence unit was in contact with their counterparts in New York and were getting good information on the Yippies' anarchistic behavior. They were told that the Yippies would confront the city with everything from "long distance conga lines" and "flying pigeons" to "petty thievery" and "defacing public property."[62] The department was also collecting Yippie threats against the city.

As Deputy Superintendent Rochford said later, the department knew that most Yippie threats were just "put-ons." Still, he and his fellow officers believed that to be totally safe every threat had to be checked out.[63] So in late May, when the department learned that the Yippies threatened to dose the city's water supply with LSD, they checked it out.

A police lieutenant was assigned to contact the commissioner of water and sewers, inform him of the situation, and get sufficient information to protect the city's water. Even after Commissioner Jardine ascertained that it would take five tons of LSD—enough LSD to make nine billion tabs—to effectively contaminate the water, the police continued to guard pumping stations and the filtration plants. To the police, there just wasn't anything funny about threatening the people of Chicago with a dangerous narcotic.[64]

Most of the news during the early spring, however, was good. Intelligence reports indicated that the Chicago protest plans were in disarray. By late May, the city was even hoping that there would be no protests. May 23, an aide reported to President Johnson that party Chairman John Bailey, who was in close contact with Mayor Daley, "is optimistic and expects none of the major groups that originally planned demonstrations to go through with them, but precautions will be taken. [He says] those attending the convention will leave Chicago remembering it as a friendly city."[65]

Just when everything seemed to be going right for the city, Robert Kennedy was assassinated. The Mayor was hit hard by the tragedy, but for a variety of reasons he had not supported Bobby the way he had Jack. By the Mayor's logic, Kennedy should not have challenged the incumbent Democratic president; it was unloyal. As Kennedy himself said, Daley "has been a politician for a long time. And party allegiance means so much to him. It's a wrenching thing for him." For the Mayor, Bobby's refusal to wait his turn for the party's nomination felt like a betrayal of the party politics to which the Mayor had dedicated his life.

On the bottom line, Kennedy's death seemed to make Humphrey's nomination a sure thing. Even before Kennedy's death, Humphrey, without entering a single primary, had been fast moving toward a first-ballot victory. With Kennedy out of it, few in the know doubted that the vice-president had the whole thing sewed up. Still, the Mayor played it close to the chest and refused to come out foursquare behind Humphrey. He was not very excited by a Humphrey ticket and, by waiting, he hoped to have more say over the second place on the ticket. It also gave him an out if something better came along.[66]

Kennedy's death also, intelligence reports indicated, revitalized the antiwar movement's plans to march on Chicago. This news, combined with increased Secret Service fears about the safety of other presidential aspirants, rekindled the city's drive to insure that the convention would not be disrupted and that all participants in it would be free from attack.

On June 19, Mayor Daley called in Brigadier General Richard T. Dunn, head of the Illinois National Guard. The Mayor wanted to know how he could get the Guard in Chicago before and not after violence erupted. How could he avoid, in other words, a repeat of the King riots situation?

Dunn laid out three possibilities: call up the National Guard in advance of trouble, plan large-scale "training assemblies" in Chicago during the convention, call up the men as soon as trouble breaks out. Dunn recommended the advance call-up if trouble seemed likely and the "training assembly" option if no trouble was expected. Either way, Dunn told the Mayor, the orders would have to come from the governor.

Dunn had been far from surprised that the Mayor had called him in to talk about mobilizing the Guard. Since March, by orders of the adjutant general of Illinois, the Guard had been preparing for convention duty. Dunn and his staff had been receiving weekly intelligence briefings and had been represented at the Police Department Convention Planning Committee. Urban riot duty, after all, had been since 1965 the central preoccupation of the Illinois National Guard which was trained and organized for it.

The Mayor, at this point, decided against an advance call-up of the Guard but did ask Dunn to begin planning for the "training assemblies." Dunn and his staff, working out of the Illinois National Guard Emergency Operations Headquarters (EOH) at the Chicago Avenue Armory (located just east of fashionable Michigan Avenue about a mile north of the Loop), began to plan. Dunn also made sure that his men would be prepared for Chicago.[67]

During the Guard's summer camp training, forty-four out of eighty-eight training hours were devoted to "disturbances and disorders" training (later, in weekend training, they would spend twenty hours in review). The guardsmen, working solely within their ten-man teams, each of which was closely supervised by an officer, practiced riot control formations. They were taught how to set up a "holding action," which, like the formations, was based on using the appearance of force to forestall the actual use of force. Deadly force, they were told, was to be used only if they were attacked. They were also told to leave all arrests to the police. Based on a military model, the guardsmen were taught to obey orders, not to make personal decisions and not to leave "the protection of . . . [their] team."[68]

Many of the guardsmen spent part of their summer training time in an elaborate role-playing drill designed to accustom them to the kind of activities they might expect in Chicago. The men were divided into two groups. One group dressed up as hippie demonstrators complete with long-haired wigs, ponchos, funny hats, picket signs, and other "hippie" paraphernalia. The other group played themselves. The "protesters" marched along chanting "We shall overcome," flashing peace signs, and using bullhorns to lead chants and insult the guardsmen. The weekend soldiers did a first-rate impression of their likely foes. Eventually, the marchers converged on a building labeled City Hall and began chanting "Bring out the Mayor." After a few minutes, someone came out role-playing Mayor Daley and announced—parodying the city's 1967 black policy—"We let you swim in our pools on the fourth of July." To this, one group of protesters threw a bucket of water on a group of guardsmen and began trying to break through the Guard formation. A fairly realistic melee ensued during which the guardsmen playing guardsmen practiced firm but controlled measures—such as, in formation, lowering their bayonets. They succeeded in restoring order.[69]

At approximately the same time, mid-July, the Justice Department also began to worry about the maintenance of order in Chicago. Attorney General Clark had been aware for several months of the convention protest plans. But until July, his only intervention into the Chicago affair had been to deny the FBI the right to wiretap the Mobe offices.

Attorney General Clark, as his lack of trust in J. Edgar Hoover's FBI indicates, did not march to the "law 'n order" tune. He held what had become by July 1968 extremely moderate and temperate views. He supported the Kerner Report and he had opposed the federal conspiracy to create a riot law. Clark believed that "the notion that you can control dissent by convicting a few of the most outspoken radicals is, you know, absurdly naive. . . . They're nothing but the most extreme manifestations of a very general unrest and turbulence."[70] Such views caused Clark to be regarded as soft on lawbreakers by a great many prominent politicians, including Richard Nixon, who made a regular practice of blasting Clark by name.[71]

Since 1966, the Justice Department had had a unit, the Community Relations Service, that specialized in intervening in local, potentially violent, usually racial, disputes. Senator Lyndon Johnson first introduced the legislation that eventually produced the service in 1959. At the time, Johnson explained his idea: "A conciliator [is] . . . worth his weight in gold. . . . I have a deep and abiding faith in the ability of people to solve any problem—as long as they are in communication."[72] The idea was that a federal government official or team of officials could, with cool heads and no allegiances to anything but the law, move into a troubled community, open up lines of communication, and help the locals settle their differences. In theory, Attorney General Clark liked the unit, but in practice he knew it was too small and underfunded to do much good—meaning it had too little leverage on uncooperative local office-holders. He also saw a problem in locating the unit in the Justice Department: "[It's] a little hard for the same hand to prosecute and conciliate."[73]

July 17, Roger Wilkins, head of the Community Relations Service, met with protest leader Rennie Davis, at Davis's request, in Chicago.[74] After the meeting, Wilkins sent Clark, his boss, a long memo outlining the problem in Chicago:

> No matter what we do, the Mobilization and other organizations cited above will indeed produce in Chicago tens of thousands of people who are hostile to the Democratic Party, to President Johnson, and to Vice-President Hubert Humphrey; that Rennie Davis is an honest, intelligent man who was being candid with me in our conversation; that large scale violence in Chicago at the time of the Convention would be a national disaster and a national disgrace; that such violence is possible and that our best chance of averting violence is to develop the closest possible working relationship between the Chicago authorities, the Democratic Party officials, federal officials and the Mobilization.
>
> I therefore recommend that the President and Vice President be appraised of the plans of the Mobilization, as we now know them at the earliest possible time. . . . That one of them or some one clearly acting in their behalf call Mayor Daley to appraise him of that point of view and that the Mayor be advised that I will be coming to Chicago next week to inform him of the Mobilization's plans and . . . to set up a continuing working relationship between the city officials and the Mobilization.[75]

Attorney General Clark liked and respected Roger Wilkins. But he did not call up the president and ask him to tell Mayor Daley how to run Chicago.

Someone did, however, set up a meeting between the Mayor and Wilkins. Wilkins went into the meeting hoping he could convince the Mayor that Rennie Davis was an honest and intelligent young man committed to a peaceful demonstration. Wilkins wanted to strengthen Davis's hand and thus insure that the peaceful elements at the protest would be able to maintain control.

The Mayor was gracious and cordial, at first. But when Wilkins began to describe the Mobe plans, the Mayor cut him off and said quite simply that the city of Chicago would take care of the city of Chicago. There would be no lawbreaking in Chicago, he said. And if there was any trouble it would come from outsiders, not from city residents. The Mayor then described how in Cleveland—and he had just talked with Mayor Carl Stokes—all the troubles during their recent difficulties were caused by outsiders and not Cleveland residents. He then excused Wilkins and his aides. The meeting lasted less than fifteen minutes.

Later, Wilkins reported that he and the Mayor did not have "a meeting of the minds. . . . I did not have the feeling that the Mayor understood the points I was trying to make. As a matter of fact, I did not have the opportunity to make all the points."

Before leaving Chicago, Wilkins talked with Tom Foran, the local U.S. attorney. He asked Foran, who'd be seeing the Mayor later, if he would try to talk to Daley about making some sort of compromise with the Mobe. But Foran, while polite, was a Daley man and was in fact closer to Daley's perspective on the protests than he was to the Justice Department's. He was not interested in telling the Mayor things he didn't believe in himself and knew were things the Mayor didn't want to hear. Wilkins left Chicago and did not come back.[76]

By this time, late July, the Mayor had a more serious problem on his mind than how to appease outside agitators. The International Brotherhood of Electrical Workers had been on strike in Chicago for better than a month and no end was in sight. Without some kind of settlement no new telephone service could be installed in the Amphitheater or the big Loop hotels, and no live television coverage of the convention could be provided. Since late June, the Mayor had been telling the Democratic National Committee that he'd have the strike settled "in a couple of days."[77] By late July, rumors were abounding that, without an immediate strike settlement, the convention would be moved to Miami. On July 22, party Chairman John Bailey flew into town to confer personally with Daley. After the meeting, Baily expressed his concern over the strike but insisted that the convention would be held in Chicago no matter what. The Mayor added that the convention was going to be held in Chicago "with or without television"; a remark that did not endear him to the networks.[78]

Behind the scenes, the Mayor was trying to settle the strike or at least to negotiate a deal. It was one of the things he did best and the DNC and the television networks knew it. Finally, at the end of July, with barely enough time to wire up the Amphitheater, Daley succeeded in working out a deal. The electrical workers, on a voluntary basis, would rig up the cables and other equipment inside the convention hall necessary for live television coverage of the Convention proceedings. The electrical workers would also allow Western Union to set up teletypes between the Amphitheater and the downtown hotels where the reporters and delegates would in the main be staying. The union would not, however, allow the microware relays necessary for live TV to be installed anywhere outside of the Amphitheater. If the networks wanted to cover demonstrations or backroom deal making in the Loop hotels, they'd have to use videotape or film. The film or tape would then have to be sent by courier to the broadcast facilities, processed, and then put on the air, a procedure that would cause delays of an hour or more depending on traffic and other uncontrollable delays.[79]

The networks did not like the deal at all. David Brinkley, the NBC nightly news and soon-to-be Convention anchorman, suggested that the arrangement was deliberately crafted by Mayor Daley to "greatly curtail" coverage of the convention.[80] After the convention, Earl Bush, the Mayor's loyal director of public relations, denied Brinkley's charge, calling it "nonsense." He also stated that the networks didn't need live cameras outside of the Amphitheater, that "live cameras are rarely used" for TV news.[81]

Over the next few weeks, however, Daley, the DNC, and the Chicago Police Department made a number of decisions that did seriously interfere with the networks' ability to cover the convention and the convention protests the way they wanted to do it. Especially galling to the networks were the decisions to reduce convention floor passes from the thirty-one they received in 1964 to seven in 1968 and to ban network television mobile units outside of the major hotels.[82] Richard Salant, president of CBS, said all of the actions formed "a pattern well beyond simply labor disputes, logistics and security problems."[83] Of course, he was right. But in the eyes of the Mayor and many other leading politicians, he was right only if you accepted the fact that the networks had the right to cover the convention any way they wanted.

The networks first started televising gavel-to-gavel coverage of the national conventions in 1952. By 1956, the politicians had begun to get angry about how they were being made to look. The networks did not simply follow the proceedings; they cut away from the podium to reporters on the convention floor or to the anchor booths or to commercials whenever they wanted. They decided for the American people what in the parties' proceedings was worth listening to and what wasn't. And, some politicans insisted, instead of letting the American people decide for themselves what was happening, the TV men hunted down every little rumor they could find and turned them into major stories. Television crews roamed the convention floor and delegate hotels with, some politicians believed, impunity, and tried to make what were by necessity private, political conversations into public spectacles. The networks, many politicians thought, were doing their best to turn the business of politics into show business. Mayor Daley and a number of other Democratic officials thought it was about time that the elected officials put some controls on the unelected newsmakers. Many Americans felt the same way.[84]

While Daley and the DNC were wrangling with the networks, the Police Department and the other security forces were implementing their final convention preparations. Officially, Robert Burke of the Secret Service was coordinator of all security and, indeed, he did have final say.[85] But, in general, it was up to the police to plan and implement security measures.

The police intelligence unit had a major role in these measures. More than a month before the convention, police in the unit began preventative surveillance of almost every important black leader in the city. There was nothing subtle about the surveillance; the whole idea was to let the blacks know they were being carefully watched. The city knew by this time that local and national black leadership was not interested in the antiwar, Mobilization-led protests. Still, one of the city's biggest fears was that the white protesters would be able to spark "spontaneous disorders" in the black communities. By putting the heat on the black leadership, police intelligence figured they could give influential blacks just a little more reason to keep clear of the protests and to use their influence in keeping things cool during Convention week. The intelligence unit also kept tabs and kept up the pressure on the white protest leaders by tailing them whenever they were in the city. Combined with the intelligence they were getting from their undercover agents and FBI reports, the police felt they had a good idea of what to expect from the protest mobs.[86]

At the Amphitheater, in the year of the assassinations, every effort was being made to provide airtight security. A barbed wire fence 2136 feet long was erected around the Amphitheater parking lot and every manhole cover in the area was tarred shut or watched. Elaborate credentials were prepared and special credential checking machines were installed. Aircraft were banned from flying under 2500 feet in a five-mile radius around the convention hall. Roadblocks were to be deployed to limit access to an area several blocks wide and long. Hundreds of police would patrol the area, dozens would be on the convention floor in plainclothes. Next door to the convention hall, the police and other security forces would operate out of an elaborate headquarters which included sophisticated radio equipment supplied by the army, hot lines to the White House and the Pentagon, and an eight-foot by twelve-foot magnetic map of the city, complete with a zoom lens television camera for closeups, that could show where every police officer and other security force was located at all times.[87]

The city was not going to be taken by surprise. If, somehow, the professional agitators were able to ignite Chicago's blacks, an overwhelming force would be on hand to stop the rioters. Unlike April, the national forces of security and order were to be mobilized before any troubles began. The U.S. army had 7500 men at Ford Hood in Texas go through an exercise, similar to the one engaged in by the National Guard at Camp Riley, called Operation Jackson Park. The soldiers divided into rioters and riot control troops and worked on strategies of containment. Jackson Park is located in a black area of the south side of Chicago and the army indicated by the title of the operation what the soldiers' likely mission was to be—to stop black riots. A group of forty-three black soldiers responded to Operation Jackson Park by announcing that they would not go to Chicago to put down ghetto rioters. They were arrested. Preparations were made for the troops to be deployed outside of Chicago before the convention began. By having the troops on hand, the city hoped that the agitators interested in sparking trouble, as well as their potential audience, would be fully intimidated.[88]

In mid-August, Daley, the governor of Illinois, and the Pentagon generals in charge of civil disorders planning decided to mobilize the National Guard a week before the convention. In part, the decision to mobilize early was mandated by legal requirements; in order to use the army in Chicago, the Illinois National Guard first had to be mobilized. But more important, Mayor Daley had simply decided to use all possible security measures to insure a safe and orderly convention. When he announced the advance mobilization of August 20—which had been decided in secret a few days earlier—the Mayor said, "[An] ounce of prevention is worth a pound of cure. . . . This is a precautionary measure." Then, picking at an old scab, he joked, "We don't anticipate or expect [trouble] unless certain commentators and columnists cause trouble."[89] The Mayor had put together a security force of approximately forty thousand armed men—enough, he believed, to keep a lid on any troublemakers.

To sometimes hostile questions from the mass media about the city's failure to provide the protesters with permits, the Mayor maintained: "We are talking to the hippies, the Yippies, and the flippies and everything else. . . . We are talking to the newspapers and some of them are hippies and Yippies. And to the TV and radio, and a lot of them, I guess, are the leaders in these movements."[90] He was kidding on the square. The Mayor was feeling good; these were ugly times but he was doing everything possible to insure that the city was under control.

Publicly, the Mayor stated he would welcome all "reasonable" protests at "reasonable hours." And he told the press, "It is only fitting that during this dynamic democratic process there is present in our city a cross section . . . liberal, moderates, conservative and radical . . . hippie and square. . . . This is the way it should be."[91] But privately, the Mayor had no intention of allowing disruptive elements to participate in the convention process.

By early August, city officials were talking with the antiwar protest leaders but they did so not so much in hopes of reaching agreement as they did in hopes of hearing what the protesters intended to do. The city's position was the same as it had always been.[92] As the Mayor put it on August 16, "People in Chicago behave themselves. It is only some people who might come to the Convention from outside Chicago that might bring trouble."[93] These outsiders, the Mayor and his people believed, had no right to interfere with the right of Chicago's citizens to enjoy a safe and orderly community. That was fact number one.

The Mayor was kept more or less abreast of the negotiating sessions but, in the main, he let his subordinates take care of business. As Tom Barry, acting superintendent of the Park District later said, it was not necessary for the Mayor to issue directives or supervise the negotiations since "the Mayor knew me and I knew what the Mayor wanted."[94]

What the Mayor wanted in late August was the same as what he always wanted: that there would "be no trouble in Chicago."[95] City Corporation Counsel Raymond Simon, who did most of the real negotiating with the protesters, explained, "They [city government] were striving as hard as they could and in as deep earnestness as they could to have it be orderly in the city. They didn't want another Robert Kennedy assassination here [or] . . . have a young girl supporter of Senator McCarthy killed."[96] Or, he could have added, another ghetto riot.

For almost eight months, as Corporation Counsel Simon later reported, "We had been reading intelligence reports about the tremendous combat that was going to happen to Chicago, that there would be the battle of the century."[97]

Police intelligence was reporting that the Black Panther party, a violent revolutionary group, was planning "the creation of incidents in Negro area and involvement of white policemen to initiate complaints of police brutality . . . to employ the use of incendiary devices, to employ prostitutes to solicit delegates." The report stated that Chicago Project Director Tom Hayden was directly linked to these plans.[98]

The FBI had proof that the same Tom Hayden was going around the country telling people they should be prepared to shed blood and be arrested in Chicago.[99] Police agent Bock had heard Rennie Davis tell people that Chicago would show the world that there would be war in the streets until there was peace in Vietnam and that the world would see that it took the entire police force and National Guard to protect the Democratic National Convention. Bock was also able to tell his superiors that the Mobe was planning to train 2500 marshals to be used in direct actions with the police.[100] Intelligence reports also indicated that the protesters were amassing huge medical and legal groups to assist them in their altercations with the police. Throughout August, police and FBI agents watched the protesters brazenly practicing karate, snake dancing, and other offensive, violent maneuvers. Bock was able to identify several known Communist party members in leadership roles in these various preparations. Reports came in from all directions stating that the protesters would block the expressways, dose the city's water with LSD, storm the Amphitheater, set fires, vandalize buildings, invade the Loop hotels, jam key city streets, and pour into Loop department stores.

The city, in early August was being told by the Mobe leaders that they had better be ready to deal with two or three hundred thousand protesters. The city was also told that the protest would take place with or without legal permits; the protesters were quite prepared to break the law. Yippie leaders made it perfectly clear that they were "prepared to tear up the town and convention" and even "to die in Lincoln Park."[101]

Less than a week before the convention was to begin, the most feared of all reports was brought to the Mayor's attention. Three inmates of the Cook County jail stated that members of the Blackstone Rangers, Chicago's largest street gang, had been hired by revolutionaries to assassinate the Democratic presidential candidates, Mayor Daley, and perhaps others. Although the inmates did not pass polygraph tests, a grand jury was immediately formed to investigate the allegations. Although no proof was found, and although the FBI declared the whole thing to be just "loose talk or braggadocio," the police made sure that the leaders of the Rangers found it convenient to be out of town convention week. There had been no substantiation of the inmates' allegations but still—Kennedy had been killed only two-and-a-half months earlier.[102]

Besides such threats and reports of planned violence and disruption, the Mayor and his people had to react to the black riots that had occurred in Miami during the Republican convention. Although the riots occurred over ten miles from the convention hall and were not directly linked to it, the fact that three blacks had been killed by the police, forty-eight wounded, and two hundred and twenty-two arrested was a foreboding sign of what Chicago's blacks might do.[103] More concretely, the city was also rocked by a last-minute taxi strike which idled 75% of the city's cabs.[104] The strike created a wealth of transportation problems and made delegates all the more vulnerable to attacks of all kinds.

The city's rank-and-file police officers paid close attention to all of these well-publicized threats and dangers. Well in advance of the convention, they knew that convention week they would be putting in twelve-hour-plus shifts. Members of the task force knew that they would be riding three to four men to a car in anticipation of danger. At roll call,

August 21, 22, and 23, every police officer was instructed in the use of the gas mask. August 22, Superintendent Conlisk issued Special Order 68-48 which outlined "motion picture documentation of demonstrators and civil disorders," procedures that would insure that good evidence would be available for the expected slew of court cases. The same day, General Order 68-13 was put into effect outlining the use of aerosol tear gas weapons (Mace and Federal Streamer); weapons that caused an intense burning sensation and temporary blindness when sprayed in or near the eyes. The order stated that the sprays, with which all police had been hurriedly outfitted, were to be used only when physical force was necessary.[105]

Shortly before the convention, the rank and file were cheered by strong backing from the Mayor. Openly and loudly he came out foursquare against an ACLU-sponsored report that criticized police handling of the April 27 peace march. The Mayor blasted the report as "not true" and announced that he was "just sort of amazed [at] the constant efforts of these people [peace marchers] to confront the police department."[106]

Only days before the convention, the president of the Chicago Patrolman's Association told the press that the Chicago Police Department would not play the old game of looking the other way during a tense confrontation with rioting protesters. He concluded, "We feel that the insane tactics shown by some groups are getting out of hand. We want the public to know this and to back the policeman in this fight."[107]

Superintendent Conlisk knew that his men were anxious and angry about the upcoming struggles with an unknown number of assailants, some of whom, they were certain, would be armed and dangerous. August 21, in a special letter to all police personnel, Superintendent Conlisk, a solid professional, trained by the best police mind in the country, told the men what was at stake:

> The eyes of the nation and the world will be on our city
> and our Department. . . . Our skills, our dedication and our
> professionalism will be tested. . . . To a substantial
> degree it will be our actions that the rest of the world will
> judge Chicago and to some degree our nation itself. . . .
> We must be examples of courtesy and we must act with
> efficiency and assurance. And above all we must be confi-
> dent—confident about ourselves and about our leadership.
> . . . Day by day, year by year this Department has moved
> forward. All of us have shared in this progress. Now we
> face a test which will show the world our quality. We
> must continue to be constantly mindful of the welfare of
> others, never act officiously, and never permit personal
> feelings, prejudices or animosities to influence our deci-
> sions or our acts.[108]

The Mayor and his men had done what they could to control the protesters and to strengthen the Police Department's ability to maintain law and order. The Mayor had brought in the National Guard and the army to back up the police. He personally had convinced Senator McCarthy to ask his people to stay away from Chicago.[109] To protect the convention from disruption and to limit the number of demonstrators the city negotiators had refused to allow a march to the Amphitheater. At the same time, in an effort to be fair, the city had offered the protesters alternative sites for marches and rallies. But when the protesters refused the city's offers (except for accepting the use of the Grant Park bandshell on the 28th) and made a series of threats, the city refused to back down one inch. The city would not be threatened, its negotiators said. The city would not allow the protesters to disrupt Chicago's right to law and order.

Corporation Counsel Raymond Simon, who directed the city's protest policy the week before the convention, put the matter very simply: "What I am saying is you have got to be responsible when you are in charge of the government. You can't afford the luxury of the liberalism of saying: 'Be more and more permissive.' "[110] The Mayor would not compromise the safety of his citizens or their right to public order. He would not allow a mob of unruly and disrespectful outsiders to come to the city of Chicago and make a violent mockery of the National Democratic Presidential Nominating Convention. They had no right and they had no place in his city.

In August 1968, the year of the assassinations, the Columbia University uprising, the ghetto riots, massive civil disobedience and increasingly violent antiwar protests, the city of Chicago, speaking in the name of law and order, said: Enough.

7 The Streets Belong to the People

> Callias, I said, if your sons had been colts or calves, we should have no difficulty in finding and engaging a trainer to perfect their natural qualities, and this trainer would have been some sort of horse dealer or agriculturalist. But seeing that they are human beings, whom do you intend to get as their instructor? Who is the expert in perfecting the human and social qualities?
>
> Socrates, "Apology"

On August 20, Soviet troops ended the Prague spring. Czechoslovakia's experiment with freedom was over. A few young Czechs challenged the tanks that rolled down their streets. Several of them were killed.

The same day, in Washington, D.C., the Democratic Party Platform Committee hardened in their opposition to any criticism of President Johnson's Vietnam policy. When the committee reconvened in Chicago two days later, they passed, with Hubert Humphrey's blessings, a pro-Johnson, anti-McCarthy Vietnam platform plank. Humphrey had the nomination sewed up.[1] (A Gallup poll released a few days later showed that 53% of adult Americans thought that sending troops to Vietnam was a mistake; two years earlier, only 25% had thought so.)[2]

In Chicago, the week before the convention and the protest were to formally begin, Mobe and Yippie stalwarts braced for what they knew was going to be a dangerous confrontation. They had lost all of their court fights. The protests would go on without legal permits. A marshal trainer, in from Los Angeles, wrote to his girlfriend: "I realize at this time that there are very good chances that I may be injured or arrested because I am here. . . . I believe that I along with many thousands more will be stopped from demonstrating our opposition to the war."[3]

Very early Thursday morning, August 22, a few blocks from Lincoln Park, two policemen stopped two long-haired teenagers for curfew violation. One of the boys, Dean Johnson, a seventeen-year-old runaway/drifter from South Dakota, seemingly in town either for the Festival of Life or the protests, drew a handgun. According to the police, he pulled the trigger but the gun misfired. They shot him three times and he died.[4]

Abbie Hoffman and some of the other Yips were in the *Seed* office, not far from Lincoln Park, entertaining some CBS newsmen, when they got word of the shooting. Hoffman was appalled and raged around the office shouting, "Don't let them kill no more people. We've got to stop them killing our people."[5] Keith Lampe and some of the *Seed* people decided to hold a funeral service for Johnson. Still at least two days before the protest crowds were due to arrive, it would be the first convention protest.

Lampe wanted to combine the Johnson service with a memorial for the Czech dead, and a Yippie flyer to that effect was handed out in Lincoln Park and Old Town. But Lampe, in search of allies, had also contacted Tom Neuman of the Lower East Side's SDS chapter—the Up Against the Wall Motherfuckers (many of whom were already in town for the protests). Neuman had opposed combining the two events, explaining that there were two diametrically opposed positions on the Czech question in SDS.

Lampe couldn't understand Neuman's reservations—to him the issue was old people killing young people. Nonetheless, at the service that night, Neuman and his people took over and ignored the Czechs. In Lincoln Park, to a small crowd of longhairs, SDSers, partying motorcycle gang members, and a host of security agents and mass media representatives, Neuman announced that Dean Johnson "died of pig poisoning . . . and the story [that Johnson pulled a gun] was probably written at one central office downtown. . . . We're suffering from pig poisoning and media poisoning." Several of the policemen in attendance found Neuman's constant usage of "pig" grimly amusing. Mockingly, they began calling each other "pig." It was not exactly the kind of protest Lampe had had in mind.[6]

By this time, the Yippies had set up shop in Lincoln Park. Through the good offices of a local theater person they had a parkside headquarters. In the park itself, they had established a "communications center"—a couple of folding tables—and had begun distributing hundreds of mimeographed flyers, including "A. Yippie's" eighteen-point program, the Yip map and program, and a request for "chicks who can type (and spell), cats who have wheels and want to do a digger trip to feed the masses." The Yips also gave out lists of the hotels in which the delegates were staying and maps of the International Amphitheater. The Yips scrawled across the maps, "Break in Break in Break in . . . Security precautions taken by Convention big wigs are a farce."[7]

While the Yippies and, to some extent, SDS began concentrating their energies on Lincoln Park, the Mobe was still working out of their downtown office trying to figure out what to do now that they had no march permit and no clear protest focal point. The same night that the Yips organized the Dean Johnson funeral service, the Mobe Steering Committee, project directors, and a few other key organizers met to discuss day-to-day tactical decision making. A leading marshal argued that the marshals should decide tactics; Davis and Hayden declared that they would make tactical decisions; Paul Potter, head organizer of the movement centers, suggested that a committee of movement center representatives and Mobe leaders should make consensual decisions. After much debate David Dellinger, chairman of the Mobe, said that he would make all tactical decisions after consulting with Davis and Hayden. But as to what the actual strategy of the Chicago protest would be, that was still undecided. Dellinger and the other Mobe organizers were still trying to figure out exactly what the city would and would not allow.[8]

Friday, with protesters easily outnumbered by reporters, Jerry Rubin and a band of Yips decided to cash in on the mass media's hunger for news by staging their own presidential nominating convention. Their candidate was Pigasus the pig and they decided to run him at the Chicago Civic Center plaza.

The original Pigasus was a California hog owned by the Hog Farm, a hippie theater group. But as with so many others, the Hog Farmers had canceled out at the last minute and Rubin and his friends had been forced to search the countryside for a farmer willing to sell them a suitable beast. Rubin wanted a real big, ugly pig.

At approximately 10 A.M., at the Civic Center, Rubin, Phil Ochs (who'd actually paid for the new pig), Stew Albert, Wolf Lowenthal, and a few other Yips jumped out of a small truck with Pigasus, a two-hundred-pound castrated hog. A crowd of television cameramen, press photographers and reporters who had been tipped off were there waiting. At almost the same moment, ten policemen led by a police commander converged on the scene. Minutes before Rubin and the police arrived, a long-haired man had gone up to a young woman spectator, given her a small brown paper bag and told her to give it to Jerry Rubin as soon as he arrived. The woman had looked in the bag, seen a large quantity of marijuana and hashish, and had immediately dropped the bag. Rubin, Pigasus and his friends, upon arrival, moved quickly into the crowd of newsmen and spectators. The police began shoving the crowd away from the Yippies. A policeman began shouting, "Get Rubin! Make sure we get Rubin." Rubin began a speech nominating Pigasus. The police grabbed him. He, Pigasus, and six others were arrested and charged with disturbing the peace. Pigasus was a mass media hit.[9]

There was a reason that Hoffman hadn't been at the pig bust. A few days earlier, he and Rubin had had a showdown on convention week tactics. Rubin had argued that during the convention he and Hoffman and the other leading Yips should fade into the crowd, allow the people to act collectively, and not allow the mass media to pay special attention to any single personality. Hoffman disagreed and felt that his personality and the other Yips' personalities were their weapons and a key part of Yippie theater and that it would be irresponsible to simply fade away into the crowds. Rubin accused Hoffman of letting Yippie become a personality cult. Hoffman belittled Rubin's "Marxist approach." In the heat of the preconvention tensions, the two men who'd been working together on a daily basis for better than eight months began to call each other names. They cooled down after a while but decided to divide responsibilities and keep their distance in Chicago.[10]

Despite the feud, after Rubin and company's arrest, Hoffman and approximately twenty-five Yips mobilized to get their comrades out of jail. Abbie told a large group of newsmen that if the Yips couldn't get Pigasus out of jail (he was being held by the Chicago Humane Society) they would run a lion instead. Despite or because of all of this, Rubin and the others were released on twenty-five-dollars bond only a few hours after their arrests. Rubin's police tails went back to work, waiting for his next illegal activity.[11]

Shortly before Rubin and friends—but not Pigasus—were released, approximately twenty-five SDSers, led by Kathy Boudin, made their way to a CIA front in the Loop. In the presence of reporters they spray painted "CIA" and "CIA Sucks" on the wall outside of the office. The special convention issue of *Rat* listed one hundred such "targets" for symbolic attacks or delegitimizations. Still four days before the Chicago protest was to formally begin, Boudin and her comrades wanted to give the people an idea of how it could be done.[12]

While the protest vanguard began to flex its muscles, the rest of the Mobe spent the day trying to get organized. Fearful of a far smaller turnout than planned—already there were way too few people in town—the Steering Committee wrote a last-minute plea to Mobe supporters asking them to come to Chicago: "Dear Friend . . . Chicago is fast becoming the Prague of the middle west. We disagree with those who have urged their supporters to stay away because of the danger of violence. . . . We will not lose our democratic rights by default." The letter went on to announce a "mass people's assembly" on August 28 for which permits had been granted. It was hoped that people too afraid to come for protest actions where no permit had been granted would show up for the one permitted assembly.[13]

By August 23 the police too were trying to get organized. Super-
intendent Conlisk issued his final commands on area responsibilities.
He also formally opened up the Convention Command Center at the
Amphitheater.[14]

At a city park not far from the Amphitheater, also on the twenty-
third, a special platoon made up of tactical unit officers practiced riot
control formations and marching. Not too good at the marching, the
officers enjoyed themselves making up army-like marching cadences
like, "Captain Hines is leading us; he trained us to do our stuff." The
men were supposed to be learning how to work as a unit.[15]

Several miles away, in Lincoln Park, Commander Robert Lynsky set
up his command post in the Cultural Arts Center, which was just a
few hundred yards away from the Yippies' "communication center."
Lynsky had approximately four hundred police officers assigned to
his command, including several in plainclothes. Lynsky had also requested and received the services of several intelligence officers, whom
he hoped could photograph and point out protest leaders.[16]

Other security forces, too, were now making their final plans. Approximately 5600 National Guardsmen began mobilizing at armories
around the city at 8 A.M. on the twenty-third and immediately began
practicing their civil disturbance procedures. The soldiers were armed
with M-1 rifles, army carbines, shotguns, and tear gas. The Guardsmen were also equipped with gas masks and had limited access to
armored vests. To support the Guard in street actions, twenty-five
jeeps were equipped with concertina wire-cage fronts—the jeeps could
be used to stop and then move crowds.[17]

While the Guard made their very public preparations for the protests, America's intelligence agencies proceeded with their secret ones.
J. Edgar Hoover had made it very clear he believed that "it is absolutely essential that we utilize every means at our disposal to keep the
intelligence community advised of the day to day plans and activities
of these dissident groups."[18] Several hundred FBI agents were in
Chicago, spying on the protesters, aiding the Secret Service, and con-
tributing to convention security. Hoover had also arranged with President Johnson to provide Vice-President Humphrey with special
intelligence reports. Unlike 1964, however, when Hoover provided
President Johnson with the secret plans of Martin Luther King, Jr.,
and other civil rights leaders assembled at the convention to protest—
information gathered with the aid of electronic surveillance—the
information given to Humphrey would not be "political" but would
only warn of "extreme" or "violent" protest actions. Hoover was angry
because Johnson's attorney general would not let him bug the Mobe's
headquarters.[19]

Also present in strength, even before the convention formally began, was the Army Security Agency under the control of the U.S.
Army Intelligence Command (USAINTC). Beginning the week before
the convention, military intelligence teams began sophisticated electronic surveillance of demonstrators, McCarthy workers, and the air-
waves—in search of secret communications either from abroad or from
protest leaders to one another. Military intelligence also put a number
of undercover agents into the field; some were assigned to the ghettos,
others to the Loop and the parks. Some agents worked directly on
protecting the presidential candidates. In part, their presence in Chicago was due to the Secret Service's post–Kennedy assassination requests for help. But all of the information the military intelligence
agents gathered went directly to the Pentagon where it was routed to
the "Left Wing Desk" of the Office of the Assistant Chief of Staff
Intelligence (OACSI).[20]

By the time the convention began, there were approximately one
thousand federal agents in Chicago. By midweek, military intelligence
estimated that one in six demonstrators was an undercover government agent.[21]

Six A.M., Saturday morning, the police started full-strength, twenty-
four-hour surveillance of Lincoln Park. Commander Lynsky began
operations by talking to his men. He told them that he expected nothing less than professional conduct at all times, that it was their job to
preserve law and order and to protect lives and property. The convention would be a total success, he said, if there were no arrests, no
disorders, no incidents. He told the men to circulate through the park
and use loose surveillance to keep an eye on things. He warned them
not to try to make any arrests alone, that if they made an arrest they
would in all likelihood be subject to baiting. Avoid borderline arrests,
he concluded—when in doubt consult a superior or the corporation
counsels who would also be circulating through the park.[22]

Later in the day, the men were also warned that police intelligence
had reported that demonstrators had bought large quantities of oven
cleaner and ammonia to use as weapons. This news, in combination
with all the preconvention reports on potential violence and the likelihood that some demonstrators would be armed, had many of the
officers on edge.[23]

Despite police concern, Lincoln Park, the Saturday before the convention, was the scene of very little action. For several hours there
were more police than demonstrators.[24]

By late afternoon, however, there were approximately two thousand
people—many of them from the surrounding neighborhood—in the park.
Most of the people congregated in small groups, listened to each other

play guitars and bongo drums, danced, and shared food, drink, and drugs. The vast majority of the policemen spent the pleasant summer day wandering around idly and making small talk with the "hippy" girls.[25]

At around two o'clock, the Mobe's regular marshal training session began. In front of the crowds and police, the five or six dozen marshals practiced karate, snake dancing, and various crowd protection formations. For a short while, Abbie Hoffman led the enthusiastic group through some karate exercises. Barbara Britts, in charge of the Mobe's medical contingent, lectured on first aid. At one point during the training a police helicopter swooped down to get a close look at the action which precipitated a lot of arm waving and swearing but nothing else happened. While the marshals practiced, Yippie Brad Fox brought "Mrs. Pigasus" to Lincoln Park to plead for her husband's release—the Yippies had been released on bond but Pigasus had been put into the pound. Although he had been warned that releasing the pig in the park was a criminal offense, Fox let Mrs. Pigasus loose. After capturing the pig, Fox and the "Mrs." were arrested. The crowd that gathered around the incident did not respond to the arrest.[26]

Approximately three miles away, in the heart of the Loop, another peaceful protest went on most of the afternoon. Women for Peace, a moderate group of middle-class women, picketed the Conrad Hilton, where many delegates and Democratic party bigwigs were staying. There were only sixty or so women on the picket line. The police treated the picketers cordially and the ten Mobe marshals assigned to protect and help coordinate the picket were left with very little to do. Both the picketers and the marshals knew that something very wrong was happening. Hundred of picketers had been expected.[27]

Women for Peace had arranged to bring people by bus from several cities around the country to Chicago. But come the convention, the buses were empty. As the American Friends Service Committee—a strictly pacifist group—reported, "There was despair at how middle class peace people were being scared off." Without permits and with the threats of violence from both the radical protesters and the security forces, a good many moderates decided they could not participate in the Chicago protests.[28]

For Tom Hayden, such a turn of events was predictable. Hayden, in the first edition of the *Ramparts Wall Poster* (a two- to six-page newspaper put out daily during the convention week, sponsored by *Ramparts* and heavily influenced by Hayden), told those who had already shown up Saturday that in Chicago "the American reality is stripped to its essentials . . . a confrontation between a police state and a people's movement." Comparing the United States to Germany in the

1930s, Hayden added, "Our victory lies in progressively demystifying a false democracy." The lack of permits, the failure of the moderates to face the danger, all of it was for Hayden an acceptable stage in that struggle to "de-mystify."[29]

The SDS leadership, in their wall poster, *Handwriting on the Wall 1*, said the same basic thing Saturday: "The pigs on the street are talking about power, finally, because we've forced them to make that clear. Chicago has made that come down." SDS, too, noted that "our 'liberal base' has finked out big." Like Hayden, they celebrated the polarization: "The real strategy for Chicago has always been disruption." And while endorsing the idea of a multitactical protest, the SDS leadership specifically endorsed attacking "the nightclubs, the offices, the stores, the theaters and restaurants where the bourgeoisie live their lives."

Earlier in the day, before putting together the wall poster, the SDS organizers already in town, approximately one hundred, had met at their Lincoln Park movement center, the Church of Three Crosses. There, they had debated strategy for several hours. The first problem they faced was what to do about the Lincoln Park curfew. Before actually arriving in Chicago, SDS, like the Yippies and the Mobe, had said that the people's right to sleep in the city parks was basic and worth struggling for. However, once in Chicago and aware that the protesters simply didn't have the numbers to support a frontal confrontation, most of the organizers thought it would be stupid to try to stay in Lincoln Park after curfew and fight the police. Better, they decided, to fight elsewhere: "In parks, ain't no place to go. Can't fight battles on a grassy plain. No ammunition (unless you carry it)."

Leaving the park was not, however, simple retreatism. Before the curfew, the organizers would form affinity groups of four to five people—a tactic first used in Berkeley earlier in the year—and take to the streets. Once there, the SDS affinity groups would lead disruptive activities: stopping traffic, starting trash fires, breaking windows, stoning cops, or whatever. Specific tactics would have to emerge from the specific situation—"Got to be cool, fast, and see exactly what the situation is at every moment. No bullshit. This is a tight game. . . . Never Go Alone, Never Leave Someone Who's Been Spotted Alone."

Some thought the plan a little overheated. They wanted to stick to the preconvention plan which was to organize the McCarthy Kids. Others thought the street tactics were unrealistic and elitist. In the end, the organizers decided to pursue both street tactics and recruitment of the McCarthy Kids. All agreed that the most important thing they could do was to avoid going to jail and to lead people out of the park at curfew before the police stormed through it.[30]

Around the city, other demonstrators began to trickle into the movement centers set up in Hyde Park, the Loop, the near west side, and the north side. Approximately twenty-five centers were in operation Saturday, including the Radical Organizing Committee (the non–Old Left splinter of the Student Mobilizing Committee), Resistance (draft resisters), Vets for Peace, Concerned Clergy and Laity, Committee of Returned Volunteers (ex–Peace Corp volunteers), Womens' Peace Groups, New University Conference, Medical Contigent, and High School Students. Although the total number of people was far smaller than expected, many at the centers were still optimistic that they'd have enough people on hand to make a successful protest. However, lack of permits and the small turnout had most of the protesters still confused about what to do convention week.[31]

Midday, after a series of meetings with the Mobe Steering Committee and other demonstrators, David Dellinger held a press conference and announced that the Mobe would march to the Amphitheater with or without permits on the twenty-eighth. Dellinger's statement gave everyone something to organize around.[32]

Allen Ginsberg flew into town in the late afternoon. While still airborne, worried, he wrote a poem and called it "Going to Chicago." "Remember the Helpless order the / Police armed to protect / The Helpless Freedom the Revolutionary / Conspired to honor," he wrote.[33] Ginsberg's worries were not dispelled by what he heard when he arrived in Lincoln Park.

At their parkside headquarters, just before dark, the Yips met to decide what they should do that night and the next day. Abbie reported that he'd talked to a police commander who told him that the Yips could not hold their music festival on Sunday. Sanders said that Commander Lynsky hadn't been as negative. They all decided to just go ahead with the festival and see what happened; they'd been through this game before.

The park curfew issue was not so easily resolved. At first, both Rubin and Hoffman felt that the park should be defended. Rubin thought that if there were enough kids in the park the police wouldn't attack. And Hoffman said that if the police tried to close down the park at 11 P.M. there'd be bands of people "going out from the park to loot and pillage." Ed Sanders was appalled and exclaimed, "I'm sick and tired of hearing people talk like this. . . . You're urging people to go out and get killed for nothing. Man, that's like murdering people." Ginsberg tried to put it into perspective: "The park isn't worth dying for." After hashing it over, Krassner, Sanders, Ginsberg, Rubin, and Hoffman drafted short statements urging the kids in the park to leave if the police enforced the curfew. Like SDS, all of the Yips rejected the idea of holding the park. But whereas Krassner, Ginsberg, and Sanders all promoted leaving the park peacefully, Rubin and Hoffman, working together in a rare bit of convention collaboration, more closely followed the SDS line: "The cops want to turn our parks into graveyards. But we, not them, will decide when the battle begins. . . . If the cops try to kick us out of the park we have sleeping places. . . . Leave the parks in small groups and do what is necessary—make them pay for kicking us out of the park."[34]

Commander Lynsky had definitely decided to clear the park at 11 P.M. The decision, at least formally, was his. He had talked "informally" with his superiors, Deputy Superintendent Rochford and Chief Kelly, about the situation and he had told them that he intended to enforce the curfew ordinance. They had not overruled him. As Lynsky saw it, any backing off by the police "would be interpreted by the demonstrators as a sign of weakness and would only lead to further confrontation." For Lynsky the problem was crystal clear; if you let people break any laws they want, what you'll get is a breakdown in law and order. Lynsky, his men, and the city corporation counsels— who were on hand in force—were ready to make mass arrests.[35]

By 10:30, there were between five hundred and a thousand people in Lincoln Park. For most of the evening, small groups of people had debated what they should do come the curfew. SDS organizers promoted street action. A few local people, unaffiliated, insisted that they had the right to stay in the park. Undercover agents listened carefully. A line of policemen formed at the east edge of the park, near the Outer Drive, which separated the park from Lake Michigan and the North Avenue Beach. At approximately 10:30, a small group of policemen, acting on their own initiative, moved into the demonstrators' territory and began kicking over several bonfires set by the protesters. The policemen then retreated but people were frightened.

Allen Ginsberg, who'd come into the park only a few minutes earlier, watched the police. Then with Ed Sanders at his side he sat down and began to chant: "Ommmmmmmm, Ommmmmmm, Ommmmmmm . . . " For over twenty minutes he chanted "Ommmmmmmm." A hundred or so people joined him. The chant calmed people. At exactly 11:00, Ginsberg and Sanders led the people out of Lincoln Park.

Over bullhorns, the police announced that the park was closed. Twenty officers, led by Commander Lynsky, cleared a few dozen diehards out of the park without incident. Once out of the park, however, SDS organizers helped to lead several hundred people through the nearby streets of Old Town, clogging up traffic for a few minutes. The crowd chanted, "Peace Now!" A few yelled, "Stop the Democratic Convention!" Most of the park people soon blended into the Saturday night crowd on Wells Street—Chicago's main "hip" scene. In the main, the police left well enough alone. Eleven people, though, were arrested for blocking a sidewalk. That night seventy-five police guarded the park.[36]

In the weekend *Chicago's American*, Jack Mabley, in his featured column, told his readers why Chicago needed every soldier, cop, and guardsmen it could get:

> Every one of the following acts of sabotage had been
> threatened by black or white militants: . . . guerilla nails
> . . . spread by the thousands on expressways . . . could
> jam the whole expressway system . . . natural gas lines
> coming into the city may be dynamited and set afire . . .
> militants have said they will put agents into hotel or res-
> taurant kitchens where food is prepared for delegates and
> put drugs or poison in the food . . . the water supply has
> been threatened . . . forged credentials to get saboteurs
> past the security lines at the Amphitheater . . . yippie
> girls would work as hookers and try to attract delegates
> and put LSD in their drinks . . . a hijacked gas tanker
> truck can be put into gear and aimed at a hotel . . .
> threats to the Amphitheater include gas in the air condi-
> tioning system, shelling it with mortar from several miles
> away, storming it with a mob, cutting the power and
> phone lines. . . . How many other sophisticated schemes
> of sabotage exist may only be imagined.[37]

Sunday marked the Mobe's first organized event, a "Meet the Delegates March." The protest targets were the three main Loop hotels in which the delegates were staying. The Mobe marshals had been told the previous day to show up at their assigned hotels around 12:30 and organize a picket line. They should march from about 2:00 to 4:00 and then disperse—a simple, peaceful march, nothing more. The marshals were to go then to Lincoln Park and help get things organized there.[38]

Tom Hayden and Rennie Davis were basically giving the marshals their orders. By Sunday, they were in general agreement about what form Chicago needed to take. Hayden got the message across in the second edition of the *Ramparts Wall Poster:* "We are forced into a military style not because we are 'destructive' and 'nihilistic' but because our normal rights are insecure and we must be able to survive in the Jaws of Leviathan." Hayden was also very aware that the protesters were not going to have the numbers they needed to force the city into giving them what they wanted. Thus, he warned the protesters to leave Lincoln Park at night even though "Lincoln Park is our territory

. . . [and] a specific example of the freedom and community our move-ment seeks." He hoped that later in the week "we will grow strong enough to hold the park even at night." But for the here and now, Hayden advocated three basic tactics which seemed to define what he called "a military style": mobile and dispersed actions, challenges to the security system, and disruptions of the delegates' fun. He also promoted the movement centers and suggested that everyone get involved in a center in which they could come up with their own actions. Hayden knew that the movement centers were floundering for lack of people.[39]

David Dellinger was, that morning, still hoping he could finesse the permit snafu. He and Eric Weinberger thought that they had man-aged to set up a breakfast meeting with Deputy Mayor Stahl to discuss the problem. But Stahl simply didn't show up, sending in his place flack catcher Al Baugher. Nothing happened.[40]

Around noon, a Mobe marshal, Lee Weiner, sporting a black armband, showed up at the Conrad Hilton on South Michigan Avenue. He found a police sergeant and asked him for permission to picket. The sergeant suggested that the picket be set up across the street from the Hilton on the sidewalk just west of Grant Park. Weiner agreed. Slowly, a small crowd began to gather. By 2:00, approximately three hundred people were slowly marching in a circle. Ten members of the Rapid Transit Guer-rilla Communications wearing skull masks and paper mache masks of LBJ and Humphrey entertained the crowd by mocking the convention and chanting, "LBJ all the way . . . Humphrey Dumphrey . . . Negotiate with bombs . . . Shoot to Kill." Approximately seventy-five police stood across the street from the marchers, guarding the hotel against any at-tempt to storm it.

In Lincoln Park, at around 2:00, Rennie Davis and Tom Hayden were promoting the Meet the Delegates March. Using a portable speaker, they rounded up approximately five hundred people. Most of the marchers had long hair and were between eighteen and twenty-five. A number of them sported Yippie! buttons, others McCarthy; some had on both. A few people waved red banners and Viet Cong flags. There were few straight people marching. Jerry Rubin, Keith Lampe, and Mobe functionary Eric Weinberger helped lead and co-ordinate the march. Due to the small turnout and the lack of city cooperation, the Yippies and the Mobe were now working closely together. Reporters, city corporation counsels, and a number of po-licemen accompanied the marchers who stayed on the sidewalk and obeyed traffic signals.

Davis was surprised that the police were letting them march. But Hayden took it matter-of-factly: "There was nothing else they could do. We had the power in the situation." The crowd chanted, "Hey, hey LBJ, how many kids did you kill today." Once in the Loop, they began screaming their chants, enjoying the echos they made among the skyscrapers.

Shortly before they arrived at the Hilton, the police rushed two busloads of men to the scene. Lee Weiner feared that the police were setting up for a mass arrest and quickly moved the picket away from the Hilton and into Grant Park. A few minutes later, Davis and the five hundred or so protesters joined the picketers. So did a large group of policemen. Davis spoke to the crowd of eight hundred or so and called the march and picket a success. Hayden reported the same to a crowd of reporters and TV men. A few minutes later, the crowd broke up, word being passed that the Yip music festival was about to begin in Lincoln Park.[41]

Abbie Hoffman, Ed Sanders, and a dozen or so other Yips worked all morning and early afternoon on setting up the festival. They got together a free store, a hospital, a theater, and a music area. To get electricity and permission to use amplified sound in the park, Hoffman, Sanders, Rubin, and other Yips independently worked out deals with whatever city and police officials they could find: making threats, using one official's okay against another's intransigence, doing whatever it took to get the festival started. While Sanders, Hoffman, and the others dealed, the MC-5—a Detroit rock bank managed by John Sinclair, an early exponent of rock 'n roll radicalism and the only band to show up for the festival—began to set up their equipment.

At approximately 4 P.M., the Festival of Life officially began. Instead of a hundred thousand people, there were, at 4:00, maybe two thousand. But there was free food, there were balloons in the trees, and there were plenty of drugs.

Ed Sanders welcomed the small crowd and read a bit of his poetry. Then Bob Fass, disc jockey on WBAI in New York, introduced the MC-5, best known for their hard-rocking tune, "Kick Out the Jams, Motherfucker." The MC-5 played loud and hard and people started to crowd around, dancing and yelling and letting the music move them.

By 5:00, several thousand more people, most of them locals, had been drawn to Lincoln Park by the rock 'n roll sounds of the MC-5. Few of them could see the musicians.

The police had refused to allow the Yips to use their flatbed truck as a stage for the musicians. The police had been worried that a stage would afford the Yips too good an opportunity "to incite the crowd." So the MC-5 were playing right on the grass which meant that the crowd could not see them, which in turn meant that people on the periphery kept pushing the people in front of them, which in turn was fast leading to a lot of tension. About thirty minutes after the MC-5 began playing, there was a mix-up about electricity and, amid much confusion and some anger, the band was cut off. While new deals were being worked out, Abbie Hoffman decided that the Yips had to have their stage. Hoping that in all the confusion he could just force the police to let him bring the truck into the park, he had Yippie Super Joel drive it into the festival site. As the truck drove in, dozens of kids jumped up on it, escorting it to the band site. But the police, sticking to their orders, refused to let the truck be used as a stage. The crowd became angry. Hoffman and the police argued. Hoffman tried to get the crowd to bring the truck in. Super Joel led the crowd in taunts.[42]

At 5:18, Super Joel was arrested and the crowd began to rage. The police made a couple of other arrests and the crowds began to swirl around the police screaming obscenities: "Pigs eat shit! Pigs eat shit!" Several policemen used their clubs to keep the crowd back. Some shouted back at the crowd: "Get the fuck out of town . . . go back where you came from, fags." A few in the crowd shouted back, "Prague! Prague!" One group of young people sat down and began singing, "My country 'tis of thee. . . ."[43] A few people threw bottles and stones at the police. A couple of policemen used the occasion to strike out at particular targets; Yippie stalwart Stew Albert was smashed in the back of the head. With difficulty the police were able to keep their prisoners, make a retreat, and form a skirmish line.

Commander Lynsky, on the scene, called for reinforcements. He also asked Corporation Counsel Richard Elrod if he could close the park but Elrod said no.[44]

Less than a mile away, the 6:00 o'clock shift of police officers were reporting for their twelve hours of duty. They were warned that serious trouble was brewing in the park. And indeed from where they assembled they could see people streaming into the park "dressed for trouble," wearing helmets, goggles, and gloves. The officers, many of whom had never dealt with demonstrators before, also noted that many of the young people wore peace symbols that "seemed to be a recognition symbol and appeared to be freshly painted on some shirts." The police felt they did not know what they were up against and many were worried about facing protesters armed with unknown weapons.[45]

Abbie Hoffman declared that the music festival was over, stopped by the police. The crowd, now numbering around five thousand, wasn't sure what to do. Most of the people had watched the confrontation between the police and the protesters avidly but had not participated in it. Still, many in the crowd were angry if not also anxious.

Allen Ginsberg tried to start a calming chant. But he was immediately surrounded by photographers and cameramen who made it almost impossible for him to establish a meditative circle. The "om" chant was not as successful in calming the crowd as it had been the previous day. But Ginsberg kept at it; he chanted nonstop for the next seven hours.[46]

Hoffman led a group of several hundred over to the baseball diamonds just east of the park fieldhouse and through a workshop in "dispersal-group tactics"—the name taken from the North Vietnamese tactic used to handle U.S. air attacks. The idea was to prepare for police attacks. One young woman became worried about the flock of newsmen who were covering the training, worried that they would inform the police of what they were doing. Hoffman reassured her: "There are no secrets. The pigs got paranoia. They're going to lose. Right? We don't get paranoia. We win. Right?"[47]

As night fell, people lit bonfires and in small groups began to discuss what they should do. Hundreds of people shared dope. Periodically, the police would rush in and stomp out the bonfires, pushing and shoving people around in the process. Several people, scattered around the park, turned over trash barrels and banged on them like drums, hour after hour. SDS organizers, now numbering several hundred, traveled around in groups of four and five and argued against staying in the park after curfew. Take to the streets, they urged. It was a cool night and people sitting on the ground were cold. Hoffman moved from group to group suggesting that they test the curfew but that if the police came they should all retreat. Some kids argued, saying that they should stay and fight. Hoffman said it was the wrong time. There were dozens of young teenagers in the crowd, some of them working-class kids from the neighborhoods west of the park. They were having fun.

At approximately 9:00, a police squad that had decided to form a skirmish line around the park bathrooms became surrounded by angry, taunting young people. Other people, seeing something happening, wandered over to check things out. Soon, several hundred young people surrounded the policemen. "Motherfuckers," they screamed. "Oink, oink . . . shithead." A few people threw stones at the police. For a few minutes, the policemen just stood there and took it. Then suddenly they charged out, smashing everybody they could reach. Heads were bloodied and the young people ran. The cops then went back to the bathrooms. Most of the policemen had removed their nameplates. The process repeated itself twice more.

Word of the incident spread around the park. Rumors abounded. A policeman back in a staging area heard that "a squad had been ambushed by the ball diamond . . . 5500 to 7000 people surrounding the squad." The same policeman was sent out with his squad to help save the surrounded officers. When they arrived on the scene they could find no sign of trouble but "it appeared as if girls came up and counted how many police officers were present as if to prepare for an attack against the police."[48] Everywhere the police turned they were taunted, "Pigs eat shit! Pigs eat shit!"

In the dark it was impossible to count numbers. A police officer figured there were six or seven thousand demonstrators in the park. Others put the number at one or two thousand. Rumor had it that there were a thousand policemen. There were less than two hundred uniformed police in the park. Some thought that a thousand National Guardsmen were hidden around the periphery of the park and that at exactly 11:00 they and the police would arrest and beat everyone in the park.

Reporters swarmed through the park. Occasionally television lights would illuminate a swath of the park, capturing a group of young people debating the night's action. One reporter asked a police lieutenant how he and his men could clear the park. The lieutenant said: "[By] whatever means are necessary. I'll have enough people. They are outnumbered and outmaneuvered. This isn't New York, this is Chicago."[49]

Since approximately 8 P.M., Rennie Davis and Tom Hayden had been wandering around Lincoln Park talking to people about testing the curfew. They were followed for most of the time by their police tails; every so often a group of people would deliberately block the police and keep them away from Hayden and Davis. At approximately 10:15, the police tails noted two figures letting the air out of the tires of their police car. They ran over and spotted Tom Hayden and Wolf Lowenthal near the car. Lowenthal started to run away but stopped. Hayden waited. The cops grabbed them both. They struggled, Hayden yelling for help. Immediately a huge crowd formed, surrounding the police and their prisoners so tightly that the police couldn't even lift their arms. Maintaining their cool, the police were forced to let Hayden and Lowenthal go but assured them that they would arrest them the first chance they got. Word of the near arrest spread through the park.

At 10:30, a traffic safety educational car with a mobil speaker unit moved slowly through the park. The police officer announced that the park would close at 11 P.M. and warned journalists and demonstrators that they would be arrested if they did not leave the park at curfew.

Mobe marshals moved through the crowd urging everyone to leave the park at 11. Others screamed, "Fuck the marshals, the park is ours!" Over a bullhorn, SDS organizers yelled, "Break up. Don't bunch up. They'll trample us if we bunch up. If you want to stay in the park, break up into small groups."[50] Several of the organizers wore helmets. The drums beat on. Groups of teenagers chanted, "Revolt! Revolt!" A helicopter flew just above tree level.

At 11 P.M., Commander Lynsky formed a skirmish line of one hundred and twenty men. Approximately two hundred and fifty other officers were held in reserve. Eighty-three plainclothes task force police officers were also on hand. Most of the men were nervous and unenthusiastic. A few, an assistant U.S. district attorney noticed, were "in a state of excited anger . . . [and] stated in strong terms how they wanted to bust the heads of the demonstrators."[51] Almost all of the police were angry and worried about getting hurt.

At exactly 11, herded by eight policemen on three-wheel motorcycles and a small force of plainclothes task force police, all but a hundred or so of the several thousand young people retreated to the westernmost edge of the park. Occasionally, a group of people would run back into the park and then soon retreat. These forays were lead by "unaffiliated spontaneous leaders." One of the most brazen of these was a fourteen-year-old boy.

At 11:40, warned by intelligence that the crowd would resist, the police skirmish line moved out at a "stroll." As the police approached, the crowd chanted over and over, "Hell no, we won't go!" Hundreds of people screamed "Fuck you!" and "Pigs!" at the police in a kind of litany. Slowly, in formation, the police kept coming.

The police reached Stockton Avenue, the street that marked the western border of the park, without incident. For a moment the two groups stood face-to-face: the police just to the east of the street, the demonstrators in a large parking lot that stood between the park and Clark Street, a large commercial and residential street. There were approximately two thousand young people facing less than two hundred police.

Then, suddenly, the police moved forward, some screaming, "Get the fuck out of here." A police captain tried to restrain his men, "Don't leave the line. . . . Get back." He raised his own club to one of his men who was threatening a photographer.[52] But he had lost control. The crowd bolted, moving into Clark Street. A few police gave chase, clubbing people in the head and in the back. A police lieutenant, acting on his own initiative, ordered a group of approximately forty policemen to "clear" Clark Street in order to keep traffic flowing. With this break in the line, the skirmish formation dissolved. The police began to methodically club people. Most of the police used their clubs to move people, jabbing them in the back or chest.

Some police beat people bloody. Some demonstrators fought back. They were beaten to the ground and then beaten some more; one of the policemen involved said "no attention was paid to the amount of violence used" on these resisters.[53] People chanted that "the streets belong to the people." And they refused to clear the streets. Many wanted the confrontation.

Occasionally, the police officers in charge were able to re-form the police into a stationary skirmish line. But then an individual officer or group of officers would react to taunts or be hit by a rock or bottle and the line would fall apart. As one police lieutenant admitted, "This is not a military unit. There is no stockade that the men can be thrown into if they chose not to follow an order. . . . The men are trained to act as individuals, not as a group."[54] A team of Justice Department officials and U.S. assistant district attorneys roamed through the streets trying to stop enraged policemen from beating people. Amazed but far from displeased, Tom Hayden and a small group of Mobe marshals watched the fight unfold from a doorway.

Photographers, who attempted to take pictures of the police in action, were clubbed in turn—"Get the bastard with the camera"[55]— and their cameras smashed. A reporter for *Newsweek*, when told to get out of the street, flashed his credentials. "Newsweek fuckers," the cop replied and then clubbed him on the head, neck, back, and upper thigh.[56] Other credential-waving reporters who would not leave the streets were treated similarly. An assistant U.S. attorney general, in a suit and tie, was clubbed. Three ministers were harangued by a group of officers: "You bastards. What are you doing here? You belong back at your church."[57] Members of the Mobe medical contingent, dressed in white, were beaten as they gave first aid. Mace was sprayed indiscriminately. The Task Force lobbed tear gas into crowds. Policemen chased people for blocks in order to club them to the ground. The conflict spread to sidestreets. Many of the policemen had removed their nameplates and badges.

Police reinforcements arrived continuously, the new police unsure of exactly what was going on. Helicopters flew overhead. The police announced on bullhorns, "Clear the streets." Demonstrators screamed and chanted and swore at the police. Dozens of motorists trapped in the melee honked and honked their car horns. Jerry Rubin watched from a distance and told a friend, "This is fantastic and it's only Sunday night. . . . They might declare martial law in this town."[58]

One large group of close to a thousand, led by SDS and Yippie organizers, fled the street battle and began a march toward the Loop. They chanted, "Ho Ho Ho Chi Minh." They dumped garbage cans into the street, pounded and jumped on stopped cars, threw rocks and bottles as they moved through the streets. The police waited for them on the Wacker Street bridge that spans the Chicago River and separates the Loop from the North Michigan Avenue area. Through threats of gas, the very public display of loaded shotguns, and a small amount of clubbing, the police were able to stop the mob and force them to disperse. Many ran back to the Lincoln Park area and rejoined the fray.

Not until approximately 2 A.M. were the streets cleared of demonstrators and order restored.[59]

The next morning and early afternoon, small groups of people made their way back into Lincoln Park. The more militant demonstrators were very pleased by the Sunday night fight. SDS, in their *Handwriting on the Wall*, waxed poetic: "11:01 and Wells Street was ours. . . . The rest of us just kept going, no idea where. Great surging feeling. Fantastic when we took Michigan Avenue, so surprised . . . fantastic. Finally the drawbridge. Those with a sense of history remembered Leningrad, 1917."[60] Tom Hayden, in the *Ramparts Wall Poster*, said much the same, calling the confrontation a "100% victory in propaganda." Hayden had heard NBC call the convention an "armed camp."

Hayden also saw the confrontation as a necessary step for the movement: "People have to be faced with the existential question of giving their life . . . forced into a moral squeeze, forced to decide whether they're chickenshit, asked what they are willing to do to stop the war." Lincoln Park, at least until the Wednesday march on the Amphitheater, would be the demonstrators' focal point, a position Hayden went on to announce formally in the *RWP*.

The Yippies responded to the sanctification of their park struggle by announcing that they had "decided to march on the Amphitheater. . . . We support our brothers and sisters in the MOB[E]. . . . We all fight in different ways; we all have respect for each other's decisions."[61] Thanks to the police attack, the demonstrators were, though small in number, at least formally now united. This unity was challenged almost immediately with the arrest of Tom Hayden and Wolfe Lowenthal at approximately 2:30.

Hayden and Lowenthal were arrested by the two plainclothesmen who'd tried to arrest them the previous night. The officers were furious with the two protesters whom they said had tried to get them killed. Lowenthal tried to explain that they'd been just as scared but communication was not really possible. At police headquarters, Hayden and Lowenthal were told to sit on the floor, a number of policemen then took turns threatening them; however, neither man was struck.[62]

Word of the arrest spread quickly through the fifteen hundred or so demonstrators already gathered in the park. Rennie Davis and a number of Mobe marshals quickly began to organize a march to protest the arrests and within a half hour a thousand young people—both long-haired Yippie types, SDSers, radicals, and McCarthyite moderates—accompanied by a host of reporters, police, and various law enforcement observers began moving along the sidewalks toward the police headquarters just south of the Loop. Police intelligence agents rushed back to police command warning that the mood of the crowd was extremely hostile and that if Hayden wasn't released police headquarters would "be stormed."[63]

In general, the marchers were extremely well-behaved, keeping to the sidewalks and following the marshals' instructions. Several of the marchers sported red and black flags and, at various times, groups of people chanted "Ho Ho Ho Chi Minh," "Dump the Hump," and other slogans.

As the group marched, Rennie Davis tried to work out a deal with Corporation Counsel Elrod. Davis wanted to have an assembly near the police station. Elrod wouldn't have it. As the group approached police headquarters they were shocked to find dozens of police officers surrounding the building. Davis, after a very quick stop in front of the station, kept the crowd moving away from what he saw as a very dangerous setup and back toward the Loop.

Specifically, Davis was leading the group to the section of Grant Park that faced the Conrad Hilton Hotel. But not all the people were interested in following Davis.

Several hundred yards short of the Hilton, but already in Grant Park, a group of several hundred broke away from the march and began the kind of symbolic action that most appealed to most of the protesters; screaming "take the hill," the group ran up a small knoll and seized a large equestrian statue of Civil War General John Logan. Waving Viet Cong flags and flashing peace symbols, the crowd climbed and clambered around the statue until about one thousand people covered the knoll.

The police on the scene, who had been warned that the crowd was very hostile and perhaps dangerous, reacted strongly to the protesters' taking of the hill. Approximately sixty of them began pushing and shoving people away from the hill. Within ten minutes the police had succeeded in clearing the statue of protesters although in the process they made a few arrests, clubbed a few youths, and broke the arm of one teenager who wouldn't get off the statue.

Rennie Davis, at the first sign that the police intended to clear the statue, had begun to reform the protesters on the parkside of the Hilton. Eventually, a small rally was held there without conflict; a rally Rennie Davis concluded by advising everyone to go back to Lincoln Park in small groups and work from there.[64]

During all of this activity, two policemen, separately, sidled up to a local ABC reporter, a friend of theirs, and warned him to "be careful, the word is out to get newsmen."[65]

By 9 P.M., approximately three thousand people were gathered in Lincoln Park. The crowd now included more locals and older people as well as a few blacks and west side teenagers there for the fun. A group of close to eighty north side ministers had also arrived to lend their support to the demonstrators and to hold a worship service around an eight-foot wooden cross.

Commander Lynsky was told by his intelligence agents that the crowd was far more hostile than on the previous night and prepared to resist the police. The agents reported that there were rumors of armed protesters and black militants prepared to shoot policemen. Lynsky called for reinforcements and before the park was to be closed had added several dozen task force members to his force. There was never any question about whether or not to enforce the park curfew. As one officer said, "If we back down here, the whole town goes."[66]

Around bonfires, small groups of protesters debated strategy. Abbie Hoffman, anonymously, went from group to group advising people to leave the park at 11 P.M. SDS organizers advised the same, pushing for action in the streets. Others, however, demanded that the park be defended and the police be made to pay for the clubbing they'd visited upon the protesters. Several radicals and street kids began to build a barricade made out of park benches, trash baskets, branches, and whatever else they could find. The barricade was to stand between the protesters and the police line that was forming on the eastern boundary of the park.

Periodically, groups ranging in size from a few dozen to several hundred left the park and ran through the streets, overturning garbage cans, disrupting traffic and occasionally throwing stones and bottles. Television crews and photographers, in the park in strength, followed the rock throwers around. As the police confronted these roaming bands and stopped them, violence flared up. Almost always the police attacked the cameramen as they attacked the demonstrators. The police did not want their work to be filmed.

At 11:30, the police announced over and over that the park was closed. The official announcement stated: "We have information that there are weapons in the hands of persons in the park to be used against the police officers, we intend to take every step to see that police officers are not injured. This is the final warning, move out of the park."[67] Most people, maybe two thousand, left the park between 11 and midnight, many of them only moving to the streets that bordered the park. About one thousand refused to leave altogether. Most of them decided to make their stand around the flimsy barricade.

At 12:20, after a police car had blundered into the barricade and had its windows shattered by barrages of rocks, the police attacked. Approximately three hundred policemen, led by task force officers outfitted with gas masks, moved into the protesters. They had been specifically ordered to fire their guns only if fired on. Two fire trucks were used to light up the demonstrators' territory. The task force men shot four gas and four smoke grenades at the barricade and the protesters, gagging and choking, ran for the streets. A few members of the task force took after the fleeing protesters. Most of the officers had to wait for the gas to clear before they could walk in formation through the park and after the protesters. For the next several hours the protesters and the police fought.

Like the previous night, the demonstrators ran through the streets. This night, even more took to throwing rocks and bottles at police. Several police cars had their windows broken. Cries of "dirty pigs," "fuckers," and other taunts were repeated endlessly. Several protesters attacked lone police officers and succeeded in hurting several—according to the police, fifteen officers needed medical assistance.

The police, too, turned meaner. Without their nameplates or badges, policemen beat people arbitrarily, clubbing women on the sidewalks, middle-aged people watching from their front steps, girls already lying bleeding on the ground. Many police were enraged.

A seventeen-year-old hippie girl was ordered to move by a middle-aged police officer. She replied that she had a right to be on the sidewalk. He screamed, "You hippies are all alike. All you want is free love." He knocked her to the ground with his club and then pinned her to the ground with his club and said, "Free love, free love, I can give you some free love."[68] A group of eight policemen surrounded three teenage girls and screamed and screamed at them, "Pig! Pig! Pig! Bitch! Bitch!"[69] A black reporter was knocked to the ground by a police officer. On the ground, he waved his press credentials. The officer said, "That don't mean anything to me nigger," and beat the reporter several more times with his club.[70] Screaming, "Get the fucking bastards!" five policemen grabbed a young man and woman north of the cleared park area. Four of them threw the man in the park lagoon. Then they clubbed the woman senseless, screaming, "How do you like this, huh!" Everytime the man climbed out of the lagoon they clubbed him and threw him back in until he was finally able to grab his friend and pull her into the water.[71] A minister wearing his clerical collar had his skull fractured by a policeman wielding a carbine.[72] Four policemen beat a photographer who refused to give them his film while a crowd chanted, "Give him back his film."[73] Several other members of the press were singled out for punishment. Policemen sprayed Mace at people along the sidewalk while they pleaded. Police violence was commonplace.

The Mobe's white-coated medics, themselves targets, treated over eighty people for serious scalp wounds. Others who were hurt went to area hospitals for stitches. Most of the police had removed their badges and nameplates. Many of the Task Force officers carried riot guns and other policemen had carbines but not a single demonstrator was shot and not a single demonstrator was seriously injured. The police arrested around seventy people. After the park was secured and the streets were cleared, a gang of approximately a dozen policemen systematically slashed the tires, broke the windows, sprung the trunks, and broke off the aerials of several dozen autos, many of them festooned with McCarthy for President stickers, that had been left in the Lincoln Park parking lot.[74]

Back in the Loop, Tom Hayden had been released from jail. But a few hours later, still in the Loop, he was rearrested for supposedly spitting on a police officer. An ABC camera crew that attempted to film the arrest was attacked by police who succeeded in smashing the camera. After making bail a few hours later, Hayden decided to go underground for the next few days.[75]

The Democratic convention had formally begun that night. Mayor Daley had welcomed the delegates by praising his party, a party he said that welcomed protest and dissent but not people "who seek to destroy instead of to build . . . who would make a mockery of our institutions and values."[76] Daley was going to hang tough and he wanted the delegates and the American viewing public to know it.

The Mobe, too, wanted the American viewing public to know that they would not be intimated. At 9 A.M., Tuesday morning, the Mobe sponsored a press conference. Close to one hundred reporters and photographers showed up. A dozen television cameras covered the action. As the Mobe's press liaison later said, "It was like the White House during an international crisis."[77]

Rennie Davis acted as Mobe spokesperson and announced that the protesters would not be stopped by police brutality. "The whole world's watching" what the police and Mayor Daley and the Democratic party were trying to do to the antiwar movement, he said. And they wouldn't get away with it. August 28, the Mobe would march on the war makers in the Amphitheater. Other Mobe leaders reiterated the protesters' commitment to marching on the Amphitheater.

Later, Abbie Hoffman, who'd wandered over to Mobe headquarters looking to talk with Davis, spoke to the reporters. Wearing a yellow helmet and carrying a good-sized tree branch, Hoffman said:

> What we saw last night was a demonstration of police
> stupidity and anarchy, it is the stupidity in driving city
> folks, you know, city yippies out into the streets of Chi-
> cago, you know, when if they were allowed to sleep in
> the rural area, you know, the park, the way we want to,
> and establish our community, you know, everything
> would be cool.[78]

Hoffman was not the only one angered by the police actions in the park. Early Tuesday morning, editors or executives of CBS, ABC, *Newsweek*, all the main Chicago newspapers except the *Tribune*, and other news media organizations all sent letters or telegrams to Mayor Daley protesting the beating and intimidating of reporters, photographers, and cameramen. A large group of media representatives demanded a meeting with Superintendent Conlisk.

Daley responded to the protests by holding a press conference and announcing: "We ask the men of the news media to follow the instruction of the police as other citizens should . . . and that they not join the running and rushing which is part of these disorders." The *Chicago Tribune* backed the Mayor's approach, declaring in an editorial that "some of the newsmen looked like hippies and perhaps they refused to obey police orders to move. If so the police perhaps were justified in using force."[79]

The Police Department, however, took a less hard-line approach to the problem. In a meeting with the editors of Chicago's four main newspapers and other media representatives, Superintendent Conlisk promised that orders would be issued to improve police-media relations. He also assured the angry media officials that he would investigate reports of police officers removing their badges and of police officers using their clubs in violation of proper procedure, that is, of smashing people on the head. Indeed, after the meeting, Conlisk issued a series of orders that provided special police protection of reporters and warned police not to remove their badges or nameplates, or to intimidate reporters, confiscate film, or damage camera equipment. The orders were to be read out loud at roll call every morning, all week.[80]

During the day, small groups of protesters engaged in a variety of actions—often planned at the Movement Centers—including a picketing of the Polish consulate in protest of the Soviet invasion of Czechoslovakia, a draft board demonstration, and a pacifistic "Walk and Vigil of Mourning," during which approximately two hundred Quakers and other adherents of nonviolence walked from the Loop to the Amphitheater.[81]

The vast majority of the protesters spent the day recovering from the previous night's bedlam, many of them doing so in Lincoln Park. Several hundred others, many of them disconsolate teenage and college-age supporters of Senator McCarthy, gathered in Grant Park across from the Conrad Hilton. It was a cool day for sitting in the park. Most people sat in small groups, talking about their adventures, considering their options, and waiting for the evening to come.

Abbie Hoffman spent most of the afternoon in Lincoln Park, rapping to a group of several hundred young people and, undoubtedly, mystified undercover agents. He tried to explain Yippie, Chicago, and his kind of revolution:

> I mean shit, you know, long hair is just another prop. You go on TV and you can say anything you want but people are lookin' at you and they're looking at the cat next to you like David Susskind or some guy like that and they're sayin' hey man there's a choice, I can see it loud and clear. But when they look at a guy from the Mobilization and they look at David Susskind, they say well I don't know, they seem to be doing the same thing, can't understand what they're doin'. 'Cause they say we're like exploiting, we're using the tools of Madison Avenue. But that's because Madison Avenue is effective in what it does. *They* know what the fuck they're doing. Meet the Press, Face the Nation, Issues and Answers—all those bullshit shows, you know where you get a Democrat and a Republican arguin' back and forth, this and that, this and that, yeh, yeh. But at the end of the show nobody changes their fuckin' mind, you see. But they're trying to push Brillo, you see, that's good, you ought to use Brillo see, and 'bout every ten minutes on will come a three minute thing of Brillo. Brillo is a revolution, Brillo is sex, Brillo is fun, Brillo is bl bl bl bl bl. At the end of the show people ain't fuckin' switchin' from Democrat or Republicans or Commies, you know, the right wingers or any of that shit. They're buying Brillo. I mean, can you imagine if they had the Beatles goin' zing zing zing zing, all that jump and shout, you know, and all of a sudden they put an ad where the guy comes on very straight: "You ought to buy Brillo because it's rationally the correct decision and it's part of the American political process and it's the right way to do things." You know, fuck, they'll buy the Beatles, they won't buy the Brillo.[82]

At around 7:00 P.M., most of the crowd of two or three thousand people in Lincoln Park gathered round to hear a special speaker, Black Panther party National Chairman Bobby Seale. Seale was a straight-out violent revolutionary and the crowd, after its own baptism by clubbing, was ready for his fiery rhetoric.

Seale had flown to Chicago at the invitation of Tom Hayden and the Mobe. But due to Hayden's police troubles, Seale was introduced by Jerry Rubin, who was involved with Black Panther Eldridge Cleaver in the Peace and Freedom party.

Seale's message was simple: the people had to organize against a racist, oppressive power structure. And because that power structure maintained itself through force, the people, too, had to be willing to use force: "If a pig comes up to us and starts swingin a billy club and you check around and you got your piece—you gotta down that pig in defense of yourself."[83]

Seale's message, while simple, was presented in a jumble of words that opened themselves to many interpretations. He told the angry crowd, "Pick up a gun, and pull that spike out of the wall. Because if you pull it out and you shoot it well, all I'm gonna do is pat you on the back and say, 'keep shooting,' "[84] He also said, "Now there are many kind of guns. . . . The strongest weapon that we each individually have is all of us . . . united with revolutionary principles. What we gotta do is functionally put ourselves in organizations."[85]

The crowd of young people cheered Seale's revolutionary message. Seemingly, after three days of police brutality, they felt themselves equal to the challenge Seale was offering them. They felt solidarity with the Panthers, who were, in California and elsewhere, meeting the police in armed confrontation.[86]

After Seale's impassioned address, the crowd split up. Rubin led several hundred to a nearby CTA bus barn in support of striking black workers. Others marched toward Grant Park; others split for the Colosseum, site of the Mobe-Yippie antibirthday party for President Johnson. Approximately two thousand people, many of them locals—and a number of them older residents—stayed in Lincoln Park.[87]

At the Colosseum, for most of the night, approximately four thousand protesters, including an increasing number of young McCarthy workers, vented their spleen against LBJ. In a carnivalesque atmosphere, created in the main through the daylong preparations of Ed Sanders, local music groups played and speakers railed against LBJ, racism, and the war in Vietnam. "Fuck you, LBJ," the crowd chanted. And "Hell no, we won't go." When Phil Ochs sang, "I Ain't Marching Anymore," people wept with frustration, anger, and bitterness. Draft cards and draft notices were put to flame while Ochs sang: "Call it peace or call it treason / Call it honor or call it reason / But I ain't marching anymore." David Dellinger told the crowd that they would march on the Amphitheater the next day. Shortly before midnight, Rennie Davis ended the show by advising the crowd to make their way in small groups to Grant Park, where they could greet the returning delegates in front of the network television cameras.[88]

In Lincoln Park, as the 11 P.M. curfew approached, there were approximately two thousand people still arguing about what was to be done. Close to a thousand people, led in part by Mobe marshals who'd decided on the strategy at a meeting with Davis and Hayden earlier in the day, had already marched out of the park headed for Grant Park, where they could protest in front of the television cameras set up outside of the Conrad Hilton Hotel—due to the electrical workers strike, the only television cameras set up outside of the Amphitheater. A large group of local clergymen and lay people—around two hundred—had set up an eight-foot cross in the middle of the park and told the crowd that they intended to hold a prayer service and stay in the park. Most of the two thousand or so demonstrators were gathered together near the giant cross. SDS organizers, who'd already spent a part of the evening leading forays out of the park and into the streets, argued for taking the action into the streets. Others demanded that the park be held. Though there was much arguing about strategy, there was a tremendous feeling of group solidarity and goodwill among the protesters.

The police, too, enjoyed a feeling of group solidarity. As an official observer for the Chicago Bar Association reported:

> There seemed to be almost without exception, an attitude or mentality of impatience of "getting started" and it was the normal thing for policemen to talk about how anxious they were to crack some heads. . . . Those who were saying anything seemed obsessed with getting a "commie" or "hippies." . . . There was almost a circus air about the hoped for opportunity to show the protesters what they thought of them.[89]

Commander Lynsky also had a surprise in store for the protesters; from the U.S. army he had borrowed a special gas-dispensing mechanism—which he had rigged to a garbage truck—and powerful CN tear gas. The park would be cleared. .

And at approximately 12:30, Lynsky had Task Force officers start the action by lobbing tear gas grenades at the protesters gathered around the cross. Then the garbage truck moved forward and officers released clouds of CN gas which sent the protesters running. Task Force officers, equipped with gas masks, pursued them, beating several people and knocking a minister unconscious.

Once again, the crowd took to the streets, and once again, the police cleared them out, swinging their clubs. There were more stones and bottles thrown at the police than on the previous nights. The police used more gas to drive the protesters out of the area. The gas drifted into apartments, cars, and residential streets, temporarily blinding people, burning at people's lungs, eyes, and throats. Police fired several shots in the air. Several police cars were pelted with rocks, bricks, and bottles. Most people on both sides accepted violence as normal. The police had far the better weapons. For the night, about one hundred arrests were made, seven policemen were injured, and over sixty demonstrators needed medical assistance.[90]

In Grant Park that night a very different scene unfolded. The police let the demonstrators spend the night.

By 12:30 A.M., about four thousand demonstrators had gathered in Grant Park across from the Conrad Hilton and the network television cameras. Several hundred police, eventually about seven hundred, guarded the Hilton and prepared for a confrontation with the protesters. Deputy Superintendent Rochford commanded the officers.

The Grant Park crowd differed from the Lincoln Park crowd. There were far more clean-cut McCarthy volunteers and older demonstrators who'd come to town for the legal rally the next day; there was also a growing number of McCarthy and Kennedy delegates joining the crowd. Arthur Waskow, a McCarthy delegate from Washington, D.C., and a committed leftist intellectual, surveyed the crowd and told a reporter that the Chicago protest was becoming "a complete victory . . . the difference between the movement and the liberals in the Party is declining, disappearing."[91]

For several hours a great variety of speakers used a portable public address system to talk to the protesters. Some counseled working within the system, others demanded a violent overthrow of the government. Tom Hayden, who was wearing a pork pie hat as a disguise, told the crowd:

> We have found that our primary struggle has not been to
> expose the bankruptcy of the Democratic Party; they have
> done that for themselves—but our primary struggle is a
> struggle for our survival as a movement. . . . Tomorrow
> afternoon we are to gather here for that march on the
> Convention that Daley and Johnson have brought out all
> their military strength to stop. . . . We are going to gather
> here and make our way to the Amphitheater by any
> means necessary.[92]

At about 1 A.M., Deputy Superintendent Rochford had his men find Rennie Davis and set up a meeting. Rochford asked Davis what he and his people intended to do—Rochford feared that the crowd meant to attack the Hilton and perhaps returning delegates who were still in session at the Amphitheater. Davis replied that they meant only to stay in the park and continue their rally. Rochford told Davis that he would allow the rally to go on. He was waiving the park curfew. He had decided that trying to clear the park of the relatively peaceful protesters in front of the TV cameras, returning delegates, and the late night Loop crowds was not worth it.[93]

Rochford also decided that he would have to find relief for his men, who, by 2 A.M., had been on duty for fourteen hours. The officers' tempers were growing thinner and thinner under the constant barrage of verbal taunts and the occasional thrown rock or can. Some officers were sure that demonstrators were throwing excrement and bottles filled with urine at them. The police had set up a line just feet away from the demonstrators.

Sometime around 2 A.M., Rochford got hold of Mayor Daley, who at 1:17 had made the motion that led to the adjournment of the day's proceedings at the Amphitheater. The mayor decided to have the National Guard relieve the police.[94]

Shortly after 3 A.M., the thirty-third Military Policy Battalion, six hundred strong, arrived. They came in jeeps armored with barbed wire and in army green transport trucks. They leapt from their vehicles in full battle gear, bayonets affixed to their carbines, shotguns and M-1s in hand, gas masks on their belts.

For a long minute the raucous crowd was almost silent; many wondered if the Guard would open fire or charge the crowd with their bayonets. Indeed, as the Guard formed a skirmish line in front of the police, they used their bayoneted carbines to force the crowd back and away from Michigan Avenue.

As the Guard forced the crowd back, more militant protesters began to swear at the guardsmen; the now familiar cries of "motherfuckers" and "pigs" rang out. General Dunn tried to inform the protesters that he had no intention of trying to remove them from the park. But in an attempt to gain the attention of the protesters he stood on his barbed wire–equipped jeep with his arm raised over his head. The crowd immediately, en mass, began chanting, "Sieg Heil Sieg Heil!" Dunn was drowned out by the chants and by the protesters' p.a. system, over which singers Peter, Paul, and Mary (in town to give support to Senator McCarthy) sang, "This Land is Your Land, This Land is My Land."

Dunn could not speak to the protesters but he did order his men to remove their bayonets and to make sure that their weapons were not loaded. The men were then ordered to maintain their line. Despite an unceasing barrage of taunts, the Guardsmen, without exception, did maintain their line. For the next hour, speakers continued to orate against the war and the system. Slowly the crowd drifted away until by daybreak only a couple of hundred sleeping protesters and approximately three hundred guardsmen remained.[95]

August 28, shortly after 8 A.M., while eating breakfast at a Lincoln Park Restaurant, Abbie Hoffman was arrested for having the word FUCK printed on his forehead. He was charged with disorderly conduct and resisting arrest. The police were making sure that he would not be involved in the Grant Park rally and convention march. Hoffman was shunted from jail to jail and kept incommunicado until his release some thirteen hours later.[96]

At 9:20 A.M., General Dunn of the National Guard was informed by the police that a rally and march would take place at the Grant Park bandshell commencing at 2 P.M. The police requested the assistance of one battalion. General Dunn began issuing orders and making plans for a parkside command post.[97]

Under the direct command of Deputy Superintendent James Rochford, the police too began mobilizing their forces. Close to six hundred officers were assigned to the bandshell area, which was located perilously close to the Loop and the delegates' hotels. Police intelligence agents were warning their superiors that a group of militant protesters planned to invade the Loop and wreak havoc. Police command also prepared thousands of leaflets upon which were printed an unequivocal warning that a march on the Amphitheater was illegal and that anyone attempting such a march would be arrested.[98]

At Mobe headquarters, in the midst of several dozen people, a group of fifteen or so debated tactics. Dellinger wanted to focus the rally around the victims of U.S. government policy: black people, draft resisters, Vietnam vets, people beat up by the police. Hayden wanted strong, militant speakers who would talk about issues.

Hayden also wanted a planned alternative to the march on the Amphitheater. He believed that the march would be stopped and that the protesters would be arrested en masse unless they left the rally site. Dellinger hoped that Daley would be reluctant to order mass arrests on the day Humphrey was to be nominated. After some debate, Davis, Hayden, and Dellinger decided to end the rally by offering demonstrators three choices: line up for a march to the Amphitheater, leave the park and mass in front of the Hilton, go home to avoid the probable confrontation with the police.[99]

At 1:00, antiwar convention delegates began their final arguments for the peace plank that had already been rejected by the platform committee. For the next three hours, the delegates debated. Pierre Salinger called on his ex-boss's name, "If Senator Robert Kennedy were alive he would be on this platform speaking for the minority."

Congressman Wayne L. Hays branded the peace plank a sop to radicals, whom he said,"would substitute beards for brains, license for liberty. They want pot instead of patriotism, sideburns instead of solutions. They would substitute riots for reason." The peace plank was defeated 1567 to 1041.[100]

By 3:00, between ten and fifteen thousand people were gathered around the bandshell in Grant Park. Compared to the crowds earlier in the week, many more of the rally goers were older and more conservatively dressed. Some of the antiwar movement's older, nonviolent members had come to Chicago just for the legal rally and hoped-for march on the Amphitheater. There was also a larger number of increasingly bitter McCarthy supporters. Some in the crowd who had confronted the police in Lincoln Park resented the unseasoned newcomers. Several of the more militant "veteran" protesters came to the rally wearing helmets and carrying rocks, pieces of concrete, and balloons filled with urine or caustic liquids. A few carried Viet Cong and red flags.[101]

Police surrounded the bandshell area on three sides. A small group of uniformed officers, most of them black, handed out leaflets warning the protesters that they would be arrested if they attempted to march. Dozens of plainclothes officers traveled in groups of eight to ten through the crowds, pushing people and threatening them. A few hundred yards to the south, National Guardsmen were visible on the rooftop of the Field Museum—more guardsmen were stationed in a large parking lot nearby.[102]

The rally began slowly and somewhat chaotically. David Dellinger acted as the master of ceremonies. Jerry Rubin was one of the first to speak. Influenced by Bobby Seale's recent speeches (Seale had left Chicago in the late morning), Rubin declared his solidarity with the Black Panthers and then said, "It has been shown that white people are going to take to the streets to become fighters . . . and that's how we are going to join the blacks, by joining them on the streets. See you on the streets tonight."[103]

At approximately 3:30, after a variety of speakers, and just as Carl Oglesby, ex-SDS president, began to speak, a teenage boy climbed the flagpole to the south of the bandshell and began to lower the flag. Police, assuming the young man intended to desecrate the flag, immediately pushed their way through the crowd and arrested the teenager. While beating him with their clubs and fists and struggling to drag him back behind the police line, the officers were pelted with food, rocks, bags of urine, chunks of concrete, and other debris.

While the police dragged off the teenager, a group of young men, including at least one undercover police officer, surrounded the flagpole and took down the flag. In its place, they raised a red t-shirt. A group of approximately eight police officers followed by several others tore into the crowd, once again, in an attempt to arrest the red flag raisers. They beat several bystanders with their clubs while chasing the perpetrators.

Over the p.a. system, Sid Peck attempted to calm the crowd, most of whom were standing in a vain attempt to see what exactly was happening. Many chanted, "Sit down, sit down." Rennie Davis ran over to the flagpole area in an attempt to set up a line of marshals between the crowd and the angry police.

A number of police reacted to the marshal formation by charging it. Under the direction of a sergeant, a group of approximately thirty enthusiastic police, clubs in hand, attacked in "a punitive assault."[104] Five of them spotted Davis. In a rage, they beat him to the ground with their clubs. They kept clubbing him as he crawled on all fours until he was able to escape under a chain link fence. Unconscious, his head, shirt, and tie covered with blood, Davis was rushed to the hospital for stitches (thirteen) and bandaging. Dozens of other protesters, most of whom were simply seated in the area around the flagpole, were clubbed around the head and shoulders. As quickly as they came, the police retreated. Demonstrators threw rocks, bottles, food and anything else within reach at the retreating officers.[105]

While the police attacked, David Dellinger and Tom Hayden fought for control of the rally. Dellinger, with the aid of Sid Peck, was doing his best to calm the crowd, stop the rock and bottle throwing, and get on with the speeches and, eventually, the nonviolent march. Hayden was furious. He couldn't believe the impunity of the police and wanted to urge the crowd to physically resist such invasions of their space. Dellinger won and kept the microphone, at least temporarily, away from Hayden.[106]

As people began picking themselves up from the police attack and returning to the benches they had fled, Carl Oglseby gave his speech:"We see the way it is in Saigon, we see the way it is in Bolivia, in Peru, in South Africa, we need no more illusions now. There is a fight going on. . . . We understand that nothing less than a fight can even insure our survival."[107]

Hayden then spoke. Informing the becalmed crowd that his friend Rennie Davis was hospitalized with a "split head," Hayden lost his cool:

> This city and the military machinery it has aimed at us
> won't permit us to protest. . . . Therefore we must move
> out of this park in groups throughout the city and turn
> this excited, overheated military machine against itself.
> Let us make sure that if blood is going to flow let it flow

all over this city. If gas is going to be used, let that gas
come down all over Chicago and not just all over us in
the park. That if the police are going to run wild, let them
run wild all over this city and not over us. If we are going
to be disrupted and violated, let this whole stinking city
be disrupted and violated. . . . Don't get trapped in some
kind of large organized march which can be surrounded.
Begin to find your way out of here. I'll see you in the
streets.[108]

Soon after Hayden's furious words, David Dellinger attempted to
calmly outline the day's protest options. There were three: line up for
a nonviolent march to the Amphitheater, leave the park and reassemble
across from the Hilton, or stay in the park and avoid any confrontation.
Dellinger announced that he would lead the march. He then
introduced Tom Neuman, whom Dellinger said would lead the other
action.[109] Neuman spoke to the point: "We have decided, some of us,
to move out of the park in any way we can, to move into their space
in any way that we can and to defend ourselves in any way we can."[110]

While Dellinger and Neuman were making their speeches, the National
Guard began moving into the area in force. Warned by the police
that demonstrators had been breaking up benches to use as weapons,
the guardsmen were armed with M-1 rifles, grenade launchers, gas
dispensers, bayonets, and .30 caliber machine guns. They had been
asked by the police to guard the series of bridges that spanned a block-
wide set of deeply sunk railroad tracks and connected the Grant Park
bandshell area with the Loop. While some police remained massed to
the south and southeast of the demonstrators, other police formed a
line west and southwest of the bandshell area, the directions in which
the marchers wanted to go.[111]

With the police and Guard surrounding the demonstrators on three
sides, Dellinger, several other ranking Mobe officials, and almost all
of the marshals attempted to organize the vast majority of the willing
demonstrators into a line. Over and over, Dellinger and the others
yelled into bullhorns that the march was to be nonviolent and that
anyone who could not abide by such a rule should leave the march.
Police officers used their bullhorns to tell the demonstrators that they
were participating in an illegal assemblage and were involved in an
arrest situation.

Tom Hayden saw the whole thing as one big trap. Working independently, he and a small group of militants, no more than a few
hundred, decided to move immediately into the Loop area. They were
able to get across the bridges before the Guard was fully deployed.

Several companies of police lined up directly in front of at least
six thousand protest marchers and kept the marchers from moving.

David Dellinger attempted to negotiate with Deputy Superintendent of Police James Rochford. But Rochford had no intention whatsoever of allowing the march to proceed toward the Amphitheater or the Loop. Based on intelligence reports, he was totally convinced that the demonstrators fully intended to "invade the hotels, invade the Amphitheater . . . disrupt the Convention."[112]

Rochford and City Corporation Counsel Richard Elrod were willing to work out a compromise. They told Sid Peck and David Dellinger that the demonstrators could remain in the bandshell area or they could reassemble in the park area east of Michigan Avenue and the Hilton, or they could march north to Lincoln Park. Dellinger was not interested.[113]

While the negotiations wore on, the demonstrators sat down and waited. They chanted and sang. The marshals told them to wait and they waited over an hour. Police vans and a special bus for prisoners arrived. A sound truck warned reporters that they were in an arrest situation. A line of police moved in and bisected the massed marchers.[114]

The march began to break up. Several dozen militants who had crossed over the bridges earlier had moved up behind the National Guard lines and called for the others to join them. Some of the marshals, worried about the increasing probabilities of a mass arrest, began to tell people to leave the line and make their way to the Hilton. People became frightened and started to leave the line, with more and more following.

There were no more leaders on either side. David Dellinger, dejected and angry by what he saw as "the absence of most of the movement's pacifist leadership," simply stayed at the march site until everyone got away.[115] Hundreds and then thousands of people rushed toward the Balbo bridge. Many simply wanted to leave the area; others were aiming for the Loop. They were met by two .30 caliber machine guns and a small number of confused and frightened National Guardsmen. The police rank and file, in formation, didn't know what was happening.[116] People in the crowd, many not from Chicago, were unsure of where to go. Many moved north to the next bridge.

Eighteen Guardsmen waited there. The first fifty or so people were allowed to go through the Guard line. But then an officer ordered the men to hold their line and when a huge mob of three or four thousand rushed up to the Guardsmen they used their bayonets to stop the crowd. A few protesters fought their way through. Guardsmen used their rifle butts to stop others. Four plainclothes policemen charged the crowd and clubbed any protesters they could reach. Guard reinforcements rushed to the scene and deployed heavy doses of tear gas into the mob. A car driven by a well-dressed, older woman and containing two gassed protesters inched up to the Guardsmen and attempted to pass through. In full view of a mobile TV cameraman, the very scared soldiers stuck a grenade launcher into the car and pointed their bayonets at the car tires. Frantically, the crowd took off to the north, many vomiting, others temporarily blinded and in agony. The heavy curtain of gas drifted into the Loop and eventually into the office buildings and hotels along Michigan Avenue.[117]

The Jackson Street bridge had been left unguarded. And word spread quickly and helter-skelter the crowd ran for the bridge. The Loop was on the other side.

Just as the wave of protesters made their way onto Michigan Avenue, the three-wagon mule train of the Poor People's Campaign, sponsored by the Southern Christian Leadership Council, was moving south past the intersection of Jackson and Michigan. Joyously, the white protesters attempted to join the train which had a permit to march. Slowly, to the encouragement of several of the wagon drivers, thousands of people filled Michigan Avenue and surrounded the slow-moving train. Militants, carrying red flags and Viet Cong flags, paraded on Michigan Avenue. Ralph Abernathy, in charge of the mule train, was afraid of the consequences of the spontaneous alliance.

For a few minutes, the police just tried to contain the demonstrators. One line, on the sidewalk west of Michigan Avenue, guarded the Hilton; another stood on the east side of Michigan Avenue between a large group of demonstrators and the street; a third group of officers formed a diagonal line in the intersection of Balbo and Michigan and thus prevented the crowd from moving south toward the Amphitheater.

At 7:30, there were approximately seven thousand people in and around the intersection. They were, as Hayden and others had wanted when they planned to mass in front of the Hilton, directly in front of the only fixed network cameras set up outside of the Amphitheater. There were also mobile television camera trucks set up in the intersection. Over and over demonstrators chanted, "Dump the Hump," "Fuck the pigs," "Fuck you LBJ," "Hell no, we won't go," "Peace Now," "Ho Ho Ho Chi Minh." Several demonstrators taunted policemen; others threw rocks, bottles, and garbage at officers.

Deputy Superintendent Rochford rushed to the scene and, after a hurried conference with an SCLC representative, ordered officers to free the mule train and allow it, and only it, to continue down Michigan Avenue. He ordered up busloads of reinforcements and vans for transporting prisoners. Upon freeing up the mule train and the arrival of reinforcements, Rochford ordered his men to clear the streets. His reasoning was elemental: "I had no intention of allowing a mob to take over the street."[118]

At the very first, for a period of twenty or thirty seconds, all went smoothly. Protesters were ordered to leave the streets and many began to do so.

Some policemen then proceeded with great discipline. Endlessly, they requested protesters to move onto the sidewalks. Led by Deputy Superintendent Rochford, they arrested those who would not comply. They used their clubs only to prod reluctant protesters in the chest or back.[119]

But almost from the start, other policemen lost all control. In a matter of minutes, hundreds of people—some just bystanders, some peaceful protesters, some violent militants—were beaten, bloodied, or Maced.

While Rochford coolly used a bullhorn to tell his officers to "hold your men steady there" and to order the protesters to "disperse,"[120] dozens of enraged officers, screaming curses, used their clubs, fists, knees, and Mace to hurt people.

Some demonstrators met the charging police head-on. Armed with caustic sprays of their own, sticks, rocks, concrete chunks, they ganged up on isolated police or picked out a target in a line. Policemen were punched, kicked, and struck.

Each injured policeman further enraged already furious officers. People were beaten to the ground and then hit again and again. The TV cameras filmed the beatings. In front of the hotels in which Hubert Humphrey, George McGovern, and Eugene McCarthy were staying, the police ravaged protesters and bystanders alike while the TV cameras recorded the violence. Some people, not on the front lines, chanted, "The whole world is watching, the whole world is watching."

Policemen came at the tightly packed crowd from all sides. Some officers attacked people watching from the sidewalks. Others pursued fleeing demonstrators for blocks. One of the first groups of police reinforcements, furious over reports of injured comrades, stormed off their bus chanting, "Kill! Kill! Kill!" A police lieutenant sprayed Mace indiscriminately at a crowd watching the street battle. Policemen pushed a small group of bystanders and peaceful protesters through a large plate glass window and then attacked the bleeding and dazed victims as they lay among the glass shards. Policemen on three-wheeled motorcycles, one of them screaming, "Wahoo!" ran people over. A group of officers cheered and protected a soldier (a deserter, as it turned out) as he beat up a white-coated Mobe medic; and when a photographer took pictures of the event the police beat him up.

Often indiscriminately, people were arrested. Some, as an assistant U.S. attorney reported, for saying "pig," others for walking on the sidewalk, and others for just being in the area.[121] As the police dragged people into the squadrols, they beat them with their clubs and fists and knees. The rock throwers and police attackers, usually younger and more agile, in the main, escaped capture.

Although the police succeeded in clearing the Balbo and Michigan intersection in about twenty minutes, the violence went on for hours. Militants and other enraged protesters ran through the Loop setting trash fires, blocking traffic, setting off stink bombs, throwing rocks and bottles, jeering, and, on a few occasions, attacking policemen. Policemen grabbed and beat up and arrested people. Occasionally, frustrated or angry police charged at the growing number of taunting, cursing protesters who were gathering in Grant Park, across from the Hilton. By 9:00, the National Guard was present in the Loop and Grant Park area in force. At 11:55, with the Loop essentially cleared of protesters, the National Guard took over completely, setting up a line between the several thousand protesters gathered in the park and Michigan Avenue.[122]

Senator George McGovern watched much of the violence from the fourth floor of his hotel room. Furious, he asked the flurry of visitors to his suite, "Do you see what those sons of bitches are doing to those kids down there?"[123] Distractedly, Senator McCarthy, who had also seen much of the fighting, told a reporter that the street fight looked "like a Breughel."[124] The senator allowed his fifteenth-floor suite of rooms at the Conrad Hilton to be used as a clinic for injured protesters. Very late the next night, the police attacked occupants of the suite of rooms after having noted a number of objects being thrown from the Hilton's fifteenth floor.[125]

Though the battle on Michigan Avenue started shortly before 8:00 P.M., the first shots of the violence weren't seen on television until approximately 9:30 pm. Not until then were the taped shots available for network transmission. The films galvanized the antiwar delegates in the convention hall. Connecticut Senator Abraham Ribicoff used his nominating speech for George McGovern to tell his audience, "With George McGovern we wouldn't have Gestapo tactics on the streets of Chicago." The live television cameras in the hall zeroed in on Mayor Daley's purple-faced rage. Off microphone, the Mayor cursed. The Democrats were divided for all to see.

At 11:20, the balloting for presidential nominee began. As expected Humphrey breezed to a first-ballot victory: Humphrey $1760\frac{1}{4}$, and McCarthy 601, McGovern $146\frac{1}{2}$, and others $114\frac{1}{4}$. At his moment of victory, Hubert Humphrey dashed to the television set and kissed an image of his wife that had been flashed onto the screen. The corps of photographers captured the moment.[126]

In response both to their defeat and events in the Loop, many of the antiwar delegates decided to march from the Amphitheater to their Loop hotels across from the demonstrators' assemblage. Eventually, over five hundred held a candlelight vigil down Michigan Avenue and many of the delegates joined the protesters in Grant Park.

The protesters stayed in Grant Park all night. As many as four thousand listened to a broadcast of the roll call vote, heard speakers, sang songs, and chanted. They heard a black Vietnam vet: "I was wounded in the back with a .30 caliber and I say let's end the war."[127] Arthur Waskow told them, "Delegate after delegate . . . has realized what your presence has made clear: the war is continued not only at the point of a gun in Vietnam, but at the point of a bayonet in Chicago."[128] Other delegates begged the crowd not to give up on the Democratic party. Norman Mailer and Julian Bond saluted the protesters. People chanted, "We want Gene," "Black Power," "Peace Now." McCarthy workers and other sympathizers in the Hilton blinked their hotel room lights in solidarity with the demonstrators. People sang "America the Beautiful" and accompanied Mary Travers and Peter Yarrow as they played "This Land Is Your Land." Hundreds of delegates and McCarthy supporters mixed with militants and others who'd been through the week's protests.[129]

Tom Hayden, keeping a low profile, told reporters: "What we have gained here is the bringing into fruition of a vanguard of people who are experienced in fighting for their survival under military conditions."[130] The battle on Michigan Avenue was more than Tom Hayden had dreamed possible.

Mayor Daley was outraged at the mass media coverage the battle on Michigan Avenue was given. He felt that his police, his city, even he had been unjustly vilified and slandered. The next morning, the Mayor began to make sure that the delegates and the mass media knew the Mayor's side of the story. A three-page handout was placed on every delegate's chair in the convention hall. One page contained a copy of a *Christian Science Monitor* article by the well-respected Richard L. Strout which blasted mass media coverage of the convention and accused the press of being too easily manipulated and misled by the "youth" protesters. Daley's statement then went on to accuse the protesters of being nothing but "groups of terrorists . . . equipped with caustics, with helmets and with their own brigade of medics." Daley then praised his police force and pointed out that they dutifully followed Kerner Report recommendations; manpower and not gunpower had been used to neutralize the rioting protesters. The statement closed: "This administration and the people of Chicago have never condoned brutality at any time but they will never permit a lawless violent group of terrorists to menace the lives of millions of people, destroy the purpose of this national political Convention and take over the streets of Chicago."[131]

Early in the evening, the Mayor appeared on CBS in a live interview with Walter Cronkite. In a twenty-three-minute interview, the acquiescent Cronkite allowed the Mayor to tell the American public why his police had found it necessary to be so tough with the protesters:

> It is unfortunate and we can't say it, that the television
> industry didn't have the information I had two weeks
> ago. These reports of intelligence on my desk that certain
> people planned to assassinate the three candidates for the
> presidency. Certain people planned to assassinate many
> of the leaders including myself and with all of these talks
> of assassination and it happening in our city I didn't
> want what happened in Dallas or what happened in Cali-
> fornia to happen in Chicago. So I took the necessary pre-
> cautions. No mayor wants to call the National Guard. In
> the interest of the preservation of the law and order for
> our people, and I don't mean law and order in itself in
> the brutal way, I mean law and order with justice—that I
> would call up the National Guard.[132]

Though the Mayor knew that the assassination plot he was referring to had been dismissed by the FBI as nothing but the "loose talk or braggadocio" of three Cook County jail inmates,[133] he also knew that Walter Cronkite would not challenge his veracity in front of the viewing public. The Mayor also knew that in 1968 to call on the threat of assassination was to draw the public's sympathy and understanding to his side. The Mayor went on to commend his police force and to attack the "terrorists" and outside agitators who'd attempted to disrupt his city and convention.

All day Thursday, the "outside agitators," antiwar convention delegates, local protesters, and a variety of celebrities spoke to a mixed crowd of militant protesters, rank-and-file demonstrators, temporary supporters, and an increasing number of spectators. While hundreds and then, as the day drew to a close, thousands of out-of-state protesters left town, others stood in Grant Park and began trying to figure out what had happened and what it meant.

David Dellinger decided to call it a "tragic victory." "Millions of people have been educated and horrified by this experience," he reported.[134] Rennie Davis spoke to the crowd of five or so thousand just after ex-governor of Massachusetts Endicott Peabody was booed for pleading, "Whatever you do, stay in the political process." Davis's advice was more warmly regarded: "Don't vote . . . join us in the streets of America. . . . Build a National Liberation Front for America."[135] Tom Hayden read a telegram from an SDS member in Cuba: "While we heard of the revolution in Cuba you held it sacred in Chicago. Create two, three Chicagos." To which Hayden added, "Only in the mood here it's become create two hundred or three hundred Chicagos everywhere."[136] The more radical the speaker the more gleeful he was. Jeff Jones, master strategist for the most militant faction of SDS, told his fellow neophyte revolutionaries, "Fight it out—build a strong base and knock those mother fuckers on their ass."[137]

Eugene McCarthy, too, spoke to the crowd across from the Conrad Hilton. He indicated to the crowd, which he called "the government in exile," that he would not support Hubert Humphrey for president. He quoted Robert Lowell, "Only man thinning out his kind / sounds through the Sabbath noon, the blind / swipe of the pruner and his knife / busy upon the tree of life."[138] McCarthy received the mixed crowd's applause.

During the day and night several futile marches to the Amphitheater were organized by the more peaceful elements within the protesters' ranks. They went nowhere. Black activist Dick Gregory, who'd first promoted the idea of protesting at the convention and then backed off, helped lead the two major marches. Some of the demonstrators hoped that at long last Chicago blacks would join them in their protests. But, as was true for the previous few days, few blacks joined the Gregory-led parades. As a local black leader said, "This was whitey's demonstration and Convention. . . . It's your turn now, whitey."[139]

The marches ended with hundreds gassed. Eventually, Gregory, nine convention delegates, and dozens of others were arrested, bringing the total number of protest-related arrests to almost seven hundred.[140]

At the Amphitheater, Thursday, the Mayor packed both the press and spectator galleries with his supporters. Waving banners announcing "We Love Mayor Daley," the patronage workers and loyalists chanted, "We want Daley, We want Daley," over and over. Before this highly supportive group and not a few hostile delegates, Hubert Humphrey gave his acceptance speech. Having "literally prayed" that antiwar delegates would not walk out on his speech, Humphrey quoted St. Francis of Assisi: "Where there is hatred let me sow love. Where there is injury, pardon." Treading carefully, Humphrey condemned all violence and all brutality and called out for party and national unity. Years later, he recalled the moment of his speech: "The whole environment of politics had come apart, I mean had become polluted and destroyed and violent and bad and I tried to put it together."[141]

Shortly after midnight, August 29, the convention was adjourned. By Friday afternoon, the protests and rallies and demonstrations were over and the Mobe had closed down its Chicago headquarters. The Yippies went back to New York. The Pentagon announced that in the previous week three hundred and eight Americans had been killed and 1144 had been wounded fighting in Vietnam.[142] Dean Johnson, the seventeen-year-old runaway who pulled a gun on two policemen, was the only fatality of the convention protests.

It's hard to say when Chicago '68 ended. Over the next few weeks, the nation debated just what went on in the streets of Chicago. An estimated eighty-nine million Americans had watched the convention proceedings Wednesday night. Mayor Daley and the demonstration leaders fought a propaganda war over the events of the week and neither side worried about the literal truth.[143]

Several Democratic congressmen and senators from around the country demanded that Attorney General Ramsey Clark prosecute the "outside agitators" that "conspired" to create the "riots" in Chicago. Other senators and congressmen, including Gerald Ford, blasted Mayor Daley and his police force for their handling of the protests.[144] Attorney General Clark, dubious about the new conspiracy-to-riot law and unable to find any proof that there had even been such a conspiracy to create a riot in Chicago, refused to prosecute anyone.[145] But later in the year, the new attorney general John Mitchell, under President Nixon, helped by an enraged J. Edgar Hoover of the FBI, charged Rennie Davis, Tom Hayden, David Dellinger, Bobby Seale, Abbie Hoffman, Jerry Rubin, and, somewhat mysteriously, Mobe marshals Lee Weiner and John Froines for conspiring to cause a riot, a charge that carried a penalty of up to five years in jail. Their trial would become the cause célèbre of 1969.

Letters poured into the networks, blasting their coverage of the convention confrontation—CBS received nine thousand and by an eleven to one ratio they were against the network's coverage.[146] On September 14, the Federal Communication Commission told ABC and CBS to answer "100s" of complaints on unfair coverage of the convention in twenty days.[147] Later in the year, the National Commission on the Causes and Prevention of Violence held two days of public hearings to determine if the print media or television contributed to the violence in Chicago and other cities. In the end, the press went formally uncharged. But the debate Chicago stirred up tore through the profession and pubic discourse for the next several years and helped create a new consciousness about the impact of the mass media on society.[148]

Mayor Daley claimed that he received 135,000 letters supporting his actions and only five thousand against.[149] Indeed, public opinion polls quickly established that most Americans approved of the Mayor's handling of the protesters. In a Survey Research Center poll taken shortly after the events in Chicago, only a little better than 10% of all whites thought that the police or the Mayor had used too much force; 25% of all respondents thought that not enough force was used. On the other hand, 82% of college-educated blacks felt that the police had used too much force, as did 63% of all blacks polled.[150] Even among those who opposed the Vietnam War, 50% reacted negatively to the Chicago protesters and 23% reacted with extreme hostility. However, 12% of those opposed to the war gave "extreme sympathy" to the protesters. This group was overwhelmingly young, college educated, urban, pro–civil rights, and Jewish.[151] It is worth noting that at the time of the convention, according to a Harris Poll, only 24% of Americans even supported the ceasing of bombing of North Vietnam.[152]

Hubert Humphrey spoke for the Mayor and many others when he gave his response to the confrontation: "The city of Chicago and the people of Chicago didn't do a thing that was wrong. . . . There are certain people in the United States who feel that all you have to do is riot and you can get your way. I have no time for that."[153]

While most Americans agreed with Humphrey's assessment of the convention violence, the immediate impact of convention week on his candidacy was disastrous. A range of influential liberals, including Senators McCarthy and Ribicoff, angered both by the means by which Humphrey won the nomination, the convention violence, and Humphrey's role in both, refused to support the party nominee. And while almost all returned to their standard-bearer in the end, their divisive behavior severely weakened Humphrey's fall campaign. The electorate, too, turned away from Humphrey. Many, in revulsion to what they saw as the riotous conditions created by a liberal administration, turned to the law-and-order candidacy of George Wallace. Others responded to the bloody convention by joining ranks with conservative supporters of Richard Nixon. A September Gallup Poll showed Nixon leading Humphrey 43% to 28%, with Wallace trailing Humphrey by only 7%.

Slowly, as the passions stirred by the convention violence faded, Democrats coalesced behind Humphrey and his support grew. Nixon just managed to hang onto his September lead. He edged Humphrey by five hundred thousand votes, a margin of .7%. Wallace received 9.9 million votes—13.5% of the total. Richard Nixon was elected to the presidency with the support of just 43.4% of the electorate.[154]

Among those who helped to lead the movement, Chicago produced a variety of responses. Todd Gitlin, ex-president of SDS, wrote, "There's nothing like a week in Chicago to clear the mind of adolescent machismo fantasies." However, as he went on to say, others left Chicago with a very different feeling, a feeling Gitlin labeled "fetishism of the streets."[155] Indeed, the most militant leaders of SDS left Chicago more excited about the possibilities of unleashing the anger of the poor and the alienated—"greasers," dropouts, gang members, and other street people—in the streets in spontaneous and anarchic acts of revolution.[156]

Older, far more moderate movement figures came away with a different lesson. Just after the convention, Arthur Waskow wrote that Chicago "challenged the most important liberal dogma, the one that America is a free and democratic country with only a few major faults that need to be reformed." For Waskow, "the lesson of Chicago" was clear, "guerrilla politics, not guerrilla war" was the right path. "Our armies of the night need new recruits—to get them we must invent a political course of action, not street tactics."[157] Waskow's voice, however, was not to be a dominant one in the post-Chicago years.

For Tom Hayden and Rennie Davis, Chicago brought together the Yippies, the New Left, and the McCarthy Kids. It drove a wedge between the mass media and the state, discredited the Democratic party, and humiliated the United States internationally.[158] Best of all, in their eyes, Chicago taught "the cutting edge" of the movement that there could be no "change without pain, without loss of life, without prison sentences."[159] Chicago succeeded "by sharpening the battle within the heart of the Mother Country." Chicago pushed Hayden and Davis further down the road toward revolutionary violence.

For the most militant movement people, a group that included Hoffman, Rubin, Hayden, and Davis, the violent confrontation in Chicago with its three or four thousand hard-core protesters was indeed what Yippie Stew Albert called "a revolutionary wet dream come true."[160] They worked to make Chicago only one violent confrontation among many. They succeeded. The movement, while growing in numbers of moderate antiwar proponents, also edged further toward violence. Chicago stood as a symbol to many of that turn toward violence in the streets.

Courtesy of the Kaye Miller Collection, 1968 Democratic Convention, Northwestern University Library.

*Courtesy of the Kaye Miller Collection,
1968 Democratic Convention,
Northwestern University Library.*

Michigan Avenue, August 28, 1968 (*Chicago Historical Society*. Photographer unknown. ICHi-14786)

Preceding pages: Chicago Ampitheatre, August 1968 (*Chicago Sun-Times, Inc. 1987*); Michigan Avenue, August 28, 1968 (*UPI photo*)

Michigan Avenue, August 1968 *(Chicago Historical Society.* Photographer unknown. ICHi-19630)

Above: Street demonstration, August 1968 (*Chicago Historical Society.* Photographer unknown. ICHi-18354)

Below: Tear gas in Grant Park, August 28, 1968 (*UPI Telephoto*)

Analyses

The case is different in an absolute democracy. . . . The object of the opposing minority is to expel the majority from power, and of the majority to maintain their hold upon it. It is on both sides a struggle for the whole. . . . Its regular course, as has been shown, is excessive violence—an appeal to force.

John C. Calhoun, "A Disquisition On Government"

8 Inside Yippie!

Young men are not effected so much by results. They are not held
responsible. They make a certain show-parade. They are judged
by its worth.[1]

Tom Watson

As I hope my story of Yippie made clear, Yippie was many different
things to many different people. This was the intention of its founders
and, in this at least, they succeeded. Virtually everyday Yippie was
refigured as its leaders or spokespersons reacted to the immediacy of
political situations or to the rush of personal vision. Then, too, Yippie
evolved, splintered, and went through some heavy changes as critics
complained, supporters suggested, adherents acted, the mass media
defined, and events unfolded. Fortune as much as intention decided
what Yippie was on any given day.

Still, beneath or perhaps even motivating many of these refigurings
and regroupings were certain visions, certain ideological dreams—to
say ideas would be to make the process more formal than it really
was. At least in the eyes of Rubin and Hoffman, these visions gave
Yippie coherency and purpose, and revealed to them when Yippie
was succeeding and when it was failing. Theirs was a complex vision,
a vision that never attained the clarity of a lucid programmatic statement or escaped puzzling, even damaging internal contradictions.
What follows is an attempt to formalize a part of that vision and to
take on more complexly a few of the questions I hope the story of
Yippie in 1968 raised. To do so, I am superimposing a vocabulary on
Yippie not necessarily natural to it, but a vocabulary that I believe can
make clearer what was at stake in the Yippies' experiment in American
political culture. In the main, my source for the assessments that follow is the text on Yippie I have already synthesized.

More than anything else, what characterized Yippie was its acceptance of the paradox most of the rest of the New Left fought to escape.
Yippie, unlike the New Left, believed that American society's ability
to reproduce all change in it own image need not be problematic but
could be the very means by which America could consume itself and
create its own rebirth. In the name of a revolutionary content, the
Yippies (with a few critical exceptions) accepted the structure of Amer-

ican modernization with its awesome ability to integrate change into the existing system. They accepted and attempted to use the culture's technical sophistication and dependence, its interdependent and increasingly homogenous form, its shift from a production ethic to a consumption ethic, its reification of mass-mediated information, and, in the end, its pattern of charismatic leadership and an abstracted mass following.

They did so because they believed, or at least acted and talked like they believed, that these social forms did not determine political content but could be manipulated to produce a political outcome radically different from their historically specific usage. This belief, in turn, depended on the Yippies' understanding that consciousness was created through cultural production. The Yips felt that by exploiting those forms of cultural production that they believed determined the consciousness of young people in particular—television, the music industry, FM radio stations, teen and youth magazines—they could subvert the ideology that gave credibility to America's entire pantheon of political symbols and master signifiers. In sum, the Yippies, playing in costumes as court jesters and fools, believed they could make a revolution by simulating a revolution that looked like fun. The simulation would play to the mass media and through the mass media it would be made available to apolitical youth.

Thus, whereas the New Left staked its fortunes on the belief that through new or recovered forms of political organization like local organization, collectivities, consensual decision making, and direct rather than mass-mediated information processing the People could regain sovereignty over their own lives, the Yippies staked their political fortunes on the primacy of consciousness over social forms and structure. For the Yippies, social forms such as the mass media, the youth market, and celebrityhood were not part and parcel of the dominant ideology but could be used to open people's eyes to the repression they were made to suffer. These forms, said the Yippies, had no inherent meaning; they were tools that revolutionaries could use as well as the State.

The Yippies believed that by using key parts of the system that were already in existence, they could activate a revolutionary consciousness already present, albeit dormant, in young people—present because of the breakdown in social formation produced by a society rife with contradictions. This is not to say that the Yippies thought that young people were right in there feeling the oppression of black people in a country that claimed equality for all, or that the young people, like the Yippies, could see that atheistic, totalitarian Soviet expansionism and American support of "friendly" Third World dictators were not so very different.

What the Yippies believed was that young people were seeing that there was something wrong when a Bridgeport, Connecticut, judge could rule that it was perfectly legal for four boys to be denied admission to their high school until they got their hair cut while in their civics class they learned that what made America great were the constitutional guarantees of free speech, free press, and freedom of religion.[2] Hair length, dress, drug laws, sex restrictions, the demands youth culture made for more pleasure and more self-expression in a society built around work and conformity—these were the kinds of contradictions the Yippies hoped to heighten and build on. Given the right ideological focus, they thought, the young people would see right through the myth of the State.

The Yippies then could accept the tools of the system because they believed the tools were without imperatives of their own. In the Yippies' hands the same tools that were used to deceive could become the means of empowerment. Daniel Cohn-Bendit, a.k.a Danny the Red, the nonleader leader of May '68 in Paris, gave an offhand intellectual justification to this kind of revolutionary practice when he said: "Some people have tried to force Marcuse on us as a mentor; that is a joke. None of us have read Marcuse. . . . Nearly all the militants . . . have read Sartre."[3] The Yippies, like Danny the Red, believed that the will to power and not the mechanisms of state power stood in the way of revolutionary change.

The Yippies were a very optimistic group. And they knew it. That was one of their gambles; that is what Abbie Hoffman meant when he retorted to an interviewer's probe as to how many people showed up in Chicago: "Well, who gives a shit. I mean if you're a revolutionary artist, you just do it."[4] The Yippie revolution centered on people's self-conception of their own desires and wishes, not on programmatics or structures. In practice, this meant that recontextualization and defamiliarization were the Yippies modes of resistance and affirmation; the Yippies meant to show young people that it was not their desires that were strange; what was strange—even evil–was the rigid society that kept the young from exploring their "natural" feelings.

The real joke the Yippies played on a fascinated society was that they meant not what they said but what they did. And what they did, as they knew, was in a great American tradition, a tradition they recast to fit their radical political needs and their antipolitical audiences' amorphous understandings and expectations. The Yippies played the part of showmen and con men in order to bring to their audiences a faith in their own natural democratic skepticism and a confidence in their own ability to discern that all was not what it seemed to be.

Historian Neil Harris tells us that in the early nineteenth century "the rituals that had once comfortably protected social convention disappeared or decayed. When credentials, coats of arms and university degrees no longer guaranteed what passed for truth, it was difficult to know whom and what to believe. Everything was up for grabs."[5] Alexis de Tocqueville, in describing this same period, asserts that Americans replaced the traditional sources of authority and judgment Harris lists, in part, with what he called "the tyranny of the majority," which could also more benignly be called an absolute hegemonic faith in the Democracy's own ability to decide not only it's own political destiny but also what counted as the True, the Good, and even the Beautiful. And while no historian accepts the totality of the Democracy's power, even at the height of the Jacksonian ascendency, few doubt that this powerful democratic faith was a hegemonic value that few could afford to ignore.[6] Of course, the question of whether this sort of democratic faith is equivalent to a workable will to power and control is in Tocqueville, at least, left unanswered. It is a question that will come to haunt the Yippies. But that's getting ahead of myself.

At any rate, it is this extreme democratic skepticism, be it mythical or historically verifiable, that the Yippies were seeking to recover. They wished to reach back to a time when, as Tocqueville says, "The people reign in the American political world as the Deity does in the universe . . . everything comes from them, and everything is absorbed by them";[7] to a time when, Harris says, "Secret information and private learning were anathema."[8]

The Yippies, like much the New Left, believed that the twentieth-century apotheosis of expertise, specialization, and certification had overwhelmed the actuality of mass sovereignty and had created in its place a caste of authority that decreed in its own name what was True and Good; a caste moreover that Yippie saw as fostering alienation and anomie as it reduced the Democracy's faith that it could understand and control the world around it. The Yippies were looking for an explosion of democracy; for an America where even epistemology flowed naturally from a democratic ideology. This, in part, is what is encoded in Yippie's dramatic declaration, "We will create our own reality. We are Free America. . . . We will not accept the false theatre of the Death Convention."

In this dramatic and dramaturgical phrase, "the false theatre of the Death Convention," lies much of Yippie's attitude toward and understanding of the counter discourse or epistemology that had, in their eyes, so ruthlessly overwhelmed and displaced the democratic practices and visions they sought to resurrect. And though the Yippies use a very different language, this understanding they share with the New Left.

Both the Yippies and the New Left believed that the American Democracy had been subverted by a power elite served by experts, technocrats, and other loyal retainers who in fact had no greater power in understanding the world than did the plain people of America. Vietnam and the continuing presence of poverty and racism seemed to the New Left and the Yippies to bear witness to the fact—indeed to prove—that the technocracy of a MacNamara and the idealism of a Kennedy were in practice only smoke screens for an Americanism based on elitism, exploitation, and ruthless materialism. This was the ideology they sought to replace and it was an ideology that seemed open to attack and exposure.

It seemed to the Yippies that the hyperrationality of a MacNamara was being proved by the Viet Cong to be only another form of superstition, only another puppet show used to fool the populace. Which isn't to say that the Yippies saw the whole thing, at least usually, as some vast conspiracy designed to fool the People. They assumed that the experts and the policymakers believed in their magic, believed, as the Yippies saw it, that their mixed bag of methodological tricks and rationalized guesses were the real thing, were indeed reality itself. But to the Yips it seemed but a "false theatre," and what was even worse was that the actors didn't know the full extent of the story they were playing, they didn't even know it was only a play contrived by themselves.

In this view, the Yippies had gone further than the New Left. The New Left, in the main, believed that if only policymakers and planners—indeed the entire discourse and practice of "scientism"—began with entirely different premises and let their work be governed by the values of cooperation, radical equality, and community, then their results and the very form of "scientism" itself would be radically transformed. The Yippies, however, maintained that the very construct of truth-seeking had to be reevaluated. In their promised land of anarchism and libertarian hedonism, it would be necessary to recast what counted as "real" and what counted as only "playful fantasy." As Keith Lampe said, "logic and proportion and consistency, often even perspective are part of the old control system and we're done with the old and done with the control system." But before I play that out, the Yippie vision of "Free America," it is critical to add that Yippie and the New Left differed substantially on the tactics by which the Democracy could be made aware of the ideology that had made of it only a pawn in the power elite's game.

Abbie Hoffman said it very plainly when he compared the Mobilization to End the War in Vietnam and the Johnson administration ideologues: "They understand each other. They all wear suits and ties,

they sit down, they talk rationally, they use the same kind of words."
Hoffman went on to tell the government investigator interviewing
him: "We don't understand what you're talking about and you don't
understand what we're talking about. . . . There's no such thing as
truth, therefore [you] can have a whole lot of fun."[9] The Yippies believed that the antidemocratic power elite established their ideological
hegemony in two ways. First through a rational, scientific discourse.
And second, through the more ambiguous machinery of mass culture.

As the Yippies saw it, the New Left sought to dispute the power
elite on its own ground—rational, scientific discourse—and, thus,
necessarily in its own terms. The Yippies, on the other hand, looked
to mass culture. They believed that it was by undermining the content
but not the basic structure of the mass culture "propaganda machine"
that the consciousness of youth, in particular, could be reached and
changed. The Yippies believed that they could forge a mass radical
political consciousness only by using the Establishment politicians'
own cynical methods against them; not through platforms, debates,
or careful policy formulations but through image building, charisma,
and sloganeering. Most concretely, they'd fight for control of, or at
the very least, exposure on, the mass media where to some degree
they could operate on their own terms. As Abbie Hoffman said, tongue
firmly in cheek (more on that below), "I fight through the jungle of
TV."[10]

Thus, while Yippie maintained a certain rhetorical allegiance to the
New Left's high valuation of what were, in corporate, centralized
America, the anachronisms of local organizing and community activism, in practice Yippie redefined community and locale. Here, too,
Yippie was accepting modernization, rejecting the New Left's anti-
progressive dream of a return to a physically immediate community.
Yippie recognized that community in America was more dependent
on self and social definition than it was on geographical location—
they knew that consciousness and not proximity produced community. Just as doctors formed a tight, working community so, too, the
Yippies hoped, might turned-on youth.

Abbie Hoffman is talking about the production of this youth consciousness when he declares: "Fuck Viet Nam is as real to me as the
Empire State Building, or as unreal, you know. Viet Nam is more real
than New Jersey. . . . I know more towns in Viet Nam, you know. I
see it all the time."[11] The real, Hoffman is saying, cannot be determined by materiality, by mere presence.

Instead, he implies, the information we receive determines what
we know. And Hoffman believed that for many young people that

information came less and less from the "scientific" discourse drilled into kids at school, even including the universities. More and more, the Yippies believed, young people received information from the mass media, especially television, and critically from the self-referential system of youth culture with its special privileging of drug experiences and rock music. In this system of knowing, reason and causality were replaced by a faith in intuitive understanding based on the immediacy of total presence. This is the message Rubin was hammering home again and again in his writings and speeches, and it's what Abbie Hoffman means when he declared to a confused interviewer: "You need three hundred pages, you know, beginning with a capital letter ending with a period. Young kids don't need that, they don't even want it."[12]

In part, the Yippies borrowed this epistemological model from the extremely popular aphoristic thinking of mass media guru Marshall McLuhan. And as I demonstrated earlier, the Yippies were not above calling on him to verify the truth of their argument (a hypocrisy they didn't let bother them). But in the main, this epistemology was based on the Yippies' own experiences and observations. They were already sophisticated observers when John Kennedy turned on a nation with his face, his family, and his sweeping rhetoric of idealism and endless progress.

The Yippies, like the New Left, believed that democracy had become, by 1968, less a system of government based on the sovereignty of the people and evermore a governmental obligation handled by teams of professionals, expert at manipulating the symbols and images that convinced the people they were still in control. While the Yippies knew that such manipulation was far from being an invention of the last few years, they also knew that the quality and significance of such manipulations had changed so dramatically as to make its current appearances significantly different.

As long as the Yippies had been old enough to know, since 1952, when Dwight D. Eisenhower's election team put Batten, Barton, Durstine, and Osborn on retainer, advertising agencies had been openly selling the president to the people—just as Leonard Hall, the onetime national Republican Party chairman said, "the way a business sells its products." The Yippies knew and believed what Marshall McLuhan said about modern politics and television: "The party system has folded like the organizational chart. Politics and issues are useless for election purposes since they are too specialized and hot. The shaping of a candidate's integral image has taken the place of discussing conflicting points of view."[13]

Much of the New Left and the vast majority of America's intellectual establishment condemned or mourned this practice and were learning to recognize and define it as an integral component in the establishment of an increasingly, dangerously powerful presidency. The Yippies accepted the electronic image making. It was, they believed, when you got down to brass tacks, the only way to reach out to a vast electorate. And, especially, it was the only way to reach out to those young people who, in essence, knew no other way of processing information. Again, the Yippies believed that it was not the technology per se that created a problem; the same TV formula that sold the war in Vietnam could be made to sell a revolutionary consciousness. There was a contradiction or at the very least a paradox inherent in this view—the TV system seemed to maintain the unequal power relationship of manipulator and manipulated and thus was apostate to an ideology where truth emerged spontaneously from a self-willed, anarchistic, hedonistic vision of the ever amorphous Free America—but this understanding the Yippies chose to ignore. Instead, they accepted the TV system as a practical necessity.

To some degree, the Yippies believed that youth culture itself could prevent their seeming media manipulations from being just another con job. The Yippies seemed to believe that the "blank space" advertising, the mass media huckstering, and the contradictory manifestos and slogans they promulgated—even the highly charismatic leadership role they cavorted in—that all of it could be seen through for what the Yippie really intended it to be. At their most hopeful and committed, the Yips really believed that the turned-on generation they were playing to could use their acid vision and dope dreams, the energy of their rock 'n roll hearts, and even the jaded sophistication of their TV souls to take the Yippies' mixed fantasies for their structural riches and absurdly correct political message. They hoped, at least sometimes, that young people could accept their posturing, contradictory content, and wild hyperbole as just a lot of noise aimed at putting on the straights, making the six o'clock news, and giving them all something to laugh along with rather than at. The Yippies had faith in the richness of youth culture. Hoffman and some of the others really believed that they shared a counterculture, a counterepistemology, with a whole generation who were just waiting to turn their truths into workable power.

And most certainly the Yippies weren't all alone. Yippie fellow traveler John Sinclair, who managed the MC-5, one of the best hard rocking bands of the 1960s, moved to the same message and tried to distribute the same truths through music, his writings, and political organizing: "We wanted them [young people] to see that if they could relate to the MC-5 and all the stuff we had been talking about before, then they could relate to the Black Panthers and the rest of the Movement too, because it was all part of the same thing and it all had to do with FREEDOM, which is what everybody wanted in the first place."[14]

Though many historians would look much farther back than the 1960s for the origin of an American youth culture—many pointing to the 1920s, some even earlier—what is more important in understanding the 1960s is the fact that so many people then believed that the youth culture around them was new, even unprecedented.[15] And they believed that it portended revolutionary change.

Certainly, those young people who grew up in the 1950s and came of age in the 1960s were a part of something new. First of all, there were more of them. The postwar baby boom produced an unprecedented number of young people. Their numbers alone might not have mattered so much had it not been for the radical restructuring of the American educational system. The huge increase in young people attending universities and colleges is well-known—from 1963 to 1973 enrollment jumped from 4.7 million to 9.6 million. Even more striking is the huge increase in those attending all four years of high school; in the pre–World War II years a little better than a third of all high school students received a diploma, while in the 1960s approximately three quarters of all students graduated from high school. The youth cohort had not only grown in size but simultaneously it had been given by the State years and years of semi-isolation and special status.

American youth had also become by the 1950s "the biggest market in history." American teenagers in the economic boom years of the early to mid-1960s were purchasing 55% of all soft drinks, 53% of all move tickets, and 43% of all records. Twenty percent of all high school seniors owned their own cars. Teenage girls while only comprising 11% of the population bought 20% of all cosmetics. And as marketing consultant Eugene Gilbert authoritatively declared: "An advertiser who touches a responsive chord in youth can generally count on the parent to succumb finally to purchasing the product."[16] Gilbert's statement reiterates that more than mere numbers defined this socially cohesive youth cohort as it approached adulthood. It was the first generation born and bred to consume above all else; and it elders demonstrated everyday that they respected its postscarcity, age of abundance consumption sensibilities.

For complex reasons stemming in large part from the imperatives of corporate capitalism and the development of the modern industrial state (which had resulted in social instability, rapid technological and cultural change, the breakdown of traditional and religious cultures, and so much else), older Americans looked, at least in matters of life-style and mores, to the young. They did so, in part, because the young seemed to be less afraid and more at home, even if by virtue of having fewer changes to make or old values to discard, in the fast-changing world that seemed to be thrust upon those too busy working in it to have the time to understand what it all meant.

This was the power the Yippies were looking to tap. A couple of years after Chicago, Jerry Rubin said it straight out:

> Those who grew up before the 1950s live today in a men-tal world of Nazism, concentration camps, economic depression and communist dreams Stalinized. A pre-1950s child who can still dream is very rare. Kids who grew up in the post-1950s live in a world of supermar-kets, color TV commercials, guerrilla war, international media, psychedelics, rock 'n roll and moon walks. For us *nothing is impossible.* We can do *anything.*[17]

Yippie's gamble was that the consumer sensibilities and arrogant, blind optimism that permeated some members of the tightly inte-grated postscarcity generation could be led to the radical political-cultural ideology Yippie was in the business of advertising. And this is where the importance of youth culture's own special objects of consumption enters in.

Theoreticians of social change have long pondered how a dissident political consciousness is produced; how an individual or group comes to the conclusion that the dominant ideology they have been raised to see as reality is only chimera, is only a contrived system of meanings used to control their own more "natural" desires and interests. It is one thing to say that an ideology is transparently rife with internal contradictions; it is another thing to explain why some people see those contradictions and others do not. In Marxian terms this is the realm of class consciousness and, even more problematic, false consciousness.

For the Yippies, who eschewed Marxian terminology but very much recognized the problem of producing a revolutionary consciousness, drugs, above all, seemed to deliver the possibilities of the kind of consciousness raising that could provoke revolutionary insight. Jerry Rubin, in the hyperbolic style of the TV pitchman, writes:

> Marijuana makes each person God. . . . Pot transforms environments. All the barriers we build to protect our-selves from each other disappear. . . . All appointments and schedules, times and deadlines disappear. Man can do what he wants whenever he wants to do it. Marijuana is the street theater of the mind. Marijuana is destroying

the schools. Education is conditioning. Pot deconditions. School makes us cynics. Pot makes us dreamers. Education polarizes our brains into subjects, categories, divisions, concepts. Pot scrambles up our brains and presents everything as a perfect mess. . . . Marijuana is a truth serum. . . . "Why die on Hamburger Hill?" asks the pot smoking Amerikan soldier, as he points his gun at the head of the Captain who orders him to take a hill only the Viet Kong want.[18]

And as Rubin said, by keeping marijuana illegal while a whole system contrives to sell more and more alcoholic beverages: "Grass teaches us disrespect for the law and the courts. Which do you trust Richard Milhous Nixon or your own sense organs." For Rubin, the revolutionary message of marijuana was simple enough, "Pot heads smoke together. We get high and get together. Into ourselves and into each other. How can we make a revolution except together? Make pot legal and society will fall apart. Keep it illegal and soon there will be a revolution."[19]

LSD took the mind's eye even further. It broke the teacher's reality into a dazzling kaleidoscope of multiple realities. It made the linear world of cause and effect into just another float in the soft parade. As John Sinclair declared, "Acid blasted all the negativism and fear out of our bodies and minds and gave us the vision we needed to go ahead, the rainbow vision which showed us how all people could live together in harmony and peace." As Sinclair goes on to explain, it wasn't so much that LSD revealed that something was wrong out there as it was that the acid provided the confidence to do something about the mess. The acid seemed to demonstrate that the way things were was not the way things had to be: "LSD brought everything into focus for the first time in our mixed up lives. . . . Until we started eating all that acid we couldn't figure out what was happening—we knew things were all wrong the way they were but we didn't know how they could be different. . . . LDS cleared all that up."[20]

I began my story of Yippie by writing: Yippie began as a dope joke. As my text showed, I meant it literally. But as I hope is now clear, I also meant it emblematically. Yippie and the drug culture so many young people were discovering and celebrating in the 1960s were intertwined. Yippie was an acid flash and it depended on the kind of vision marijuana supplied. To make drug consciousness—or even worse, a faith in the instrumentality of drug consciousness—a major force in the youth movement in the 1960s is not something that comes easily to an academic historian, but those academicians who have written about the 1960s without any attempt to seriously or analytically relate drug consciousness to the events of the 1960s have done so at the cost of warping and misconstruing much of what went on.

Psychedelic drugs shatter reality. At a time when so much seemed so wrong with the world, drugs taught many people in the 1960s that there were visions truer than Vietnam, more beautiful than a Cadillac, and more honest than a money exchange. But it is crucial to add that the drugs of choice—marijuana and LSD—more than anything else intensify experience and perceptions rather than radically change them. The boon they offer, more often than not, is clarity, whether in the form of a reductio ad absurdum or in the second sight of a hidden truth already in place but underdeveloped or unexposed.

This was the world the Yippies performed in and it was the world they expected their adherents to see. It was a world they hoped would arm their mass followers, teaching them to take the wisdom and to laugh along with their fellow actors as they all played as hard as they could to escape, to destroy the "false theatre of Death" that had been erected in steel, plastic, and concrete by those who lacked the vision to see that there was more to life than money and power.

All during the 1968 Democratic Convention the national press routinely referred to the thousands of assembled demonstrators, many of them short-haired, clean-cut, and most of them affiliated with a variety of New Left or even liberal causes or organizations, as hippies and Yippies. So, too, did Mayor Daley and the Chicago Police Department.[21] By the late 1960s and early 1970s, Yippie was a household word and Jerry Rubin and Abbie Hoffman were probably the two best-known radicals in the United States. Yippie was indeed, as its founders had dreamed, a perfect "media manipulator." Yippie, unlike much of the New Left, was able to pierce the mass media veil that so enshrouded the antiwar and social change movement in the 1960s and broadcast its message loudly enough for almost all to hear. This, in itself, was a kind of success.

Yet, almost twenty years later, it is fairly easy to judge Yippie and its two most flamboyant leaders harshly. Considering that they mouthed words to the effect, and at times surely must have believed, that the youth movement should have no leaders, it is hard to understand their incessant posturing and hungering for attention. Similarly, it is hard to see their voracious need to control situations and people as anything but hypocrisy and deception. Hoffman's admonition that "we're not leaders, we're cheerleaders," seems to be just a sly way to say that whatever happens it's not our fault or responsibility. On the other hand, the obsessive fear of leadership that typified much of the movement in the sixties was, at least somewhat, an overreaction to the felt treachery of establishment leaders and a too optimistic, naive faith in the abilities of the naturally less sophisticated and thoughtful rank and file. The leadership bugaboo was a fault of the entire movement, and it might be fair to say that Yippie leaders Hoffman and Rubin were more victims of a paradox than exploiters of the situation.

For a historian, Yippies' tactical reliance on what can be summed up as mass mediated spectacle is not easily judged because it is not always easy to determine what, in fact, the Yippies meant to produce with it. Certainly the Yippies succeeded in one of their central purposes: they helped turn Chicago '68 in the eyes of both the movement and the establishment into a mythic battle between the young who wanted change NOW! and the old establishment who stood for law and order above all else. The Yippies, by hook or by crook, got the image they set out to establish.

But obviously, if Yippies' goal was to produce a workable myth that could mobilize young people into acting out their fantasies so that they would topple the "Death" culture and replace it with a more humane, antimaterialistic, egalitarian society, well, then they failed. And—taking as a premise that the essential reason they failed was because most young people were perfectly happy to be upstanding citizens looking out for number one–critically they failed because Yippies' reliance on image produced no reality to match it.

Todd Gitlin has explained this brilliantly in his *The Whole World Is Watching*, probably the most insightful book yet written about the New Left:

> Rubin's confusion between image and reality was shared
> by much of his youthful audience, raised on television as
> it had been. . . . In his conception, the revolutionary
> mass was just that, a *mass* to be "turned on" by media
> buttons. Since in this view the revolutionary task reduced
> itself to mobilizing that mass for a specific action—an as-
> sumption similar to conventional marketing assump-
> tions—the problem of the mobilizer was simply
> instrumental: not whether or why to mobilize for a news-
> worthy action, but *how?*[22]

Although my story of Yippie indicates that Rubin and Hoffman did worry about "whether" and "why" to mobilize, Gitlin's major point rings true: Yippie exchanged the political practice of people working together for social change for a fantasy of a mass youth culture already primed for revolution and just awaiting a TV commercial to tell them to be about their bloody business. Singer Gil Scott Heron would seem to be right: "The revolution will not be televised."

Be like us, the Yippies seemed to be saying. But they never really took the time or the effort to explain to their audience how you got there. Julius Lester, as I described in Chapter 2, compared the Yippies to a Zen monk, but I think it is more accurate to say that the Yippies' style was really just like the TV commercials they dreamed of emulating. Like the TV commercial, Yippie obfuscated the process in the name of the product. They, too, promised what the vast majority of their audience would never have: a kind of never-never land of consumption without limits and freedom without responsibility. This is what the mass media responded to and insomuch as Yippie had followers it was what they reveled in. Yippie was fun as long as its politics remained just an afterthought.

The Tom Watson epigram I started this chapter off with is meant to be more than a reflection of one historian's sense of the ironic. The Yippies in some ways are reminiscent of the strange career of Tom Watson, the great Populist rhetorician and leader.

Watson began in great earnestness. He felt from the heart the plight of the poor farmers and was, in the deepest part of his soul, angered by the new class of capitalists that he believed were destroying the truths and beauty of the Old South while they plundered and exploited her plain people. And yet, Tom Watson, too, had an overly large ego that needed constant attention. And Tom Watson, too, in the end, allowed the simple path to the lesser parts of his large vision rule. As time went on, Watson turned more and more to the hysterical rhetoric of race and religious hatred to reach his constituency and turned less and less to the complex task of instructing, organizing, and leading his people from their troubled world of powerlessness, ignorance, and fear to a better place of autonomy, understanding, and courage.[23]

Democracy allows for many paths. The easiest one, the one usually traveled, demands only that leadership cater to the masses' most shortsighted self-interest and their most immediate sensations, and all this in a language that claims to be speaking only of the highest truths and the noblest causes. This is the path the Yippies tried to take.

They gambled that youth, interested above all in the pleasures of the body and the delights of forbidden consumption, would fight for their right to pursue such a plain dream. What the Yippies refused to see was that this youth vision or youth fantasy, which really amounted to consumption without limits, was something that society was more and more willing to give—or at least promise to give—just as Tom Watson's enemy, the New South, was happy to give the blacks to the poor whites in order to keep them pacified. Yippie failed to do the hard work, the educational work, that cannot be finessed through the manipulations of simple images. They failed to do the slow, hard work that would have given richness and depth of understanding to their potential followers' dope dreams and naive fantasies.

The Yippies—Jerry Rubin much more than Hoffman, Sanders, Lampe, or Krassner—played the game of fascism when they aestheticized politics. They played the game of fascism when they used facile slogans instead of careful explanation and caricatured images instead of potent critiques. This is not the game they meant to play—although Rubin, at times, embraced it as a salve to a damaged, voracious ego. By pretending, even to themselves, that the wisdom they themselves had earned through years of hard work and challenging experiences was nothing but child's play, they turned what could have been a visionary experiment into what was often a corrupt self-aggrandizement that led nowhere.

These are harsh words and I would not end with them. What the Yippies did took courage, discipline, intelligence, and a great hope in the goodness and possibilities of young people. In 1968, the Yippies were, in the main, men of conviction, and they were fighting a system that was alive with ugliness, brutality, pettiness, and hatred. Their vision had much that was beautiful and good to commend it. But their means of achieving it, I write almost twenty years later, seemed to contradict what was best about it.

9 Thinking about the Mobe and Chicago '68

In Chicago, the militant organizers of the Mobe realized a dream; they were in an open conflict with the armed forces of the State. They proved their point with their bodies. There were people (The People, they said) opposed to the way things were.

How an affluent and privileged group of young people had come to hold and realize such a dream is largely the story of a grandiosity shared in the 1960s by many who were both the enemies and upholders of what went by the name of the System. Both generations— the young militants and the national elite of Establishment elders who had tried to teach and lead them—lived a vision of America based on the victory of World War II, the rush of the Cold War (and the discrediting of the Soviet Marxist–Leninist State), and the stupendous success of the postwar economy. The grand vision of an all-powerful, endlessly prosperous America that helped to create Vietnam contributed to the grand design of Chicago '68.

The vision of the United States shared in by both generations drew on a revision of a centuries-old privileged notion of American exceptionalism and national self-discovery. In America there was consensus, they all claimed; already manifested according to the intellectual and power establishment; inchoate according to the young militants. Both sides believed themselves to be outside of a national history defined by conflicting forces that dictated change within the confines of temporal continuity.

For the upholders of the System, this sense of being at the end of history was cause for celebration. America—"the new technocratic society," as Zbigniew Brzezinski called it[1]—marked the triumph of reason in the world. Internally, America was fixed and needed only for its young and idealistic "sons" to adopt the "ethics of responsibility" and to join in the management of "a society where there is a shared consensus."[2] There was no need and no reason to expect change in this finally formed American way. As Daniel Bell reported as the decade began: "Today, intellectually, emotionally, who is the enemy that one can fight?"[3] For Bell and other celebrants of "the new technocratic society" the clear answer was, No one.

The young militants, however, could not agree. They rebelled against what they saw, in their overheated way, as an absurd world that old men were trying to lock into immoral patterns. They seemed to rebel against their teachers who insisted that American consensus was a historical verity. Instead, they looked for wisdom among the angry blacks who seemed to be proving that there was no consensus. They rebelled against the cold war internationalists who ran their government and insisted that all the world stood as battleground between forces of light and forces of darkness. And instead they turned to those "victims" of imperialism who seemed to be struggling for independence from both superpowers. Vietnam and the civil rights movements seemed to belie all that the young militants had been taught. The world the young radicals thought they were seeing simply didn't fit the ideology they thought they were being offered.

But in the end, instead of rejecting the ideology of consensus, they refigured it, positing a counterconsensus. They matched the grand claims of their teachers and leaders—the claims built around "the new technocratic society"—with their own grand claims. Strikingly, those claims mirrored the driving vision of an earlier generation of radical and liberal Christians, the very generation their teachers and leaders had, by and large, themselves repudiated. They would create just what an earlier generation had sought to produce, "a future cooperative commonwealth that would transcend the brutal confines of industrial society." The present, they orated, created by an older generation, was an abomination that the young must sweep aside and replace with a future uncontaminated with the racist, imperialist, materialist past.

How such a future could be created out of such a past remained a dim vision. But one bright light prevailed; the true Democracy was a participatory rather than an electoral one. And the best means for practicing such a democracy was through long debates in which all voices were heard and during which all decisions were reached through consensus. The goal was clear—in the end, all would determine all and all would agree that the determination was right.

One side believed that in America consensus on the fundamental questions of life, liberty, and property had already come. The other side believed that a consensus on fundamental matters of social life had been thwarted but would prevail. One way or the other, both sides believed, the united will of the American people was extant and capable of determining the course of human events.

Both sides wished to live within a society in which conflicting interests were subsumed by a shared consciousness. Both sides believed that in America the people's interests could be collectively realized. Both sides looked at the political struggles of the postwar years with distaste, viewing them as narrow and partisan reactions to large-scale changes.

The partisans of the new technocratic state looked increasingly to a centralized and centralizing executive branch to control the new mass society. The militants looked to an all-knowing and all-powerful People who would figure their collective fate through consensual decision making. Politics, narrowly defined as the competition between conflicting interest groups or individuals for power and leadership, was increasingly becoming discredited by both sides. In its place, both sides posited a faith in the exercise of power itself—either executive power built on a consensual society, or the Power of the People based on a Rousseauian General Will.[4] For many in the 1960s, the erotica of power replaced the practice of politics.

> One document after another was signed Shuvalkin . . . Shuvalkin . . . Shuvalkin.
>
> Walter Benjamin, "Kafka"[5]

What is hardest to remember or to imagine about the protest actions taken at the National Democratic Convention in Chicago is that the militant organizers believed that what they were doing was challenging the authority of the State. They were adamant about this fact in all their speechmaking and preconvention communications. They insisted to reporters and to each other that they were not interested in pressuring the convention delegates to include a liberal peace plank in their party platform and were unconcerned about whether McCarthy or Humphrey won the nomination.[6] They were in Chicago out of disrespect to the convention itself and to the political system that could perpetrate Vietnam and perpetuate racism and inequality.

They did not accept the claim of the Democratic party (the same went for the Republican party) that it was a proper institution for selecting one of the two candidates for the nation's highest political office. They didn't accept party politics. After viewing public policies and the state of the union, they didn't accept the idea that electoral politics represented democratic practice. They had other plans, other ideas. They said, "The government of the United States is an outlaw institution . . . under the control of war criminals."[7] At the convention, the epitome, they believed, of a closed system masquerading as a democracy, they would protest and, they figured, do something about the State's "illegitimacy and criminality."[8] On this, the militant organizers of the Mobe agreed.

On August 26, in response to reporters' questions about the confrontation in the parks and on the streets, Tom Hayden said, "It shows the bankruptcy of the political system."[9] That a demonstration has resulted in a stark, brutal confrontation between the police and the protesters was for Hayden representative of American political reality

("Its need to use force to deal with people," is how he phrased it).[10] In 1968, Hayden and his fellow activists were not interested in reforming the particular policies of Johnson or the tactics of Daley, they were hammering away at the system. They were not debating policy, they were insisting that the American political system was not good, that "it," as Rennie Davis told a couple of hundred young people just before the convention, "is unrepresentative of the interest of vast numbers of people."[11]

What would replace that system was never very well described. It went under the rubric of participatory democracy and suggested something that combined the collective, egalitarian, humanistic spirit of a socialism that had never been, with the individuality and forthright citizenship of Jefferson's vision of yeoman democracy.[12] Linda Morse, head of the Radical Organizing Committee in 1968 and a strong supporter of the Chicago protest, described this alternative system at the trial of Hayden, Davis, Dellinger, and others accused of conspiring to create a riot in Chicago: "A good society . . . a society that meets the ideals that the country was founded on years ago . . . a society that is a free society . . . a joyous society where everyone is fed, where everyone is educated . . . has a job . . . has a chance to express himself artistically or politically or spiritually or religiously."[13] As to how that system would be better representative of the American people, it was only clear that the poor would be determining their own future—that was the lesson learned, if not always observed, in the civil rights movement—and that wars in support of Third World dictators who opposed nationalist, socialist revolutions would be ended—no more Vietnams, anywhere, anytime.

But what would replace the "illegitimate" system was, to many of the radical organizers, not that important to what was going on in the Chicago protest.[14] What mattered was that people could get together from across the country, run and march through the streets, disrupt, confront the armed might of the State, chant and make speeches, insist that the way things were done and therefore what got done in America was fundamentally wrong and had to be radically changed. People could act out their anger. They could show the managers of the system—which to them meant their professors just as much as their elected officials—that American life could be lived outside of what they saw as the technocratic warfare state.

From the militants' perspective, protesting the Democratic National Convention was ideologically about bringing down the capitalist, welfare state, and politically about rejecting established authority in the name of a vision of something better. To give it a label appropriate to the times, call it Castroite. The protesters expected that they would learn by doing. They didn't need a fixed ideology because the situation would suggest the solution and the program. They believed that in the process of taking on the authority of the system they would discover their new system by embodying it. Staughton Lynd, older but not too old to be a New Leftist, wrote in mid-1967, " . . . a method of struggle [and he had a specific one—decentralization—in mind] creates new experiences that point toward a new society."[15] Greg Calvert, an SDS leader, wrote a little earlier, "While struggling to liberate the world, we create the liberated world in our midst. While fighting to destroy the power which had created the loveless anti-community, we would ourselves create the community of love—The Beloved Community."[16] The key to the riddle of the right tomorrow was to oppose the right problems today. By opposing evil, these people believed, one could learn how to become good.

Before developing the problematic aspects of such an approach, it need be said that, in adopting an almost Rooseveltian faith in the transformative power of pragmatic action, these New Leftists did break the chains of dogma that had imprisoned much of the anticapitalist left in the United States. Hayden and his allies were free to avoid the binds of a rhetoric inappropriate to their situation, a rhetoric that would have privileged class war above all else. Before Chicago, Hayden made some effort to make clear that the movement must find its allies and build its revolution where it could, not just where dogma said it must.[17] More important, by believing that through experience and struggle the good society could be both envisioned and lived in the here and now, some movement people did find transforming experiences and were able to establish a set of values that survived the antiwar movement. Their experiences did lay the groundwork for other political/cultural struggles, which while not as well publicized as the confrontationalism of the 1960s continue to enrich many lives and many communities.[18]

But the problem with a radical politics that looked to experience and the struggle itself to create direction and provide answers was, as Chicago demonstrated, that it defied certain practical considerations. And certainly by 1968, many in the movement were reeling under some of these practical considerations. To be in opposition, to define oneself in opposition, usually binds one to one's opposition. When one's opposition is brutal and uncompromising, as it was in Chicago, the tendency is, as the action in Chicago's streets evidenced, to adopt the tactics of the opposition while decrying the ideology that produced such tactics in the first place. It was Tom Hayden, enraged by police attacks and the callous authorities that had authorized such attacks, who told the largest assemblage of Chicago protesters that "if blood is going to flow, let it flow all over this city. If gas is going to be used, let that gas come down all over Chicago. . . . If we are going to be disrupted and violated, let this whole stinking city be disrupted and violated."[19] Opposing a system that can and will use overpowering force to stifle protest does not usually, as Lynd, Calvert, and so many others hoped, produce "experiences" that suggest both how to live and how to manage a revolutionary society.[20] This is all the more problematic in a loosely organized coalition that has no clear sense of how to produce change or even what changes are being fostered by the coalition's struggle. In discussing Chicago seven years later, David Dellinger observed, "Some of the now disillusioned leaders of the early New Left found it hard to move from protest to resistance without adopting some of the cynicism and *realpolitik* of the society we were resisting."[21]

Confrontation can create polarization—it did in Chicago. But it doesn't necessarily "point toward a new society." SDS leadership, indeed, left Chicago pointed toward the oldest society of all—the lawless one where any means available could be used to enforce one's will.[22]

> To perceive the aura of an object we look at means to invest it
> with the ability to look at us in return.
>   Walter Benjamin, "On Some Motifs in Baudelaire"[23]

Many who were a part of the Mobilization to End the War in Vietnam did not look at the Chicago protest as a political struggle per se. They saw themselves operating less in a political discourse than in a spiritual, moral realm where the corruption inherent in unequal power relations—indeed, by their definition, in all power relations—could be exposed and somehow be done away with. Just after Chicago, David Dellinger explained, "Our aim is to destroy power, dissipate it, decentralize it, democratize it, if you will."[24] To some degree, Dellinger is suggesting something akin to Marx's final stage of history; the timeless period in which the State has withered away and all men are free to be. But Dellinger would have his peaceable kingdom without any intermediary stage; he rejects any interim dictatorship of the proletariat or any other group. He leaves out any and all stages of political control. Moral vision alone, he seems to suggest, can get us from here to there. Dellinger's avowal indicates much about the moral activists' constant struggle to pose a political message on a moral landscape that provided no ground for the legitimacy of conflicting interests. Dellinger begins, after all, by advocating the destruction of power, but he ends this declaration of his single most important revolutionary goal by equating the destruction of power to the democratization, "if you will," of power. Beneath the fog of this sentence lies a simple truth (and I can never tell—even today—if Dellinger understands what he implies)[25] that only in a society where all agree on all can power be both destroyed and democratic. "Do what you will," as long as what you will is always already what all would will. It is the lesson of the Chinese reeducation camps which existed contemporaneously with the antiwar movement.

In the 1950s, such a decidedly and dangerously antipolitical message could be seen as a valuable step in creating a movement for social change. Moral critiques could be used to delegitimize entrenched "natural" power relationships. At a time when many of America's most influential intellectuals were declaring the end of ideology and the endless ascension of America to a technocratic state dedicated to affluence,[26] moral rather than political criticism supplied an opening to a morally vulnerable, politically complacent society.

In part, as Christopher Lasch argued in the 1960s,[27] such antipolitical language and understandings were a part of the legacy many of the best of post–World War II, American intellectuals bequeathed to the younger generation. The cold war and nuclear brinkmanship contributed to a feeling that conflict between self-interested parties could not be at the base of a morally defensible politics. In such an environment a moral critique based on the apotheosis of international harmony and national consensus alone seemed to carry resonance and reason.

Such a critique well served the civil rights movement in the 1950s. Indeed, such feelings contributed to the federal government's decision made at the end of World War II to push, cautiously and slowly, for racial integration. Some national security advisors realized that cold war international politics necessitated the removal of America's internationally embarrassing "Negro problem."

But the civil rights movement in the 1950s was above all else about being included in society. It was not an ideological rejection of American society's form and function. For white people, already free to participate in existing American society, such a moral critique provided no basis for reworking political claims.

The moral critics of the 1960s, dedicated in theory to disproving the Establishment's claim that America was a consensual society, operated interior to the very same claim. Instead of offering an answer to the real, ongoing problem of political conflict, they insisted that beneath the corruption of power relations lay a harmonious society. They ignored their own organizational struggles, as well as the lessons the implementation of federal civil rights laws offered, in order to cling to a moral vision of an absolutely cooperative society, peopled by angels. Though most in the movement would not have welcomed the comparison, such feelings closely resemble those held by late nineteenth-century American utopianists like Edward Bellamy and his adherents, who insisted that a nonpolitical cooperative society was necessary and was obtainable if only the right form of social organization would be adapted; for the movement radicals such organization usually revolved around the amorphous participatory democracy; for the Bellamy adherents it was the incorporation of society.

An even closer parallel existed, as I already suggested, between the antiwar movement and the vibrant liberal and radical Anglo-Saxon Protestant peace movement of the early decades of the twentieth century. In 1966, A. J. Muste, the patron saint of the moralist protesters and revered chairman of the Mobe in 1966 and early 1967, whose roots lay firmly in this older radical Protestant tradition, could still call out to the movement, "Let there be voices crying out in the wilderness."[28] When Muste talked about American politics, he was prone to decry its "wickedness and stupidity."[29] Muste died more than a year before Chicago, but his influence, his understandings were well-represented by David Dellinger, who had long worked with Muste. So, too, did many of the young protesters carry a Mustian perspective. They may have known little or nothing about Muste but some shared, if not his biblical language, his emphasis on reverentiality and deliberate witness. And with him and many of his generation, they hoped for and believed in the possibility of launching "a community of love."

But most of the younger militant movement people had, by 1968, gone past a belief that moral witnessing could produce social transformation. They had tried civil disobedience and mass marches—the tactics of moral witness—and had found them lacking in efficacy. It was this frustration that had produced the slogan "from protest to resistance" in 1967. It had produced the confrontations at the Pentagon, at the Oakland Induction Center, and at the Whitehall Induction Center in New York. The militants believed they had somehow to directly engage the war makers. They had to do more than passively resist. Unlike Dellinger and Muste, they wanted to do more than declare the immorality of what was. They wanted to demonstrate their own legitimacy. They wanted "To travel a road to power."[30]

By the time of Chicago, the dedicated militant activists felt themselves to be deeper in a struggle than Muste's image of a Jeremiah crying in the wilderness allowed. Moreover, *they wanted to be inside*, in the cities and on the streets. They wanted to be in the thick of a fight for power as well as about power. The time for prophecy, they believed, was over. It was time to confront, not merely to exhort. They were fighting to bring the whole thing down.

Surely, a good deal of this confrontational attitude that sought control in the name of moral authority came from the Black Power movement, which by 1968 had turned from what the black militants had come to see as the reformist path of civil rights. Black Power, which had become by the summer of 1966 the dominant strategy of the younger leaders of the black movement, insisted that its goal was black control and black authority over the black community's daily life and political and economic future; a goal not unlike that offered in the on again–off again Communist party policy of self-determination or in Marcus Garvey's domestic policies. To achieve this goal, Black Power leaders turned from confrontation and exhortations to violent armed struggle.[31]

Listen to Stokely Carmichael, SNCC leader and practically an icon to white militants, just after Martin Luther King, Jr.'s assassination: "White America has declared war on black people . . . today the final solution is coming . . . and black people are going to have to find ways to survive. The only way to survive is to get some . . . [guns]."[32] Or the Black Panther party ten-point platform, item 6: "We will protect ourselves from the force and violence of the racist police and the racist military by whatever means necessary."[33] And blacks were rioting in core city after core city, burning down buildings, looting stores (all in their own ghetto neighborhoods), and on a few occasions sniping at police. Such actions had produced violent reactions. In 1968, George Wallace, governor of Alabama, was running for president on one basic issue—keeping the niggers down. And Nixon, playing it closer to the chest, called for law and order, which to black militants and a lot of other people was just the permissible way to say, Get the niggers. Special federal laws had been passed to stop the likes of Stokely Carmichael, and Huey Newton, chairman of the Panthers, was in jail in Oakland, being tried on the dubious charge of having murdered a policeman. For the blacks, the struggle was palatable, it was happening.

The most militant whites wanted that experience. They wanted that revolutionary reality to be theirs. They worked on it in Chicago.

National SDS, and that is not at all the same thing as saying all SDS members, worked the rhetoric of revolution harder than all the others. On Chicago, they concluded, "Yeah we did all right this week. . . . We won. . . . We have a base in the millions of young people who have no place and want no place in plastic poverty pig America. . . . Call us revolutionary communists—you better. But you better call us the people because that's who we are."[34] They laughed at the liberals: "Those of us who have been on the streets for the past five days didn't give a flying fuck whether McCarthy would win or lose; and now that he's lost, still don't."[35] They could issue, in good faith, mimeographs that read, "The man has guns. We don't have our guns with us. . . . Be cool. . . . Keep going."[36]

Now the line, "We don't have our guns with us," was not, could not be taken seriously as a literal assessment of the situation. It was really a kind of direct emulation of the Black Panther's anthematic demand that "all black people should arm themselves for self defense." What it meant was that these militant SDS leaders wanted to be positioned alongside the Black Power forces in an armed struggle against the State. They wanted (even if most were not quite ready for the actuality of it) to be in battle with the American State and its crushing security forces. "We came to town to show the world that the rotten empire is no longer going to be tolerated by the people it's been fucking over these many years."[37]

"The people," they keep saying. "You better call us the people." "No longer going to be tolerated by the people." The People seem to be the poor and the oppressed. What that makes a number of other Americans is unclear. Nor is it clear why the SDS figures had adopted such an aggressive but beseeching tone of voice. "You better"; "No longer going to be tolerated"; "A flying fuck." They are both obnoxiously rude and in direct, clamorous, one-sided conversation with their enemies. Yelling lustily, they beg for attention. One is hard-pressed not to find something infantile in their tone, something speaking of a great insecurity.

Undoubtedly, a part of that insecurity stemmed from making what was in normal American political discourse such an absurd claim. How can the white, middle-class, college-educated SDS leaders be the People? How can one tie this claim back to the seed idea of participatory democracy? Revolutionary agency (i.e., if it wasn't going to be the working class, who was going to make the revolution?), as many other observers of the New Left have commented, was by the time of the Chicago protest one of SDS's most urgent concerns.[38] By 1968, for many of SDS's leaders, the only possible answer was to become increasingly "objective" (i.e., if the present situation doesn't fit revolutionary needs, then it is the present "subjective" situation and not the "objective" necessity of revolution that needs adjustment): "The People" were the revolutionary force and so whoever made the revolution were "The People."

Chicago, with its emphasis on street fighting and clear polarization, pushed many of the militants toward an increasingly "objective" position. Chicago demonstrated that the state could be met in battle and that unexpected allies such as street gangs, "greasers," and other *lumpen* types could be counted on in such a battle. Chicago, combined with the "success" of Columbia and the increasing militancy found on a few college campuses and in many urban ghettos, demonstrated to many members of SDS that revolution was a real possibility. They felt that with such a possibility at hand it was time to become more "disciplined"; it was time to find an ideological guide to the upcoming struggle.[39] SDS was turning toward an increasingly strident Third World Marxism—in which Marx's urban workers had been replaced by poor people of all kinds—in which the vast majority of Americans were seen as the enemy. The radicals were finding a History but in the process were losing the specificity of their own past. Working democracy of any kind was fast being dismissed by the radicals in the name of revolutionary necessity. Like the most short-sighted kind of early twentieth-century Progressive, the radicals had begun to ignore the practice of democratic decision making while claiming to be working for the good of society as a whole.

The SDS was, of any major presence at the Chicago protest, the most militant force. Their brand of militancy was not at all wholly representative of the multiconstituent Mobe coalition. However, their general sense of alienation from the American system was representative of a feeling shared by many who protested at Chicago. An editorial in the SDS convention week poster newspaper, *Handwriting on the Wall*, read, "If we are 'outside' here, it is because we have always been outside. . . . We are excluded because we refused to be good Germans."[40] "We are excluded," not we reject or we refuse but instead the nauseating feeling that It—what they claimed was a consuming, racist, and imperialist society—out of bad conscience, had kept the moral protesters out.

There is in this SDS statement still the remains of a wishful liberalism, a liberalism of the same kind that a few years earlier had Tom Hayden trying to convince Bobby Kennedy that the Vietnam War was wrong.[41] But it is a liberalism gone sour. Perhaps the equation of liberalism with a rationalist's trust in the goodwill of those in power is overly simplistic. But if one equates revolutionaries with those who believe that a system needs to be changed not because it doesn't work but because it works for the wrong people, then there is still something about even the militants that smacks of a dispirited liberalism. The protesters do talk about the system and not simply about corrupt officials but the germ remains; the protesters still wonder if they have been kept out only because they are too good.

For the militants, confrontation had replaced moral witness as a tactical necessity. But for many of them political struggle—which would have made them examine just who were the American people and assess how they could be reached—had not replaced a rigid, moral absolutism. By holding onto such a moralism in a society where politics were pervasive—unlike, say Poland in the 1980s or even Cuba in the 1950s—the militants guaranteed their own isolation from the vast majority of the American people. They also revealed their own distaste for the realities of democracy.

> Man's inner concerns do not have their issueless private character by nature. They do so only when he is increasingly unable to assimilate the data of the world around him by way of experience.
>
> Walter Benjamin, "On Some Motifs in Baudelaire"[42]

Andy Warhol told an underground newspaper reporter, "I don't know where the artificial stops and the real starts. . . . If you look at something long enough, I've discovered, meaning goes away. I'm so empty."[43] Few people were so decidely alienated from the world around them as Andy Warhol. But almost all the young people in the movement who maneuvered through radical politics in the 1960s worried at the subject, at the personal certainty that they were alienated from American institutions and perhaps from the entire American way of life.[44] The political implications of such a feeling are volatile. As many critics of the New Left have mournfully written, such estrangement leads young people to believe that they need not play by the rules of the American political game.

Before exploring the political implications of such estrangement and alienation further let me begin here by presenting, just emblematically, something from the surface world from which the activists who were to gather in Chicago felt themselves estranged.

Time Magazine, in its review of 1966, named "Twenty Five and Under" as its "Man of the Year." The cover featured a collage of hopeful young faces. American youths, the cover story explained, were men (women were fundamentally ignored) the whole country could be proud of. *Time* explained:

> He has a unique sense of control over his own destiny— barring the prospect of a year's combat in a brush-fire war. . . . He stalks love like a wary hunter, but has no time or target—not even the mellowing communists—for hate. . . . Far from "disaffiliated," they are more gregarious than any preceding generation. . . . [He] has known all his life that he must serve a military tour of duty, indeed has planned it along with college, marriage, and choice of vocation. From the moment he arrives (usually aboard a comfortable troop ship) . . . to combat itself (as intense as any in history but brief), he is supported by the best that his country can offer. . . . It is little wonder that he fights so well, and quite comprehensible that his main concern in off-duty hours is aiding the Vietnamese civilian.[45]

The weight of the world the militants felt themselves skidding away from becomes more apparent when one adds onto this curious hymn to American youth Zbigniew Brzezinski's spring 1968 dismissal of the student protest movement:

> Some of the recent upheavals have been led by people who increasingly will have no role to play in the new technocratic society. . . . Thus, rather than representing a true revolution, some recent outbursts are in fact a coun- terrevolution. Its violence and revolutionary slogans are merely—and sadly—the death rattle of the historical irrelevants.[46]

Know that Brzezinski is not talking about ghetto looters. He is writ- ing in the *New Republic* most specifically about the just concluded Columbia University protests. He knows that the militants were com- ing from Columbia, Berkeley, Harvard, Ann Arbor, the University of Chicago—what *Fortune* magazine, based on a series of polls and sur- veys taken just after Chicago, would call the "Forerunner" colleges and universities.[47] Historical irrelevants? And/or the best and the brightest of the new generation?

When the most thoughtful in the movement read that the American soldier's "main concern in off-duty hours is aiding the Vietnamese civilian" and that "the American Youth" has known all his life and contentedly planned for "a year's combat in a brush-fire war," they felt that what they were reading was not of "their" world. And they felt that when Zbigniew Brzezinski, a foremost American social sci- entist and policy analyst, called them "historical irrelevants" because they did not accept the inevitability of "the new technocratic society," that what had been declared reality by those who had been duly authorized by society to make such declarations was not a reality they could embrace as their own. Paul Potter, head organizer of the move- ment centers in Chicago, relates this feeling directly to the Chicago confrontation. Writing about Chicago soon after the protest he states, " 'Our' level of rationality and 'theirs' had drifted so far apart that we just couldn't even guess at what theirs was anymore."[48]

More than ten years later, when Tom Hayden was asked to recon- sider what he did in 1968 and at the convention protest, he quietly told a CBS reporter, "The things you have to do to be heard in a closed society will make you seem preposterous, crazy and subject you to labels of all kinds."[49] And not too long after Chicago, David Harris, leader of Resistance (the draft resisters who caravaned to Chicago from California, singing and acting out antiwar protests as they went), wrote in prison, "We no longer carry out our intentions but make our actions a tool of the state in hopes it will realize them. . . . We are the recipients of reality rather than its source. We become strangers in a strange land."[50]

Michael Rossman, a prominent Berkeley radical who approached Chicago with considerable caution, tried in early 1968 to describe what it meant to believe in a radical alternative in an America so unwilling and so unprepared to consider such a possibility. Writing for the Catholic magazine, *Commonweal*, he titled his piece, "Look Ma, No Hope." He said, referring all the way back—four years—to the Free Speech Movement in Berkeley, "Our hopeless beauty, then, flowed from a barren landscape of Impossible. . . . Our motion . . . grew . . . not out of hope, but because we had to, because that context of Impossible granted us a weird sort of freedom."[51]

In 1934, Reinhold Niebuhr had carefully sketched out the utility and the danger of that landscape of Impossible for the embattled radical:

> In the task of that redemption the most effective agents
> will be men who have substituted some new illusions for
> the abandoned ones. The most important of these illu-
> sions is that the collective life of mankind can achieve
> perfect justice. It is a very important illusion for the mo-
> ment; for justice cannot be approximated if the hope of
> its perfect realization does not generate a sublime mad-
> ness in the soul. Nothing but such madness will do battle
> with malignant power and "spiritual wickedness in high
> places."[52]

Niebuhr concludes: "The illusion is dangerous because it encourages terrible fanaticisms. It must therefore be brought under the control of reason. One can only hope that reason will not destroy it before its work is done." Such similar words from such different men speak tellingly to the bind the twentieth-century American radical who challenges feels locked within. To challenge Power is often to challenge reason, or, at the very least, reasonableness itself.

Many in the movement in 1968 fully felt the weight of such a challenge. To some extent, the movement in the 1960s was a continuation of the liberal and radical Anglo-Saxon Protestant tradition that had sustained Norman Thomas and many other native Socialists and had been revived in the civil rights movement. The "illusion" of some of the younger members of the movement was remarkably similar to the "dream" held by that earlier generation; the "dream," as historian Richard Fox put it, "that an organic community would one day displace the impersonal mechanisms of modern capitalism."[53] This dream was in part transmitted directly or indirectly to many young people through the church-led and inspired civil rights movement. However,

young members of the movement were making their challenge to
Power without the firm faith in either God or History that guided
earlier generations. Starring out into their own landscape of Impossible, many in the movement in 1968 believed themselves to be in an
unprecedented bind.

They felt faced with a system that seemed to deny the possibility
of substantial internal alternatives but not change along an already
determined line; as Brzezinski suggests when he reprises the para-
doxical anti-Marxist message the "end of ideology" proponents had
long been hammering home to many of these superior college students. They saw themselves not in a world from which ideology had
been banished but in one where ideology had become seamless. And
they were caught outside of it, rejecting the rules of the American
political system but not, for the most part, accepting any other system
in its stead. The result of this exile was, to continue Rossman's met-
aphor, a trip to a mental landscape where there was great freedom—
there were no rules, no foreordained paths to follow—but no model
for relating freedom to power.

This was, as other historians of the New Left have noted[54] and I
have been arguing, a freedom of the alienated—a freedom not foreign
to several generations of artists and independent intellectuals. It was
a freedom bitterly celebrated in the books, movies, and music the '60s
generation grew up on: *Rebel without a Cause*, "Blue Suede Shoes,"
Catcher in the Rye, *On the Road*, "Rollover Beethoven," *Wild One*. It was
the freedom that prompted Tom Hayden to buy a motorcycle and to
make his way catch-as-catch-can to Berkeley where he found the people he was looking for—people who were tired of feeling like numbers
and who were, in the midst of the multiversity, trying to use their
alienation from the system as a weapon to reconceive that system.

Being outside (which is not at all the same as dropping out) did
provide a certain amount of individual liberation. It meant that the
system's arsenal of rewards and punishments were less efficacious. It
also meant that the alienated radicals were prepared to reject the causal
chains of events that suggested, as Brzezinski and so many others
declared, that all that is, is what must be. To be alienated was to at
least be in a psychological position that allowed one to see that reality
might only be the predictably corrupt product of a sick society.

Distanced from the regularized struggles of everyday life, searching
for alternatives that would turn America's unrealized ideals of equality
and democracy into a way of life, many in the movement felt they
could, indeed must, operate outside of established norms. For them,
the codes of civility, sociality, and legality underpinned what seemed
to be an undemocratic, racist society in which the people's powerlessness was institutionalized. For the militants, freedom meant not,

as it normally did in America, the ability to choose so much as it meant beginning without the constraints, the lessons, even the understandings of what they called the Establishment or the System. Being alienated from society seemed to free one from its formulaic demands if not from its problems.

In part, this is what Rossman is suggesting when he says that the movement began in a barren landscape of Impossible. For him and others, what was, was simply unacceptable. For the young radicals, who in a typically American understanding, saw no need to read the actual rather than the figurative claims of the past on the future; the rhetorical sweeps of the New Deal and even the New Frontier were unkept moral promises rather than precarious, ongoing excursions into conflicting political claims. Alienated from the racist, imperialist society that they were soon supposed to manage, the young militants, as has happened before, turned toward an idealism often uncluttered by any knowledge of American history. Later, after Chicago and the frustrations of Nixon's first two years in office, as so often happens to the alienated when their idealism is shattered by the rush of experience, many in the movement, though hardly all, would turn to idealism's twin: cynicism.

As Rossman's image suggests, the young radicals believed that the social landscape they sought to create existed only dimly in their own collective minds' eye. In part, this almost arrogant dismissal of previous political writings is indicative of the anti-intellectual strain typical of most practitioners of both established and radical American politics. It is also indicative of the fact that most of the leaders of the movement were young men, who looked with particular scorn upon the generation of cold war intellectuals as sellouts.

Indeed, many intellectuals, ranging from the very sympathetic Paul Goodman to the more critical Harold Cruse, agreed that older thinkers and writers had, as Goodman wrote in the *New York Times Magazine*, February 25, 1968, provided the young with "no persuasive program for social reconstruction."[55] Christopher Lasch, a younger intellectual, concurred. At approximately the same time as Chicago '68, he wrote that "my experience and the experience of many of my friends and contemporaries fully bears out the contention that the intellectual acquiescence in the premises of the cold war made it unusually difficult to get a political education in the 1950s."[56] Many political theorists tried in the 1960s to make up for this felt absence of grounding ideas but as Harold Cruse wrote (and Lasch quoted as the epigram to his 1969 *The Agony of the American Left*), "These young intellectuals are the victims of historical discontinuity. . . . As a result this new generation is called upon to make up for lost time—about forty five years of it."[57]

Perhaps more important, for the young white radicals of the early
and mid-1960s there was no Marx or Mao. Protesting against a feeling
of dehumanization as much as anything else, state socialism was not
a vision these young people found appealing. Only toward the end
of the decade, in the need to find program and connections, did parts
of the movement reach out toward the coherency of Marxism and
neo-Marxism. For several years, there was only the inspiration but
not at all the practice of John Kennedy, a heartfelt understanding of
America's founding documents, a few texts that described the enemy—
power elites and corporatized bureaucracies—and, most important,
the awesome example of old and young black people taking their lives
into their own hands.

More than anything else, as I have already been claiming, the black
movement (especially early on for the veterans of Mississippi, the
example of Bob Moses and the Student Non-Violent Coordinating
Committee who were organizing, against all odds, sharecroppers in
Mississippi) gave the nascent radicals a seed vision that they thought
they could make flower on the barren landscape they had been given
by their elders. But to translate the dream of participatory democracy
and the experience of a Mississippi summer into the realities of the
multiversities and the military-industrial complex, to even believe that
the sacrifices in Mississippi could change fundamental problems, was
to know that one was only twenty or twenty-five and operating outside of American political and moral reality.[58] To be in such a place,
as Rossman suggested, was to have freely chosen an Impossible mindscape. For those who could remember that their vision was impossible
but that their actions could have political impact, this mindscape was
tenable. Perhaps Tom Hayden, who many distrusted as a political
opportunist, exemplifies such a position. For too many others, operating in a Land of Impossible only produced a typically American
response: frustration, boredom, cynicism, and reaction.

Some have charged that the alienation that seeded much of the
movement contributed to its "failure" and "excesses." They have
charged that alienation created and, I suppose they would still say,
creates an emphasis on "personal heroism" rather than on "analysis
of the sources of tension in American society and the possibility of
change."[59]

To some degree, as I hope I have made clear, I agree. But these
young people did found a politics of morality that existed outside of
instrumental limitations. Alienated from normal schemas of political
outcomes that could have stopped them from ever trying to create
changes, many in the movement could begin at what they saw as the
beginning, laying out a course of events that originated with a shared

feeling of being morally superior outsiders. To do so was, as David Harris said, to say "No" to the state's demand that every individual realize his destiny only as a tool of the state's reality. It was also to insist that one's own reality was as valid, and more justified morally than the state's, which as Hayden knew could only be done at risk of being labeled crazy and preposterous. French students in the May '68 uprising, intensely influenced by their American counterparts, had a slogan that translates, "I take my desires to be reality because I believe in the reality of my desires."[60]

The clearest, albeit still nascent, presentation of this reality is in the Port Huron Statement, which links the failures of the American system with its loss of a captivating vision. It clearly marks off alienation and not political claims or even economic class and/or self-interest as the harbinger of a revolutionary (which is, for 1962, really too radical a word) consciousness. The better part of a decade after the manifesto, Davis and Hayden, as they planned and executed Chicago '68, still rejected traditional Marxist dialectics, just as they rejected liberal pluralism. But by 1968, they were able to combine a radical American faith in democracy with a loosely constructed theory of liberation that suggested that the alienated of the world—be they white middle-class college students, ghetto street-corner men, or Cuban peasants—could and would unite, consensually determine their own revolutionary path and collectively overthrow their capitalist and/or bureaucratic oppressors.

Hayden and Davis, in 1968, believed that to produce a revolution the standing order still need not be shown to contain internal contradictions so much as it would have to be demonstrated to be containing its own nullity, its own process that drove the young out just as it kept out blacks and the poor of all races. Ugliness and scabrousness and not a class structure per se, were the system's politically reprehensible qualities. To turn the private, individual revulsion of middle-class people, to make the inner, psychological condition of alienation into or onto a concrete public set of meaningful, collective actions was thus still the practical task the Chicago project directors faced. And still faced without any sure sense of direction, stability, or reassuring dogma. In lieu of such guides, polarization, Hayden well knew, would have to serve. As self-defined outsiders who lacked faith in any dialectical principle of social change except direct power, they knew, as they knew from the start, that mass rejection was the only significant leverage they could have on the American political system.

It was not a strong position. Without a viable alternative culture or a coherent politics, without a concrete place for most people to practice or "live" the revolution, the alienated were, in the face of a long-term

process, atomized and left to the freedom to choose their own modes
of consumption that the American system so eagerly offered to the
well-educated, potentially affluent malcontents. But those commentators and citizens who see the success of Reagan and the extreme
right wing, the reintegration of many alienated militants, and the
ethos of the present college generation as the absolute repudiation of
the 1960s movement for social and political change are not being realistic. The successes of the movement are legion. They range from
the deauthorization of the government and most other American in-
stitutional bases of power and authority among a sizable number of
Americans, to the creation of a whole range of new political forces
and approaches, to the legitimization of leftist and other alternative
critiques in the universities, to the ongoing declaration to the warmakers that they will not be able to wage a war without facing a
skeptical and even resistant force of American people.

> It is as if something that seemed inalienable to us, the securist
> among our possessions were taken from us: the ability to ex-
> change experiences.
>
> Walter Benjamin, "The Storyteller"[61]

Chicago '68 was a heady success for those who participated in it
directly or vicariously. Above all else, it gave the militants—labeled
"historical irrelevants" and worse by their critics—a sense that what
they were doing was real, that they could affect how things really
were, and that it took tens of thousands of security forces to keep
them down. In Chicago, at the nationally televised convention, people
in the movement were able to make their presence felt and they were
able to feel themselves in active confrontation.

By the summer of 1968, the movement needed such concrete acts.
Movement people needed to feel themselves part of a collective struggle. They needed, as Tom Hayden said just before the protest, "dramatic national experience as a common point of reference, as a way
to make a leap of consciousness."[62] For Americans raised to accept
representative democracy and economic atomization, especially for
those young Americans who responded to such societal expectations
with feelings of alienation, such a concrete experience of resistance
was invaluable. It fostered a sense of control and powerfulness. In
these ways, Chicago '68 was a good idea. For many who participated
in it, it worked. As Tom Hayden hoped, it did produce a shared
experience; it produced a sense of history.

Most Americans, however, didn't like what they saw and heard.
The protesters' radical presence threatened them. It alienated them.
And the radical protesters gave most Americans little chance to un-

derstand them. So unsure of their own presence, the protesters offered no space in their Impossible landscape for the experiences of others. The police baiting that went on throughout the week was the most obvious example of this inability to see the other in its own terms. The radicals' desire for polarization in Chicago marked the end of the dream of a participatory democracy.

Chicago '68 was plagued with the problems that would eventually finish off the 1960s-style movement for social change. But without most of those problems—naivite, alienation, anti-intellectualism, stubborness, extreme moralism, youthful ignorance—there would not have been a movement in the first place. At Chicago, the movement displayed its courage and its heart even as it revealed its unworkable politics.

10 Public Feelings

> In what order should one describe those profound and confused impressions which assail the traveller when he first arrives in a village where the native culture has remained comparatively untouched?[1]
>
> Claude Levi-Strauss

> I don't hear much about what is going on around the country. I'm strictly a local boy serving the great city of Chicago and the state of Illinois.[2]
>
> Richard J. Daly

The demonstrators who came to Chicago did so in order to confront a national symbol. They came in order to use the Democratic National Convention, which happened to be located in Chicago, as a local marker in the national moral challenge they saw themselves waging. They were, as they said over and over, not interested in influencing the convention; they were in Chicago to demonstrate their refusal to accept the American political system. Their concerns were abstract and long-range. For them, the particular configuration of the Democratic Convention in Chicago only mattered insomuch as it interfered with their plans for a symbolic protest. Their Chicago shared little with the Chicago the Mayor and his people sought to protect.

For those who felt charged with maintaining order, the Chicago confrontation felt completely different. For them, the well-functioning system of political control and public order that maintained a stable life came before all else, and so came before discussion or consideration. Politics was what made sure that things stayed about the same. In Chicago, such politics, naturally enough, was known as "machine" politics.

All during the campaign of 1968, Richard Nixon tried to find the words that would express his constituents' feelings. He knew that the turmoil of the 1960s—the rioting and burning and Black Power Negroes, the students storming around their universities telling everybody what was right and wrong, the protest marchers carrying Viet Cong flags and saying that American boys were dying in vain—was making the "silent majority" of good Americans angry and afraid. In a position paper he wrote for the 1968 Republican Platform Committee, Nixon reached for this feeling: "The first right of every American, to be free from domestic violence, has become the forgotten civil right of the American people."[3]

The state, Nixon is suggesting, was formed to protect individuals from the unwelcome violent attentions of others. The state was invented (he is implying mythically with his call on the preamble to the Constitution) to insure that citizens' right to domestic tranquillity remained inviolate. The national Democratic party's welfare state, Nixon is saying, has forgotten that it is obliged to protect an individual's right to be left alone. Instead, that state has pledged itself to a policy of inclusion, a policy that insists that the state has the right to intrude in local affairs and order private citizens to accept the right of other citizens—the blacks, the Latinos, the poor, the protesters—to intrude on their privacy. Such a policy, Nixon is implying, naturally leads to a situation in which certain citizens would intrude violently into other people's lives, marching and sitting in and taking over streets and even burning and destroying private property. Americans' most important right, the right to "domestic tranquillity"—the right to be left alone—Nixon is telling his followers, has been overridden by secondary concerns.

Nixon believed that when he spoke of such feelings he was reaching the "silent majority"; and when Nixon used the term "silent majority" it had resonance for many Americans. In terms of Chicago '68 though, Nixon's phrase, "free from domestic violence," is still too removed from concrete experience to explain what the Mayor and his people felt.

Chicago newspaper columnist Mike Royko, in an interview he gave on NBC the day after the convention closed, comes much closer. The Mayor, Royko says, believes in "the fantasy that we are the middle of everything."[4] Perhaps Royko is right to call such a feeling a fantasy but most of the time the feeling worked for the Mayor and his people.

First and foremost, the Mayor and his people thought about the convention, the protests, the TV cameras, *"everything"* in terms of the city; by which they meant themselves, those they owed and those they knew or cared about. While the protesters saw the city government and police only as a problem that stood between them and meaningful action, only as an obstacle in the way of their symbolic protest, the local authorities saw only their obligations, their streets and their houses and their parks. To the degree that the Mayor and his men did embrace and were embraced by symbolic politics—both as represented by the flag and labels like hippie and commie—they did so only inasmuch as they represented the conflict between local order and external threats. For the city what was most immediate was most real. What was plainly ideological, symbolic, and abstract to the demonstrators was only fantasy and without the weight of real concern to the Chicago authorities.

Again, Richard Nixon, in his position paper for the Republican Platform Committee, aimed to voice the same concern. He wrote, "We must cease . . . the granting of special immunities and moral sanctions to those who deliberately violate the public laws—even when those violations are done in the name of peace or civil rights or anti-poverty or academic reform."[5] Only days before the Chicago convention the presidents of both the Chicago and New York City Patrolmen's Benevolent Associations said almost the same thing. Acts, Nixon is saying, are always only acts. Their context, their symbolic freight, their situational frame are irrelevant to the fact that they interfere with the laws that keep us all safe.

In Chicago, the question of the law and its relation to order came to be raised most explicitly around the issue of the protesters' right to sleep in the parks. The subtlety of the Mayor's feelings on the issue is stated most succinctly in his August 22 statement: "We don't permit our own people to sleep in the park, so why should we let anyone from outside the city sleep in the park. We don't permit our own people to march at night, so why should we let a lot of people do snake dances at night thru the neighborhoods."[6] What makes the statement so subtle is the fact that the Mayor knew full well that some Chicagoans did sleep in the parks on hot summer nights and that the National Guard and the Boy Scouts had been allowed to camp out in the parks. Indeed, before, during, and after the convention many of the Mayor's critics took him to task over that very fact. But from the Mayor's perspective such critics were missing the point.

The poor Chicagoans who slept along the lakefront on hot summer nights were not permitted to do so; they asked no one for permission and they had none. They acted sub rosa; their presence in the park was not "real" because they had not been, up until the convention, in a space where they could be noticed. Public laws had not been invoked. The Mayor believed in privacy, even on public land, just so long as it stayed private. For it—the act—to remain private, however, the actors must remember to stay out of public notice and to avoid turning an immediate response to concrete conditions (the weather) into an abstract statement about power relations (the parks belong to the people). As long as people respected the public laws when the public authorities needed to invoke them, then people had not broken city ordinances and thus had not formally, declaratively slept in the city parks after curfew. It was just a practical response, on both sides, to particular concrete problems.

The fact that the National Guard and the Boy Scouts slept in the parks also had for the Mayor little to do with people's right to sleep in the park. The National Guard and the Boy Scouts were not individuals seeking public property for symbolic stands against other individuals. They were clearly public institutions acting in accordance with authorized activities. To compare the demonstrators to the public institutions was to confuse categories and to deal with abstractions.

For the Mayor and his people, the issue of space as a concrete sphere of activity—for which the parks stood as synedoche—and not as a realm in which symbolic confrontation could occur with legitimacy relates to the problem of indigenousness. No cry was more common after a ghetto riot or student demonstration than that of "Outside Agitator!" Student protests, governors and college presidents always said, were caused by "nonstudents." This was always a critical fact in the minds of the besieged. Over and over, before, during, and after the convention, the Mayor said that any and all trouble was or would be caused by outsiders, non-Chicagoans.

Certainly, such a concern with indigenousness relates to the earlier cry of the forces of law and order that all domestic troubles were caused by Communist agents who take orders from the Soviet Union. Evil is always a product of the Other. And certainly the FBI during the 1960s continued to inform presidents, newspaper publishers, and all who would listen that black leaders and New Leftists were either dupes or agents of international Communism. Mayor Daley's people, too, tried this line of reasoning. Somehow it made all the difference if the obviously American protesters were or were not linked to another nation.

But even more, the Mayor of Chicago and so many other local officials had something else in mind when they exclaimed, "outside agitators." They meant to suggest that problems of a national or international or even regional nature had no jurisdiction over their locality. They meant to suggest that issues that assembled constituencies by virtue of race or class or ideology had no place, literally, to operate in their space. The city or the university was not the place for such activities. The city or the university, they would say, quite simply served other purposes. Thus, the Mayor to Senator Abe Ribicoff when the Connecticut senator challenged the Mayor's use of force during the convention: "Fuck you, you Jew son of a bitch, you lousy motherfucker go home."[7] Not, you lie, or you're wrong, but "go home." The Jew part too—sworn out at a time of extreme visceral anger—with its medieval sense of condemning the stateless, wandering heretic who cringingly claims allegiance to a God before any particular spot of ground. What's at stake, the Mayor rages, is not right or wrong, but jurisdiction.

This same feeling underlies the police and city response to the mass media coverage of the convention protests. One policeman said so very straightforwardly. When asked why the police treated reporters so harshly, he sneered, "The reporters act like they own the streets."[8] For the policeman, it was enough of an explanation. The streets, the policeman might almost have been saying, belong to the people. And the policemen are those people. They walk and drive those streets. They act in those streets, enforcing the law. Unlike the reporters who claim only to observe, who claim only to be reporting on what they see, the police are there day in and day out, living with the crime and the victims. They see the results of violence as it affects other people and not just as it affects the abstract manipulations of policy or as it forms itself into a genre suitable for a news hole.

As the demonstrators stormed onto Michigan Avenue, one police officer said to another, "If they'd get the hell out of Chicago with those fucking cameras this wouldn't be happening."[9] The police and city authorities, when they said that the mass media created the confrontational, symbolic national protest that put them into twelve-hour shifts and frightening, disgusting situations, are not far from being absolutely right. Indeed, during Chicago '68, both the mass media and most of the protest movement operated according to the rules of newsworthiness.

The Chicago demonstrators reveled in the simulated world of the mass media. Their efforts were aimed not at concrete changes so much as they were toward changing people's images and understandings—somehow those ideological changes would produce something better. The SDS didn't accept such a nebulous plan but most of the Mobe and Yippie leaders, at least for the Chicago action, did. Their goal was to create a visual image of the State in action, a kinetic image that would be useful to their purposes. The protesters were interested in shaping information to their own purposes. As Mayor Daley observed, in the main accurately, the demonstrators came to Chicago to "assault, harass and taunt the police into reacting before the television cameras."[10] But for the Mayor and the police, the main problem was not that the press recorded such a reaction; it was that the networks, in particular, refused to show or state why the police had to react.

"This administration and the people of Chicago," the Mayor stated the day after the Michigan Avenue confrontation, "will never permit a lawless, violent group of terrorists to menace the lives of millions of people, destroy the purpose of a national political Convention and take over the streets."[11] For the Mayor, the protesters were not dealing in mass-mediated images, suitable for ideological battle. The protesters were pushing their bodies into spaces in which they did not belong. But the mass media, rather than explain that (as the President of the Chicago Fraternal Order of Police said) "the police could never let a mob take over,"[12] accepted the demonstration and even promulgated the demonstration as a symbolic act. In essence, the Mayor and the police were right when they declared that many members of the mass media were a part of the movement. But it wasn't exactly the same movement to which the demonstrators would have thought they belonged.

Both the mass media and the demonstrators were more interested in the configurations of information than they were in the traditional work of American politics, especially traditional municipal politics. This feeling was stated by the protest leaders who denied that they were in Chicago to affect the convention in any way. They were, they said, in Chicago to rip away the mask the Democratic party hid under. The television networks expressed a similar feeling in a very different way. Among the networks NBC did so in the most brazen manner.

The main feature of the August 29 NBC Morning News was a poetic montage of the previous day's convention "highlights." Back and forth NBC cut from the convention hall celebrations that followed Hubert Humphrey's first-ballot victory to footage of protesters being beaten, clubbed, Maced, and gassed by hordes of clearly enraged, out-of-control policemen. They showed this while the conventioners cheered and paraded and sang. They showed the "kids" being knocked to the ground, kicked in the face while the delegates whooped and hollered with joy. NBC cut back and forth, back and forth, from the terror in the streets to the festivities that followed Hubert Humphrey's victory.[13]

The events were not going on at the same time. NBC superimposed them. NBC liked the dramatic effect. Indeed, it made for powerful television and, indeed, it certainly was how the demonstrators would have seen the situation. But it wasn't literally, physically happening like that. For NBC and for those viewers who did not perceive news information as only a chronicle of objective facts but instead as a synthesis of information carefully edited to provide the most impressive images, reordering the chronology of events to supply the symbolic thrust of the convention was a meaningful act. The networks, bound by time and structure to an encapsulation rather than a mirroring of reality, looked for those images that would represent rather than merely replay the totality of what they were observing. For them, trained in the art of the forty-five-second piece, distance would always have to lend enchantment.

For the Mayor, such coverage was only a "distorted and twisted picture." He said that the network's manipulation of the convention was a dangerous failure to provide the truth.[14] He and a number of Democratic congressmen called for and got an FCC investigation.

As the Mayor saw it, "The television industry is part of the violence and creating it all over the country."[15] Richard Nixon agreed. He would say over and over again, from August until his victory in November, the real newsmaker in America was the hardworking American, who went to work, raised his family, and supported the boys in Vietnam: the average American, the "silent majority." No news was the real news, said Nixon.

The mass media, one police spokesman said, " . . . [were] assiduously stoking the fires of unrest" by overpublicizing those few militant leaders and those few demonstrators who were not satisfied with the American system.[16] The mass media, Daley, Nixon, and other spokesmen for law and order were saying, paid too much attention to the rhetoric and the symbols of protest and not enough, not nearly enough to the real lives of most Americans. The news, they were saying, did not picture reality, it created its own separate world—a world in which trouble, conflict, and the sensational were treated as normal and acceptable. And instead of treating those people who perpetrated such problems as wrongdoers who were causing mental and sometimes, albeit very rarely, physical anguish for the "average" American, the mass media treated them as citizens acting or reacting reasonably to large-scale social forces. In the mass media, these people felt, the scale was all off. What was rare and different was treated as if it were normal and regular, which in turn challenged what was supposed to be normal and regular. The mass media made the protesters an official challenge to normalcy—they were news.

For the Mayor and his people such a simulated world, in which actions were supposedly perpetrated to demonstrate ideas and relay information that was supposed to be nothing but objective, seemed suspect. Actions should produce concrete results, not pictures to consider. "What Trees Do They Plant," was the name of the movie the Mayor had made about the Chicago protests. Reasonable men worked in the here and now for what good they could get. Treating reality in any other fashion struck the Mayor and his people as irrational and counterproductive.

In such feelings, the Mayor and his people were not alone. To a large degree, these feelings were shared by many American intellectuals; the same intellectuals, naturally, who were chastized by New Left members or sympathizers. Writing at the cusp of the fifties and sixties, Daniel Bell calls on Max Weber to validate the "ethics of responsibility" practiced by those who know that in politics "one's role can be only to reject all absolutes, except pragmatic compromise."[17] Bell and the cohort of intellectuals he seems to be speaking for had reached such a position in their graying years after experiencing the brutal failure of their own Communist revolutionary dreams and after having lived through the horrors of the Nazi ideology machine. History had taught such intellectuals what Mayor Daley and his people knew as the facts of everyday life.[18]

Other intellectuals who had studied such facts of everyday life were prone to agree with the Mayor's practical wisdom. Scholars like Edward C. Banfield and James Q. Wilson, by inclination distrustful of machine politics, had through their research moved close to a full endorsement of Daley's political operations. As Banfield and Wilson wrote in their compelling study *City Politics* (1963):

> Even though in the abstract one can prefer a government
> that gets its influence from reasonable discussion about
> the common good rather than from giving jobs, favors
> and "friendship" . . . he may nevertheless favor the ma-
> chine in some particular concrete situation. . . . The polit-
> ical indifference of the machine may be preferable to any
> likely alternative.[19]

As Banfield and Wilson saw it, in the concrete, "the decentralization of authority in the city must be overcome in one way or another if public undertakings are to be carried forward."[20] Machine politics, with its practical emphasis on centralized authority, in a time of declining, fragmenting urban environments, seemed to offer urban citizens and industries at least the possibility of receiving the services and acts they needed to function. The vast majority of Chicago voters and businessmen clearly agreed with these scholars. As long as the machine provided some degree of social and economic stability, its democratic failures could be forgiven.

Others extended this faith in the pragmatic approach to the national and the international political arenas. During the 1950s and 1960s, hosts of historians and political scientists, many of them a part of the "non-Communist left," were extolling the "pragmatism" of Theodore Roosevelt, Franklin Roosevelt, and even Boss Tweed. An impressive array of intellectuals celebrated the arm-twisting "pragmatism" of John F. Kennedy and Lyndon Johnson. They believed that in the face of the Soviet threat, domestic reactionaries, and the chaotic thrust of the wayward, modern State, a pragmatic, forceful governmental presence was a necessity.

The Mayor, the voters, and the established intellectuals all seemed to agree: political ideology was less important than practical considerations. The protesters in Chicago disagreed; they said that ideology determined practical considerations. The battles of the 1960s—and Vietnam more than anything else represented this—revolved around this question of how to define the relationship of ideology and pragmatic considerations.

Mayor Daley's understanding of what constituted realistic responses to practical problems also played a critical part in how the
forces of law and order justified the policeman's role in the convention
confrontations. The Mayor's logic was simple: "If someone walks into
you and shoves ya and spits in your face or calls you a four letter
word, what would you do or what would anyone do?"[21] Or put another way, "What would you do if someone was throwing human
excrement in your face, would you be the calm, collected people you
think you are? What would you do if someone was biting you. . . .
What do you think they [the police] were supposed to do?"[22] Speaking
directly to his fellow citizens and then to reporters, the Mayor tried
to make people understand what it was really like to be standing there
facing a swarm of angry, crazy protesters. It was only reasonable, the
Mayor was implying, to react to such immediate provocation with
anger and with force.

The Mayor was saying that the policeman was no different from
anybody else—"What would you do . . . what would you do . . .
would you . . . would you?" An abstract notion like police professionalism was not as important as the concrete experience of being
provoked, being sworn at, having your mother called a nasty name:
"the foulest language that you wouldn't hear in a brothel hall."[23]

J. Edgar Hoover, the nation's number one police professional, when
he testified before the National Commission on the Causes and Prevention of Violence in regard to the behavior of the Chicago police,
said the same thing: "The police are human. They are supposed to be
both lawyers and sociologists, as I said, but they are still human. I
don't think any of us in this room would be restrained if we had been
hit with some of the things they have been hit with."[24] Of course, most
of the police who attacked demonstrators had not been literally hit
with anything. But as the judge who presided at the trial of three
policemen who had brutally beaten a newspaper photographer said,
"The language that Mr. Linstead used . . . was vile and degrading to
the officers . . . gutter language which I suggest would be provoking
in such a manner that any red-blooded American would flare up."[25]

A New York police officer, just after the spring 1968 Yip-In at Grand
Central Station, goes even further. He speaks for many of his fellow
officers when he explains why he and the other police attacked the
Yip-In:

> Here's a bunch of animals who call themselves the next
> leaders of the country. . . . I almost had to vomit. . . . It's
> like dealing with any queer pervert, mother raper, or any
> of those other bedbugs we've got crawling around the
> Village. As a *normal human being,* you feel like knocking

every one of their teeth out. *It's a normal reaction"* (emphasis added).[26]

In a sense, the Mayor, the police, and the other police defenders have joined hands with the demonstrators. The demonstrators, too, were saying that ideas like professionalism were just screens to hide behind, that social scientists and bureaucrats who claimed they were just doing their jobs were not facing up to the human, existential task they were performing. The Mayor asked, "What would *you* do?" Not what does the job, the profession, or the boss *insist* you do. The Mayor, in his defense of his police, rejects the professional training that told them not to react to provocation. The police, the Mayor said, had the right to act like men and not like some abstract figure—a "professional." And men, as the judge and the others insist, have the right to react "normally" to outrages.

Certainly, during much of the 1960s, the police acted "normally." The behavior of the Chicago police—clubbing and gassing white protesters—was far from exceptional. Police in Berkeley, Los Angeles, San Francisco, and New York, as well as a good many less "sophisticated" cities, both before and after the Democratic Convention, acted in almost exactly the same way as the Chicago police.[27] What was different about Chicago was that the mass media were present in unprecedented numbers to witness the beating, and, much more important, the press was unmistakenly being singled out by the police for the same sort of treatment as the demonstrators.

The two feelings—that the mass media paid too much respectful attention to protesters and advocates of change and that the policeman had as much right as anybody else to react to provocations—are certainly linked. Both stem from a mistrust of disembodied authority. Both feelings come from a suspicion that some outside, elite power has taken control of what should be commonsensical and local.

Mayor Daley could never quite understand what right the mass media had to come into his city and frame reality. Frank Sullivan, the official police spokesman, came out and said it: "The intellectuals of America hate Mayor Daley because he was elected by the people, unlike Walter Cronkite."[28] The Mayor, in a more politic fashion, made a similar statement to members of the Democratic National Committee shortly before the convention began. In private, as they all prepared to face a large assemblage of reporters, Daley explained to the DNC officials that they, not the press, were the representatives of the people and that, quite simply, "you just don't have to answer every question they [the press] ask."[29]

The Mayor's politics was built around public works, patronage, precinct workers, and the exchange of public services for support. The

Mayor's politics was not organized with mirrors or simulated with photo opportunities and paid political advertisements. What national political influence the Mayor exerted was not based on his grasp of issues—though he was respected for his views on urban problems— but on his ability to control his political territory. When the federal government, in the form of the Justice Department, tried to intervene in Chicago and told the Mayor that he should compromise with the demonstrators, he made it clear that *he* would decide what needed to be done in *his* city. What Mike Royko described as "the fantasy that we are the middle of everything" prevailed over the Justice Department's belief that conflicting perspectives could be reconciled.

As Royko implies, the Mayor and his people did not believe that Chicagoans had to share their streets with intruders. For the Mayor, the fact that the nation was being torn apart by an unpopular war and racial conflict was simply irrelevant to Chicago politics. Even more, these issues were not as important as local concerns: it was far more important to keep Michigan Avenue free of demonstrators than it was to allow a group of outsiders to protest in a disruptive way. Similarly, it was far more important to keep the demonstrators from marching through the ghettos and possibly igniting a riot than it was to allow such people their right to protest a distant war. It was even more important to the Mayor to keep the "outside agitators" out of the city parks and out of the city streets than it was to maintain as placid an environment as he could for the Democratic National Convention. For the Mayor, the state of his streets and his parks and his neighborhoods was far more important than abstract ideas about free speech, free assembly, or even national stability and calm. For the Mayor, the world was Chicago, and those forces—the Justice Department, the national mass media, the antiwar movement—that sought to subordinate the city of Chicago to larger concerns or issues or jurisdictions were simply trying to undermine that life-sustaining vision.

Richard Nixon, throughout his 1968 and 1972 campaigns, called on this vision. His political brilliance allowed him to relate such a vision to national politics by imbuing national symbols like the flag with the desperate pride of local satisfaction and the certainty of unchallenge-able American integrity. In his speeches and advertisements Nixon created a land of endless local pride and loving community. The place was called Middle America and it was populated with people called the "silent majority." Nixon, like Reagan after him, understood that most Americans were proud of the lives they had produced and wanted above all else to be free to enjoy both the bounty and strength of the American dream they felt they lived within.

Hubert Humphrey, too, during the crisis of national faith that po-larized many Americans, tried to call up such associations. But he had to overcome the frightening convention images of confrontation that belied a rhetoric of national pride based on success and glory. And perhaps more important, he had to overcome the Democratic war that more and more found unwinnable.

Very few of the young protesters who came to Chicago believed that the United States really consisted of satisfied Americans whose communities offered each and every one of them opportunities for rich and rewarding lives. Paradoxically, perhaps, they wanted to believe in that vision; they wanted a nation made up of workable, highly autonomous communities, governed by proud and active citizens. But while hoping to reclaim this familiar American territory they had to wrestle with the fact that the most intellectually gifted and/or economically advantaged of them had been brought up to assume a national, even international, outlook. National culture, national politics, and national celebrities *were* their frame of reference, their reality. "Vietnam" *was*, by and large, more real to them than the lives of their neighbors. In unprecedented numbers they had been trained at colleges and universities, taught by television, and even given the experiences via a transportation revolution, youth fares, and their parents' wealth to understand that they lived in a world in which global and national interconnectedness were the immediate facts of life. The information age they grew up experiencing demonstrated daily that the abstractions that allowed for the management of state and corporate control were as real as the concrete streets they protested on or the transparent windows they managed to smash.

For some, college, with its easy homogeneity and emphasis on self and social discovery, presented a middle ground between their vague dream of "beloved community" and the fixed presence of a corporatized America. It was an opening where the physical intimacy of a late-night rap session could compete with and sometimes even triumph over the society-wide intimacy offered by presidents and name brand products. But college was also, as many knew, the last stop in the social process that moved them from the protection of family life to the vagaries of the corporate world—from the singular realm of the private to the conscious and conscientious bifurcation of life into public and private spheres.

A few—SDS-ERAP—left the "false security" of the university in order to engage themselves politically in the "real world" of communities in which people were struggling to make a living and a life. Others fled their formally constructed community—school—for ones more of their own making—Haight-Ashbury, the Lower East Side, underground press collectives, draft-resister and antiwar organizations.

In their struggles to find free spaces from which to build a new political consciousness, those members of the generation that came of age protesting in the 1960s were caught between the imperfect reality of community men like Mayor Daley sustained and the simulated world of technocratic internationalism they had been raised to manage. Neither possibility seemed to offer them an opportunity to create a sustainable public life. In Chicago, August 1968, a few thousand came to seek an answer to their bind. "Ride, boldly ride the Shade replied, if you seek for Eldorado."

Notes

Chapter 1

1. The beginnings of Yippie have been deliberately enshrined in myth and mystery by the founders. My version of Yippie's first night is based on several accounts including interviews, sworn trial testimony, and various firsthand accounts. I attempt to present a factual rendering of events but I doubt I have fully succeeded in establishing "things as they really were," which is probably how it should be. Yippie deserves a history that does not totally reject its mythic concerns. See Paul Krassner, R052A, Box 40, Records of the Chicago Study Team Investigation, National Commission on the Causes and Prevention of Violence (NCCPV), Lyndon Baines Johnson Library (LBJ), pp. 5–6 (hereafter I will refer to the Records of the Chicago Study Team located at the LBJ by the abbreviations NCCPV, LBJ); Abbie Hoffman, R051A, Box 40, NCCPV, LBJ, pp. 1–14, 26–30; *U.S. v. David T. Dellinger and Others*, Transcript of proceedings, United States District Court, Northern District of Illinois, Eastern Division, Docket 69, C.r. 180, Chicago, 1970, pp. 12496–12501, 12600–12604, 16930–16938; Jerry Rubin, *Do It!* (New York: Ballantine Books, 1970), pp. 81–82; Milton Viorst, *Fire in the Streets* (New York: Simon and Schuster, 1979), pp. 431–432; David Lewis Stein, *Living the Revolution: The Yippies in Chicago* (Indianapolis: Bobbs-Merrill, 1969), pp. 5–7.

2. For descriptions of the Lower East Side hippie community see the *East Village Other* in 1967 and 1968 and *Rat* in 1968. See also Elia Katz, *Armed Love* (New York: Holt, Rinehart and Winston, 1971)—a truly strange book that effectively describes the counterculture love-hate relationship with madness and fantasy. See also Abbie Hoffman's informative autobiography, *Soon to Be a Major Motion Picture* (New York: G. P. Putnam's Sons, 1980), pp. 92–98.

As suggested in my Preface and Introduction, throughout my two narrative chapters on Yippie I have made recourse to language like "stoned," "rapping," "talking up," and other nonacademic terms. One of the trickiest stylistic and epistemological questions involved in writing a historical narrative is what voice to use. In each of my three narrative sections I have attempted to use a different voice that my historical research indicates is most appropriate to the historical actors I am seeking to portray. My language is meant to suggest the reality the historical figures thought themselves living in; for me to write that Abbie Hoffman was "rapping" to runaways is to indicate what all involved in the act thought to be happening—they were not conversing or arguing and he was not lecturing or speaking; he was "rapping." In some ways, such word choices and the narrative voice they help create do indeed only confuse a historian's simulations of what happened with what each and every participant in the historical act thought to be happening. Still, I think to write a narrative history is to dedicate oneself to more than just a distanced attempt at an orderly recreation of events. The historian who narrates is not merely linking scenes together—leaving out what doesn't follow the flow of his or her "story"—he or she is also sketching out the rules, the signifiers, the terms by which the characters give meaning to their actions. Their language must creep into even the historian's expository passages because that language is offering historical meanings that a more academic or professorial or "objective" language deliberately and misleadingly suppresses.

3. Hoffman, *Soon to Be a Major Motion Picture*, p. 92.

4. Ed Sanders, R548, Box 42, NCCPV, LBJ, pp. 1–2; *U.S. v. David Dellinger and Others*, pp. 14520–14527.

5. Ellen Sander, *Trips* (New York: Charles Scribner's Sons, 1973), pp. 125–129.

6. In interviews and in his writings, Hoffman was never uptight about his age. See Hoffman, *Soon to Be a Major Motion Picture*, p. 93.

7. Hoffman, *Soon to Be a Major Motion Picture*, pp. 15–16.

8. Arthur Liebman thoroughly explores this subject in chapter 9 of his *Jews and the Left* (New York: John Wiley and Sons, 1979). See also John Murray Cuddihy, *The Ordeal of Civility* (New York: Basic Books, 1974).

9. Most of this information is culled from Hoffman's autobiography, *Soon to Be a Major Motion Picture*, pp. 2–87. See also *U.S. v. David Dellinger and Others*, pp. 12403–12439; and Abbie Hoffman, "Liberty House/Poor People's Corporation," *Liberation*, April 1967, p. 20.

10. Hoffman, *Soon to Be a Major Motion Picture*, pp. 87–126; Free (Abbie Hoffman), *Revolution for the Hell of It* (New York: Pocket Books, 1970), pp. 13–24, 27–29; *U.S. v. David Dellinger and Others*, pp. 12434–12541. For Hoffman's statement on language see Hoffman, R051A, Box 40, pp. 6–7. For the Diggers see Emmett Grogan, *Ringolevio* (New York: Avon, 1973); and Charles Perry's excellent history *The Haight-Ashbury* (New York: Random House, 1985), esp. pp. 103–105 for a prime example of Digger Street Theater. For a notable perspective on the art/theater/culture scene in the early 1960s see Susan Sontag, *Against Interpretation* (New York: Dell, 1966), esp. "Happenings: An Art of Radical Juxtaposition."

11. Jerry Rubin, *Growing Up (at 37)* (New York: M. Evans and Company, 1976), pp. 60–73. Rubin, *Do It!* pp. 12–13. J. Anthony Lukas's portrait of Rubin's early years in *Don't Shoot We Are Your Children!* (New York: Dell Publishing Company, 1972), pp. 323–369, is masterfully written and superbly researched.

12. Stein, *Living the Revolution*, p. 7.

13. Fred Halstead, *Out Now!* (New York: Monad Press, 1978), pp. 54–55, 69–71, 85–88; James F. Petras, "Berkeley's Vietnam Days," *Liberation*, August 1965, pp. 31–32.

14. Jerry Rubin, "Alliance for Liberty," *Liberation*, April 1966, p. 9.

15. Halstead, *Out Now!* pp. 85–86.

16. Ibid., pp. 11–12. For more on this see also p. 165.

17. Todd Gitlin, *The Whole World Is Watching* (Berkeley: University of California Press, 1980), p. 171. Rubin, *Do It!* pp. 60–62.

18. Jerry Rubin, "For Mayor—Jerry Rubin," Box 5, 1968 Democratic National Convention (DNC), Northwestern University (NU).

19. Rubin, *Do It!* pp. 48–51. Compare this to Rubin's attitude in 1966 on radicals and electoral politics in regard to Bob Scheer's bid for Congress—Jerry Rubin, "Alliance for Liberty," *Liberation*, April 1966, p. 12.

20. Rubin, *Growing Up* (at 37), p. 79.

21. Halstead, *Out Now!* pp. 312–315.

22. See n. 1. All of the listed sources are in agreement about the general flow of the conversation.

23. *U.S. v. David Dellinger and Others*, pp. 12495–12496. Also Michael Rossman, *The Wedding within the War* (Garden City, Doubleday and Company, 1971), pp. 223–226.

24. *U.S. v. David Dellinger and Others*, p. 12499.

25. Ibid., pp. 12475–12477, 12489–12492. See also Norman Mailer, *The Armies of the Night* (New York: New American Library, 1968); Halstead, *Out Now!*, pp. 312–323; David Dellinger, "Resistance: Vietnam and America," *Liberation*, November 1967, pp. 3–7; Martin Jezer, "Postscript: Mobile Tactics," *Liberation*, November 1967, p. 11; Abbie Hoffman, "How I Lost the War," *The Realist*, August 1967, pp. 15, 20–23. A perusal of the *Village Voice, Berkeley Barb, Liberation,* and even more counterculture underground papers reveals how effective the Pentagon demonstration was in capturing the imaginations of a great variety of people.

26. See n. 1. See in particular Abbie Hoffman, R051A, Box 40, pp. 1–14, 26–30; and *U.S. v. David Dellinger and Others*, pp. 12496–12501, 12600–12604. Also see Stein, *Living the Revolution*, pp. 5–7.

27. Free (Abbie Hoffman), *Revolution for the Hell of It*, pp. 36–37; Hoffman, *Soon to Be a Major Motion Picture*, pp. 100–102.

28. This information is compiled from all of the sources listed in n. 1.

29. *U.S. v. David Dellinger and Others*, pp. 14530–14531.

30. Ibid., pp. 12620–12622.

31. Ibid., pp. 14614–14618. Stein, *Living the Revolution*, pp. 6–7.

32. *U.S. v. David Dellinger and Others*, p. 12605.

33. Ibid., p. 12612.

34. Ibid., p. 12610.

35. Yippie, "For Conscription into the Yippie Army," Box 5, DNC, NU.

36. Fred Halstead, *Out Now!* p. 316.

37. Jerry Rubin, "What a Day at White Haul," *East Village Other*, December 15–30, 1967, pp. 5–7. For an opposing view see Halstead, *Out Now!* pp. 354–356. He saw mobile tactics and Whitehall as counterproductive and anarchistic.

38. Jerry Rubin, "And in America We Are All Becoming Viet Cong," *Berkeley Barb*, January 5–11, 1968, pp. 8–9. Jerry Rubin, "I Am the Walrus," *Win*, 4, no. 2:2. Jerry Rubin, no title, *LA Free Press*, February 23–29, pp. 1, 5–8. For Halstead's views on the debate see Halstead, *Out Now!* pp. 406–407.

39. Jerry Rubin, "Rubin Raps," *Berkeley Barb*, January 19–26, 1968, p. 2.

40. Ibid., February 2–8, 1968, p. 7.

41. Ibid., p. 7.

42. Ibid., March 8–14, 1968, p. 11.

43. Jerry Rubin, "Year of the Yippies," *Berkeley Barb*, February 16–22, 1968, p. 4.

44. Stein, *Living the Revolution*, pp. 11, 25. Halstead, *Out Now!*, pp. 321–322. Keith Lampe, R494, Box 42, NCCPV, LBJ, pp. 1–3.

45. Keith Lampe, "The Honkie Rebellion," *Liberation*, August 1967, p. 14. See also Keith Lampe, "From Dissent to Parody," *Liberation*, December 1967, p. 20.

46. For a few autobiographical details see *U.S. v. David Dellinger and Others*, pp. 14505–14520. See also Ed Sanders, *Tales of Beatnik Glory* (New York: Stonehill, 1975), esp. the last chapter on the impact Allen Ginsberg's *Howl!* had on Sanders; the stuff on A-heads is also useful for understanding life on the Lower East Side. The "Fuck-In" is particularly promoted in the June 1965 *Fuck You*, which opens with Sanders's declaration: "It makes us puke green monkey shit to contemplate Johnson's war in Vietnam."

47. *Berkeley Barb*, "The Fugs," May 12, 1967, reprinted in John Hopkins, ed., *The Hippie Papers* (New York: New American Library, 1968), pp. 213–214.

48. Jim Tankard, "The Fugs on Good Friday: Their Bag Is Crucifixion," Liberation News Service, May 6, 1967.

49. *U.S. v. David Dellinger and Others*, p. 14518.

50. *U.S. v. David Dellinger and Others*, p. 16924; Paul Krassner, R052, Box 40, NCCPV, LBJ, p. 108; Stein, *Living the Revolution*, p. 10; "The Digger Papers," published by *The Realist*, August 1967.

51. Paul Krassner, R052, Box 40, p. 108.

52. Ibid., pp. 10–11, 16.

53. *U.S. v. David Dellinger and Others*, pp. 10453–10457; Michael Ochs, "War Is Over," press release, exhibited at the Peace Museum, Chicago, Illinois, Spring 1984. For more on Ochs see *U.S. v. David Dellinger and Others*, pp. 10494–10495.

54. Jane Kramer, "Profiles: Paterfamilias—II," *New Yorker*, August 24, 1968, p. 40.

55. Ibid., p. 41.

56. Allen Ginsberg, "Public Solitude," *Liberation*, April 1967, p. 32.

57. Ibid.

58. Hoffman, R051A, Box 40, p. 72.

59. Bradley J. Fox, R549, Box 42, NCCPV, LBJ, p. 1; *U.S. v. David Dellinger and Others*, p. 16458; Sally Kempton, "Yippies Anti-Organize a Groovy Revolution," *Village Voice*, May 21, 1968, p. 30; Stein, *Living the Revolution*, p. 12.

Chapter 2

1. *U.S. v. David Dellinger and Others*, p. 12626.

2. For the meetings in general and the Yippie organizers see Stein, *Living the Revolution*, p. 17. For the activities, setting, and dialogue of the March meeting see Naomi Fogelson, *The Underground Revolution* (New York: Funk and Wagnall, 1970), pp. 88–91; and more important, Sally Kempton, "Yippies Anti-Organize A Groovy Revolution," pp. 5–6, 30. See Abe Peck, *Uncovering the Sixties* (New York: Pantheon, 1985), p. 102, for the press treatment of the conference. March 18, the *New York Post*, for example, said, "They plan mad

antics which with their thousands of young adherents will compel the networks to cover them."

3. Clark Whelton, "Sweep Out on Third Street Garbage Is Their Bag," *Village Voice*, February 15, 1968, pp. 1–2.

4. Don McNeil, "The Grand Central Riot Yippies Meet the Man," *Village Voice*, March 28, 1968, p. 1. On the planning and formulating of the Yip-In see Stein, *Living the Revolution*, p. 13; *U.S. v. David Dellinger and Others*, p. 12638; and Howard Smith, "Scenes," *Village Voice*, March 21, 1968, p. 38.

5. *U.S. v. David Dellinger and Others*, p. 12637.

6. Most of this comes from McNeil, "The Grand Central Riot Yippies Meet the Man," pp. 1, 13–14. See also *U.S. v. David Dellinger and Others*, pp. 12641–12648, pp. 14553–14556, 11685–11692.

7. New York Civil Liberties Union, "Report to the Mayor," A208, Box 7, NCCPV, LBJ, p. 1.

8. McNeil, "The Grand Central Riot Yippies Meet the Man," p. 14.

9. Jerry Rubin, "Letter to the Editor—Liberty or Death," *Village Voice*, April 18, 1968, p. 4.

10. *New Left Notes*, editorial, March 4, 1968, p. 2.

11. Julius Lester, "From the Other Side of the Tracks," *Guardian*, March 30, 1968, and reprinted as a Yippie flyer, A182, Box 7, NCCPV, LBJ.

12. Jon Moore, "Yippie," *Rat*, March–April 4, 1968, pp. 5–6.

13. Lawrence Lipton, "Yippie: A Conversation with Anon," *LA Free Press*, March 1, 1968, p. 4.

14. *U.S. v. David Dellinger and Others*, p. 3845.

15. Abbie Hoffman, Jerry Rubin, Ed Sanders, and Paul Krassner, "Yippie," "Convention Notes," n.d., A294, Box 8, NCCPV, LBJ. "Convention Notes" was put out by the National Mobilization to End the War in Vietnam.

16. The quote is from Hoffman, R051A, Box 40, p. 22.

17. For Yippie in Lake Villa see Hoffman, R051A, Box 40, pp. 22–23; *U.S. v. David Dellinger and Others*, pp. 12650–12655; Ray Mungo, "Red Get Together at Camp," Liberation News Service, March 25, 1968, pp. 9–10.

18. Abe Peck, "Yippie Here It Is," *Seed*, March 15–29, 1968, p. 1; Steve Mrvos, "A Day and a Half in the Life," *Seed*, April 1968, p. 9; Abe Peck, R231, Box 41, NCCPV, LBJ, pp. 1–2; *U.S. v. David Dellinger and Others*, pp. 12655–12665, 16951.

19. *U.S. v. David Dellinger and Others*, pp. 14534–14535, 14539.

20. Ibid., pp. 11693–11696, 11705–11706.

21. Howard Smith, "Scenes," *Village Voice*, April 4, 1968, pp. 26–27.

22. "Sit-In at Mayor's Office," Liberation News Service, April 10, 1968.

23. "Yip-Out," Liberation News Service, April 16, 1968; *U.S. v. David Dellinger and Others*, pp. 11709–11710.

24. Sally Kempton, "Sunday in the Park: Yip Out or Has Been," *Village Voice*, April 18, 1968, pp. 1, 18.

25. Abbie Hoffman, "The Yippies Are Going to Chicago," *The Realist*, September 1968, p. 1.

26. Ibid., p. 23. Hoffman's comment comes before the miracle Mets of 1969.

27. Jerry Rubin, "Elections in America Are a Mind Poison," Liberation News Service, March 25, 1968; also in *Village Voice*, March 21, 1968, p. 10.

28. Hoffman, "The Yippies Are Going to Chicago," p. 23.

29. Ibid., p. 10.

30. Hoffman, R051A, Box 40, p. 100.

31. *Chicago Tribune*, April 26, 1968, p. 3. The *Tribune* called the meeting a hippie party. See also Joseph Ettinger, R484, Box 42, NCCPV, LBJ, p. 1.

32. Abe Peck, "Open Letter to Mayor Daley," Liberation News Service, May 9, 1968.

33. Ettinger, R484, Box 42, pp. 2–3; Peck, R231, Box 41, NCCPV, LBJ, pp. 2–4; Carl Burnette, "The Free City Survival Committee Is Alive and Well in Chicago," Liberation News Service, June 7, 1968.

34. Ettinger, R484, Box 42, p. 4.

35. Peck, R231, Box 41, pp. 3–5; Al Baugher, R595, Box 42, NCCPV, LBJ, p. 7.

36. *U.S. v. David Dellinger and Others*, p. 16736.

37. Ibid., 11716–11717, 17233–17235, 16533–16534.

38. Ibid., pp. 12680–12683.

39. Ibid., pp. 12686–12690.

40. Peck, R231, Box 41, pp. 5–6.

41. Hoffman, R051A, Box 42, p. 92; see also Hoffman, *Soon to Be a Major Motion Picture*, pp. 139–142. On Columbia see the Cox Commission Report, *Crisis at Columbia* (New York: Vintage Books, 1968).

42. Stew Albert, "Manhattan PFP Convention Dull Despite Yippies," *Berkeley Barb*, July 26–August 1, 1968, p. 3; Stew Albert, "Then Eldridge Blew Their Minds," *Berkeley Barb*, August 23–29, 1968, p. 5; *U.S. v. David Dellinger and Others*, pp. 16535–16537.

43. Don McNeil, "Summer's a Bummer When the Heat's On," *Village Voice*, June 20, 1968, p. 16; Martin Jezer, "Rubin Yippies to Appear in Court," Liberation News Service, July 2, 1968; Jerry Rubin, "The Yippies Are Going to Chicago," *The Realist*, September 1968, pp. 1, 21–23; Stew Albert, "Jerry . . . My Jerry," *Rat*, July 1–5, 1968, p. 6; Stein, *Living the Revolution*, p. 25.

44. Hoffman, R051A, Box 40, p. 102.

45. Rubin, *Do It!* p. 167.

46. Abbie Hoffman, "The Yippies Are Going to Chicago," *The Realist*, September 1968, pp. 1, 23–24.

47. Free City Survival Committee, Letter to Commissioner of the Chicago Park District, July 15, 1968, RG283, Box 6, NCCPV, LBJ. For another example of the Free City's careful, polite language see Free City Survival Committee, Letter to Deputy Mayor David Stahl, n.d. (late June 1968[?]), A215, Box 7, NCCPV, LBJ.

48. I have used a somewhat less militant version of the speech provided by the sympathetic James Kunen, *U.S. v. David Dellinger and Others*, pp. 15599–15632. For the more militant, FBI version see Robert Casper, *U.S. v. David Dellinger and Others*, pp. 3005–3011—the language quoted by Casper just doesn't sound like Jerry Rubin.

49. Abe Peck, "Street Survival Directory," *Seed*, August 23, 1968, n.p.; Hoffman, R051A, Box 40, p. 115.

50. Abe Peck, "A Letter from Chicago," Liberation News Service, August 6, 1968.

51. *U.S. v. David Dellinger and Others*, pp. 12715–12717.

52. Ibid., pp. 16955, 12717–12723, 13159, 512–514, 592–594, 706–708, 713, 14560, 9400–9407, 9510–9511.

53. This account is based on Richard Goldstein, "Prelude to a Convention: Marking Time at Pig Sty," *Village Voice*, August 22, 1968, p. 22. See also Hoffman, R051A, Box 40, p. 123; and Krassner, R052A, Box 40, pp. 34–35. Abe Peck, in his *Uncovering the Sixties*, gives the same basic story but has Hayden blasting Peck and not the Yips in general. See pp. 99–119 for Peck's version of the Chicago–New York conflicts.

54. Nixon is quoted in Lewis Chester, Godfrey Hodgson, and Bruce Page, *An American Melodrama* (New York: Dell, 1969), p. 556.

55. *U.S. v. David Dellinger and Others*, pp. 12725–12731, pp. 515–517, 84–89, 303–304.

56. *Chicago Sun-Times*, August 9, 1968, p. 29.

57. *U.S. v. David Dellinger and Others*, pp. 12730–12732; Allen Ginsberg, *Chicago Trial Testimony* (San Francisco: City Lights, 1975), p. 22.

58. Hoffman, R051A and R051B, Box 40, pp. 124–131. The "honky revolution" comment is the same basic message Hoffman had used back in March when straight reporters, still not aware of how separate the white and black movements had become, had asked the Yippies at a press conference why they didn't have any black members. Allen Ginsberg justified the fact by saying that Black Power leader Stokely Carmichael had told him, personally, that the best thing he could do to help blacks was to work with whites. Hoffman added that whites must work from within their own experiences to wake up America—see Feigelson, *The Underground Revolution: Hippie, Yippies and Others*, p. 91. Feigelson gives a very interesting account of the March 17, 1968 straight press conference at the Americana Hotel in New York that I have not included in my account.

59. Hoffman, R051B, Box 40, pp. 128–129; *U.S. v. David Dellinger and Others*, pp. 12733–12739.

60. Free City Survival Committee, "Don't Go to Chicago," *Avatar*, August 16–29, 1968, p. 1. See also the Free City, Letter to Mayor Daley, Deputy Mayor David Stahl and Park District Commissioner McFetteridge, August 8, 1968, RG283, Box 6, NCCPV, LBJ. In it the locals withdraw their permit application.

61. Peck, "Street Survival Directory," p. 2.

62. "All Set to Surge: The Festival of Life," *Berkeley Barb*, August 16–22, 1968, p. 5. The cover of the *Barb* has a picture of a pig wearing a Yippie banner. See also the *Chicago Sun-Times*, August 21, 1968, p. 18, which presents a half page reproduction of the Yippies' map of Lincoln Park.

63. The first quote is from "All Set to Surge," *Berkeley Barb*, p. 7; and the second is from "Bay Area Yippies Set to Go No Matter What," *Berkeley Barb*, August 2–8, 1968, p. 3.

64. *U.S. v. David Dellinger and Others*, pp. 12738–12741, 13651–13653.

65. Ed Sanders, "Predictions for Yippie Activities," *Berkeley Barb*, August 2–8, 1968, p. 13.

66. *U.S. v. David Dellinger and Others*, p. 14628.

67. See for example Judy Collins's testimony in ibid., pp. 17240–17241.

68. Stein, *Living the Revolution*, pp. 34–35; *U.S. v. David Dellinger and Others*, pp. 16538–16539, 12743–12751.

69. Parts of the document appeared in most major newspapers. The entire document can be found in *U.S. v. David Dellinger and Others*, pp. 12751–12761.

Chapter 3

1. Maris Cakars, "From Dissent to Resistance," *Mobilizer*, September 1, 1967, p. 6.

2. David Dellinger, "Resistance: Vietnam and America," *Liberation*, November 1967, p. 37. Dellinger discusses the Pentagon action and explains what he means by "Gandhi and Guerrilla." See also Arthur Waskow, "Gandhi and Guerrilla," *Liberation*, November 1967, pp. 26–27.

3. This is all explicitly stated in the September 1, 1967, *Mobilizer*, which was an extremely militant document, so militant, in fact, that as is reported in Halstead *Out Now!* pp. 322–323, moderate Mobe leaders scrapped the issue after only a few were distributed. Nonetheless, at the Pentagon protest the Mobe did sanction all levels of protest.

4. Cakars, "From Dissent to Resistance," p. 6.

5. Lawrence S. Wittner, *Rebels against the War* (Philadelphia: Temple University Press, 1984), p. 154.

6. For the clearest and most thoughtful statement of this see Tom Hayden, *Rebellion in Newark* (New York: Random House, 1967).

7. Jerry Rubin, project director of the Pentagon protest, gave this statement to the press August 28, 1967, and then printed it in the September 1, 1967, *Mobilizer*.

8. Ibid., p. 1.

9. All of this comes from Halstead, *Out Now!* pp. 322–323.

10. Dellinger, "Resistance: Vietnam and America," p. 7.

11. Ibid., p. 6.

12. According to Marty Jezer—an upstanding contributor to the Liberation News Service, editor of *Win*, and later a communard—in "Pentagon Confrontation," *Liberation*, November 1967, p. 8, the Revolutionary Contingent was composed of members of the Black Mask—a Lower East Side artists' group, some of whose members would soon form the Up against the Wall, Motherfuckers—and the Committee to Aid the NLF.

13. The best history of the Pentagon action is Norman Mailer's *Armies of the Night* (New York: New American Library, 1968). Marty Jezer's much shorter treatment, "Pentagon Confrontation," in the November 1967 *Liberation*, pp. 8–11, is an excellent example of a young radical's description of the Pentagon as a turning point—as "the last sit down for many of us" and the beginning of a "clenched fist of struggle"—p. 11. The entire November 1967 issue of *Liberation*, edited by David Dellinger, is devoted to assessing the Pentagon. The commentators range from proto-Yippie Keith Lampe to intellectual Arthur Waskow—which is another indication of the movement's desire to be as inclusive as possible. For the planning and discussion of the multitactical, confrontational style see *Mobilizer* September 26, 1967, and October 16, 1967.

14. The West Coast movement was almost always more militant than the East Coast. This fact will create tensions for the Chicago '68 protest planners, most of whom are easterners, interested in acting like west coasters while operating in the more conservative midwest.

15. Sidney Lens, "State of the Movement," *Liberation*, November 1967, pp. 24–25. For more on Lens see his *Unrepentant Radical: An American Activist's Account of Five Turbulent Decades* (Boston: Beacon Press, 1980)—an autobiography full of good anecdotes and leftist critiques but thin when it comes to giving the reader even a glimpse of the inner man.

16. Dellinger, "Resistance: Vietnam and America," p. 4.

17. Eric Weinberger, R066, Box 40, NCCPV, LBJ, p. 2.

18. *Mobilization Report*, n.d., Box 1, Fred Halstead Papers, Wisconsin State Historical Society (WSHS).

19. David Dellinger, "Statement on Entering Prison," in David Dellinger, *Revolutionary Nonviolence* (New York: Bobbs-Merrill Company, Inc., 1970), pp. 7–8.

20. Ibid., p. 8. (See also the statement signed by Staughton Lynd, Dellinger, Tom Hayden, Paul Krassner, Paul Goodman, Sid Lens, and others protesting Soviet treatment of dissidents in the tenth-anniversary issue of *Liberation*, March 1966, p. 23, for an update on anti-Soviet feelings shared by Dellinger and almost all other antiwar leaders.)

21. David Dellinger, "An Integrated Walk through Georgia," in Dellinger, *Revolutionary Nonviolence*, pp. 240–241.

22. Ibid., p. 242.

23. David Dellinger wrote constantly in the late 1950s and 1960s in *Liberation*, the movement magazine he co-edited. In short editorials and occasional articles Dellinger maintains a running commentary on all aspects of the movement including civil rights, antiwar work, socialism, and internal politics and debates. *Liberation*, in general, is the most useful magazine for understanding what the older and/or more traditional movement people are up to.

24. Fred Halstead's *Out Now!* is an extremely well-researched book. In addition to his fine work, Halstead has helped all historians of the period by taking the rather unusual step of depositing all the documents he used in writing *Out Now!* at the Wisconsin State Historical Society in Madison, under his name—the Fred Halstead Papers. This allowed me, and allows any other interested party, to check out his facts and assessments as well as use the documents for other scholarly purposes. All historians of the 1960s owe Mr. Halstead their thanks. Halstead was a major, behind-the-scenes antiwar activist. He was also, in the 1960s, the moving force of the Socialist Workers party. His account of the 1960s positions the Old Left—particularly the SWP and its youth affiliate, the Young Socialist Alliance, right in the center of the antiwar movement. And while most accounts of the 1960s—excepting Kirkpatrick Sale's outstanding account of the SDS, *SDS* (New York: Random House, 1973)—pay too little attention to the Old Left, Halstead tends to pay them too much. The SWP and YSA did provide a number of excellent organizers and were not an insignificant presence in Berkeley; still their numbers were small and their influence less than decisive

in most organizations and events. Also, Halstead gives his people the benefit of the doubt in every instance. For example, his pro-YSA treatment of the Student Mobilization Committee split (pp. 367–404) is not fair to Linda Morse and her nonaligned supporters and comrades. See Student Mobilization Committee Papers, Box 1, Folder 5–6, WSHS.

25. Halstead, *Out Now!* pp. 67–75.

26. Sale, *SDS*, pp. 169–192; Gitlin, *The Whole World Is Watching*, pp. 53–56.

27. Halstead, *Out Now!* p. 44.

28. Ibid., pp. 73–75.

29. Ibid., pp. 89–90.

30. Nelson Blackstock, *Cointelpro* (New York: Vintage Books, 1976).

31. Halstead, *Out Now!* p. 196. The summary of the November 5–8 Mobilization and the Cleveland conferences also come from Halstead, *Out Now!* pp. 187–215. See also Lens, *Unrepentant Radical*, p. 311, on the Inter-University Committee which sponsored the conference.

32. Halstead, *Out Now!* p. 215.

33. David Dellinger, "North Vietnam: Eye-witness Report," *Liberation*, December 1966, pp. 3–15.

34. David Dellinger, "Vietnam and the International Liberation Front," *Liberation*, August 1965, pp. 14–16.

35. A good example of this passion is seen in David Dellinger, "Indomitable Vietnam—a Fresh Look," *Liberation*, May/June 1967, pp. 14–26, in which he describes his May 26–June 9 visit to North Vietnam—a trip on which Dellinger invited Nick Egleson, SDS president.

36. Harrison E. Salisbury, "A Visitor to Hanoi Inspects Damage Laid to U.S. Raids," *New York Times*, December 25, 1966, pp. 1–2.

37. Halstead, *Out Now!* pp. 274–275.

38. *Mobilization Report*, n.d., Box 1, Fred Halstead Papers, WSHS.

39. Rennie Davis and Others, S017, Box 44, NCCPV, LBJ, p. 5.

40. Ibid., p. 6.

41. *U.S. v. David Dellinger and Others*, pp. 17354–17358, 17392–17393, 1260–1266, 1311.

42. Ibid., pp. 17347–17352; John R. Rarick, *Congressional Record*, April 10, 1968, pp. E2901–E2902. Rarick represents a Louisiana district.

43. For more on ERAP see Sale, *SDS*, chap. 7.

44. See Gitlin, *The Whole World Is Watching*, pp. 167–170.

45. David Dellinger, "Unmasking Genocide," *Liberation*, December 1967, p. 3. The same article discusses Lynd's decision. Dellinger was also at the first session of the Tribunal in Stockholm in the spring of 1967. See David Dellinger, "Report From the Tribunal," *Liberation*, April 1967, pp. 7–13; also David Dellinger, "Report from the Tribunal II," *Liberation*, May–June 1967, pp. 8–11.

46. *U.S. v. David Dellinger and Others*, p. 17394; Sid Lens, R238, Box 41, NCCPV, LBJ, p. 1.

47. National Mobilization, Minutes, December 27, 1967, Box 2, Fred Halstead Papers, WSHS. See also Halstead, *Out Now!* pp. 368–369; and *U.S. v. David Dellinger and Others*, pp. 17394–17396.

48. Jack Newfield, "Tom Hayden—Saigon Will Fall in the Dry Season," *Village Voice*, July 18, 1968, p. 3.

49. All of this is culled from Steven V. Roberts, "Will Tom Hayden Overcome?" *Esquire*, December 1968, pp. 176–179, 208–209.

50. Students for a Democratic Society, "The Port Huron Statement," in Massimo Teodori, ed., *The New Left: A Documentary History* (New York: Bobbs-Merrill, 1969), p. 164.

51. Tom Hayden and Staughton Lynd, *The Other Side* (New York: New American Library, 1966).

52. Roberts, "Will Tom Hayden Overcome?" p. 208.

53. Ibid., p. 208. See Tom Hayden, *Rebellion In Newark: Official Violence and Ghetto Response* (New York: Random House, 1967).

54. Roberts, "Will Tom Hayden Overcome?" p. 208. See also Tom Hayden, *Rebellion and Repression* (New York: World Publishing Company, 1969), pp. 138–141, which is the part of Hayden's December 2–3, HUAC testimony relevant to the Bratislava and 1967 Vietnam experiences.

55. Tom Hayden and Rennie Davis, "Discussion on the Democratic Convention Challenge," A175, Box 7, NCCPV, LBJ. (See *U.S. v. David Dellinger and Others*, pp. 17836–17837 for a brief discussion of the paper and its distribution.)

56. Tom Hayden and Rennie Davis, "Discussion on the Democratic Convention Challenge?" p. 1.

57. Ibid., p. 3.

58. Ibid., pp. 3–4.

59. *U.S. v. David Dellinger and Others*, p. 18184; David Dellinger, *More Power Than We Know* (Garden City, Anchor Press/Doubleday, 1975), p. 121.

60. Dellinger, *More Power Than We Know*, p. 121.

Chapter 4

1. National Lawyers Guild, "Open Letter," January 19, 1968, A213, Box 7, NCCPV, LBJ.

2. National Lawyers Guild, "Minutes—January 26," A213, Box 7, NCCPV, LBJ. I have quoted Hayden's remarks as reported in the minutes. The other summarized statements come from the minutes as does the list of participants.

3. *U.S. v. David Dellinger and Others*, pp. 17397–17407, 14087–14095.

4. In Wini Breines, *Community and Organization in the New Left* (New York: Praeger, 1982), p. 94.

5. Halstead, *Out Now!* p. 311.

6. "Coalition Convention Demonstration and Youth Festival," *New Left Notes*, January 8, 1968, p. 3.

7. *U.S. v. David Dellinger and Others*, pp. 15454–15460.

8. Ibid., p. 14779; Rennie Davis and Others, S017, Box 44, NCCPV, LBJ, p. 7.

9. *U.S. v. David Dellinger and Others*, pp. 17458–17460, 2483, 2485–2486; Dwayne Oklepek, memos to Jack Mabley, S117a–j, Box 45, NCCPV, LBJ.

10. Oklepek, memos to Jack Mabley, S117h, Box 45, p. 2.

11. Ibid., pp. 1–3.

12. The minutes of the February 11 meeting are recorded in National Mobilization to End the War, "Convention Notes," February 17, 1968, A294, Box 8, NCCPV, LBJ. See also U.S. v. David Dellinger and Others, pp. 17409–17418, 13557–13565, 18346–18347.

13. National Mobilization, "Convention Notes," February 17, 1968.

14. National Mobilization, Mobilizer, 3:1, Box 4, DNC, NU.

15. National Mobilization, "Convention Notes," February 27, 1968, A294, Box 8, NCCPV, LBJ.

16. Resistance, "The Long March," A300, Box 8, NCCPV, LBJ.

17. National Mobilization, "Convention Notes," February 27, 1968.

18. See Arthur Herzog, McCarthy for President (New York: Viking Press, 1969), pp. 91–99. See also Eugene McCarthy, The Year of the People (Garden City: Doubleday and Company, 1969).

19. National Mobilization, "Statements Passed at the March 22–24 Movement Conference," A222, Box 7, NCCPV, LBJ.

20. Lew Jones, "Report on the Lake Villa Conference," March 28, 1968, Box 2, Fred Halstead Papers, WSHS.

21. Mike Klonsky, "A Report on the Proceedings of the National Interim Committee Meeting of March 9–10, 1968," Box 35, SDS Papers, WSHS.

22. Weinberger, R066, Box 40, p. 52.

23. Ibid., pp. 42–43.

24. Jones, "Report on the Lake Villa Conference."

25. David Dellinger, "Commentary," Liberation, March–April, 1969, pp. 45–46.

26. "Hear Plans to Disrupt Convention," Chicago Tribune, March 24, 1968, p. 1.

27. Rennie Davis and Tom Hayden, "Movement Campaign 1968: An Election Year Offensive," March 1968, A192, Box 7, NCCPV, LBJ.

28. Ibid., p. 19.

29. Ibid., p. 4.

30. Ibid., p. 3.

31. This statement from the paper is quoted by Rennie Davis in his trial testimony; see U.S. v. David Dellinger and Others, p. 17478.

32. Davis and Hayden, "Movement Campaign 1968," pp. 6–9, 16–19.

33. Rennie Davis and Others, S017, Box 44, pp. 12–13.

34. U.S. v. David Dellinger and Others, pp. 13585–13591.

35. National Mobilization, "Statements Passed at the March 22–24 Movement Conference."

36. Quoted in Chester, Hodgson, and Page, An American Melodrama, p. 4. Slightly different wording is given in Lyndon B. Johnson, The Vantage Point (New York: Holt, Rinehart and Winston, 1971), p. 435.

37. Chester, Hodgson, and Page, An American Melodrama, p. 5.

38. Johnson, The Vantage Point, chap. 18. Johnson argues that his decision was based on his failing health, family pressures, the need to push through a tax increase, and his desire to end the war. In Vaughn Davis Bornet, The Presidency of Lyndon B. Johnson (Lawrence: University Press of Kansas, 1984), pp. 298–305, a strong argument is made that it was indeed health concerns

that drove LBJ to withdraw. In his argument, however, Bornet points out that LBJ had suffered from serious health problems for better than a decade. Yet, he hadn't withdrawn from any other elections. Something must have given him the push he needed to put his health and the concerns of his family first, I would argue.

39. See Chester, Hodgson, and Page, *An American Melodrama*, pp. 8–11.

40. Ibid., p. 7.

41. *U.S. v. David Dellinger and Others*, pp. 11223, 11234.

42. Lens, *Unrepentant Radical*, p. 328.

43. J. Anthony Lukas, "Dissenters Focusing on Chicago," *New York Times*, August 18, 1968, p. 64.

44. *Chicago Daily News*, April 17, 1968, p. 1.

45. For a good account of the riot see Bill Gleason, *Daley of Chicago* (New York: Simon and Schuster, 1970), pp. 50–63.

46. *New York Times*, April 22, 1968, p. 16. For the reactions of the Mobe team in Chicago see *U.S. v. David Dellinger and Others*, pp. 15463–15464. Chicago SDS was involved in a joint leafleting with some of the Mobe activists in Chicago; see SDS, "Wanted: Inciting to Riot," Box 3, DNC, NU. This leaflet has a picture of Mayor Daley and the slogan, "eleven dead Chicago / aren't enough / for Mayor Daley alleged Mayor of Chicago." See also Marty Jezer, "Black Rebellion around U.S.," Liberation News Service, April 8, 1968.

47. Halstead, *Out Now!* pp. 386–388; and Sale, *SDS*, pp. 428–430.

48. Otto Liljenstolpe, R422, Box 42, NCCPV, LBJ, pp. 2–3.

49. *U.S. v. David Dellinger and Others*, pp. 15467–15469.

50. Thomas Powers, "Anti-War Protesters Battle Police," *Chicago Tribune*, April 28, 1968, pp. 1, 8, provides the information and the quote on police, FBI, and Army Intelligence. See also *Chicago Tribune*, "Loyalty Day Marchers to Show Colors," April 26, 1968, p. 12, for background. The most comprehensive piece on the demonstration is by Joseph Sander, "Battle of Chicago: A Study in Law and Order," *Nation*, May 20, 1968, pp. 655–657. For an overview see *Dissent and Disorder: A Report to the Citizens of Chicago on the April 27 Peace Parade*, August 1, 1968.

51. Powers, "Anti-War Protesters," pp. 1, 8.

52. *Dissent and Disorder*, p. 30. Sidney Lens and Jay Miller of the American Civil Liberties Union had prompted the investigation that resulted in *Dissent and Disorder*. The investigation and report were funded by the Roger Baldwin Foundation. See Lens, *Unrepentant Radical*, p. 325.

53. C. Clark Kissinger, R385, Box 42, NCCPV, LBJ, p. 1.

54. Liljenstolpe, R422, Box 42, p. 18.

55. American Civil Liberties statement (untitled), A256, Box 8, NCCPV, LBJ, p. 1.

56. Roberts, "Will Tom Hayden Overcome?" p. 176.

57. Quoted by Congressman Ashbrook in his questioning of Hayden, December 3, 1968, at the House UnAmerican Committee hearings—see Hayden, *Rebellion and Repression*, p. 182.

58. Donald Kalish, OR181, Box 34, NCCPV, LBJ, p. 2.

59. See Chester, Hodgson and Page, *An American Melodrama*, pp. 108–11, 142–157.

60. Halstead, *Out Now!* p. 405.

61. All of this is in Sale, *SDS*, pp. 451–457.

62. Harvey Stone, "G.I. Coffee House for Peace," Liberation News Service, July 17, 1968; *U.S. v. David Dellinger and Others*, pp. 17462, 11770–11773, 17236–17237.

63. See Legal Defense Committee, "Instructions to Volunteer Attorneys," Box 3, DNC, NU; Medical Committee for Human Rights, "Chronology," A185, Box 7, NCCPV, LBJ.

64. Chester, Hodgson, and Page, *An American Melodrama*, p. 393.

65. The Reagan quote and correction comes from my favorite account of the 1968 campaign trail—Chester, Hodgson, and Page, *An American Melodrama*, p. 405. The three authors covered the campaign trail for the Sunday *Times* of London.

66. Newfield, "Tom Hayden: Saigon Will Fall in the Dry Season," p. 3; *U.S. v. David Dellinger and Others*, pp. 16108–16109; Roberts, "Will Tom Hayden Overcome?" p. 209.

67. Don Kalish, OR181, Box 34, NCCPV, LBJ, p. 2.

68. Weinberger, R066, Box 40, p. 60.

69. Quoted in Bob Greenblatt, "Coordinator's Report—Steering Committee of the National Mobilization," Box 2, Fred Halstead Papers, WSHS.

70. Ibid.

71. Paul Offner, OR119, Box 34, NCCPV, LBJ, p. 2. See also Coalition for an Open Convention, news release, July 30, 1968, Box 1, DNC, NU; Al Lowenstein, OR121, Box 34, NCCPV, LBJ; Clinton DeNaux, OR120, Box 34, NCCPV, LBJ.

72. *U.S. v. David Dellinger and Others*, pp. 17485–17486, 15110–15116.

73. Ibid., pp. 17207–17211, 17492–17493.

74. Newfield, "Tom Hayden," p. 3. See also *U.S. v. David Dellinger and Others*, pp. 13611–13617.

75. Lucy Montgomery, R384, Box 41, NCCPV, LBJ; C. Clark Kissinger, R385, Box 41, p. 2. Kissinger says the entire Mobe budget was around $15,000 and that money wasn't much of a problem.

76. *U.S. v. David Dellinger and Others*, pp. 17493–17495, 16618–16624.

77. National Mobilization to End the War in Vietnam, "Summary of Administrative Meeting Held at the Ohio Area Peace Council," Box 45, SDS, WSHS. See also *U.S. v. David Dellinger and Others*, pp. 17488–17514, 14654–14662. Most of this comes from the Mobe, "Summary," including Davis's and Hayden's comments on blocking the convention hall.

78. Sale, *SDS*, p. 664.

79. All of this material, including all quotations, comes from the SDS-NIC Minutes, July 19–21, 1968, Box 36, SDS, WSHS.

80. Mike Klonsky, "View of Chicago," *New Left Notes*, August 5, 1968, pp. 1, 4.

81. Wayne Heimbach, Jo Horton, Hamish Sinclair, Mike Klonsky, "Democratic Party Convention—Chicago," August 11, 1968, Box 45, SDS, WSHS.

82. *U.S. v. David Dellinger and Others*, pp. 11237–11244, 15891–15903, 4067. The trial testimony on p. 4067 is by Frank Sweeny, a New York ad man who worked for the FBI.

83. *U.S. v. David Dellinger and Others*, pp. 2898–2983. This testimony also comes from an FBI informant, a TV news cameraman in San Diego who worked for the FBI.

84. Weinberger, R066, Box 40, pp. 62–65.

85. *U.S. v. David Dellinger and Others*, pp. 16300–16314, 16648–16651.

86. National Mobilization Committee (Mark Simon), "City Negotiation Notes," July 27, 1968, A191, Box 7, NCCPV, LBJ. See also Mark Simon's trial testimony, *U.S. v. David Dellinger and Others*, p. 15113.

87. *U.S. v. David Dellinger and Others*, pp. 16892–16893, 17537–17542, 15123–15128.

88. National Mobilization to End the War in Vietnam (Paul Potter), "Dear Friend . . . Movement Centers in Chicago" (Mid-August, 1968[?]), Box 4, DNC, NU. See also National Mobilization to End the War in Vietnam, "Volunteer Check List," Box 4, DNC, NU.

89. Otto Liljenstolpe, R422, Box 42, NCCPV, LBJ, pp. 9–11.

90. See National Mobilization to End the War in Vietnam, "City Negotiation Notes," July 27, July 31, August 6, 1968, A191, Box 7, NCCPV, LBJ.

91. *U.S. v. David Dellinger and Others*, pp. 507–509, 17547–17555, 15417–15454.

92. Most of this is from the National Mobilization to End the War in Vietnam, "Summary of Administrative Meeting Held in Chicago, August 4, chaired by David Dellinger," A265, Box 8, NCCPV, LBJ. See *U.S. v. David Dellinger and Others*, pp. 14664–14667. The Hayden remark is from Rennie Davis's trial testimony, *U.S. v. David Dellinger and Others*, p. 17659.

93. *Chicago Sun-Times*, August 6, 1968, p. 22. The quote is from the National Mobilization to End the War in Vietnam, press release, August 5, 1968, S109, Box 45. See also the *Chicago Tribune*, August 6, 1968, p. 6.

94. *U.S. v. David Dellinger and Others*, pp. 17571–17573, 15160–16164.

95. National Mobilization to End the War in Vietnam—Mark Simon to James Conlisk, letter, August 5, 1968, A191, Box 7, NCCPV, LBJ.

96. *U.S. v. David Dellinger and Others*, pp. 17579–17581, 15763–15782. They did change their permit application the next day—see Mark Simon's trial testimony, *U.S. v. David Dellinger and Others*, pp. 15322–15327.

97. Ibid., pp. 15162–15167.

98. Ibid., pp. 14462, 6194; Benjamin J. Radford, R412, Box 43, NCCPV, LBJ, pp. 1–3, and R761, Box 43, NCCPV, LBJ, pp. 8–9; American Friends Service Committee—Kale Williams to members, memos, August 14 and September 18, 1968, A300, Box 8, NCCPV, LBJ.

99. National Mobilization to End the War in Vietnam, "Policy," Box 4, DNC, NU. See also National Mobilization to End the War in Vietnam, "Introduction to Marshalls," Box 4, DNC, NU; Stephanie Miller, monitor notes, Box 4, DNC, NU; *U.S. v. David Dellinger*, pp. 2515, 2654–2660.

100. *U.S. v. David Dellinger and Others*, pp. 17602–17608, 17614–17617.

101. *Chicago Tribune*, August 13, 1968, p. 8.

102. Ibid., August 17, 1968, p. 10; Ibid., August 21, 1968, p. 20; Lowenstein, OR121, Box 34, p. 1; Offner, OR119, Box 34, pp. 1–3; American Civil Liberties Union, press release, August 14, 1968, Box 1, DNC, NU; *U.S. v. David Dellinger and Others*, pp. 16067–16068.

103. Weinberger, R066, Box 40, pp. 48–49.

104. *U.S. v. David Dellinger and Others*, pp. 17585–17591, 15178–15190, 15782–15790, 521–529, 555, 600–601, 9408–9411, 9540–9543, 9555, 9619–9621.

105. National Mobilization to End the War in Vietnam, letter, August 10, 1968, Box 4, DNC, NU.

106. *U.S. v. David Dellinger and Others*, pp. 17622–17627, 16812–16815, 16822–16825, 16841–16847.

107. American Friends Service Committee—Kale Williams to members, memo, August 14, 1968.

108. *U.S. v. David Dellinger and Others*, pp. 2496–2500, 2521, 2527–2528, 2837. Irwin Bock, a Chicago Police Department spy, confirms all of this, but as will be seen in Chaps. 6 and 7 he claims that Davis and Hayden went even further—see Irwin Bock's trial testimony, *U.S. v. David Dellinger and Others*, pp. 6212–6213, 6217.

109. *U.S. v. David Dellinger and Others*, pp. 17633–17643, 17648, 17685, 10530–10538, 93–116, 205–262, 283–284, 375–378; Simon, R467, Box 42, pp. 22–24; *New York Times*, August 20, 1968, p. 25.

110. *New York Times*, August 20, 1985, p. 25.

111. *U.S. v. David Dellinger and Others*, p. 11265; Weinberger, R066, Box 40, pp. 80–81; Kale Williams, David Finkle, James Reddy, R632, Box 43, NCCPV, LBJ, p. 1; Committee of Returned Volunteers, "Suggestions on Mobilizing," August 15, 1968, A287, Box 8, NCCPV, LBJ; *Think!* August 23, 1968, A217, Box 7, NCCPV, LBJ; Movement Center in Boston, "Come to Chicago," A219, Box 7, NCCPV, LBJ; Ann Arbor Anti-War Mobilization, "Confrontation in Chicago," Box 4, DNC, NU.

112. *New York Times*, August 23, 1968, p. 20.

113. Ibid., p. 22.

114. American Friends Service Committee—Kale Williams to members, memo, September 18, 1968.

115. The slogan was printed—white letters on a pink background—on 1½ × 3-inch pieces of paper with an adhesive on the back—copies of which can be found under National Mobilization, Box 4, DNC, NU.

116. *Mobilizer*, August 15, 1968.

117. *Chicago Sun-Times*, August 23, 1968, p. 20.

118. Tom Hayden, "The Cops and the Convention," and "Democracy Is . . . in the Streets," *Rat Convention Special*, pp. 2, 4–5.

Chapter 5

1. The facts, figures, statements, and chronology of the convention selection are culled from William King, "Chicago Still in Running," *Chicago Tribune*, October 7, 1967, p. 6; William King, "Democrats Name Chicago," *Chicago Tribune*, October 9, 1967, pp. 1–2; John Elner, "How Mayor Got 1968 Convention for City," *Chicago Tribune*, October 10, 1967, p. 1. See also ibid., pp. 12 and 10; *New York Times*, February 13, 1968, p. 16. See also the *Chicago Sun-Times*, *Chicago Daily News*, and *Chicago's American*, October 7–10, 1967.

2. Quoted by Theodore White, *The Making of the President 1968* (New York: Pocket Books, 1970), p. 329.

3. For a particularly celebratory summary of such feelings see White, *The Making of the President 1968*, pp. 328–329.

4. Leon Despres, "Your Alderman Reports," n.d., DNC, NU.

5. Mike Royko, *Boss: Richard J. Daley of Chicago* (New York: New American Library, 1971); Bill Gleason, *Daley of Chicago* (New York: Simon and Schuster, 1970); Milton L. Rakove, *We Don't Want Nobody Nobody Sent* (Bloomington: Indiana University Press, 1979); Milton L. Rakove, *Don't Make No Waves, Don't Back No Losers* (Bloomington: Indiana University Press, 1975); Len O'Conner, *Clout* (New York: Avon, 1976). Rakove's books more than the others describe and explain how Chicago politics worked in the Daley years. *We Don't Want Nobody Nobody Sent* is a collection of oral histories that together superbly recount precinct and ward politics. Veteran Chicago newspapermen Royko and Gleason both provide thoughtful, well-written biographies of Daley. Royko's better-known work is highly critical of Daley while Gleason's work is more temperate in its criticisms. Royko's book is the best at stripping away Daley's facade, while Gleason, by concentrating on black-white relations in the city, effectively shows the organization at its worst. Both are extremely well-researched and very sensitive to the nuances of Chicago politics. O'Conner, a veteran Chicago television reporter, writes a more respectful biography of Daley and has the advantage of covering Daley's last years. It too is solidly researched and sensitive to city politics. At times, however—and the 1968 Democratic Convention is one of those times—O'Conner seems less aware of events and pressures outside of the city and so presents a slightly out-of-focus account. For a solid account of Daley's last year and death see Len O'Conner, *Requiem* (Chicago: Contemporary Books, 1977).

6. See T. N. Clark, "The Irish Ethic and the Spirit of Patronage," *Ethnicity* 2 (1975), pp. 305–359.

7. See Royko, *Boss*, pp. 30–64; Gleason, *Daley of Chicago*, pp. 111–146; O'Conner, *Clout*, pp. 16–105.

8. See Rakove, *We Don't Want Nobody Nobody Sent*, pp. 159–189, on the organization blacks. In 1965, 82.3% of all the city's elementary schoolchildren went to totally segregated schools—Gleason, *Daley of Chicago*, p. 37.

9. For a good account of early efforts by blacks to gain political power in Chicago see Joe Matthewson, *Up against Daley* (La Salle, Ill.: Open Court, 1974), pp. 121–134.

10. *Chicago Tribune*, December 27, 1967, p. 10.

11. Edward Scheiber, "Daley Hits Street Crime," *Chicago Tribune*, December 28, 1968, p. 1.

12. One indication of the American people's fear of disorder and rioting in the streets was the rise in the sale of firearms. According to the Stanford Research Institute, in 1967, the majority of firearms purchasers said that they bought their weapons for protection against rioters. See *Chicago Tribune*, August 18, p. 13.

13. Richard Elrod, R580, Box 42, NCCPV, LBJ, p. 1.

14. Donna Gill, "LBJ-Humphrey Slate Seen by Party Leader," *Chicago Tribune*, January 9, 1968, p. 2.

15. Royko, *Boss*, pp. 201–202.

16. Elrod, R580, Box 42, p. 1.

17. "Counselor for the City," *Chicago Police Star*, February 1968, pp. 6–7.

18. James Conlisk, Jr., "Report of the Superintendent to the Police Board," January 12, 1968, Chicago Police Board (CPB).

19. See William J. Bopp, *O. W. Wilson and the Search for a Police Profession* (Port Washington, N.Y.: Kennikat Press, 1977).

20. Seymour Martin Lipset, "Why Cops Hate Liberals—and Vice Versa," in *The Police Rebellion*, ed. William J. Bopp (Springfield, Ill.: Charles C. Thomas, 1971), p. 35.

21. James Q. Wilson, "Police Morale, Reform and Citizen Respect: The Chicago Case," in *The Police*, ed. D. Bordua (New York: John Wiley and Sons, 1967), p. 145.

22. Lipset, "Why Cops Hate Liberals—and Vice Versa," p. 35; see also Bopp, *O. W. Wilson*, pp. 96–97.

23. Bopp, *O. W. Wilson*, pp. 84–87; Wilson, "Police Morale," pp. 142–154; and Barbara R. Price, *Police Professionalism* (Toronto: D. C. Heath and Company, 1977), pp. 30–32, 52.

24. Bopp, *O. W. Wilson*, p. 95.

25. Robert M. Fogelson, *Big City Police* (Cambridge, Mass.: Harvard University Press, 1977), p. 257. Fogelson quotes from a study done by Albert J. Reiss and Donald J. Block that showed that three quarters of white Chicago, Boston, and Washington, D.C., policemen were racists.

26. William W. Turner, *The Police Establishment* (New York: G. P. Putnam's Sons, 1968), p. 107.

27. Bopp, *O. W. Wilson*, pp. 134–137.

28. Turner, *The Police Establishment*, p. 110.

29. See n. 23.

30. Wilson, "Police Morale," pp. 145–147.

31. Charles Grutzner, "Leary Asks Albany to Draft Guidelines for Police in Riots," *New York Times*, July 3, 1968, p. 8.

32. Fogelson, *Big City Police*, p. 239.

33. O. W. Wilson, "Police Authority in a Free Society," *Journal of Criminal Law, Criminology and Police Science*, June 1963, pp. 176–177.

34. Lipset, "Why Cops Hate Liberals—and Vice Versa," p. 32.

35. Wilson, "Policy Authority in a Free Society," p. 176.

36. James J. Allan, "The Public Attitude toward Police," in *Police and the Changing Community*, ed. Nelson A. Watson (Washington, D.C.: International Association of Chiefs of Police, 1965), pp. 23–25; Rodney Stark, *Police Riots* (Belmont, Calif.: Wadsworth, 1972), pp. 60–61, 92; Lipset, "Why Cops Hate Liberals—and Vice Versa," pp. 28–29, 32.

37. Quentin Tamm, "Police Professionalism and Civil Rights," in *Police and the Changing Community*, ed. Nelson A. Watson, p. 145.

38. Arthur Niederhoffer, *Behind the Shield* (Garden City, N.Y.: Doubleday, 1967), p. 142.

39. Ibid., p. 90.

40. Wilson, "Police Morale, Reform and Citizen Respect," p. 154.

41. The best summary of these expert views by an expert is in Jerome Skolnick, *Justice without Trial: Law Enforcement in Democratic Society* (New York: John Wiley and Sons, 1966), pp. 42–70; see also Lipset, "Why Cops Hate Liberals—and Vice Versa," pp. 29–35; Stark, *Police Riots*, pp. 86–96; William A. Westley, "Violence and the Police," *American Journal of Sociology*, August 1953, pp. 34–41; and William A. Westley, "Secrecy and the Police," *Social Forces*, March 1956, pp. 254–257.

42. Charles E. Moore, "The Rebels and the Law," in Watson, *Police and the Changing Community*, p. 51; see also Fogelson, *Big City Police*, p. 147.

43. Lipset, "Why Cops Hate Liberals—and Vice Versa," pp. 23–24.

44. Leonard Ruckleman, *Police Politics: A Comparative Study of Three Cities* (Cambridge: Ballinger Publishing Company, 1974), p. 75.

45. Turner, *The Police Establishment*, p. 294.

46. Fogelson, *Big City Police*, p. 147.

47. Ramsey Clark, "The Year of the Policeman," *Police Chief*, May 1968, p. 12.

48. And so he called his 1968 book on what it was like being a New York City cop—Herbert T. Klein, *Damned If You Do, Damned If You Don't* (New York: Crown Publishers, 1968).

49. Bopp, *O. W. Wilson*, pp. 115–121; see also Turner, *The Police Establishment*, pp. 125–129.

50. Turner, *The Police Establishment*, p. 140.

51. "Miami," *Liberation News Service*, January 5, 1968.

52. *Chicago Tribune*, January 8, 1968, p. 7.

53. R. E. Anderson, "Are Our City Police Departments Being Neutralized?" *Police*, July–August 1968, p. 14. For a similar comment see Quentin Tamm, "Justice Now!" *Police Chief*, July 1968, p. 12; also Stark, *Police Riots* in its entirety, which argues that this feeling of being forced into law enforcement permeated urban police departments across the country.

54. His biographer, William J. Bopp in *O. W. Wilson*, pp. 122–123, says it's true and that he was not pressured into retirement.

55. Royko, *Boss*, p. 165.

56. Bopp, *O. W. Wilson*, p. 106.

Chapter 6

1. Chicago Police Department Convention Planning Committee (CPD-CPC), minutes, January 29, 1968, A108, Box 5, NCCPV, LBJ.

2. CPD-CPC, minutes, February 13, 1968 and February 27, 1968, A108, Box 5; CPD-CPC, memo from Chief of the Patrol Division to Deputy Superintendent Bureau of Staff Services, February 13, 1968, A094, Box 5, NCCPV, LBJ; CPD-CPC, "Memo to All Concerned," February 21, 1968, A094, Box 5, NCCPV, LBJ; CPD-CPC, memo to Lt. McDonald from A. J. Hinkens (Central Detention), February 28, 1968, A118, Box 5, NCCPV, LBJ.

3. *Chicago Tribune*, February 14, 1968, p. 1.

4. Ibid., p. 1.

5. Ibid., March 1, 1968, p. 4.

6. CPD-CPC, transcribed notes—Professor Miesner, February 29, 1968, A081, Box 5, NCCPV, LBJ.

7. Thomas Powers, "Chicago Trains Policemen in Control of Mobs," *Chicago Tribune*, March 3, 1968, p. 3. For more on this see James Conlisk, "Report of the Superintendent to the Police Board," April 5, 1968, Chicago Police Board (CPB).

8. James Conlisk, "Report of the Superintendent to the Police Board," April 5, 1968; Chicago Police Department (CPD), General Order 67–18c, "Official Uniform and Equipment," March 11, 1968, effective April 1, 1968, CPB.

9. National Advisory Commission on Civil Disorders, *Report of the National Commission on Civil Disorders* (New York: Pocket Books, 1968), pp. 18–19. President Johnson formed the commission on July 29, 1967, after the summer 1967 urban riots.

10. Ibid., pp. 10–11.

11. Gleason, *Daley of Chicago*, p. 266. The Mayor's statements are also from Gleason, *Daley of Chicago*, pp. 265–266.

12. *Chicago Tribune*, March 2, 1966, p. 8.

13. Donna Gill, "LBJ-Humphrey Slate Seen," *Chicago Tribune*, January 9, 1968, p. 2.

14. This account is taken directly from Gleason, *Daley of Chicago*, p. 258.

15. See Daley, Richard J., January–March 1968, Diary Back Up Card Files, LBJ.

16. *Chicago Tribune*, April 1, 1968, pp. 1–2. A *Chicago Tribune* editorial, April 1, 1968, p. 14, agreed.

17. Marvin Watson to Juanita Roberts, memo, April 3, 1968, Daley, Richard J., Name File, LBJ.

18. Ruckelman, *Police Politics*, pp. 75–76.

19. Lyndon Baines Johnson to Brother H. Basil, night letter, April 1, 1968, Daley, Richard J., Name File, LBJ.

20. George Tagge, "Johnson and Daley Weigh Candidates," *Chicago Tribune*, April 2, 1968, p. 2.

21. *Chicago Tribune*, April 3, 1968, p. 3. It is important to note that there was no presidential preference ballot in Illinois' June 11 Democratic primary, which meant that the delegates slated by the Mayor would easily dominate the Illinois convention delegation.

22. *Chicago Tribune*, April 1, 1968, p. 24.

23. Ibid., April 5, 1968, p. 1.

24. This quote comes from Royko, *Boss*, p. 150. For Daley and King in general see Royko, *Boss*, pp. 149–158—it's Royko at his best. The best treatment of Daley and the civil rights movement in general and the King Chicago Project in particular is in Alan B. Anderson and George W. Pickering, *Confronting the Color Line* (Athens, Ga.: University of Georgia Press, 1986). Also see Lois Wille, "Confrontation in Chicago," *Nation*, August 20, 1965, pp. 92–95. For the rioting elsewhere in the country see *Chicago Sun-Times*, April 5, 1968, p. 1.

25. Peter Yessner, comp., *Quotations from Mayor Daley* (New York: G. P. Putnam's Sons, 1969), p. 115; said July 27, 1967, at a press conference. Yessner's little book is a gold mine of source materials.

26. Quoted in Gleason, *Daley of Chicago*, p. 52—Gleason is very good on the riot.

27. My account is based on three major sources, Gleason, *Daley of Chicago*, pp. 53–61; "Criminal Justice in Extremis: Administration of Justice during the April 1968 Chicago Disorders," *University of Chicago Law Review*, Spring 1969, pp. 470–481; and newspaper accounts: *Chicago Tribune*, April 6, 1968, pp. 1–2, 8; John McClean and Bernard Judge, "Mayor Keeps Vigil in City Hall Office," *Chicago Tribune*, April 6, 1968, p. 5; Bruce Engle, "Looters Have a Grim Carnival," *Chicago Tribune*, April 6, 1968, p. 5; *Chicago Tribune*, April 7, 1968, pp. 1–3, 5. When there was a factual discrepancy I accepted the *Law Review* statistics and account. The Mayor's April 5, 4:20 speech is from the *Chicago Tribune*, April 6, 1968, p. 1, as is the Mayor's response to reporters immediately following the radio and television speech. The material on police strategy and concerns is mainly from the *Law Review*, pp. 477–480, as is the policeman's statement about "one good crack on the head," p. 481.

28. *Chicago Tribune*, April 7, 1968, p. 28.

29. Ibid., April 8, 1968, p. 1—for the statistics see n. 81.

30. Ibid., April 11, 1968, p. 2.

31. Paul McGrath, "U.S. Bares Plot to Turn Riot Rites into Chaos," *Chicago Tribune*, April 9, 1968, p. 1.

32. *Chicago Tribune*, April 9, 1968, p. 14.

33. Ibid., April 11, 1968, p. 2.

34. See Gleason, *Daley of Chicago*, pp. 74–75.

35. Ibid., pp. 75–76. One of the several good parts of Gleason's work is his inclusion of long quotes not available elsewhere.

36. Ibid., p. 74.

37. Ibid., p. 80.

38. Royko, *Boss*, p. 169.

39. *Chicago Sun-Times*, April 18, 1968, p. 1.

40. Gleason, *Daley of Chicago*, pp. 78–79.

41. CPD, Special Order 68–26, "New Ordinances Governing Disorderly Conduct, Trespass, and Resisting Arrest," April 12, 1968, CPB.

42. American Civil Liberties Union, *Dissent in Crisis* (New York, 1969), p. 9; J. Anthony Lukas, *The Barnyard Epithet and Other Obscenities* (New York: Harper and Row, 1970), p. 4; William Higgs and Guy Smithe, "Brief Analysis of Civil Rights Act of 1968," Liberation News Service, April 15/17/19, 1968; Sale, *SDS*, p. 221. For an understanding of the constitutional questions raised by the bill, see Thomas I. Emerson, *The System of Freedom and Expression* (New York: Random House, 1970), chap. 9.

43. James Conlisk, "Report of the Superintendent to the Police Board," June 7, 1968, CPB; and James Conlisk, "Memo to Police Board," August 8, 1968, CPB.

44. Robert Wiedrich, "Unsung Heroes Invade Terror Ranks," *Chicago Tribune*, April 10, 1968, p. 3.

45. The history of the Red Squad is taken from Lois Wille, "The Secret Police in Chicago," *Chicago Journalism Review*, February 1969, pp. 1, 7–12. The phrases and words in quotes are from Wiedrich, "Unsung Heroes," p. 3. He is quoting members of the Red Squad.

46. Lens, S167, Box 45, pp. 2–4; Lens, *Unrepentant Radical*, p. 326; Turner, *The Police Establishment*, pp. 129–131.

47. *U.S. v. David Dellinger and Others*, pp. 6158–6161, 6503–6505, 6590–6618.

48. Ibid., pp. 4251–4253, 4404–4406, 4427.

49. See for example the testimony of Louis Salzberg in *U.S. v. David Dellinger and Others*, pp. 3669–3872; and also Al Rosen in ibid., pp. 16498–16508.

50. P. W. Moore, "Wiretaps: Disclosed or Leaked?" *Nation*, October 27, 1969, p. 434. The internal FBI memos are from the pathbreaking work by Arthur Theohaus, *Spying on America* (Philadelphia: Temple University Press, 1978), pp. 183–184.

51. Wille, "The Secret Police in Chicago," p. 12.

52. Richard Elrod, R580, Box 42, NCCPV, LBJ, pp. 1–3.

53. *U.S. v. David Dellinger and Others*, p. 568.

54. Al Baugher, R595, Box 42, NCCPV, LBJ, pp. 1–2, 5–7.

55. Earl Bush, R657, Box 43, NCCPV, LBJ, p. 5. For David Stahl's definition of hippies, *U.S. v. David Dellinger and Others*, p. 583. "Hippies" was what all demonstrators, regardless of age or hair length, were called by most city officials. David Dellinger, Rennie Davis, and Abbie Hoffman were all "hippies" in the eyes of the Mayor and many of his people. Many in the mass media reported it in the same way. By the late summer, hippie and yippie became fairly interchangeable and picture captions began to refer to local antiwar demonstrators as well as long-haired youths as yippies.

56. Bush, R657, Box 43, pp. 4–5; see also Raymond Simon's testimony, *U.S. v. David Dellinger and Others*, p. 338.

57. Royko, *Boss*, p. 173.

58. James Rochford, R402, Box 42, NCCPV, LBJ, p. 6; see also *U.S. v. David Dellinger and Others*, p. 8431.

59. *Chicago Tribune*, April 28, 1968, p. 4.

60. This account of the April 27 confrontation is based on Thomas Power, "Anti-War Protesters Battle Police," *Chicago Tribune*, April 28, 1968, pp. 1, 8; Joseph Sander, "Battle of Chicago," *Nation*, May 20, 1968, pp. 655–657; and Royko, *Boss*, p. 176.

61. Marvin Watson to Lyndon Johnson, memo, April 24, 1968, Daley, Richard J., Diary Backup Card File, LBJ; "The Democratic Part of Cook County Reception and Dinner Honoring LBJ," April 24, 1968, Daley, Richard J., Diary Backup Card File, LBJ.

62. "Yippie," *Chicago Journalism Review*, May 1969, pp. 1, 11.

63. James Rochford, R798, Box 43, NCCPV, LBJ, p. 2.

64. James Jardine, R694, Box 43, NCCPV, LBJ, pp. 1–2.

65. Bill Blackburn to Lyndon Johnson, memo, May 23, 1968, Daley, Richard J., Name File, LBJ. In the same memo, the president also read of and then noted approval of a draft of the speech Bailey wanted to give at a luncheon in Chicago in which Bailey confirmed that contrary to certain rumors stated after the King riots, the convention would be held in Chicago.

66. Chester, Hodgson, and Page, *An American Melodrama*, p. 134. For the RFK quote see Arthur Schlesinger, Jr., *Robert Kennedy and His Times* (Boston:

Houghton Mifflin, 1978), pp. 864–865. The question of whether RFK would have won the nomination had he lived is an intriguing one. See David Burner and Thomas R. West, *The Kennedy Brothers and American Liberalism* (New York: Atheneum, 1981), p. 220.

67. Richard T. Dunn to Richard J. Daley, letter, June 20, 1968, A148, Box 6, NCCPV, LBJ; Illinois National Guard, "Final Report," September 3, 1968, A151, Box 6, NCCPV, LBJ; Richard T. Dunn to Richard J. Daley, letter, July 17, 1968, A148, Box 6, NCCPV, LBJ; Richard T. Dunn to James B. Conlisk, letter, July 17, 1968, A148, Box 6, NCCPV, LBJ; Illinois National Guard, "INTSUM," Number 1, April 1968, A149, Box 6, NCCPV, LBJ; Major Lawrence Crimine, R748, Box 43, NCCPV, LBJ, pp. 2–4.

68. Crimine, R748, Box 43, pp. 1–2.

69. Film clips of this can be seen in Haskell Wexler, director, *Medium Cool* (1969); and in CBS News, "1968" (1969).

70. Ramsey Clark, Oral History Interviews, Interview 4, April 16, 1969, by Harri Baker, LBJ, pp. 14–15.

71. See for example *Chicago Tribune*, August 15, 1968, p. 19; Nixon attacked Clark during his acceptance speech at the Republican Convention.

72. *U.S. Department of Justice Administrative History*, vol. 7, pt. 11, pp. 1–2, LBJ.

73. Ramsey Clark, Oral History Interviews, Interview 3, March 21, 1969, by Harri Baker, LBJ, p. 13.

74. More accurately, Davis had spoken to Phillip Mason, Chicago Field representative of the Service who had contacted Wilkins. See Roger Wilkins, OR162, Box 34, NCCPV, LBJ, pp. 1–2.

75. *U.S. v. David Dellinger and Others*, pp. 16640–16641.

76. Wilkins, OR162, Box 34, pp. 3–5.

77. John B. Criswell to James R. Jones, memo, July 1, 1968, Daley, Richard J., Name File, LBJ.

78. Donald Janson, "Bailey and Daley Confer," *New York Times*, July 23, 1968, p. 23.

79. *Chicago Tribune*, August 1, 1968, p. 8.

80. Ibid., August 8, 1968, p. 9.

81. Bush, R657, Box 43, p. 3.

82. *Chicago Tribune*, August 25, 1968, p. 8; *New York Times*, August 23, 1968, p. 23.

83. *Chicago Sun-Times*, August 27, 1968, p. 11.

84. See William Small, *To Kill a Messenger* (New York: Hastings House, 1970), pp. 194–199. One of the results of Chicago '68 was a number of books that argued about the place and impact of TV news in the political process.

85. *Chicago Tribune*, August 11, 1968, sec. 1A, p. 1.

86. Thomas Lyon, R723, Box 43, NCCPV, LBJ, pp. 11–13; *Chicago Sun-Times*, August 15, 1968, p. 5. For the black perspective on this see Chester Robinson, R608, Box 43, NCCPV, LBJ, p. 1. Robinson was head of the West Side Organization and was tailed.

87. *Chicago Tribune*, August 10, 1968, p. 8; ibid., August 15, 1968, p. 5; William Garrett, "All Out Security Includes Hot Line to White House," *Chicago's American*, August 24, 1968, pp. 1, 3.

88. *Chicago Tribune*, August 21, 1968, p. 16; ibid., August 25, 1968, p. 8; Theodore Dreyer, "Know Your Enemy," *Rat*, September 6–19, 1968, p. 12; Harvey Stone, "Riot Control," *The Rag*, August 22, 1968, p. 1.

89. *Chicago Tribune*, August 21, 1968, p. 14.

90. Ibid., August 17, 1968, pp. 2, 9.

91. *Chicago Sun-Times*, August 23, 1968, p. 3.

92. *U.S. v. David Dellinger and Others*, p. 541.

93. *Chicago Tribune*, August 17, 1968, p. 9.

94. Ed McCahill, "The Liberation of Tom Fitzgerald," *Chicago*, August 1978, p. 133.

95. *Chicago Tribune*, August 17, 1968, p. 9.

96. *U.S. v. David Dellinger and Others*, pp. 371–372.

97. Ibid., p. 344.

98. Jason Epstein, *The Great Conspiracy Trial* (New York: Random House, 1970), pp. 72–73.

99. *U.S. v. David Dellinger and Others*, p. 3969.

100. Ibid., pp. 524, 4265–4266, 4273, 4299, 6161, 6212.

101. Ibid., pp. 508, 514.

102. *Chicago Tribune*, August 20, 1968, p. 3; ibid., August 23, 1968, p. 1; Lois Wille, "The Convention Plot Mystery," *Chicago Daily News*, October 8, 1968, pp. 3–4. At the same time, a prison parolee told the FBI that the Black Panthers had met in Chicago and were going to kill most of the city's black Democratic party leadership. The FBI assigned sixty agents to the case and the Chicago Police hid or protected the city's black leaders. The FBI determined that the parolee had made up the story. After the convention, the CPD leaked the story—minus the FBI conclusion—to the newspapers to help back up Mayor Daley's version of convention week. See Federal District Judge James B. Parsons, R516, Box 4, NCCPV, LBJ. Parsons was one of five black leaders named by the parolee.

103. *Chicago Sun-Times*, August 9, 1968, p. 2; ibid., August 10, 1968, p. 10. Twenty-seven out of 1333 delegates at the Republican Convention were black—*Chicago Sun-Times*, August 7, 1968, p. 38.

104. *Chicago Tribune*, August 18, 1968, p. 2.

105. Ibid., August 23, 1968, p. 7; CPD, Special Order 68–48, "Motion Picture Documentation of Demonstrators and Civil Disorder," August 22, 1968; CPD, General Order 68–13, "Aerosol Tear Gas Weapons," August 21, 1968. See also CPD, Special Order 68–50, "Command Center and Command Center Personnel," August 23, 1968.

106. *Chicago Sun-Times*, August 3, 1968, p. 24.

107. *Chicago Tribune*, August 13, 1968, p. 14; and *Chicago's American*, August 14, 1968, p. 7.

108. James B. Conlisk to All Police Personnel, letter, August 21, 1968, A143, Box 5, NCCPV, LBJ.

109. *Chicago Sun-Times*, August 14, 1968, p. 20.

110. *U.S. v. David Dellinger and Others*, p. 364.

Chapter 7

1. Lewis, Chester, and Page, *An American Melodrama*, pp. 593–596.

2. *New York Times*, August 25, 1968, p. 74.

3. Stuart Glass to Peggy, letter, August 1968, Box 4, DNC, NU.

4. *Ramparts Wall Poster*, 1:1; *Chicago Daily News*, August 23, 1968, p. 14.

5. Stein, *Living the Revolution*, p. 38.

6. Ibid., pp. 38–41; *U.S. v. David Dellinger and Others*, pp. 10219–10231; *Ramparts Wall Poster*, 1:1. See Yippie, "Pigs Kill Yippie," Box 3, DNC, NU; and Up against the Wall Motherfucker, "Pigs Murdered Our Brother," Box 3, DNC, NU.

7. Yippie, "Vote for Pig" (information packet), Box 3, DNC, NU.

8. *U.S. v. David Dellinger and Others*, pp. 6304–6305, 6884.

9. "Some News," *Chicago Journalism Review*, October 1968, p. 1; Stein, *Living the Revolution*, pp. 46–47; *U.S. v. David Dellinger and Others*, pp. 10513–10515, 16552; *Ramparts Wall Poster* 1:1; Mike Korelenko, director, *Chords of Fame* (1983); Hugh Romney, "The Hog Farm," *The Realist*, November–December 1969, pp. 18–23; *Chicago Tribune*, August 24, 1968, p. 4; *New York Times*, August 24, 1968, p. 9.

10. Stein, *Living the Revolution*, p. 33; Tom Buckley, "The Battle of Chicago: From the Yippie Side," *New York Times Magazine*, September 15, 1968, p. 137, Korelenko, *Chords of Fame*. See also Stew Albert, "Pigasus Bound to Win," *Berkeley Barb*, August 23, 1968, p. 11.

11. *New York Times*, August 24, 1968, p. 9; Bradley J. Fox, R549, Box 42, NCCPV, LBJ, p. 14.

12. *New York Times*, August 24, 1968, p. 20.

13. *U.S. v. David Dellinger and Others*, p. 14719.

14. CPD, Special Order 68–69, "Areas of Responsibility for the Democratic National Convention," August 23, 1968, CPB.

15. Hoke Norris and Mike Chiappetta, "The First Platoon," *Chicago*, August 1978, p. 136.

16. Robert Lynsky, R502, Box 42, NCCPV, LBJ, pp. 1–2.

17. National Guard, "Final Report," pp. 1–2, 10; *Chicago's American*, August 24, 1968, p. 3.

18. Theohais, *Spying On Americans*, p. 184.

19. Ibid., pp. 181–183.

20. Paul Cowan, Nick Egleson, Nat Hentoff, with Barbara Herbert and Robert Wall, *State Secrets: Police Surveillance in America* (New York: Holt, Rinehart and Winston, 1974), pp. 8–13; *U.S. v. David Dellinger and Others*, pp. 7751–7752, 8084, 8087, 8090, 9369–9379; CBS News, "1968."

21. *Chicago Tribune*, August 15, 1968, p. 20; CBS News, "1968"—according to CBS, the CIA had agents in the Mobe and Women Strike for Peace during the convention.

22. Lynsky, R502, Box 42, pp. 3–4.

23. Patrolman, R631, Box 43, NCCPV, LBJ, p. 1; Lt. Skawski, R355, Box 41, NCCPV, LBJ, p. 2.

24. Walter C. Ladwig, R604, Box 43, NCCPV, LBJ, p. 1.

25. Dennis Cunningham, R234, Box 41, NCCPV, LBJ, pp. 2–3; Ladwig, R604, Box 43, p. 1.

26. *U.S. v. David Dellinger and Others*, pp. 2535, 4212–4213; Fox, R549, Box 42, p. 1.

27. *U.S. v. David Dellinger and Others*, p. 17072; *Rampart Wall Poster*, August 24, 1968.

28. Kale Williams, David Finkle, and James Reedy, R632, Box 43, NCCPV, LBJ, p. 1.

29. Tom Hayden, "The Reason Why," *Ramparts Wall Poster*, August 24, 1968.

30. Walter Schneir, editor, *Telling It Like It Was* (New York: Signet Books, 1969), p. 14; SDS, *Handwriting on the Wall 1*.

31. Stan Plona, R033, Box 40, NCCPV, LBJ, pp. 3–4; *Chicago Daily News*, August 24, 1968, p. 11; National Mobilization, List of Movement Centers, Box 5, DNC, NU.

32. *Chicago Tribune*, August 25, 1968, p. 8.

33. Allen Ginsberg, *Chicago Trial Testimony* (San Francisco: City Lights Books, 1975), p. 57.

34. For the statements see *Ramparts Wall Poster*, August 25, 1968. The dialogue comes from Stein, *Living the Revolution*, p. 60. See also Hoffman, R051–B, Box 40, p. 144; Ginsberg, *Chicago Trial Testimony*, pp. 27–29; Cunningham, R234, Box 41, pp. 2–3; and *U.S. v. David Dellinger and Others*, pp. 14572–14574.

35. Lynsky, R502, Box 42, pp. 1–3.

36. Ginsberg, *Chicago Trial Testimony*, pp. 30–33; *Ramparts Wall Poster 2*; SDS, *Handwriting on the Wall 2*; *Chicago Tribune*, August 25, 1968, p. 8; Stein, *Living the Revolution*, pp. 61–62.

37. *Chicago's American*, August 25, 1968, p. 1, 3.

38. Stephanie Miller, monitor's notes, Box 4, DNC, NU.

39. Tom Hayden, "The Machine Can Be Stopped," *Ramparts Wall Poster*, August 25, 1968.

40. *U.S. v. David Dellinger and Others*, pp. 9414–9418, 9573–9577, 9607.

41. Frank Joseph, OR142, Box 34, NCCPV, LBJ, pp. 4–16; *U.S. v. David Dellinger and Others*, pp. 17715–17726, 14406–14411, 4316–4321, 9227–9230, 6315–6317; CPD, Planning Division (PD), Convention Log, A053, Box 5, NCCPV, LBJ.

42. *U.S. v. David Dellinger and Others*, pp. 9419–9422, 9587, 12801–12825, 16965–16966A; Stein, *Living the Revolution*, pp. 68–73; Art Goldberg, "Kids Bashed by Cops," *Ramparts Wall Poster*, August 26, 1968; Yippie, "Food Flyer," Box 3, DNC, NU; Dave Chavooshin, SOR167, Box 47, p. 13; and Lynsky, R502, Box 42, p. 5, 14.

43. *U.S. v. David Dellinger and Others*, pp. 11728–11731.

44. Lynsky, R502, Box 42, pp. 5, 14; and CPD-PD, Convention Log, A053, Box 5.

45. Patrolman, R631, Box 43, p. 1; Lt. Skawski, R355, Box 41, p. 2.

46. Ginsberg, *Chicago Trial Testimony*, pp. 35–36.

47. Shultz, *No One Was Killed*, p. 80.

48. Patrolman, R631, Box 43, p. 1.

49. Lt. Raymond Skawski according to Richard C. Longworth, S010, Box 44, NCCPV, LBJ, p. 2.

50. Mary Teetor, R789, Box 43, p. 1.

51. Richard Schultz, S064, Box 44, NCCPV, LBJ, p. 1.

52. Norman Lapping, R604, Box 43, NCCPV, LBJ, p. 3.

53. Patrolman, R631, Box 43, p. 2.

54. Skawski, R355, Box 41, p. 2.

55. Ron Grossman, R284, Box 41, NCCPV, LBJ, p. 3.

56. John Culhane, R621, Box 43, NCCPV, LBJ, p. 1.

57. *U.S. v. David Dellinger and Others*, p. 12351.

58. Stein, *Living the Revolution*, p. 77.

59. I have identified by source all quotes, except for chants, used in this section. The basic scenario was developed from a variety of sources. Most useful were the statements taken by the Chicago Study Team of the NCCPV. For the police in particular see Richard Schultz, S064, Box 44, p. 1; Braasch, R736, Box 43, p. 1, and R717, Box 43, p. 1; Rochford R402, Box 42, p. 1; Lynsky, R502, Box 42, pp. 4–7, Patrolman, R631, Box 43, pp. 1–3; Skawski, R355, Box 41, pp. 1–2; Culhane, R632, Box 43, p. 1; Lapping, R014, Box 40, p. 3; Johnson, R007, Box 40, p. 4; CPD-PD, Convention Log, A053, Box 5; Sargent Beecher, R773, Box 43, NCCPV, LBJ, p. 1; Lt. Mooney, R760, Box 43, NCCPV, LBJ, p. 1; Longworth, S010, Box 44, p. 2; James Murray, R656, Box 43, NCCPV, LBJ, pp. 2–3; *U.S. v. David Dellinger and Others*, pp. 2138–2155, 4321–4331; *Chicago Sun-Times*, August 26, 1968, p. 26. For the general scene see Robert J. Weber, S066, Box 44, NCCPV, LBJ, p. 1; Lapping, R014, Box 40, pp. 1–4, Longworth, S010, Box 44, pp. 2–3; Ruth Migdal, R009, Box 40, NCCPV, LBJ, p. 2; Maurice Collins, R687, Box 43, NCCPV, LBJ, p. 1; John Herbers, S060, Box 44, NCCPV, LBJ, p. 1; Grossman, R284, Box 41, pp. 2–6; John Burnett, ORO51, Box 33, NCCPV, LBJ, p. 5; C. Clark Kissinger, R376, Box 41, NCCPV, LBJ, p. 2; Teetor, R789, Box 43, pp. 1–5; Robert Hart, R707, Box 43, NCCPV, LBJ, p. 1; Nina Boal, S097, Box 41, NCCPV, LBJ, pp. 2–7; Hoffman, R051-B, Box 40, pp. 155–163; Paul Sills, R021, Box 40, NCCPV, LBJ, pp. 3–4; Cunningham, R234, Box 40, pp. 6–10; K. Greene, R013, Box 40, NCCPV, LBJ, p. 1; Joseph, OR143, Box 34, pp. 1–19. For police brutality see ACLU statements, Box 33–34, NCCPV, LBJ; *U.S. v. David Dellinger and Others*, 14049–14050, 11936–11940, 15401–15432, 11033–11044, 12828–12854, 11730–11734, 16699–16703, 11996–12006, 15476–15485, 7074–7081; Schultz, *No One Was Killed*, pp. 81–85; Stein, *Living the Revolution*, pp. 70–74; Katz, "Chicago," pp. 2, 10; Goldberg, "Kids Bashed by Cops"; *New York Times*, August 26, 1968, p. 25; *Chicago Tribune*, August 26, 1968, p. 1.

60. *Handwriting on the Wall #2.*

61. Ibid.; and *Ramparts Wall Poster*, August 25, 1968.

62. Wolfe Lowenthal, "A Porcine Tale," *WIN*, October 1, 1968, pp. 4–7; James Ridgeway, "The Cops and the Kids," *New Republic*, September 7, 1968, pp. 11–14.

63. Lynsky, R502, Box 42, p. 7.

64. *U.S. v. David Dellinger and Others*, pp. 17734–17760, 18149–18155, 3373–3381, 15546–15579, 16345–16350, 4332–4336, 9425, 9632, 6320–6368, 14716–14722, 3610–3622, 3489–3518—see 2092A-C for the transcript of the speech Davis gave. See also Schultz, *No One Was Killed*, pp. 94–103; Joseph, OR143, Box 34, pp.21–23, and OR144, Box 34, pp. 1–8.

65. Les Brownlee, R646, Box 43, NCCPV, LBJ, p. 1.

66. See Hal Bruno, R401, Box 42, NCCPV, LBJ, p. 2.

67. Lynsky, R402, Box 42, p. 11.

68. Dean Suffka, OR225, Box 35, NCCPV, LBJ, p. 1.

69. Katherine Chambers, SOR127, Box 47, NCCPV, LBJ, p. 1.

70. Robert Jackson, Jr., R215, Box 41, NCCPV, LBJ, p. 1.

71. Robert Skotak, OR205, Box 35, NCCPV, LBJ, p. 1.

72. Roy Reis and others, R017, Box 40, NCCPV, LBJ, p. 3.

73. Edward Shields, R545, Box 42, NCCPV, LBJ, p. 2.

74. *New York Times*, August 27, 1968, p. 29; *Chicago Tribune*, August 27, 1968, p. 5; *Chicago Sun-Times*, August 27, 1968, pp. 1, 5–6; *U.S. v. David Dellinger and Others*, pp. 12859–12887, 12109–12110, 12352–12358, 12371, 11941–11978, 11051–11052, 11282–11294, 13837–13850, 112218, 14051–14062, 17009–17032, 14118–14134, 14211, 9371–9388, 13671–13676, 13747–13765; Hall, R686, Box 43, p. 1; Herbert Davis, R018, Box 40, NCCPV, LBJ, pp. 1–4; Reis and others, R017, Box 40, pp. 1–3; Cunningham, R234, Box 41, p. 12; Joseph, OR144, Box 34, pp. 9–16, Douglas Beall, R203, Box 41, NCCPV, LBJ, pp. 4–6; Michael Simons, SOR181, Box 47, NCCPV, LBJ, pp. 3–4, Donald L. Ruf, OR150, Box 34, NCCPV, LBJ, pp. 8–9; Boal, R220, Box 41, pp. 2–3; Sills, R021, Box 40, pp. 5–6; Tom Awkwright, R663, Box 43, NCCPV, LBJ, p. 1; John Wilson, R750, Box 43, NCCPV, LBJ p. 1; Grossman, R284, Box 41, pp. 7–9; Lapping, R014, Box 40, p. 5; James Jones, R374, Box 42, NCCPV, LBJ, pp. 2–4; Robert Piekrusiak, OR017, Box 33, NCCPV, LBJ, pp. 2–4. For the police side see *U.S. v. David Dellinger and Others*, pp. 605–606, 741–753, 6488–6497, 3382–3386, 828–848, 5848–5884; Thomas Foran, S084, Box 44, NCCPV, LBJ, p. 3; Lynsky, R502, Box 42, pp. 7–15; Braasch, R717, Box 43, pp. 3–5; H. Davis, R018B, Box 40, NCCPV, LBJ, pp. 4–5; Richard Schultz, S064, Box 44, NCCPV, LBJ, pp. 2–3; Bruno, R401, Box 42, p. 3; Arthur Morradian, R603, Box 43, NCCPV, LBJ, p. 1; Jeff Kammens, R223, Box 41, NCCPV, LBJ, p. 1. See also "Some More," *Chicago Journalism Review*, October 1969, p. 5; Ridgeway, "The Cops and the Kids," p. 11; Katz, "Chicago," p. 10; Stein, *Living the Revolution*, pp. 79–85; Shultz, *No One Was Killed*, pp. 104–127.

75. *U.S. v. David Dellinger and Others*, pp. 4338–4340, 10239–10241, 16899–16903, 15249–15251, 2158–2167, 2300, 15947–15968, 17761–17765; James Burns, R008, Box 40, NCCPV, LBJ, pp. 2–5.

76. Chester, Page, and Hodgson, *An American Melodrama*, p. 565; or better see CBS, Convention Outtakes, "Daley Welcome Speech."

77. Don Rose, "The Whole World's Watching!" *Chicago*, August 1978, p. 124.

78. *U.S. v. David Dellinger and Others*, p. 5761.

79. *Chicago Tribune*, August 28, 1968, p. 16.

80. Bruno, R401, Box 42, p. 4; *Chicago Tribune*, August 28, 1968, p. 9; *Chicago Sun-Times*, August 28, 1968, p. 5; Roy M. Fisher, "Letter from the Editor," *Chicago Daily News*, September 14, 1968, p. 2. For the Daley remark see *Chicago Tribune*, August 28, 1968, p. 9.

81. Liljenstolpe, R422, Box 42, pp. 20–21; National Mobilization "WE Mourn," A279, Box 8, NCCPV, LBJ; Resistance, "Our Movement is Worldwide," Box 4, DNC, NU.

82. Abbie Hoffman, "Media Freaking," taped by Charles Harbut, *The Drama Review*, Summer 1969, pp. 361–362.

83. Jason Epstein, *The Great Conspiracy Trial* (New York: Random House, 1970), p. 78.

84. Ibid., p. 79.

85. Ibid., p. 80.

86. Arthur C. Hull, OR255, Box 35, NCCPV, LBJ, p. 1; Dale Brown, R024, Box 40, NCCPV, LBJ, p. 1; Epstein, *The Great Conspiracy Trial*, pp. 73–85.

87. Katz, "Chicago," p. 10.

88. Ridgeway, "The Cops and the Kids," p. 13; *New York Times*, August 28, 1968, p. 31; Joseph, OR144, Box 34, pp. 19–23, and OR145, Box 34, pp. 1–2; Stein, *Living the Revolution*, pp. 100–101; CBS News, Convention Outtakes, August 27, 1968; National Mobilization, "LBJ," Box 4, DNC, NU.

89. Robert K. Downs, S119, Box 45, NCCPV, LBJ, p. 2; see also Dr. Richard Levine, SOR109, Box 47, NCCPV, LBJ, for more on the policemen's attitudes.

90. Lynsky, R502, Box 42, pp. 16–18; CPD-PD, Convention Log, A053, Box 5, August 27, 1968; Braasch, R736, Box 43, p. 3; Mooney, R760, Box 43, pp. 1–2; Teetor, R789, Box 43, pp. 5–9; Steve Lerner, "A Visit to Chicago," *Village Voice*, September 5, 1968, p. 22; Art Goldberg, "Lincoln Park," *Ramparts Wall Poster*, August 28, 1968; James Shiflett, R022, Box 40, NCCPV, LBJ, p. 12; Sills, R021, Box 40, p. 1; Walter Hays, R028, Box 40, NCCPV, LBJ, pp. 4–8; Peter Martyn, OR111, Box 34, NCCPV, LBJ, p. 1; Simon, OR055, Box 33, p. 1; Davis, R018, Box 40, pp. 6–8; Victor Berkey, OR169, Box 34, NCCPV, LBJ, p. 1; R. Schultz, R064, Box 40, pp. 3–4; *New York Times*, August 28, 1968, p. 36; Buckley, "The Battle of Chicago," pp. 130–140; Schultz, *No One Was Killed*, pp. 150–153; Katz, "Chicago," p. 11; CBS News, Convention Outtakes, August 27, 1968.

91. Teetor, R789, Box 43, p. 15.

92. Ibid., p. 14.

93. *U.S. v. David Dellinger and Others*, pp. 17766–17772, 3388–3389.

94. *Chicago Tribune*, August 28, 1968, p. 1; National Guard, "Final Report," A152, Box 6, pp. 7–8.

95. Teetor, R789, Box 43, pp. 9–14; Jay Heyman, R703, Box 43, NCCPV, LBJ, pp. 1–2; Bob Vanasek, SOR115, Box 47, p. 1; Katz, "Chicago," p. 11; Foran, S084, Box 44, p. 4; *Chicago Tribune*, August 28, 1968, p. 1; Don Rose, "Up against the Wall, Chicago," p. 102; CPD-PD, Convention Log, August 27–28, 1968, A053, Box 5; National Guard, "Final Report" A151, Box 6, pp. 7–8.

96. *U.S. v. David Dellinger and Others*, pp. 12972–12979.

97. National Guard, "Final Report," A151, Box 6, pp. 8–9.

98. CPD-PD, Convention Log, August 28, 1968, A053, Box 5; *U.S. v. David Dellinger and Others*, pp. 8436–8438.

99. *U.S. v. David Dellinger and Others*, pp. 17774–17779, 2823–2824, 4365–4370.

100. Chester, Page, Hodgson, *An American Melodrama*, pp. 646–647.

101. John Beal, R333, Box 41, NCCPV, LBJ, p. 1; Lerner, "A Visit to Chicago," p. 33; J. Simon, S084, Box 44, NCCPV, LBJ, p. 1; *U.S. v. David Dellinger and Others*, pp. 7535–7536, 8231; CPD-PD, Convention Log, August 28, 1968, A053, Box 5.

102. Downs, S119, Box 45, p. 3; National Guard, "Final Report," A151, Box 6, pp. 8–9; CPD-PD, Convention Log, August 28, 1968, A053, Box 5.

103. Epstein, *The Great Conspiracy Trial*, p. 294.

104. *U.S. v. David Dellinger and Others*, p. 9829.

105. Simon, S084, Box 44, p. 1; Davis and Others, S019, Box 44, pp. 70–72; *U.S. v. David Dellinger and Others*, pp. 17796–17797, 11152–11165, 11188, 11313–11316, 15691–15721; Pfeffer, R229, Box 41, p. 2; Joseph, OR146, Box 34, pp. 20–23; Wille, "The Secret Police in Chicago," p. 11; Lens, *Unrepentant Radical*, p. 332; Frederick C. Olds, S081, Box 44, NCCPV, LBJ, p. 5.

106. Dellinger, *More Power Than We Know*, pp. 142–143; Lens, *Unrepentant Radical*, p. 332.

107. Katz, "Chicago," p. 10.

108. *Chicago Daily News*, August 29, 1968, p. 1; *U.S. v. David Dellinger and Others*, pp. 9876–9878.

109. *U.S. v. David Dellinger and Others*, p. 9910;

110. Ibid., p. 9918.

111. Ibid., pp. 14354–14359D; Dave Jackson, R292, Box 41, NCCPV, LBJ, pp. 1–3.

112. *U.S. v. David Dellinger and Others*, p. 8665.

113. Rochford, R402C, Box 43, p. 2.

114. CPD-CP, Convention Log, August 28, 1968, A053, Box 5.

115. Dellinger, *More Power Than We Know*, p. 185.

116. CPD-PD, Convention Log, August 28, 1968, A053, Box 5.

117. D. Jackson, R291, Box 41, pp. 2–7.

118. *U.S. v. David Dellinger and Others*, p. 8589.

119. John E. Harnett, Chief of Patrol Area 5, exemplifies this—see R. Jackson, R215, Box 41.

120. Rochford, R402, Box 43, pp. 3–4.

121. Nicholas Karzan, S072, Box 44, NCCPV, LBJ, p. 7.

122. The events here are drawn from many sources. The place to start is filmed accounts. See Haskell Wexler, *Medium Cool*, CBS Evening News, August 25, 1978, "Ten Years After," and the outtakes collected for the segment; see also the entire collection of CBS News Convention Outtakes of the August 28, Michigan Avenue events; also CBS, *1968: A Look for New Meanings*, p. 4: "The Battle of Chicago," shown July 28, 1978. I have only used CBS materials but certainly similar materials are available from the other networks. For Deputy Superintendent James Rochford's per-

spective, see *U.S. v. David Dellinger and Others*, pp. 8432–8475, 8521–8689, 8765–8810; also on the police see David Nystrom, R313, Box 41, NCCPV, LBJ; Foran, S100, Box 44, p. 7; Thomas Todd, S068, Box 44, NCCPV, LBJ, pp. 5–6; M. B. Nash, S071, Box 44, NCCPV, LBJ, pp. 6–10; Karzen, S072, Box 44, p. 7; R. Schultz, S064, Box 44, p. 6; CPD-PD, Convention Log, August 28, 1968, A053, Box 5; *Chicago Tribune*, August 29, 1968, pp. 1, 7; *Chicago Daily News*, August 29, 1968, pp. 1, 6; National Guard, "Final Report," A151, Box 6. For other events, see D. Jackson, R292, Box 41, pp. 2–7, and R291, Box 41, p. 1–2; for the best description of the Haymarket Bar window breaking see Earl Caldwell, S186, Box 45, NCCPV, LBJ, pp. 1–3. For an excellent description of the early events on Michigan Avenue see Richard Pfeffer, R229, Box 41, NCCPV, LBJ, pp. 7–18; for other particularly useful accounts see Mrs. Alfred Meyer, S061, Box 45, NCCPV, LBJ, pp. 1–3, Migdal, R009, Box 40, pp. 4–6. See also witness statements Boxes 31–34, 40–47, NCCPV, LBJ. In general, my account of the Michigan Avenue and Loop actions August 28 is in agreement with that given in NCCPV *Rights in Conflict* (New York: Signet Books, 1968), which details a number of instances of police brutality. In general, my primary print source material is the same as that used in the report. My account here is also based on the numerous discussions of the events of August 28 given in *U.S. v. David Dellinger and Others*.

123. Robert Sam Anson, *McGovern* (New York: Holt, Rinehart and Winston, 1972), p. 210.

124. Chester, Page, and Hodgson, *An American Melodrama*, p. 651.

125. For the attack, from the perspective of a National Guardsman, see Steven G. Armanino, R487, Box 42, NCCPV, LBJ, pp. 1–4.

126. Chester, Page, and Hodgson, *An American Melodrama*, p. 652. For the picture see *Life*, September 6, 1968, p. 27.

127. Joseph, OR146, Box 34, p. 9.

128. Arthur I. Waskow, *Running Riot* (New York: Herder and Herder, 1970), p. 152.

129. Joseph, OR146, Box 34, pp. 9–12.

130. *Chicago Daily News*, August 29, 1968, p. 6.

131. Mayor Richard J. Daley, statement, August 29, 1968, A231, Box 7, NCCPV, LBJ.

132. CBS News, Convention Outtakes, Daley/Cronkite Interview, August 29, 1968.

133. As I have recounted in Chapter 6.

134. *Chicago Daily News*, August 29, 1968, p. 4.

135. Lorraine Perlman, "Chicago August 1968," *Black and Red*, October 1968, p. 37.

136. *U.S. v. David Dellinger and Others*, p. 18231.

137. CBS News, Convention Outtakes, August 28, 1968. See also Schneir, *Telling It Like It Was*, pp. 142, 147; and Sale, *SDS*, pp. 475–476.

138. Chester, Page, and Hodgson, *An American Melodrama*, p. 657.

139. Chester Robinson and Reverend Henry, R608, Box 43, NCCPV, LBJ, p. 1. For more on blacks' attitudes see L. P. Palmer, "What Is Black's Mood Here?" *Chicago Daily News*, August 23, 1968, p. 3; *New York Times*,

August 23, 1968, p. 25; ibid., August 23, p. 29; ibid., *Times*, August 30, 1968, p. 14. See also Arthur Brozier, R807, Box 43, NCCPV, LBJ; and Denton Brooks, R574, Box 42, NCCPV, LBJ.

140. Rochford, R402, Box 42, pp. 4–5; Harris Wofford, R001a and R001b, Box 40, NCCPV, LBJ; CPC-PD, Convention Log, August 29, 1968, A053, Box 5; Strayhorn, R552, Box 43, pp. 1–4. Officially, 668 were arrested, 75.8% were twenty-five or under, 41.5% were residents of Chicago—see NCCPV, *Rights in Conflict*, pp. 320–321.

141. CBS News, "Ten Years After," Outtakes.

142. CBS Morning News, August 29, 1968.

143. The Mayor's staff immediately put out a booklet called *Strategy of Confrontation* and a movie *What Flowers Do They Plant?* The one-hour film was shown on independent television stations in seventy-four cities. For a discussion of the film and its showing see the *Chicago's American*, September 13, 1968, p. 38. The TV viewer number comes from White, *The Making of the President 1968*, p. 397.

144. For a good summary see Tom Littlewood, "Senators Assail and Defend Daily and Video Networks," *Chicago Sun-Times*, September 5, 1968, p. 17; and *Chicago Tribune*, August 31, 1968, p. 11.

145. For a good summary of Clark's feelings see his forward to *Contempt* (Chicago: Swallow Press, 1970).

146. William Small, *To Kill a Messenger* (New York: Hastings House, 1970), p. 210.

147. *Chicago Daily News*, September 14, 1968, p. 1.

148. Forty-three reporters, photographers, and cameramen had been beaten by the police during the convention—see NCCPV, *Rights in Conflict*, pp. 270–296. CBS had carried twenty-eight hours and three minutes of convention coverage. Of that, thirty-two minutes and twenty seconds featured the demonstrators. The Mayor had been featured for thirty-seven minutes and eight seconds. On NBC there were sixty-five minutes on the demonstrations amid thirty-five hours of coverage —see Bill Matney, "The Shattering Effects of Television News," *Columbia Journalism Review*, August 1969, p. 3. A whole slew of books on the subject of the mass media and its impact began to appear after the Chicago events. The best of the early reactions to Chicago was Matney, "The Shattering Effects of Television News," in the pathbreaking *Columbia Journalism Review*, August 1969, pp. 3–4. For a good pro–mass media view see William Small, *To Kill a Messenger*. The conservative attack is given in Edith Efron, *The News Twisters* (Los Angeles: Nash Publishing, 1971). For the radicals' perspective see Todd Gitlin, *The Whole World Is Watching*.

149. Small, *To Kill a Messenger*, p. 210.

150. John P. Robinson, "Public Reaction to Political Protest: Chicago 1968," *Public Opinion Quarterly*, Spring 1970, pp. 1–9.

151. Philip E. Converse, Warren E. Miller, Jerrold G. Rush, and Arthur C. Wolfe, "Continuity and Change in American Elections: Parties and Issues in the 1968 Election," *American Political Science Review*, December 1969, pp. 1087–1088.

152. *New York Times*, August 20, 1968, p. 1.

153. Chesly Manly, "Hubert Backs Mayor Daley, Chicago Cops," *Chicago Tribune*, September 1, 1968, p. 4.

154. White, *The Making of the President 1968*, pp. 425, 438–479.

155. Todd Gitlin, "Plain Clothes Hoods," *Rat*, October 4, 1968, p. 7.

156. See Sale, *SDS*, pp. 476–477.

157. Waskow, *Running Riot*, pp. 154, 158.

158. Tom Hayden and Rennie Davis, "Politics after Chicago," *Rat*, October 18, 1968, p. 5.

159. Schneir, *Telling It Like It Was*, p. 123.

160. Stew Albert, "Chicago Retrospective," *Berkeley Barb*, September 6, 1968, p. 9.

Chapter 8

1. C. Vann Woodward quotes this in his *Tom Watson—Agrarian Rebel* (New York: Oxford Press, 1963), p. 82.

2. Harry Morganstern, "High School Students Get Choice: Your Education or Your Hair," Liberation News Service, February 14, 1968. There were few high school students in the 1960s who did not have personal knowledge of such practices. In girls' cases it had to do with skirt lengths and makeup. Marijuana laws, illegal searches and seizures in schools, and the confiscation of private property spoke to the same issue.

3. Danny the Red's statement is from James Joll, ed., *The Anarchists* (Cambridge, Mass.: Harvard University Press, 1981), pp. 541–542.

4. Hoffman, R051A, Box 40, p. 10.

5. Neil Harris, *Humbug* (Chicago: University of Chicago Press, 1981), pp. 3–4.

6. Marvin Meyer, *The Jacksonian Persuasion* (Stanford: Stanford University Press, 1957), is still a useful guide to how various elites maneuvered through the mid-nineteenth-century democratic discourse. Neil Harris's *Humbug* portrays how a democratic vision contributed to the everyday practices of the master showman of the nineteenth century. Harris's portrait of P. T. Barnum speaks tellingly to the tradition the Yippies sought to operate within. Karen Halttunen's *Confidence Men and Painted Women* (New Haven: Yale University Press, 1982), also in terms that portend the Yippie experience, brilliantly analyzes the uneasiness that pervaded the nineteenth-century Democracy and its rush toward information and systems that could help it resolve what Halttunen calls, "a crisis of social identity" (p. xv).

7. Alexis de Tocqueville, *Democracy in America*, ed. Richard D. Heffner (New York: New American Library, Inc., 1956), p. 58.

8. Neil Harris, *Humbug*, p. 74—see chap. 3 for an extended discussion and explanation of this.

9. Hoffman, R051A, Box 40, pp. 12–13.

10. Ibid., p. 26.

11. Ibid., p. 10.

12. Ibid., p. 13.

13. The McLuhan is quoted in Joe McGinnis, *The Selling of the President* (New York: Pocket Books, 1970), p. 21, as is the Leonard Hall statement, p. 21. McGinnis's work, while not as far-ranging as Daniel Boorstin's well known *The Image* (New York: Atheneum, 1962), is in many ways—perhaps due to the advantage of being able to discuss much of the 1960s—more sophisticated and informative. For a first-rate treatment of the joining of the mass media to the presidency, see Barry Karl, *The Uneasy State* (Chicago: University of Chicago Press, 1983).

14. John Sinclair, *Guitar Army* (New York: Douglas Books Corp., 1972), p. 45.

15. See for example Lewis A. Erenberg, *Steppin' Out* (Westport, Conn.: Greenwood Press, 1981); and Paula S. Fass, *The Damned and the Beautiful* (New York: Oxford University Press, 1977). For the "new and unprecedented" school, the exemplars are Theodore Roszak, *The Making of a Counter-Culture* (Garden City: Anchor Books, 1969); and Charles A. Reich, *The Greening of America* (New York: Random House, 1970). The best historical treatment of the American counterculture is in Lawrence Vesey, *The Communal Experience* (New York: Harper and Row, 1973), pp. 3–73. Vesey demonstrates that the main concerns of the 1960s counterculture had deep historical roots.

16. The quote and all the facts come from Landon Jones's witty and informative compendium on the Baby Boomers, *Great Expectations* (New York: Coward, McGann, and Geoghegan, 1980), pp. 43–79. The Gilbert quote is on p. 43.

17. Jerry Rubin, *Do It!* pp. 90–91. The back cover of *Do It!* warns, "This book will become a malatov cocktail in your very hand."

18. Ibid., pp. 98–99.

19. Ibid., pp. 100–101. The quotable Rubin adds, "Juice-heads drink alone. They get drunk and disgusting. They puke all over themselves. They pass out. Alcohol turns off the senses," p. 101. The fact that the government and business worlds were full of alcoholics was very important and frightening to the Yippies.

20. Sinclair, *Guitar Army*, pp. 22–23.

21. See for example the *Chicago Tribune* for the entire month of August 1968 or even CBS convention and preconvention coverage. See also the many newspaper clips gathered in Box 2 of Northwestern University's 1968 National Democratic Convention materials. The *New York Times* and the *Washington Post* did not practice this kind of labeling.

22. Gitlin, *The Whole World Is Watching*, pp. 175–176.

23. See Woodward, *Tom Watson*.

Chapter 9

1. Zbigniew Brzezinski, "Revolution and Counterrevolution," *New Republic*, June 1, 1968, p. 23.

2. Daniel Bell, *The End of Ideology* (New York: Free Press, 1960), p. 302.

3. Ibid., p. 301.

4. It is this loss of faith in the Rousseauian General Will that, in essence, drives the French New Philosophers, ex-60s radicals all, in the late 1970s, to

their extreme attacks on all "great thinkers" of collective will. See in particular Bernard-Henri Levy, *Barbarism with a Human Face*, trans. George Holoch (New York: Harper and Row, 1979); and Andre Glucksmann, *The Master Thinkers*, trans. Brian Pearce (New York: Harper and Row, 1980).

5. Walter Benjamin, *Illuminations*, trans. Harry Zohn (New York: Schocken Books, 1969), p. 112.

6. *New York Times*, August 18, 1968, p. 1. Hayden is quoted, "Our goal is not to influence the delegates in the convention."

7. Hayden, "Democracy Is . . . in the Streets," p. 5.

8. Ibid., p. 4.

9. CBS News, interview with Tom Hayden, Convention Outtakes, August 26, 1968.

10. Ibid.

11. *U.S. v. David Dellinger and Others*, p. 5746. This is from a transcript of a speech given by Davis at Case Western Reserve University, August 17, 1968.

12. For an interesting assessment of participatory democracy see C. George Bennelo and Dimitrious Roussopoulos, eds., *The Case for Participatory Democracy* (New York: Grossman Publishers, 1971). See also Wini Breines in *Community and Organization in the New Left*.

13. From Linda Morse's trial testimony—*U.S. v. David Dellinger and Others*, pp. 11361–11362.

14. As Rennie Davis said in an interview, "[The Mobe] cannot present an overall blueprint of action." See *New York Times*, August 18, 1968, p. 64. See also Tom Hayden, "Hayden Hails Chicago: The Elements of Victory," *The Movement*, October 1968, pp. 4–5, 7.

15. Staughton Lynd, "Decentralization: A Road to Power," *Liberation*, May–June 1967, p. 3.

16. Quoted in Breines, *Community and Organization in the New Left*, p. 48.

17. Hayden, "Democracy Is . . . in the Streets," pp. 4–5. Hayden calls for a coalition with liberals. More typical of the early Hayden and the early New Left is Tom Hayden, "Community Organizing and the War on Poverty," *Liberation*, November 1965, pp. 17–19. Here the emphasis is on empowering the poor.

18. Despite a spate of movies and television shows and a couple of notable exceptions to the contrary, most 1960s *radicals* did not become conservative stockbrokers or self-absorbed copouts. Many continue to be activists at local and national levels. For quantitative proof see Rex Weiner and Deanne Stillman, *Woodstock Census* (New York: Viking Press, 1979). See also John H. Bunzell, *New Force on the Left: Tom Hayden and the Campaign against Corporate America* (Stanford: Hoover Institute Press, 1983).

19. Tom Hayden at the Grant Park bandshell, August 28, 1968—recorded by security agencies and read at the conspiracy trial—*U.S. v. David Dellinger and Others*, p. 9876.

20. Experiences, that is, that lead to participatory democracy and utopian socialism. Such experiences can lend themselves to other practices—see Stalinism.

21. Dellinger, *More Power Than We Know*, p. 124.

22. I refer to the Weatherman stage.

23. Benjamin, *Illuminations*, p. 188.

24. Dellinger, "Lessons from Chicago," p. 9.

25. A speech he gave October 1984, at an anti-Nukes rally in Chicago, sounded the same chords.

26. See Bell, "The Exhaustion of Utopia," *The End of Ideology*, pp. 275–407.

27. See Christopher Lasch, *The Agony of the American Left* (New York: Vintage Books, 1969); and, more important, Christopher Lasch, *The New Radical in America 1889–1963* (New York: Vintage Books, 1967), pp. 286–349.

28. A. J. Muste, "Mobilizing for Peace," *Liberation*, December 1966, p. 22.

29. A. J. Muste, "The Movement to Stop the War in Vietnam," *Liberation*, January 1966, p. 35.

30. Todd Gitlin, "Theses for the Radical Movement," *Liberation*, May–June 1967, p. 34.

31. See Harold Cruse's brilliant analysis of this in *The Crisis of the Negro Intellectual* (New York: William Morrow and Company, 1967), pp. 544–565. Like many other historians, I am indebted to Cruse's work and to some degree my analysis of 1960s radicalism follows from Cruse's history of black activism.

32. "SNCC Press Conference," Liberation News Service, April 5, 1968.

33. Black Panthers, "Black Panther Platform," in Peter Stansill and David Zane Mairowitz, *Bamn!* (London: Penguin Books, 1971), p. 81.

34. SDS, *Handwriting on the Wall #3*.

35. Ibid.

36. Ibid., #1.

37. Ibid.

38. See for example Sale, *SDS*, pp. 338–340, 505–507; and Breines, *Community and Organization in the New Left*, chap. 10.

39. See Breines, *Community and Organization in the New Left*, pp. 119–120.

40. SDS, *Handwriting on the Wall #1*.

41. Paul Cowan, *The Making of an UnAmerican* (New York: Vintage Books, 1970), p. 287.

42. Benjamin, *Illuminations*, p. 158.

43. Allen Katzman, comp., *Our Time* (New York: Dial Press, 1972), p. 124.

44. The best scholarly work that examines this is Kenneth Kenniston, *Young Radicals* (New York: Harcourt, Brace and World, 1968); also Kenneth Kenniston, *Young and Dissent* (New York: Harcourt Brace Jovanovich, 1971). For a pathetic personal account of such worries, see Dotson Radar, *Blood Dues* (New York: Alfred Knopf, 1973).

45. "Twenty Five and Under," *Time*, June 6, 1967, pp. 18–19.

46. Brzezinski, "Revolution and Counterrevolution," p. 23.

47. "What They Believe," *Fortune*, January 1969, pp. 179–181.

48. Paul Potter, *A Name for Ourselves* (Boston: Little, Brown and Company, 1971); as truly risky and challenging a book as Radar's *Blood Dues* is not. Leni Wildflower's introduction to *A Name for Ourselves* is a superb account of the anger and frustration felt by many women in the movement in the 1960s—movement women's reality and movement men's reality were far apart.

49. CBS News, "Ten Years After."

50. David Harris, *Goliath* (New York: Richard W. Baron, 1970), pp. 47, 49.

51. Michael Rossman, "Look Ma, No Hope," *Commonweal*, April 12, 1968, pp. 101–102.

52. Richard W. Fox, *Reinhold Niebuhr*(New York: Pantheon Books, 1985), p. 139.

53. Ibid., p. 140.

54. See for example Peter Clecak, *Radical Paradoxes: Dilemmas of the American Left 1945–1970* (New York: Harper and Row, 1973), pp. 530–533.

55. Quoted in Lasch, *The Agony of the American Left*, p. vii.

56. Ibid., p. viii.

57. Ibid., p. vii.

58. Among the young radicals, it was typical to refer to one another as "kids." They felt it important to stress to each other and to outsiders that they were not adults bound by adult conventions; they were just "kids" out to remake the world they had not yet joined. See Stephen Diamond, *What the Trees Said* (New York: Delacorte Press, 1971).

59. See Clecak, *Radical Paradoxes*, who in partial agreement, outlines this position, pp. 532–533.

60. Thanks to David Cohen for the slogan—noted by him in Paris, May 1968—and its translation.

61. Benjamin, *Illuminations*, p. 83.

62. Hayden, "Democracy Is . . . in the Streets," p. 6.

Chapter 10

1. Claude Levi-Strauss, *Triste Tropique*, trans. John Weightman and Doreen Weightman (New York: Atheneum, 1975), p. 215.

2. *New York Times*, March 28, 1968, p. 5.

3. *Chicago Sun-Times*, August 1, 1968, p. 4.

4. NBC Today Show, August 30, 1968.

5. *Chicago Sun-Times*, August 1, 1968, p. 4.

6. Edward Schreiber, "Daley Blasts Suppression of the Czechs," *Chicago Tribune*, August 23, 1968, p. 11.

7. "Daley's Dirty Words," *Hyde Park-Kenwood Voices*, January 1969, p. 1.

8. *New York Times*, August 30, 1968, p. 1.

9. Female, SOR206, Box 47, NCCPV, LBJ, p. 1.

10. *New York Times*, August 30, 1968, p. 1.

11. Ibid., p. 15.

12. CBS News, Convention Outtakes, August 30, 1968.

13. NBC Morning News, August 29, 1968.

14. Harry Golden, Jr., "Daley Talks to Press," *Chicago Sun-Times*, September 10, 1968, p. 7.

15. NBC Morning News, August 29, 1968.

16. Quinn Tamm, "In the Public Interest," *Police Chief*, June 1968, p. 10.

17. Bell, *The End of Ideology*, p. 302.

18. Ibid., pp. 275–407.

19. Edward C. Banfield and James Q. Wilson, *City Politics* (New York: Vintage Books, 1963), p. 127. See also Robert K. Merton, *Social Theory and Social*

Structure (Glencoe: Free Press, 1957), pp. 71– 81; Edward C. Banfield, *Political Influence* (New York: Free Press, 1961), pp. 210–212.

20. Banfield and Wilson, *City Politics*, p. 126.

21. NBC Morning News, August 29, 1968.

22. Golden, Jr., "Mayor Talks to Press," p. 7.

23. *New York Times*, August 30, 1968, p. 15.

24. Stark, *Police Riots*, p. 58.

25. Ibid., pp. 58–59.

26. Ibid., p. 110.

27. Ibid., pp. 4–7.

28. *New York Times*, August 30, 1968, p. 14.

29. John B. Criswell to James R. Jones, memo, July 27, 1968, Name File, Richard J. Daley, LBJ.

Index